Mastering

Social Welfare

To renew please telephone: 01904 770406
with your ID card number
Or email lc-helpdesk@yorkcollege.ac.uk

Macmillan Master Series

Accounting
Advanced English Language
Arabic
Astronomy
Banking
Basic Management
Biology
British Politics
Business Communication
Business Law
Business Microcomputing
C Programming
Catering Science
Catering Theory
Chemistry
COBOL Programming
Commerce
Computer Programming
Computers
Databases
Economic and Social History
Economics
Electrical Engineering
Electronic and Electrical Calculations
Electronics
English as a Foreign Language
English Grammar
English Language
English Literature
English Spelling
French
French 2

German
German 2
Hairdressing
Human Biology
Italian
Italian 2
Japanese
Manufacturing
Marketing
Mathematics
Mathematics for Electrical and
    Electronic Engineering
Modern British History
Modern European History
Modern World History
Pascal Programming
Philosophy
Photography
Physics
Psychology
Pure Mathematics
Restaurant Service
Science
Secretarial Procedures
Social Welfare
Sociology
Spanish
Spanish 2
Spreadsheets
Statistics
Study Skills
Word Processing

Mastering

Social Welfare

Third edition

Pat Young

MACMILLAN

First edition 1985
Reprinted three times
Second edition 1989
Reprinted six times
Third edition 1995

Published by
MACMILLAN PRESS LTD
Houndmills, Basingstoke, Hampshire RG21 2XS
and London
Companies and representatives
throughout the world

ISBN 0–333–63199–4

A catalogue record for this book is available
from the British Library.

10   9   8   7   6   5   4   3   2   1
04   03   02   01   00   99   98   97   96   95

Printed in Great Britain by
Biddles Ltd
Guildford and King's Lynn

For my father

Contents

List of plates

⬡ List of figures and tables

Figures

Tables

Acknowledgements

Many people helped in the writing of this book, by giving ideas, advice, support and encouragement. Heather Roberts provided invaluable assistance by spending many Saturday afternoons reading chapters and offering constructive criticism. Others who read chapters were Arthur Rutherford, Judy Nixon, Dave Evans and Eva Garmonikow. The staff in the library at Langley College of Further Education were supportive and tolerant of my dependence on their services. Finally, I would like to acknowledge the encouragement I received from the many people who took an interest in the progress of this book.

I am very grateful to Pat Newberry for her help in updating the information for the third edition of the book. She painstakingly sought out up-to-date statistics for me and provided invaluable information on the ever-changing scene in social welfare legislation and policy.

The author and publishers wish to thank the following for permission to use copyright material, as follows: The Guardian News Service plc for graphs, 'Daycare and education for children under five', *Guardian,* 7.12.93, and 'The Richest 500 Club', *Guardian*, 3.8.94; The Controller of Her Majesty's Stationery Office for Crown copyright material from *Social Trends 1994, Britain 1994: an official handbook* and *1991 Census, National Monitor*; Routledge for tables from Stewart Lansley and Joanna Mack, *Poor Britain*, Allen and Unwin, 1985, Tables 1, 2, 3.3; and Sally and Richard Greenhill, Chris Schwartz, Popperfoto, Photofusion and Network Photographers for photographic material. Every effort has been made to trace all the copyright- holders, but if any have been inadvertently overlooked the publishers will be pleased to make the necessary arrangement at the first opportunity.

⬡ 1 People in society

1.1 Introduction

The aim of this book is to increase understanding of people, the kind of problems they encounter, the situations in which they live and the welfare provision which exists to help. People whose work involves caring for others have to be able to demonstrate an almost instant understanding of a variety of human predicaments and problems. Nursery nurses will be told that a new child is expected at the nursery tomorrow, social workers will be asked to visit new clients, residential care workers will have to welcome new people into the home. In each of these situations, which are everyday events for caring workers, strangers are meeting and one will be expecting a great deal from the other. An understanding of society and social problems can provide a background of knowledge for dealing with such circumstances. The questions which make up the first section of this chapter give an idea of the way this book approaches individual and social problems.

Activity 1.1

Think about meeting a client for the first time, it could be a child coming into care, a patient in a hospital, an older person, or an adolescent in a youth club. On a piece of paper, make a list of the sorts of things you might need to know about in order to understand and help that person. Compare what you have written with the following list.

What is the person's family background?

Most people spend some part of their lives living within a family, although family structures can vary quite considerably. Some children live in a home where there is only one adult, often the mother, but sometimes the father. Some children have step-brothers or sisters. Other families include grandparents or aunts and uncles in addition to the children and their parents. In many families the mother does a paid job, either full-time or part-time, as well as caring for the family. Some fathers participate in caring for their children, whilst in other families the father is a more distant figure. The father may be responsible for making all the decisions or the process may be more democratic. Social services attempt to work alongside the family, helping members to cope with the demands made upon them, rather than taking over those demands. For this reason, caring workers need to understand the way the family operates.

What race is the client?

Most people in caring jobs seek to treat everyone equally, regardless of race, and this, therefore, may seem an inappropriate question to ask. However, at this time, people of different races do have different experiences and it is important to be familiar with the customs and practices of the ethnic minority communities. Many Asians, for example those who are Hindus, are vegetarian and therefore there is little point in health visitors or others telling them to give their children cod liver oil, although this has happened.[1] Practices associated with courtship and marriage vary and an adolescent girl living in an Asian community in Britain may have demands made upon her which are not shared by her white friends. Discrimination and racism are, unfortunately, social and economic realities in this country and exert particular stresses and strains on members of the ethnic minorities.

Is the person employed? Is the head of the family employed?

In this society work is very important. Not only does it bring financial reward, it also gives status; when people say 'I am a teacher', 'I am a nurse', they are using their work to define who they are as well as how they spend their day and earn their money. The worries and fears brought about by unemployment are complex and involve more than financial insecurity which itself causes stress. There is a stigma attached to unemployment. This means that the person has a feeling, reinforced by society, that he or she is somehow inadequate and a failure. Whilst it is true that not everyone experiences unemployment in exactly the same way, a general understanding of the problem throws light on a particular individual's circumstances.

How old is the person?

In this society there is a tendency to group people in terms of age, therefore it is usual to want to know the age of the client. People talk about the problems of children, adolescents, teenagers, young adults, middle-aged people, elderly people. In fact many people choose to work with a specific age group, perhaps young children or elderly people. A general understanding of the needs of children, the demands made upon adolescents, the problems faced by people as they get older, will help in developing a sympathy towards a particular individual.

Is the client male or female?

Section 1.3 of this chapter looks at the different expectations society has of men and women, and the way that children learn about these differences. The differences in masculine and feminine behaviour are demonstrated in innumerable ways. A little boy and a little girl will probably react differently to coming into care, typically, one may become aggressive or violent, while the other is withdrawn and tearful. Similarly men and women react differently to stress, and social problems like alcoholism, depression and crime are not equally prevalent amongst men and women.

What class is the person?

Different kinds of work not only provide different levels of income but also are closely associated with different life-styles and expectations. This can be summarised in the concept of social class, which is explained in detail in section 1.3 of this chapter. At this point, it is enough to say that there is research which demonstrates that class differences affect people's lives from the moment of conception through to the end of their lives.[2] Social workers need an understanding of class, as they may be required to work with people whose class background is completely different from their own. Social work itself has a class dimension, with many social workers having a middle-class background, whilst the majority of their clients are working-class. This could lead to a conflict of expectations, and misunderstandings over different ways of approaching problems.

Does the client come from a rich or a poor family?

Money cannot solve all problems but it does make many problems easier to deal with. For example, a young mother with access to a car will probably not experience the same feeling of isolation as the woman who, in order to leave the house, has to cope with public transport, with young children in tow. Strange as it may sound, lack of money can make life more expensive. The person with a car and a monthly salary can buy cheaper goods in bulk at a hypermarket while the poorer person is forced to buy small amounts at a local and more expensive store. Inadequate money is obviously the key aspect of poverty, but it results in more complex forms of deprivation and suffering. It also brings about its own problems in the form of feelings of hopelessness and degradation.

What sort of education does the person have?

Since the education system in this country combines private and state sectors and is constantly in a state of change, it is hardly surprising that people's experiences of schooling are so varied. The state sector includes some selective schools although most local areas have a comprehensive system. Education provides more than qualifications in the form of GCSEs and training for specific jobs; it also leads to a set of attitudes and expectations. The person who has attended a private school and then university may have little in common with his or her contemporary who left the local comprehensive at the earliest possible date. As a less extreme example, the child who has been able to attend a nursery school or pre-school play-group may cope better with certain situations than the child who has remained at home.

What sort of environment does the person come from?

The word 'environment' includes the home itself and the wider environment of the street and the locality. People are greatly affected by their home environment. For example, in an overcrowded home, it will be difficult for a child to find a quiet place to do homework and the child's education will therefore suffer. Similarly, lack of privacy can cause strain in a marriage and perhaps lead to the breakdown of that marriage. A child growing up in a flat at the top of a tower-block will not have the same opportunities for safe exploratory play as the child with access to a garden or a street free from traffic. Social workers and policy-makers now recognise the special problems for all the members of a family living in an overcrowded home or in high-rise housing.

The wider environment is also important. Living in a rural cottage without basic amenities, such as an inside toilet, might not result in the same feeling of deprivation as life in an identical property in a run-down inner-city area. The multiplicity of problems in run-down areas are exacerbated by the fact that living in such conditions causes people to despair of improving their situation, thus leading to further deterioration of the environment and morale. The effects of the environment on individuals can be seen by the fact that sometimes problems which appear psychological in origin, such as depression, can be solved simply by removing a person from a particular environment.

These questions are intended to show that people cannot be understood solely as individuals with individual problems but must be seen in the light of social pressures and social environments. This is why books can be of help to those planning to work with people. Reading about unemployment or poverty will increase insight into the plight of a family living on income support and struggling to make ends meet.

In Britain, and indeed in most other countries, people are not allowed to do exactly as they wish, nor are they expected to cope with all difficulties in isolation. The legal system, welfare provision and voluntary organisations, will intervene in people's lives, preventing them from doing certain things, enabling and assisting them to do others. There are laws, for example, to stop parents from abusing their children and there are social workers and charitable organisations who will step in if children are thought to be in danger. There is a law which says that the local authority must house certain categories of homeless people and, again, statutory and voluntary organisations help people to obtain their rights. It is therefore important for people wanting to help others to know something of the relevant legislation, welfare provision and services provided by voluntary organisations.

It would, of course, be possible to understand all these aspects of society and still fail to understand a particular individual. However, it would be difficult to grasp an individual's needs without a general understanding of social problems, certainly without more time than most caring workers have at their disposal.

It is necessary to give two words of warning at this point. First, there is a danger in the above approach that it may appear that something called 'society' in some way causes people to do things and influences people into holding certain attitudes and beliefs. In reality, society is made up of people and it is therefore people who make society what it is. There is a two-way interaction in process, with people changing their environment and being changed by it. For example, a child will be very influenced by the family and the home in which it grows up, but the very presence of the child will have changed the family. As adults, people influence their world through their work, political behaviour and perhaps through participation in voluntary organisations.

The second point is that, for the purpose of study, it is necessary to break up the subject area into topics which may then appear to be separate. It is clear, however, that all these areas are in fact highly interconnected. Poor housing, poverty and low achievement at school tend to go together and possibly it is the very inter-relatedness of these problems that makes it so difficult for governments and social service workers to find solutions. In the same way, class is not really a separate topic, but it is significant because it is related to all the other subject-areas.

Figure 1.1 overleaf summarises this section, and illustrates the subjects covered in this book.

'Sticks and stones'

'Stick and stones will break my bones; but names cannot hurt me'. This is a saying which I often heard as a child, as adults tried to persuade me that verbal bullying could not harm me. But is it true? Is it really true that words cannot hurt?

Some people think that words can be damaging and recently the popular press have made a great joke out of so-called 'politically correct' language, poking fun out of some perhaps rather extreme attempts to avoid words with negative meanings. So-called 'politically correct' language includes avoidance of terms which might be considered sexist – suggesting that a role is limited to men or women, for example postman, dinner lady, etc. – and terms which might be considered insulting to groups such as older people, black people or people with disabilities. So does it actually matter what words we use to describe people? Has language the power to hurt or to belittle?

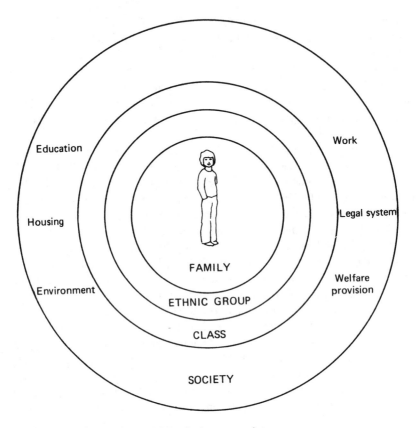

Figure 1.1   The individual in relation to society

___ **Activity 1.3** _____

Are there any words which you would avoid using, perhaps to describe
people with disabilities, people with mental illnesses, black people, women
or older people? Are there any names you would not like to be called yourself, or which you would not like to hear used about your relatives or
friends? Make a short list for yourself.

What is wrong with these words as far as you are concerned? Why do
you not use them? Compare your list with those of others. Over which
words do you disagree?

Although people do not agree about which words it is not okay to use, most
people agree that there are some words which they do find offensive. From this
it would seem that perhaps words do in fact matter.

The view taken here is that language *is* an important issue, for two reasons.
The first is that words can be negative or insulting and therefore hurtful and

damaging to the people they are used to describe. Words can make people feel in some way abnormal, or less than human. Words which are not actually insulting can still be belittling, making people feel like objects of charity, and thus not fully human. This point is fairly obvious and you will probably be able to think of words which would make you feel this way.

The second point is more subtle and harder to grasp. It concerns the way in which the terms and categories we use influence our thinking, the way we perceive the world, and most importantly ourselves and others. The following example demonstrates this point.

'The elderly need our help'

An expression may at first appear to express a positive attitude towards older people. However, it contains a number of more subtle and less positive attitudes. The term 'the elderly' implies that the fact of being elderly is the main and only thing we need to know about these people. They are being defined purely in terms of their age, as if nothing else is important. The term also creates the idea of a *category* of people who are the same or at least similar (whereas in fact people of the same chronological age are likely to differ in many more ways that they are similar). It also implies a rigid distinction between the elderly and the not-elderly, creating a division between people. It is as if some transformation occurs on the day we turn 65. Some writers and care workers have chosen to use the term 'older person' which is thought to suggest fewer rigid divisions.[3] The next point is that the idea of elderly people needing help implies that older people are incapable of helping themselves, when in fact many are carers and work for charity. Finally, 'our help' suggests again the idea of two groups: older people who are passive and helpless and the rest of 'us' who are capable of giving help.

Activity 1.4

Look in textbooks and other sources for similar statements to that analysed above and try to work out the subtle messages contained within them.

It is not possible to lay down hard and fast rules about which words are demeaning to people and which are not. Language and meanings change constantly and words which were neutral can come to have negative connotations. An interesting example here is the term 'Borstal', which was the name given to institutions for young offenders (now no longer used). Originally this was the name of a village and was chosen for its neutral meaning. However it soon came to have powerful connotations and to conjure up an image of a harsh and rather brutal regime. The word itself began to sound unpleasant.

Sometimes it is important to change terms in order to try to shake up people's attitudes and to challenge their ways of thinking. The use of a new term can have the effect of making people think in a new way. An example of this occurred when residential homes began to talk of 'residents' instead of 'patients'. Staff were reminded that their workplace was home for the people they cared for and should be treated as such, with respect for privacy and residents' rights. A number of different terms have been used in the past to describe what we now call 'learning disability' – and it is surprising how derogatory and unacceptable some of the old terms which were once current and which can still be found in older books now sound.

The issue of language will be returned to throughout this book, for example in Chapters 11–14 looking at mental illness, learning disabilities, elderly people, and people with disabilities. For now, two terms which have already been used in this chapter need brief discussion.

The first such term is 'clients' which has been used to describe the people with whom care workers are involved. There is disagreement about the most appropriate word here. Other possibilities might be 'patient', in a medical setting; 'resident' in a home; or some people have advocated the term 'user' of services. The term 'client' has been borrowed from the private sector, and for me implies choice and rights and respect. The reasons that some prefer the word 'user' is that the word is more active, suggesting involvement, whereas 'client' perhaps implies a rather passive recipient of services.

Activity 1.5 _____

What is implied in the following terms:
resident
patient
therapist
counsellor
helper
customer?
Add some terms of your own, from your own reading or experience.
In your view, which terms are most appropriate?

This may seem rather complicated and perhaps you are wondering why it matters which term is used. But think back to what was said earlier about the power of language to influence our thinking and the way we see the world. The words used in this context can influence the way the client and the worker perceive their relationship to each other. This will affect the *power dynamic* between the two – a point which is returned to in chapters 8 and 9.

The other term which has been used already and which needs some explanation is 'race'. Discussion of this and other related terms can be found later in this chapter, at the beginning of section 1.4.

All areas of study have their own language, and the area of social care and social policy is no exception. To help you get to grips with the terms used, there is a Glossary at the end of the book and list of words used at the end of each chapter.

The next section of this chapter introduces the idea of *role* as a means of understanding human behaviour. This is followed by sections on class and race – both of which are referred to again in the chapters which follow.

1.2 Understanding social behaviour

There are theories which seek to explain human behaviour and which can give an insight into why people behave the way they do. Theories can also be used to anticipate situations which will cause stress. The idea described below is useful in this way and is known as *role theory*.

Role theory

A role is simply a set of ways of behaving which are expected of a person occupying a certain position. The best way to illustrate this is with an example. When a class of students meets a new teacher, even though these people are strangers, they tend not to surprise each other. This is because the individuals concerned are behaving as others expect them to act in a particular role. The teacher does not come in, stand on the table and sing a song, neither does the teacher take a seat at the back of the classroom and wait in silence. In fact the teacher will follow the detailed pattern of behaviour which makes up the role of teacher. This involves entering the classroom, sitting or standing at the appropriate place at the front, facing the other individuals and addressing them as a group. Similarly the other people in the classroom act in accordance with their role. They become students, they ask and answer questions, accepting that the teacher already knows about the subject.

This is only one example of the roles which people take up throughout their day and during their lives. The 'students' and the 'teacher' in the classroom will act in a different way on the bus going home. The bus conductor would be rather taken aback if the teacher, instead of paying the fare when asked, proceeded to give a talk to the passengers, punctuated with requests for the passengers to stop talking, sit properly and answer questions!

__ **Activity 1.6** _____

To show that people play a number of roles, make a list of all the roles you play. Be prepared to discuss these.

There is a danger in analysing social behaviour in terms of role theory. Stressing the way in which behaviour conforms to expected patterns can lead to a neglect of individual personality factors. There is, in reality, freedom for manoeuvre within a particular role. People interpret the role of student differently. Some students are passive, preferring only to listen, whilst others are lively and challenge the teacher. The role of teacher is also interpreted in different ways by different personalities. There are teachers who are very strict and expect complete attention from students, whilst others are more democratic and encourage students to participate in the class.

Two further ideas help to explain social behaviour within the frame-work of role theory. These are *role-set* and *role-conflict*. A role-set is a collection of roles which go together. Roles only make sense within a situation, and when complemented by other roles. The behaviour which makes up the role of teacher is meaningless without the presence of people acting the role of student. A teacher alone at the front of a classroom, perhaps catching up on some marking, appears somewhat lost and lonely. The way of talking associated with teaching, addressing people as a group and asking questions whilst knowing the subject, is only appropriate in conjunction with the role of student. It would be considered patronising and condescending if used in another situation, for example at a social event, even if the same individuals were present.

The other term mentioned was role-conflict. Activity 1.6 showed that people have several roles. It is possible for two or more of these roles to come into conflict and cause problems for the individual. For example, a person who is a mother or a father may also be a daughter or a son. The role of daughter is quite different from that of mother and it may be difficult for a person to play both roles simultaneously. Family visits to grandparents may produce this tension between the roles. People who are parents themselves will resent being treated as children, especially in front of their own children. From the other side, parents of grown-up children may find it difficult to adapt their behaviour and expectations to allow for the fact that their children are themselves now parents.

An understanding of role theory gives an insight into the problems people may encounter. Adjusting to a new role is not always easy. A woman with a new baby can find it difficult to adjust to the restrictions and responsibilities of motherhood, especially if she is not adequately prepared or supported in her new role. Men suffer the same problems of adjustment when they become fathers for the first time. The problems faced by young people are partly caused by their attempts to break away from the role of child and take up the role of adult. A person who has been made redundant at work will feel the loss of his or her role as worker and wage-earner, especially as that role will have carried a certain status.

Activity 1.7

List as many examples as you can where a change in role, a role conflict or a clash of roles between individuals may cause tension.

Problems which may arise in the following situations can be analysed in terms of role theory.

Retirement

When people retire after a life-time of work, even if they have looked forward to this event, they may experience feelings of loss of purpose and loss of identity. Their work will have given them a status and may also have been a source of power and prestige. Suddenly their identity is reduced, in the eyes of society, to that of old age pensioners. other members of the household may also find this a difficult time.

Mothers who work outside the home

Women who have paid jobs as well as caring for a family may experience a conflict over which role takes priority. This can be particularly acute at times when the children are ill, or have problems which seem to demand their mother's full-time attention. Whilst such demands may be unrealistic, many mothers feel guilty concerning the care of their children and women with paid employment are particularly vulnerable. Men may also feel threatened by their wives' ability to earn an income and have an independent existence and identity. The 1990s have seen an increase in the numbers of families in which women are in paid employment and men are unemployed. Many of the jobs which have been lost over the last 20 or so years have been jobs traditionally done by men; whilst new jobs created in service industries have often been those seen traditionally as 'women's jobs'. Although this situation can result in a successful 'role-swap', with the men becoming 'househusbands'; there are many sources of strain as people try to adjust to new roles or loss of roles, and come to terms with seeing their partners in new ways.

Unemployment

In our society, particular importance is attached to work roles. The first thing we want to know about someone is what they do: work roles are a source of status. Work takes up a large part of the day, week and year; it fills people's lives. As with retirement, unemployment can mean a loss of purpose and identity (as well as the more obvious loss of income). The effects of unemployment may be different for different people, depending on the centrality of the role of work in their lives. Although things are changing, it is still perhaps the case that loss of work has a different meaning for a man than for a woman. A woman has probably been brought up to attach importance to other roles, such as mother. Children may feel differently about unemployment affecting their father than their mother. The problems faced by young people unable to find work have aspects in common with those of older unemployed people, although there are some differences. Having the status of a job and a wage is an important aspect of adult life, and young people may find it difficult to make the transition into adulthood if they are deprived of work.

Shared households

Some newly-married couples live with their parents. Such a situation may demand a great deal of compromise and flexibility over roles. Often, the difficulties cannot be overcome, and there is conflict and tension among all the people involved. Similar problems may arise when an elderly person, having difficulties in managing alone, moves in with a daughter or son. The elderly person may feel that he or she has no role at all in the new household, whilst the other adults feel there is a risk of their roles and privacy being encroached upon or taken over.

Mature students

People who return to education after years spent working or raising a family may find being a mature student more difficult than they anticipated. They may feel that teaching staff give insufficient recognition to their experience and the contribution they could make to the class. At home, women in particular, may find that the family is not supportive and does not make allowances for the demands made by studying for examinations. Similarly, teachers used to working with young and inexperienced people may feel that their traditional position of authority is threatened by the presence of a mature student.

Promotion

Promotion within a work-place can be a cause of conflict. The newly-promoted person may find that it takes time to become accustomed to the new position in the hierarchy. Colleagues may find it difficult to accept the authority of someone who was very recently an equal.

Step-parents

A new adult joining an existing family and taking up the role of mother or father may be resented by children who have been used to managing as a single-parent family. The situation is not made any easier by the fairy-tale tradition of the wicked stepmother, nor by the fact that the children may still feel the loss of the natural parent.

These are only a selection of the examples which exist of ways in which role theory can aid understanding of problematic situations. The fact that such situations are a source of tension is illustrated by the frequency with which they are used in fiction on television and other media. Much drama and comedy is based on circumstances such as young couples living with their parents or people marrying a second time.

Sex-roles

An important area of role differentiation in this society is that which exists between males and females. In every aspect of life, differences between girls and boys, and men and women, are emphasised. In the home, certain tasks are seen as more appropriate to women and others better suited to men. In employment, women are concentrated in certain types and levels of work. In sport and leisure interests, males and females follow different activities. Males and females are thought to have different personalities and abilities.

___ **Activity 1.8** _____

In groups of three or four, decide which of these words describe men, women or are equally appropriate to either sex. You may need to look up some of the words in a dictionary.

aggressive	egotistic
independent	assertive
confident	helpless
sensitive	sympathetic
perceptive	passive
domesticated	caring
gossipy	gentle
emotional	self-sacrificing
catty	reliable
logical	brave
scheming	

___ **Activity 1.9** _____

Decide which of the words listed in Activity 1.8 describe:
(a) yourself
(b) someone of the opposite sex whom you know well.

Sexual stereotypes
Ascribing characteristics to people on the basis on factors like sex, race or age is known as *stereotyping*. Sex stereotypes are applied to males and females. It is common for women to be stereotyped as domesticated, emotional, passive and gentle, whereas men are seen as more aggressive, daring, logical and egotistic. The fact that stereotypes can be misleading is seen by the extent to which people tend not to see themselves, or people they know well, in the same way.

Stereotyping limits behaviour and development and can cause unhappiness for children and adults who cannot, or do not wish to, conform to the appropriate stereotype. Boys who do not act in an aggressive way, or who prefer quiet activities to competitive sport are labelled as 'wet', or in adult life, may be believed to be homosexual. It is interesting that the word 'tomboy' is not as derogatory as the label 'wet', but as a girl moves into her teens, if she does not become interested in clothes, make-up and girls' magazines, she may find herself socially isolated. These stereotypes may also limit choice of subject in school and later on, career decisions, restricting certain types of jobs to men and others to women. This is a waste of talent and ability and also leads to the perpetuation of the existing inequality.

If it is reasonably clear that stereotypes and role divisions exist, it is less clear how this situation comes about.

Activity 1.10

In pairs or groups of three, examine each of the following statements and decide if you think each is true or false:

1   Women are naturally better at caring for babies and small children.
2   It is natural for boys to take the initiative in asking girls out.
3   Men have a stronger sex-drive than women.
4   Women are, by nature, more concerned about their appearance than men.
5   Boys are less afraid of danger than girls.
6   Women's emotional needs are stronger than those of men.
7   Boys are naturally better at scientific subjects.
8   Girls cannot do maths.
9   Males are, by nature, more aggressive than females.
10   Men are naturally more competitive than women.

Masculinity and femininity

Although many people believe that sex differences have their origins in biological factors, there is no clear evidence to prove this. For example, it may be true that women show their emotions more than men, and are less attracted to technical subjects, but it is not necessarily true that these differences exist at birth.

Studies of different societies have found that both the characteristics of men and women and notions of masculinity and femininity vary considerably across different cultures. In a tribe called the Arapesh in New Guinea,

> the ideal adult has a gentle, passive, cherishing nature, and resembles the feminine type in our culture. In the relationships between the sexes, including the overtly sexual, the Arapesh recognises no temperamental differences at all. Neither is the initiator or the aggressor. The main 'work' of both adult men and women is child-bearing and child-rearing – indeed they call sexual intercourse 'work' when the object is conception ... The verb 'to bear a child' is used indiscriminately of both sexes.[4]

Within another tribe, the Tchambuli, the situation is quite different. Here, the women are practical, and men

> are skittish, wary of each other, interested in art, in the theatre, in a thousand petty bits of insult and gossip. Hurt feelings are rampant ... the pettiness of those who feel themselves weak and isolated. The men wear lovely ornaments (the women shave their heads and are unadorned) they do the shopping, they carve and paint and dance.[5]

Finally, an example from a South-west Pacific society where

only men wear flowers in their hair and scented leaves tucked into their belts or arm-bands. At formal dances it is the man who dresses in the most elegant finery and ... when these young men are fully made-up and costumed for the dance they are considered so irresistible to women that they are not allowed to be alone, even for a moment, for fear some women will seduce them.[6]

It seem that sex roles are not in fact biologically determined, but are cultural in origin, and learned by the members of a particular society.

___ **Activity 1.11** _____

List all the ways in which you think children might learn about sex roles.

Sexual differentiation
From the moment a child is born in this society, sexual differentiation is considered very important. Babies are given different coloured clothes and toys, and people express great embarrassment if they mistake the sex of a baby. Mothers and fathers treat male and female babies in different ways and have different expectations of them. Girls are praised for being 'pretty', boys for being 'clever' and 'brave'. Parents are more protective of their daughters than of their sons. Girls are taught to stay clean and take an interest in clothes, boys to be brave and not to cry. Toys believed to be appropriate for girls and boys reflect adult sex roles, with girls being encouraged to play with dolls, and boys with building sets. Children also learn by simply observing and imitating the adults they meet, in particular their parents. Girls may be encouraged to help with housework, while boys are given other tasks around the home.

The family is not the only source of learning for children. Books, comics, magazines, computer games, videos and television shows still also portray certain activities and role as more suitable for one sex than the other.

___ **Activity 1.12** _____

Collect together as many children's books and comics as you can find. Analyse the content in terms of sex roles. Look at the roles in which adults are shown. See if girls and boys are presented playing with different toys and games. Examine the books to see which children take leadership roles and show other children what to do. If you come across animal characters, are these male, female or neutral? How does this affect the personalities and behaviour of the characters?

___ **Activity 1.13** _____

Write a story for children which does not allocate different roles to males and females, but which encourages the interest of all children in all areas of life.

Adults outside the family also tend to treat girls and boys in different ways, encouraging them to play with particular toys and to act in certain ways. Schools continue this process and chapter 7 on education contains a section on this subject.

___ **Activity 1.14** _____

If you do placements in a nursery or children's home, make an observation of any ways in which boys and girls are treated differently. Compare your findings with those of the rest of the class. What effects might such differences have on children as they grow up?

   If this is not possible, carry out the same exercise, by thinking back to your own childhood.

The gender roles learned in childhood have implications which continue into adult life. One important example of this concerns the work done by men and women both inside and outside the home.

   Inside the home women are more likely to be responsible for housekeeping and childcare, whilst traditionally men take on tasks such as car maintenance and home repairs. This division of labour means that women play a very significant role in informal caring: for example caring for young children, looking after people who are ill and providing support and practical help for elderly parents. This point will be referred to again in looking at the implications of the policy of developing community care.

Horizontal and vertical job segregation

In paid employment many occupations are, to a greater or lesser extent, segregated by sex. This means that the labour market is divided into jobs done predominantly by men and jobs done predominantly by women. *Horizontal segregation* refers to situations in which different jobs, perhaps of equal status, are done by men and women. An example of this is in residential care where cooks and cleaners are usually women whilst gardeners and handypersons are usually men. *Vertical segregation* refers to situations in which men and women are working in the same jobs, but one group tends to dominate the top positions and therefore receives greater rewards and has more power. This tends to be the case in social work where the majority of social workers are women but only 12 out of 132 directors of social services are women.[7]

Activity 1.15

Make a study of a local social services or educational establishment. Find out which jobs are done by men and which jobs by women. Include the jobs of the people with the power – up to the relevant Secretary of State. Analyse your findings and decide if horizontal and/or vertical segregation exists. Compare your findings to national statistics.

Activity 1.16

Discussion points:
1 Does it matter if men and women do different work?
2 Does it matter if one group tends to hold the position of power in a particular field of work?
3 What might be the causes of segregation in work?
4 What could be done to change the situation?

1.3 Social class

One of the ways of understanding British society today is by looking at it in terms of class. This involves a view of society which takes account of the fact that people do not have equal access to wealth, power and prestige. In Britain the majority of people recognise the existence of a class structure, although they may not agree on what determines class.[8] Also they may not be aware of all the implications of class. This section describes a scheme for classifying people on the basis of social standing in the community, and comments on some of the implications of class.

Class and life-style

An understanding of the class structure is important to those who want to bring about social reforms and to help people. For example, in the field of education, policy-makers and people working in schools have aimed for a long time at achieving equality of opportunity in education. So far, changes, such as the introduction of comprehensive schools, have had little effect and educational achievement still bears a strong relationship to social class. Chapter 7 looks at this aspect of education in some detail.

The Activity that follows demonstrates some of the less serious distinctions between different classes and serves to illustrate the relationship between class and life-style.

Activity 1.17

What class are you? Without taking the questions too seriously, tick answer
(a) (b) or (c) and then calculate your score.
1   At a party, which of the following drinks would you prefer?
    (a)   lager
    (b)   martini and lemonade
    (c)   gin and tonic
2   Which of these three names would you prefer for your daughter?
    (a)   Tracey
    (b)   Clarissa
    (c)   Hannah
3   Which of the following TV programmes would you prefer to watch?
    (a)   a ballet
    (b)   *Brookside*
    (c)   a nature programme
4   What do you call the main meal of the evening?
    (a)   tea
    (b)   supper
    (c)   dinner
5   Which of these three holidays would you prefer?
    (a)   a week at a holiday camp
    (b)   A rail trip to Birmingham to go to the 'Ideal Home' exhibition
    (c)   a week in Scotland walking and fishing
6   Which newspaper do you read?
    (a)   *Guardian*
    (b)   *Financial Times*
    (c)   *Sun*
7   To which station is your radio most often tuned?
    (a)   Radio Five Live
    (b)   Radio Three
    (c)   Four Radio
8   How would you rather spend a Saturday evening?
    (a)   Betting at the greyhound races
    (b)   Eating out at a restaurant
    (c)   At the opera
9   If you wanted a new coat which of the following would you be most
    likely to do?
    (a)   Have a look in your friend's mail order catalogue
    (b)   Go to the local High Street shops
    (c)   Wait until your next trip to London
10 After an expensive meal at a restaurant, how would you pay?
    (a)   By American Express
    (b)   By cheque
    (c)   With cash

Award yourself marks as follows and add up the total. Question 1. (a) 10 (b) 8 (c) 6; 2. (a) 10 (b) 6 (c) 8; 3. (a) 6 (b) 10 (c) 8; 4. (a) 10 (b) 6 (c) 8; 5. (a) 10 (b) 8 (c) 6; 6. (a) 8 (b) 6 (c) 10; 6. (a) 8 (b) 8 (c) 10; 7. (a) 10 (b) 6 (c) 10; 8. (a) 10 (b) 8 (c) 6; 9. (a) 10 (b) 8 (c) 6; 10. (a) 10 (b) 8 (c) 10.

Results of quiz

94–100 This scores indicates a person with working-class tastes and no desires to pretend to be anything else.

88–92 There are three possibilities to explain this score. One is that you ticked any answer at random. Second, you could have changed class: perhaps your parents are working class, but you have a professional occupation and associate with middle-class people. Or perhaps you pride yourself on doing whatever you feel like.

70–86 The nearer the score is to 80, the more the tastes might be described as lower middle-class. The person who scores around 80 is definitely not working-class in his or her tastes, but cannot be described as middle-class.

60–68 This score demonstrates a middle-class life-style. A score at the lower end of the band might qualify for another term such as upper-class or upper middle-class.

Class stereotypes

There is a set of attitudes, habits and a life-style which go to make up a class stereotype. There are, also, more serious effects of class which tend to mitigate any attempts of policy-makers to move towards social equality. Educational achievement, access to wealth and top jobs, and length of life are all statistically related to social class. Statistics show that middle-class people are more likely to use contraception effectively and to have smaller families. Such people are generally healthier and less likely to suffer from serious illnesses. Working-class people are more likely to become unemployed at some time in their working life, and to have to take time off work because of illness. Smoking is more prevalent amongst the working class, as are respiratory diseases as a cause of death. Working-class people are less likely to own their own houses, and more likely to be council or housing association tenants.[9]

Activity 1.18

Using all the information in section 1.3, together with that contained in the quiz plus any additional information you have, write a brief character sketch of a real or imaginary person. Give the person a name, a job and a life-style. Read out your description and ask others to say to which class they think the person belongs.

Up to this point, words such as 'working class', 'middle class' and 'upper class' have been used loosely without much thought as to what 'class' means. Meeting Jeremy Ponsonby-Smythe who attends a public school and enjoys a game of real tennis, it is not difficult to apply the label 'upper-class' or 'upper-middle-class'. It is more difficult to say which particular variable indicates social class. The factors which people commonly use to define social class include the way people speak, their job, their educational background, the amount of money people have or the way they spend it, including how they dress and the car they drive.

Activity 1.19 _____

Decide what class you think you are and write it on a piece of paper.

Occupation and class

In everyday conversation, it does not matter too much what people mean when they talk about class. However, compilation of statistical information linking class with factors such as educational achievement or death by different causes, requires a strict definition of the term. The indicator most commonly used is that of occupation. There are pitfalls in grouping people on this basis but it does seem that different types of work are linked with different life-styles and attitudes. One means of demonstrating this (and becoming unpopular) is to try and convince a stranger at a party that you do a job very different from the one you really do. It is probably because class and occupation are so closely related that a conversation between strangers usually begins with the question 'What do you do?'. The man in a suit, carrying the *Financial Times* at the opera, may be a coalminer but it is unlikely.

Government reports and most other surveys which relate information to class use a form of classification devised and updated from time to time by the Registrar-General (a government official). The Registrar-General has a list of some 20 000 occupational titles which are then grouped into occupational units. These groupings are intended to reflect occupational skill and qualifications. This information is then summarised to arrive at five groups, the middle one of which is commonly split into two. Table 1.1 shows this classification. Whilst it is difficult to produce a better scheme, there are problems in the Registrar-General's classification.

Activity 1.20 _____

Study Table 1.1 and decide which class you are. Compare this with your self-classification in Activity 1.19 and discuss any difficulties or variation.

TABLE 1.1 The Registrar-General's classification of occupations

Examples of occupations			Social status	Definition
Senior executives, doctors, lawyers, accountants, bank managers, chemists, University teachers	N O N	I (A)	Upper middle class	Professional, higher managerial and administrative
chiropodists, farmers, journalists police officers, teachers, nurses	M A N U	II (B)	middle class	intermediate managerial, administrative, professional
bank clerks, technicians, sales representatives, secretaries, shop assistants, estate agents,	A L	III (C1)	lower middle class	skilled, intermediate and junior non-manual
fitters, welders, bus-drivers, miners, cooks, electricians, hairdressers, carpenters	M A	III (C2)	skilled working class	skilled manual
agricultural workers, bus conductors, machine-sewers, postmen and postwomen	N U A L	IV (D)	semi-skilled working class	semi-skilled manual
labourer, cleaner, window-cleaner, railway-porter, messenger		V (E)	working class	unskilled manual

Some of the troublesome aspects of this method of determining social class are described below. Households, children, and sometimes, married women are allocated to a class on the basis of the occupation of the head of the household. Where there is an adult male and an adult female, the man is taken as the head of the household. Whilst people tend to marry within a social class, it is possible, for example, for a middle-class woman to marry a working class man. In this situation it could easily be the woman's class background which most influences the family's life-style and values.

There appears to be a group missing from the top of the scale. Whilst not numerically significant, there are titled aristocrats who live on inherited wealth. These people probably have more social standing in the community than doctors or lawyers. Also, the occupational groups are large and not clearly defined. For example, farmers vary from large-scale land-owners employing workers to tenant-farmers working a small farm alone. Their social standing and life-style cannot be assumed to be similar.

The division between non-manual and manual work also creates some problems. It is debatable whether a secretary or a shop assistant has more status than an electrician or hairdresser. More generally, using 'present occupation' as the determining factor for class analysis does not allow for the prestige a person may have through the social standing of his or her parents.

Class and economic production

There are other ways of looking at class. For example, there is a strong tradition of seeing class in terms of people's relationship to the means of economic production. This means that one class is defined as being the owners and controllers of the factories, machines and processes which produce goods and wealth. The other class is forced to sell its labour in order to survive. Whilst this analysis is very important, most of the references to class throughout this book will be using the term in the sense in which it is defined in the Registrar-General's classification.

1.4   Race and racism

This section looks at aspects of the situation of Britain's black population. It starts by looking at countries from which black people, or their parents, came to Britain and the reasons why they left their home to come here. This is followed by an examination of cultural differences between different groups. Finally the problem of racism is introduced, along with examination of some policy initiatives to combat racism. These issues are also looked at more specifically in the chapters which follow.

What is 'race'?

Section 1.1 of this chapter looked at some of the problems in finding the best words to use: these problems are especially difficult to solve in the context of talking about race. The word 'race' itself is somewhat nonsensical. It has no scientific meaning in the sense in which it was originally used to refer to genetically distinct groups. Its origins are tied up with the colonisation of other countries through the British empire and the use of the other people as slaves. The idea that some human beings were of a different 'race' – and seen at the time as inferior with less developed feelings and intellects – helped to justify slavery in white people's minds. If we actually tried to strictly divide people into racial groups – as was done under the apartheid system in South Africa – ridiculous problems of classifying particular individuals follow. However issues to do with race are significant in this society and do need to be talked about – whilst this is the case we cannot simply abandon the word race. In this book the term will be

Source: Gina Glover, Photofusion
Britain is a multi-racial society

used in the same imprecise way as it is used by the general population, to refer
loosely to people with different skin colours.

What is 'black'?

Another term which needs some explanation is 'black'. As used here, this
includes people from India, Pakistan and Bangladesh, as well as to those from
Africa and the Caribbean. This convention is followed despite a recognition that
the groups included may have little in common with each other in terms of
culture. It is also the case that some Asians would not accept the term 'black' as
applying to themselves.

UK-born ethnic groups

Another source of confusion that needs to be mentioned here concerns the convention of calling people Asian or West Indian even when they were born in the
UK. A common way to avoid some of these issues is to use the term 'minority
ethnic group', meaning a group with its own cultural background which does not
make up the majority of the population in a given country.

Origin of Britain's black population

___ Activity 1.21 _____

Make a list of countries from which Britain's black population originates.

People of Asian origin came from two parts of the world. The first is the Indian sub-continent – India, Pakistan and Bangladesh. Second, many British Asians had been living, and perhaps had been born, in East Africa. Such people came to Britain from Tanzania, Kenya, Uganda and Malawi. There is also a small number of Africans living in Britain although more important in terms of numbers are those who come from the Caribbean, also known as the West Indies. West Indian people living in Britain have come from a number of Caribbean islands such as Jamaica, Trinidad, Barbados, Grenada or Antigua.

___ Activity 1.22 _____

Have a look in an atlas to see if you know where these places are in the world.

___ Activity 1.23 _____

Conduct an informal survey in the classroom to find out what people think is the proportion of black people in the population. Guess the percentage of blacks in Britain and write it on a peice of paper, then collect together the information to establish an average.

Percentage of minority groups in the population

In 1991, for the first time, the government decided to include a question on ethnic origin in the census carried out on the whole population. The total population of Great Britain on the night of the census was 54 888 844. Of these people 94.5 per cent were white, and 5.5 per cent from minority ethnic groups.[10] Other statistical sources have indicated similar percentages. Table 1.2 shows more detail, giving percentages for different minority ethnic groups.

You can now compare these figures with your estimates in Activity 1.23. The most common result is for people to over-estimate, often hugely, the size of the minority ethnic population in relation to the white population. In my experience this is true of nearly everyone who has done this exercise, regardless of where they live. Why do people tend to do this? It is probably an aspect of racism, fuelled by the press, some politicians and general ignorance which leads people

TABLE 1.2   Percentage of the population in various ethnic groups, 1992

Group	(%)
White	94.5
Black Caribbean	0.9
Black African	0.4
Black other	0.3
Indian	1.5
Pakistani	0.9
Bangladeshi	0.3
Chinese	0.3
Other Asian	0.4
Other	0.5

Source: OPCS, National Monitor (Government Statistical Office, 1992), Crown Copyright.

to believe that there are many more black people in Britain than is actually the case.

The historical context

Why did people come to Britain?

Racism feeds generally on lack of knowledge and one particular area of ignorance concerns the reasons why people emigrated to Britain. A full understanding of this requires an explanation which goes back some 400 years and looks at Britain's role in the slave trade and the exploitation of other countries through the British empire. It is not possible to give such an account here, and whilst it should be noted that black people have been in Britain since the sixteenth century, the explanation here focuses on the period following the Second World War, which is when many Asians and West Indians arrived.

After the Second World War Britain experienced a serious shortage of labour and many employers, especially those offering low wages or expecting people to work anti-social hours, could not find workers. It was at this time, in 1948, that the Nationality Act was passed which established two types of British subject. 'Citizens of the UK and colonies' and 'Citizens of Commonwealth Countries'. Both were free to enter and remain in the UK and, by a simple process of registration, a citizen of a commonwealth country could become a citizen of the UK and colonies. One explanation for this law was that it was a token of gratitude for the large part played by the colonies in fighting the war. However, another motive was probably to allow employers to make use of workers from the poorer countries to solve the problem of not being able to attract workers in Britain.

People were actively encouraged to come and work in Britain. For example, London Transport went to the Caribbean to recruit workers. Enoch Powell, then Conservative Minister of Health, also sought West Indians to work in the National Health Service. Employers in the textile industries looked to India and Pakistan for staff. In the words of one writer:

The 'immigrants' came because they were invited. The Macmillan government embarked on a large-scale advertising campaign to attract them. They were extraordinary advertisments, full of hope and optimism, which made Britain out to be a land of plenty, a golden opportunity not to be missed. They worked. People travelled here in good faith, believing themselves wanted.[11]

People came for work, in order to send money back home or to achieve a better standard of living for themselves and their families. Some Asians also came as a result of the partition of India (in 1947) into India and Pakistan, in which Britain politicians had played a major role.

The partition caused disturbances at the border areas and led to a situation where people living on the Indian side of the border following the Muslim religion became a religious and cultural minority. They emigrated into Pakistan where they were refugees without work. Since they were already uprooted and living precariously some decided to come to Britain.

East African Asians were in a different situation. They had emigrated from India to Africa in the first half of this century, encouraged by the British who wanted a middle class to exist between the British rulers and the African populations. The Asians in East Africa were wealthy and owned many of the business enterprises. However, when the African countries achieved independence from Britain, the position of the Asians became insecure, and they were often forced to leave.

Restrictions on immigration

By the end of the 1950s, two things were happening. First, immigration was slowing down, as the demand for workers decreased. Second, racism in Britain was beginning to take on violent forms and become a subject of public debate. In 1962, legislation was passed, restricting immigration. It is ironic to note that racism and immigration laws sometimes had the opposite effect to that which was intended. For example, many Asian men came with the intention of earning some money, with which to return home. However, discrimination in employment forced them to set up businesses which, taking considerable time and investment to establish, they were reluctant to give up. Similarly, there was a tendency in some Indian families to send one son temporarily, to be replaced by another, on his return. The laws passed in the 1960s restricting entry made frequent trips to and from Britain impossible and resulted in the men staying on and sending for their wives and children.

By the 1970s, immigration of black people into Britain was practically non-existent and limited to dependents of those people already here. In 1981, a law was passed to come into effect on 1 January 1983, replacing the 1948 Nationality Act and incorporating aspects of immigration laws passed in the 1960s and 1970s. The 1981 Nationality Act set up three tiers of citizenship; British citizenship, British overseas citizenship and citizenship of the British dependent territories. Of these three, only the first gives an automatic right to enter and live in Britain, and being born in Britain is no longer sufficient to give British citizenship. People living abroad who are included in the category of

British citizen are largely white, living in places such as Canada and Australia, whereas the people in the category of British overseas citizen are mainly black.

Cultural variation

When people move to a different country, they do not somehow forget all the things they have learned in the country from which they came. People will adapt in some ways to a new way of life, but they will probably retain their values and some aspects of their life-style.

Activity 1.24

Imagine you and your family are going to live in a very different culture, perhaps in the Middle East. How much of yourself and your life-style would you want, or be prepared to change? Think about whether you would change your religion, your way of eating, your ideas about marriage and bringing up children. Would you seek out people like yourself, or would you make friends with native inhabitants of the country?

To have a better understanding of ethnic minority groups in England, it is helpful to know something of the way of life in the countries from which they originate.

Activity 1.25

In small groups make a study of one of the countries from which Britain's black population originally came, as mentioned earlier. Cover aspects such as religion, food, education and family structure. Report your findings to the class.

Asian society

A very brief and generalised account is given here of life in the Indian sub-continent. Many people, although not all, from the Indian sub-continent, come from a rural background where the main occupation is farming. In the villages, homes commonly consist of a number of rooms built around a courtyard. People live in large family groups, which incorporate three generations. When sons marry, they bring their wives into their family home, whilst daughters join the family of their husbands. Indians have strong feelings and obligations towards their families and there are also powerful kinship relations between families.

Amrit Wilson, in her book on Asian women, argues that an important factor in Indian family life is the concept of *izzat*.[12] In one sense, *izzat* means male pride, but it also refers to the honour of the family, and it is the responsibility of everyone to maintain and enhance the *izzat* of the family. In traditional Indian families, men and women have separate roles, with the women responsible for housework and child-care. Children are given a great deal of love and attention and allowed a lot of freedom. In the large families, the women provide a great deal of support for each other. Marriage is seen, not as an individual concern, but as something which affects the whole family, and as a result, marriages are arranged by the parents of the young couple.

Religion is a very important part of Indian life, affecting clothes, food and many other aspects of life. The three main religions of India are Hinduism, Sikhism and Islam.

Caribbean society

Caribbean societies are much more similar to British society, reflecting the European influence on the islands. This influence shows in the political and legal systems, as well as in education, where schools may offer GCSE examinations from the English examining boards. The language of the West Indies is English, sometimes spoken in a dialect known as Creole. The main religion on the islands is Christianity or Rastafarianism.

West Indians see the ideal for families as being a married couple and their children. However, other forms of family group are most common. Poverty means that men need to travel to find work and as a result many families consist of a woman, her children and her mother. Common-law marriage is also as common as legal marriage. This situation means that women have considerable authority in the family. Children are brought up strictly and obedience is expected, both at home and at school.

Activity 1.26

What cultural variation exists between different ethnic groups in Britain? List any you can think of.

Ethnic minorities and British society

The following section examines some way in which ethnic minorities differ from white British society. It is important to note that what is said is very much at the level of generalisation. In reality, there are wide variations between members of minority ethnic groups, and changes occurring as the generation of black people born in England grows up.

Marriage and family life

Minority groups are unusual in so far as there are fewer older people than in the population as a whole. This is explained by the fact that most people who came in the 1950s and 1960s were young and are now moving into middle age. The absence of a large number of elderly people partly explains the statistical fact that minority households tend to be larger, since in the general population elderly people make up a large proportion of one- and two-person households. However, whilst most black people live in households containing one adult couple, households with more adults are more common than in the rest of society. This is in part a result of choice, but is also related to difficulties in finding housing, shortage of money and a tendency to feel the need for support, because of the difficulties of living in an alien and sometimes hostile society.

Even where people do not live in the same house, ties and obligations between relatives are stronger than tends to be the case for white people. Relatives commonly live near each other and spend leisure time in each other's company. Having said this, it is important that social workers and others do not adopt a stereotyped view of the Asian family in particular, assuming older people will always be cared for by relatives and that services are not needed to meet their needs. One piece of research studied European, Asian and Afro-Caribbean older people in Birmingham. The study found that although 95 per cent of the Asians said that they were looked after by relatives when they came out of hospital, one quarter of the sample had no close relatives in Britain.[13]

In Asian families, there is a tendency for there to be a clear separation between male and female roles, and this is reflected in the way in which girls and boys are brought up, as well as in relationships between husbands and wives.

The Indian custom of arranged marriages continues in Britain. Whilst some young people reject the idea, most accept it as part of their culture or realise that to rebel would be to risk losing the support of their family and the Asian community. It is usual for there to be some consultation between parents and their children over arranged marriages. One Indian girl says, 'If my mum shows me a boy and I refuse, she does not mind. She asks me the reason and I tell her. If it's not my cup of tea I don't have it, and that's the case with most girls.'[14]

Young people with Asian parents live something of a double life, moving between two cultures. At home, they are expected to maintain Asian ways, whereas at school and college, they are exposed to Western culture. These two worlds are often kept strictly apart as any attempt to combine them leads to conflict. This is perhaps particularly true of Asian girls, who often have more freedom at school and college than at home. Obviously all parents want their children to be successful, but ethnic minority parents are especially ambitious for their children, wanting for them the things that they themselves could not have.

Religion and religious customs

This section focuses on people who originate from the Indian sub-continent. West Indians are mainly Christians, although Rastafarianism is becoming increasingly significant in West Indian communities.

As mentioned earlier the three main religions of India are Hinduism, Sikhism and Islam. Religious rules and customs cover many aspects of life, for example food and dress. Islamic law requires that women keep their bodies covered. Within Hinduism, a female must not show her legs, once she reaches womanhood. This at first caused problems in schools, where girls were not allowed to wear trousers or were expected to wear shorts for physical education. The clothes worn by Asian women are of several types, depending on the part of India from which they originate and the religion. Even within one kind of dress, there are many subtle variations. Examples of Asian clothes for women are saris, the *salwar-kamiz*, which is a long tunic worn with trousers and the *dupatta*, which is a long scarf worn over the head and shoulders. Sikhism demands that men do not cut their hair, and that they should wear a turban.

Food is also governed by religion. Muslims must eat *halal meat*, which is meat slaughtered according to certain rules, and pork is forbidden. Hindus are vegetarian, as are some Sikhs. All three religions require fasting on particular days of the year.

Activity 1.27

In small groups find out more about Hinduism, Sikhism and Islam. Also find out about other religions such as Rastafarianism and the Jewish religion.

In the following extract an Asian Hindu talks about her religion and her life to Julie, who is collecting information for a project as part of her Diploma in Playgroup Practice.

On religion ...
We believe in one god – Krishna. In our religion we have many gods but they are all aspects of the god Krishna. I don't find the fact that the children are taught mainly about the Christian religion a problem as we believe that all gods, the Muslim god and the Christian god, are all aspects of Krishna. I tell my children this.

Every day I have a ritual bath then I light an oil lamp to pray to Krishna. We have a special place or shrine in our house called a Mandir – the oil lamp or Dibo goes on the Mandir. When I cook I always put a little of the food on the Mandir as a 'thank you' or offering to God before we eat. If I buy fruit I always wash it and put it on the Mandir before I give it to the children to eat.

I never waste food or throw it away. I give leftovers to the birds. In India very religious people will give food to birds, cows or beggars before they eat. When I pray I say sorry to God for things that I've done wrong.

We do have a lot of festivals and sometimes we hire a hall at the college. Gorba is a kind of folk dance which carries on over nine days. The date is variable but it usually falls in October. Gorba tells the story of the Goddess Durgama or Kali who has a war with a devil. After nine days she won. We dress up in Indian clothing and dance. Diwali is another festival and there are many more.

On food ...
I am a strict vegetarian and so are my husband and children. Some Hindus will eat fish and other meats but no beef as the cow is sacred. In Gujerat where I come from people are mostly vegetarian but they will eat chicken if they live on a farm.

My best friend is a Hindu but she eats meat. She thinks that it is important to do as the English do in this country. I don't think one should give up one's beliefs and we have many arguments about it.

The children are very strict about it too. When Srina was two we went to visit a relative and she was offered curry with chicken in it. I didn't tell her not to eat it, and the relative encouraged her to try it but she refused.

Although school will provide vegetarian meals they will assume that the children will eat fish. I have to be careful to specify no meat or fish. The children take a packed lunch. Even things like biscuits have animal fats in them so I have to be careful. When the children were at playgroup I asked the staff to check the ingredients on the packet to make sure there were no animal products in the food.

On marriage and family life …
We usually have marriages arranged for us but we do have a choice. If we have a meeting with our potential husband or wife and don't like them we can refuse. My brother saw fifteen girls before he said okay.

I was born in Uganda then lived in India from age three to fourteen. My parents then came to England. My husband's family came from Kenya. I agreed to marry my husband although he was the first man I was introduced to as a prospective husband. I liked him and he was quite religious and also a vegetarian. If he was not a vegetarian I would have refused him as I could not cook meat.

We were very happy at first then we moved in with his parents and lived with them for eight years. We had three small children and slept in one room. I don't get on with my in-laws. They are very critical, particularly my mother-in-law, and I could do nothing right. When we got our own house, it was much better.

The family in Hindu life is very important but like anyone there may be personal clashes. My parents live in London but I don't get on with my mother because our temperaments are too similar. We fight quite a lot but if they needed me to look after them I would.

Caste is more important in India when choosing a husband or wife. If a man or woman really wants to marry someone of a different caste the family will usually object but come round to it eventually in this country.

I have a friend from Rajastan. Her parents objected to her marrying a Patel as they wanted her to marry from her own community. The pair insisted and now they all get on very well.

I have a cousin who married an English woman. My uncle was furious although my aunt was not so angry. They gave in the end and the couple married. Funnily enough they ended up getting divorced and my cousin married another English women. Now they are very happy and are accepted by the family.

Most Hindus will eventually accept marriage to an English woman but would object if a Hindu married an African or West Indian. This is crazy as a lot of Indians lived in Africa. How can we condemn racism if we are prejudiced ourselves? I am very against this.

Weddings are huge affairs. In India if a girl is born the family start saving for the wedding straight away as they are so expensive.

I have read about people aborting female foetuses in India. It is terrible. My husband was really pleased when Sita was born and the nurses said 'I'm surprised you're happy to have a girl, most Indian people want boys'.

Valuing ethnic culture

┌─ **Activity 1.28** ────────────────────────────────┐

What steps can be taken by a nursery school or children's home in a multi-racial area to reflect the different cultures of the children?

└──┘

It is not difficult for a nursery or other organisation, having recognised the need, to provide an atmosphere in which all children can feel at home. There is a need for teachers and other staff from ethnic minorities, and for white teachers to know something of the different cultures. Perhaps staff who speak only English could learn something of the languages spoken by people in the area, and they certainly should make sure they are able to pronounce the children's names correctly.

The nursery or other children's home should generally reflect the fact that the children are from different backgrounds. This can be done with posters, toys, dressing-up clothes, musical instruments, stories and books. It is particularly important that books and posters show black people in everyday situations in Britain. Where food is provided, different diets must be recognised and respected and all religious festivals should be celebrated, not just Christmas and Easter.

┌─ **Activity 1.29** ────────────────────────────────┐

Why is it important for a nursery, or any other provision, to reflect the different cultures its children come from?

└──┘

There are several points to be made here, all of which are very important. People settle much more quickly in a familiar environment, especially young children who may have little experience outside the home. Where a child's or adult's culture is ignored a feeling of conflict may result, or a feeling that a particular type of background is not valued by society. Also, if white and black children are educated to understand and accept different cultures, they may grow up to be more tolerant adults.

Racial disadvantage

So far, this section has looked at the reasons why black people came to Britain, the backgrounds from which they came and variations in life-style and beliefs. Little has been said about the experience and treatment of ethnic groups in this country.

```
Activity 1.30
```

Make a list of areas of life where you think black people might have suffered from discrimination.

The theme of this section is racism and ways in which society operates in such a way as to disadvantage black people. Racism and disadvantage take many forms and the aspects covered here give an indication rather than a total picture of the problem. The term racism, as used here, has several aspects. First, it refers to attitudes and behaviour of individuals who discriminate between black and white people, or who believe, consciously or unconsciously, that white people are superior. Second, racism describes procedures and practices of individuals or institutions, which, intentionally or unintentionally, work to the disadvantage of ethnic minorities.

Table 1.3 is a chart produced by an advisory committee of Berkshire County Council in 1983, showing the various aspects of racism, compared with a situation of equality.[15]

TABLE 1.3   Racism and equality

	Racism	*Equality and justice*
POWER, PARTICIPATION AND INFLUENCE	White people control all or most positions of management, government, influence and power; black people are disproportionately involved in menial work, or are unemployed or under-employed	Black people are proportionately represented in management and government at all levels, and are not over-represented in lowest-paid and lowest-status occupations or in unemployment or under-employment
PRACTICES, PROCEDURES AND CUSTOMS	Practices, procedures and customs affecting life-chances and the allocation of scarce resources benefit white people rather than black, and work to the disadvantage therefore of black	Practice, procedures and customs do not discriminate to the advantage of white people and to the disadvantage of black. On the contrary they are fair to all
BELIEFS AND ATTITUDES	White people believe in white superiority, have negative views and expectations of black, and are ignorant or indifferent with regard to the nature of racism. Black people in consequence develop negative views of white	There is mutual respect and appreciation: black people and white are ready to learn and benefit from each other's history, culture, insights and experiences, and to work together co-operatively on the solution of common problems

Source: Berkshire County Council, *Education for Racial Equality* (1983).

Black people suffer from racism in a variety of ways, they are abused and ridiculed, their culture is ignored or denigrated and they live in a society which, in terms of advertising and other media, treats them either as non-existent or in terms of stereotypes. The following extracts show how black children can feel, on realising that they are not white. This experience is particularly painful for black children who have grown up in a white world. The two women referred to in the first extract were both brought up by white foster parents.

> When Susie Crawford first went to school, she was called a wog and a golliwog. Later in the bath she scrubbed her skin until it was red. Mary Titchmarsh recalls going riding with a (white) friend on her horse. When it refused at a jump she called it a silly wog – without knowing what the word meant. Her friend said, 'My horse is not a silly wog. You're a wog'. 'That really hurt', says Mary. 'She was my best friend'.[16]

A black man who was educated at an English boarding school tells how:

> The social brainwashing has its desired effect. If I wanted to be better, to be like them, I had to be white. So I tried. At Easter 1960, when I was fourteen – Easter, because that was when Jesus was in the mood to forgive *all* sins and by now black had become a sin – I went down on my knees and prayed, real hard. Every time I was alone I prayed, sometimes for hours. I prayed with tears in my eyes, imploring God to listen to my plea. I prayed to God to make me white. The myth of black inferiority, having been preached at me for so long, convinced me that the way out was to become a white man.[17]

Activity 1.31

Susie and Mary in the first extract above were fostered by white parents. There has been a lot of debate about mixed race fostering and adoption. The Commission for Racial Equality have a booklet on this called *Adopting a Better Policy* which contains useful evidence, recommendations and further readings.

For the address of the CRE, see Further Reading section at the end of this chapter, p. 38. Do some library research on the arguments surrounding adoption and fostering of ethnic minority children and decide your own view on this issue.

Activity 1.32

As a class, carry out a survey of media to discover the way in which ethnic groups are presented or ignored by the media. Include books, comics, magazines, newspapers, television and videos in your study.

Racism does not only consist of verbal attacks and lack of respect for black people and their culture, it can also erupt in violence. It is difficult to find figures to illustrate the level of racist attacks on people in Britain. This is partly because of the way in which records are kept. The police keep statistics for 'inter-racial incidents' which not is the same as attacks motivated by racism, which is what people generally mean by 'racial attacks'. Also there is a reluctance on the part of members of ethnic minorities to report incidents to the police, perhaps because they feel the police cannot, or will not help them. Local newspapers in areas like Southall in London and Handsworth in Birmingham regularly report attacks on Asians.

Amrit Wilson, in the introduction to her book on Asian women, tells of a woman who will not open the door until she hears a greeting in Bengali and another whose child was badly beaten up on the way to school. These women feel that Asians must live near each other for protection from violence. In Amrit Wilson's book, one woman describes an incident as follows:

> It was just an ordinary evening. I had done all the cooking and was waiting for my husband to come home. Suddenly I heard a loud scream and rushed to the front door. Half a dozen white teenagers were beating someone up. There was blood on the pavement. I couldn't see who it was at first, then I realised it was my husband. He was unconscious on the ground. They were kicking and beating him. I screamed for help. the neighbours rushed out and we beat off the thugs with sticks and broom-handles. We called the police and ambulance but it was long time before the police arrived. They went to see my husband in hospital and asked him to see them when he came out. But when he did, they showed no interest at all, they just said the officer concerned was not there. They made no attempt to catch the thugs.[18]

Specific aspects of racial disadvantage, such as in housing, education and employment, are examined in Chapters 5, 7 and 4 of this book.

Policy on racism

1976 Race Relations Act

The discrimination and disadvantage suffered by black people persists despite the existence of legislation which makes discrimination illegal. The Act of Parliament which covers this is the 1976 Race Relation Act. The law makes discrimination illegal in a variety of circumstances including employment, housing, education and the provision of goods and services. The Race Relations Act is concerned with discrimination on racial grounds, which is defined in terms of colour, race, nationality or ethnic origins. Discrimination is defined in three ways. First, it is against the law to treat a person less favourably, on the grounds of race. Second, indirect discrimination consists of applying criteria which work to the disadvantage of one person over another, for no justifiable reason. An example of this might be an employer requiring a high standard of English for a job which does not need this qualification. Third, it is illegal to victimise someone for being involved in making a complaint about discrimination.

People who believe that they have been illegally discriminated against must prove in a court (or industrial tribunal in the case of employment) that they have been treated less favourably because of their race. If people are successful in proving that discrimination occurred they can be awarded compensation and sometimes have the situation put right. The Commission for Racial Equality, which was set up by the government to work towards the elimination of discrimination, can help in the preparation of Race Relations Act cases.

__ **Activity 1.33** _____

Why might the Race Relations Act have limitations as a means of stopping discrimination?

The first and most obvious problem of the existing anti-discrimination legislation is that people have to prove that the law was broken. This is extremely difficult, since few employers are going to admit that they are acting illegally. If, for example, someone is not given a job, it is difficult to prove that discrimination on the grounds of race was the reason. Also, people may feel that they will lose more than they will gain by bringing a case to court or to a tribunal. However, the 1976 legislation is important and its existence may serve to prevent some discrimination from occurring and perhaps act to change attitudes towards race.

Equal opportunities policies

Many organisations in the public and the private sectors have adopted policies to promote equal opportunities. These can cover various aspects of the organisation and the services it provides. In terms of employment practices, an equal opportunities policy could involve the following aspects. The first step might be to examine current practices in case any are discriminatory in the sense of preventing black people from competing for jobs on an equal basis with whites. Secondly, positive action can be taken in terms of advertising posts in such a way as to attract black people to areas of work where they are needed. Finally, in areas of work where a particular racial group is under-represented, training can be provided or people can be encouraged to go for training.

The following is an example of how the positive action already outlined could be used in a social services department. A social services division in an area of the country with a large population has no black social workers. When vacancies arise, the employing authority could use positive action in the following ways:

- The advertisement for posts could include a statement that applications from members of ethnic minorities are welcomed.
- The authority could encourage black people to train as social workers (although cannot guarantee a job afterwards, since this would count as unlawful discrimination).
- If there is a job which involves providing people from a particular racial group with personal services to promote their welfare, the law allows the

employer to appoint someone of the same racial group. An example of this might be a post of warden in a hostel for Asian girls.

This chapter has attempted to demonstrate the importance of recognising that Britain is a culturally and racially diverse society. Alongside this, is the necessity of understanding the causes and effects of disadvantage. This understanding is perhaps particularly important for those who work in the caring professions, whether in nurseries, children's homes or in the community. It may be that such an understanding will be the first step towards moving away from the situation, described by Salman Rushdie, where, 'Britain is now two entirely different worlds, and the one you inherit is determined by the colour of your skin'.[19]

Activity 1.34

Make sure that you understand the following expressions, which have been used in this chapter. Check the glossary on p. 363 if you need to.

census	psychological
class structure	racism
common-law marriage	role
comprehensive school	role-set
cultural differences	role-conflict
depression	selective schooling
deprivation	social services
discrimination	state sector
equality of opportunity	status
ethnic minority	statutory organisation
learning disability	stereotype
legal system	stigma
positive action	voluntary organisation
private sector	welfare provision

Further reading

There are several other introductory textbooks on social welfare. These include the following: Tony Bryne and Colin Padfield, *Social Services*, 4th edition (London: Made Simple Books, 1990); Muriel Brown, *Introduction to Social Administration in Britain*, which is regularly updated (London: Hutchinson) and Stephen Moore, *Social Welfare Alive* (Cheltenham: Stanley Thornes, 1993). An interesting book which looks at welfare more from the perspective of the services is David Tossell and Richard Webb, *Inside the Caring Services* (London:

Edward Arnold, 1986). Each year The Family Welfare Association publish a new and up-to-date edition of their *Guide to the Social Services*.

Any book in this area quickly becomes out of date as the rate of change in social policy is so rapid. Newspapers and journals are a source of more up-to-date information. The *Guardian* is a newspaper with an excellent reputation for coverage of welfare issues. Journals published for the caring professions, such as *Community Care*, contain useful and relevant articles. Other more specialist and academic journals will be available in college libraries. *Social Trends* is an annual summary of statistical data published by HMSO. It is available in reference sections of libraries.

On gender issues, the Equal Opportunities Commission is a useful source of information (the address is given below). For information on race issues, try the Commission for Racial Equality (see below). The CRE, in partnership with Radio 1, have produced an excellent booklet called *Race Through the 90s* (revised 1993). This covers many areas relevant to social welfare. Other useful booklets are *Racial Equality in Social Services Departments*, 1989, and *Race Relations Code of Practice in Primary Health Care Services*, 1992.

Useful addresses

EOC : Overseas House, Quay Street, Manchester M3 3HN
      tel. 0161 833 9244

CRE : Elliot House, 10–12 Allington Street, London SW1E 5EH
      tel. 0171 828 7022

Institute of Race Relations: 2–6 Leeke Street, King's Cross
Road, London WC1X 9HS
tel. 0171 837 0041

Joint Council for the Welfare of Immigrants: 115 Old Street, London EC1V 9JR
tel. 0171 251 8706

② Family life

The family is the most important social group in our society. Very few people do not spend at least part of their lives living as a member of a family. Although there is a tendency to regard family life as a very private area, it is a subject of concern, both to academic writers and to policy-makers. The reason for this interest is that the family plays a key role in society.

Activity 2.1

Think about the family as a social group. List all the ways in which the family meets needs of individuals, and of society at large.

2.1 Functions of the family

Social scientists talk about the *functions* of the family. This is simply a way of looking at the role the family plays in the context of the whole society. An important set of functions concern children. The family, in whatever form, is the unit which provides a home and care for dependent children. In addition to physical care, children also receive a great deal of informal education within the family. They learn to walk, to talk, and the correct way to behave in society. A teacher in a nursery school will be aware how much a child knows, on arrival. For example, most children know that chairs are for sitting on, that they should obey grown-ups, and countless other details of social behaviour. This learning process is known as *socialisation*. It is not done exclusively by the family, although the family is the key agent. The way children are brought up is of obvious concern to society, since children grow up to be future citizens. In a very real way, the future of society depends upon the family.

Adults also expect to have certain needs met within the family. The family is expected to provide for emotional and sexual needs. Family groups form economic units in the sense that income is pooled and goods consumed are shared. Physical needs – for food, and care in times of ill-health – are primarily met within the family. Finally, the family exercises control over social behaviour, for example, someone might hesitate before leaving a husband or wife, because of anticipated disapproval from relatives.

Activity 2.2 _____

In some societies – for example in the kibbutz in Israel – the family, in the sense that we understand it, does not exist. Imagine what life would be like without the family. Write an account of a day in the life of a person in such a society.

It is probably becoming clear that discussion of the family takes in many different areas. Relationships within the family include marriage, parenthood and links with other relatives such as grandparents. The relationship between the family and the state is also an area of interest. This chapter will look at different types of family, marriage and divorce, violence in marriage and the relationship between welfare provision and the family.

2.2   Family structures

Over time, between societies, and even within one society, there is variation in the way in which the family is structured. Different terms are used to describe different kinds of families. Activity 2.3 is an introduction to looking at different family structures.

Activity 2.3 _____

Take a particular family you know well. Obviously, this could be a family of which you are a member or in which you grew up. Construct a family tree, using Figure 2.1 as an example. (The symbol ○ means a female, △ means a male, and a line through the symbol △ shows that the person is deceased. I have also indicated divorce ⌊╫╫╫⌋ and you may need to add a way of showing people who are living together without being married.)

Using the family tree, consider how much contact there is between family members. Note down how near people live to one another, and how regularly they visit. Do family members support each other, for example by lending money or offering to help someone to move house? Do families rally round in the event of a death or divorce? Do people feel obliged to attend weddings and to visit on festival occasions?

Nuclear, extended and modified extended families

Families vary, both in terms of the number of people living under one roof, and the amount of contact and support given. Two common types of family are

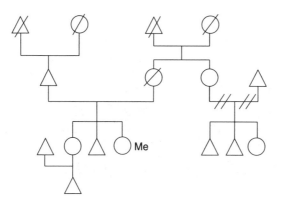

Figure 2.1   Family structures

nuclear families and *extended families*. The nuclear family consists of one man, one woman, and their dependent children. The extended family is a wider grouping, including grandparents when vertically extended, and aunts and uncles when horizontally extended. A recently-invented third term is the *modified extended family*. This consists of separate nuclear families, related to each other, who do not have a great deal of actual physical contact, but who exchange significant services. An example of this would be families who live in different

Source: Crispin Hughes, Photofusion
A nuclear family consists of two parents and their dependent children

Source: Bob Watkins, Photofusion
Most lone parents are women

parts of the country, but who help each other out, for instance, in raising money for one member to start a business.

Lone-parent and reconstituted families

Lone- or single-parent families have become increasingly common in recent years and are looked at in section 2.5 later in this chapter. The increase in divorce and re-marriage has given rise to another new term, *reconstituted families*. These are families including step-parents, half- or stepchildren.

Activity 2.4

Decide the most appropriate term for the family for which you drew the family tree in Activity 2.3. Find out which type of family is the most common in the area where you live.

Changes in family life

Whilst there is disagreement among social historians, it seems that in the past, extended families were more common than they are today. Family structures have altered as a result of changes in the wider society, for example, the economy demands that people should be prepared to move away from their relatives to find work. This trend has implications for social policy, for instance in terms of the needs of the elderly and of mothers of young children. However, extended families still exist, particularly in traditional working-class communities and among the Asian population. The ideal family, as portrayed in advertising images, consists of one man, one woman and children. In reality, only 24 per cent of households are made up of a married couple and their dependent children.[1]

Activity 2.5

What do you think are the advantages and disadvantages of living in a nuclear or extended family, from the point of view of:
(i)   a child
(ii) a teenager
(iii) a mother with young children?

Other changes in family life include the fact that most families have a smaller number of children. In Victorian times, the average family would have included about six children. The statistical average now is just over two. There are several reasons for this trend, including improved and more freely available contraception, and the fact that whereas children were once a financial asset, working on family farms, they are now a financial liability, costing their parents thousands of pounds. The trend towards smaller families, together with the tendency for elderly people to live longer, has implications for the care and support of elderly people (see chapter 13). At a time when there is an increasing expectation that relatives will care for elderly people, there are proportionately less people available to provide care.

2.3   Marriage

Types of marriage

The kind of marriage practised in our society, and enforced by law, is the marriage of one woman and one man. This type of marriage is known as *monogamy*. Other types of marriage which exist in other countries are *polygyny*, which involves one man and several women, and *polyandry*, where a woman has several husbands. The term *polygamy* is sometimes used to cover polygyny and polyandry. These kinds of marriage are often found where the population has an unequal number of men and women.

Trends concerning marriage

In the UK, statistics demonstrate changing trends concerning marriage. Marriage rates peaked in the early 1970s and have fluctuated since, with current trends showing a decrease in the number of marriages. Trends also indicate that people were marrying younger, although recent figures show a move back to later marriage.[2]

Why do people marry?

Activity 2.6

Why do people want to get married? List as many reasons as you can think of, indicating if you think that some reasons apply more to women than to men, or vice versa.

Marriage gives a sense of emotional security. Women also see marriage as a source of financial security. Married women have higher status than single women. Whether married men have more status than single men is less clear, certainly the term 'bachelor' conjures up an attractive image. People are also encouraged to marry by traditional values and religion.

It is obviously possible to have children without being married – and attitudes towards women who do so have changed a great deal in recent years (see below) – but there is still some element of social disapproval in some social groups. For men, marriage provides someone to care for them. It has been shown that married men suffer far less than single men from psychiatric problems.[3] Whilst this could be interpreted in more than one way, it is likely that men benefit from having the support of a wife.

Changing attitudes towards marriage

Attitudes towards marriage seem to be changing quite significantly with trends showing an increase in the number of people who live together. Figure 2.2 shows percentages of people living together in various age groups.[4] It used to be that people lived together before getting married and this still is the case for a lot of people, although there is a significant increase in the number of people who live together instead of getting married. A significant proportion of the people living together are people who have been married to someone else previously and are either divorced or in the process of getting divorced.

The basis for choice of a partner in marriage varies from society to society, and has changed over time. At one time, marriage was more concerned with benefits to the wider family group, such as bringing together adjoining land, than with romantic love. Amongst the Asian population in Britain, as we saw on

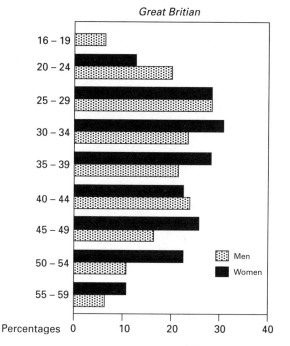

Source: General Household Survey

Source: *Social Trends 1994*, 24 (London: HMSO, 1994, © Crown copyright, p. 38).

Figure 2.2 People cohabiting as a percentage of the unmarried population, by sex and age, Great Britain 1992

p. 29, it is common for marriages to be arranged by the parents, and love is seen to come after marriage, not before. However, even for people who see romance and sexual attraction as the basis for selecting a partner, other factors intervene. For example there is a tendency for marriage partners to be of the same age, the same religion, the same race and the same class background. People do not fall in love in a completely random way.

Married working women

There has been an increase in the number of married women who work outside the home. The image of the male breadwinner and dependent housewife no longer reflects the reality of the family. In 1961, 29.7 per cent of married women were in paid employment, compared with a figure of 60 per cent of married or cohabiting women in 1992.[5] Many women leave paid employment while their children are below school-age, although a significant minority are remaining in the labour force. In 1991 13 per cent of women with children aged 0–4 were working full-time and 29 per cent working part-time.[6]

There are several explanations for the increased numbers of married women working outside the home. The two world wars brought women into areas of work previously considered suitable only for men. Although women were encouraged to give up their jobs when the wars ended, attitudes about the role of women had been challenged. The 1960s was a period of full employment with expansion in the areas of work traditionally seen as women's work, for example, in the service, commercial and administrative sectors of the economy. Even with high unemployment rates in later decades, these jobs have not been lost at the same rate as jobs traditionally done by men in areas of the economy such as manufacturing. It is becoming increasingly common for women to have work whilst their husbands are unemployed. Other explanations for the number of women in paid employment include the facts that families are smaller and that people live longer. It is no longer the case that child-bearing and child care take up the whole of a woman's life. On an individual level, women may work outside the home for various reasons. The need for money is obviously a significant factor. Other reasons might include desire for social contact, the need to have an identity other than housewife, a wish to escape from the routines of housework and, for some women the desire to use their skills in a job which they enjoy.

Women with children are often made to feel guilty about having a job. There is, however, no conclusive evidence proving that marriages or children suffer in a family where both parents are in paid employment.

Activity 2.7

Do you think married women should have careers? Give reasons for your answer and be prepared to discuss your ideas.

Segregated and joint roles

The sort of relationship a man and a woman have in marriage can, and does, vary. One way of looking at this is to talk of *segregated* and *joint* roles. In a segregated-role relationship, housework and child-care are seen as the concern of the wife only. Leisure and social activities are also separate, in that the man will have his own friends and hobbies, and the woman her own. In a marriage with joint roles, divisions are less distinct, and housework, interest and friends are shared.

There have been changes in men's and women's roles in marriage over the last 50 or so years, but there is also a tendency to exaggerate the extent of these changes.

One obvious change which has already been looked at is the increased likelihood for women to be working outside the home. This has not however been accompanied by an equivalent change in the amount of work done by men inside the home.

In 1993 Mintel, a market research company, carried out a survey on gender roles, interviewing 1500 men and women.[7] They tried to interview couples who shared equally the shopping, cooking and laundry but were forced to give up when they could only find one man in a 100 who did his fair share of housework. 85 per cent of working women said they almost always did all of the laundry and ironing and a similar number said they were entirely responsible for cooking the main meal. The consumer research manager of Mintel commented:

> Men seem to set out with good intentions to share the domestic chores but the catalyst appears to be the arrival of children. At this stage, the man appears to abdicate responsibility for his share, regardless of whether his partner is working.

Other surveys have found similar results: people tend to think that men and women should share housework, but in reality it is the women who carry the main burden, even where they have paid work.

Things have changed a little more with regard to children. Men are taking a bigger role in the care of their children than was previously the case. A study called *Looking after Baby* carried out in Bristol found that 80 per cent of fathers were involved in tasks such as bathing, walking, feeding and putting children to sleep. The study suggested that men nowadays feel able to be soft, tender and caring with their children without being seen as a 'wimp'.[8]

Activity 2.8

Carry out a survey to investigate roles in marriage. Design a questionnaire to put to married couples, including questions on housework, child care, decision-making, money management and social activities. Write up the results and conclusions in a report.

Activity 2.9

Imagine a situation where a couple are about to marry and have decided that they want an equal marriage. Draw up a contract which they could both sign. Bear in mind the areas of married life mentioned in Activity 2.8.

2.4 Divorce

Statistics show that the divorce rate has increased dramatically. In 1961, 27 000 decrees absolute were granted to end marriages in the UK, whereas in 1991 the figure was 171 000.[9] If current trends persist, one in three marriages will end in divorce. The likelihood of divorce increases where people marry in their teens.

When can people get divorced?

Under the 1969 Divorce Reform Act, divorce is allowed when a marriage has irretrievably broken down. There are several ways in which this can be said to have happened. People can get divorced if they have lived apart for two years and both agree to the divorce. Where one partner does not agree, a divorce can be granted after they have lived separately for five years. Other grounds for divorce are unreasonable behaviour or adultery which the other partner finds intolerable. Since the 1984 Matrimonial and Family Proceedings Act, couples can petition for divorce after one year of marriage.

Trends in marital breakdown

The rise in the divorce rate does not necessarily indicate an increasing disillusionment with marriage, since many divorced people remarry. Neither does the trend in divorce mean that marriages are less happy than they used to be. The reverse may be true, in that it may be that people have a higher expectation of marriage and are less prepared to remain unhappily married. Those marriages which do continue may be of a better quality. One explanation of the increase in divorce lies in the fact that people now marry younger and live longer. This means that marriages are expected to last longer. It is possible that a new phenomenon now exists which can be termed *serial monogamy*. This means that it is normal for people to have more than one monogamous marriage in the course of their life. Another possible reason for increase in divorce is the greater independence enjoyed by women, which makes it possible for unhappily married women to consider leaving their husbands.

Children and divorce

One reason why people express concern over divorce is that it may have a bad effect on children. This is a difficult area in which it is dangerous to generalise. There are situations in which children are suffering as a result of very unhappy marriages and experience relief when their parents split up. In other situations, children show symptoms of emotional distress and anxiety, perhaps in the form of bed-wetting or tantrums in a younger child. The long-term effects of divorce on children have not been sufficiently researched for any positive conclusions to be drawn.

The 1989 Children Act introduced new provisions for children in cases of divorce. These are known as Section 8 orders and can apply to others such as grandparents as well as the child's parents. The orders are made by a court after all the evidence has been heard and the aim of the court will be to provide the best for the child. Section 8 orders are only used when necessary and the court can decide not to go ahead with an order at all.

There are four types of orders which the court can make.

- A *residence order* decides where the child will live. This can be in more than one place. The order also gives parental responsibility for the child and this too can go to more than one person.
- A *contact order* replaces the old idea of 'access'. This gives a person with whom the child does not live with the right to contact with the child. The court can say exactly how much contact there will be and what conditions there might be. This might mean, for example, that the contact has to be supervised.
- A *specific issue order* takes away the parents' responsibility over particular issues and means decisions must be made by the court. An example of this could be decisions on education.
- A *prohibited steps order* stops something from being done, for example stating that the child must not be taken abroad.

Activity 2.10

Questions for discussion:
1 Should divorce be made easier, remain as it is, or be made more difficult to obtain?
2 Should divorce be allowed in the first year of marriage?
3 Should people wait until their children grow up before seeking a divorce?
4 In view of the increased likelihood of those who marry young getting divorced, should the age for marriage be increased to 21, or perhaps 25?

2.5 Single-parent families

At present, there are about 1.3 million single-parent families in Britain. They consist of people who are divorced, separated, widowed or unmarried. Families where one parent is in prison can also be considered as single-parent families, since they will experience the same sorts of difficulties.

There is a tendency to see single parenthood as something abnormal, in spite of the fact that in some areas, the majority of children in a school live with one parent only. Similarly, single-parent families are assumed to be problem families, a view which overlooks the unhappiness in many two-parent families. Both these attitudes arise from the fact that society has in the past been geared to couples and nuclear families. However, whilst single-parent families should not be characterised as problem families, they do encounter special difficulties, many of which could be alleviated by legislation and better welfare provision.

Activity 2.11

What sort of problems do you think a single parent might encounter? Make a list of them.

Problems for single-parent families

The problems experienced by widows and widowers, divorcees and unmarried parents vary to some extent, although there are common factors. The stigma attached to single parenthood has reduced very significantly but it is still there to some extent, especially for unmarried mothers. Loneliness is a potential problem for all single parents and people who are widowed have special burdens in coping with bereavement at the same time as adjusting to life as a single parent. The problems of stigma and loneliness are both the concerns of *Gingerbread*, which is a national organisation of single parents. Gingerbread campaigns for a better deal for lone parents, as well as providing local groups offering advice and support.

Other emotional problems for single parents include their feeling of guilt towards their children. Children may feel deprived and express resentment towards the parent with whom they live. This may be caused partly by treatment received from other children at school, or even by tactless comments by teachers. Concern for children can also make it difficult for single parents to form new relationships, since children may feel threatened by the entry of a new adult into their lives. These problems are too complex to be more than indicated here. More information on this, and other aspects of single parenthood, can be obtained from Gingerbread.

Single-parent families tend, as a group, to be less well-off than other families. The costs of running a home are not substantially reduced because there is only one adult. Rents, mortgages and heating bills, for example, remain the same. In addition, many two-parent families benefit from having two incomes. Single parents face extra costs for child-care, if they want to work or have a social life.

Even where a lone parent has employment, the family is likely to be less well-off than other families. There are several reasons for this. First, the majority of single parents are women and women tend to earn less than men, despite the existence of equal pay legislation. Second, working often involves paying for child-care. Work is not organised in such a way as to make running a family at the same time an easy task. Even in the best situations – for example, teaching – school holidays do not always coincide, evening meetings are held and all plans are thrown into chaos if a child is ill.

The problems of working and the limited availability of suitable child-care result in many single parents being forced to rely on income support. These benefits are means-tested and barely provide for existence. Single parents with paid employment are privileged by comparison, since they receive extra tax relief and increased child benefit. People on income support obviously do not receive tax relief, and their benefit rate is reduced to take account of the extra child allowance.

Child support and maintenance

Financial and emotional hardship for single parents has also resulted from problems concerning maintenance payments. Until April 1993, all maintenance payments to lone parents were dealt with by the courts. In many cases this system did not work and only 30 per cent of lone parents received any maintenance at all, with many others receiving only a very small amount. The result was that many lone parent families lived in poverty.[10]

Creation of the CSA

In 1991 the Child Support Act was passed. In April of 1993 the *Child Support Agency (CSA)* was set up by the government to gradually take over the task of dealing with maintenance of children by 'absent parents'. The agency uses the term 'absent parent' to describe the parent not living with the children; this is usually, but not always, the father. Fathers – who may in fact be seeing their children for several days a week – have objected to the implications of this term (see below).

The job of the agency is to assess the financial situations of both parents and to set an amount of maintenance to be paid. It is also responsible for making sure that the maintenance is actually paid. Where a lone parent is claiming income support, the maintenance is deducted from the income support paid. In most cases, lone mothers refusing to give information about the father of a child lose benefit. The law, however, states that people are exempt from assessment where there are reasonable grounds for believing that harm or undue distress will be caused by a maintenance assessment. An example of such a situation would be a case of a violent partner.

Reaction from 'absent fathers'

There has been a strong reaction from fathers to the Child Support Agency and their campaign has been well publicised in the media. It appears that the CSA targeted particular types of situations for the first wave of their assessments. These tended to be middle-class men in regular employment who were already paying maintenance. Many of these men had agreed to what were known as 'clean break' arrangements under the old system. These arrangements were favoured by the courts and encouraged in government legislation. The thinking behind a 'clean break' was that it was important for the children to have a home. Solicitors representing the husband and the wife (separately) would agree that the house – or a large part of the capital invested the house – would be given to the woman in order that she and the children should have a home. In return, maintenance payments were set very low. These arrangements were believed to be permanent and legally binding. The CSA has overturned this approach. In situations where men have already given over the house, they are now finding that they have higher maintenance costs to pay as well. In an average case, a man previously paying £80 a month for two children might now be expected to pay £300. It is argued that this has forced some fathers to give up work and go on to benefits; others say they are no longer able to afford to visit their children.

It has been stated that the views of absent fathers have been well publicised and indeed responded to by the government, with a series of amendments. Not long after the setting up of the CSA, the government announced radical changes to the formulas used to assess the amount fathers should pay for their children. This is a good example of how more powerful voices are heard. Much less well publicised has been the views of lone parents themselves – a less powerful group.

NCOPF and NACAB criticisms

The National Council for One Parent Families (NCOPF) supports the principles behind the Child Support Act, believing there is a need for more equality between lone parents and their ex-partner. They argue that for too long lone parents have lived in poverty with their children whilst absent fathers have enjoyed a higher standard of living on their own or with second families. However NCOPF are still critical of the CSA, arguing it is failing those people it was set up to help. NCOPF monitored the working of the agency and in a report published in 1994 criticised it for delays and inefficiencies. They also felt the agency was weak in enforcing payments of maintenance.[11]

The CSA has been criticised from all sides for being more concerned with saving the government's money than with helping lone parents or children. The National Association of Citizens' Advice Bureaux (NACAB) carried out a major survey of the Agency's first year. They wrote:

> It is the conclusion of the CAB service that the Government's concern to maximise public expenditure savings has serious consequences for the success of the child support scheme.

On the basis of their survey NACAB makes a number of recommendations, including that lone parents should be able to keep the first £15 of maintenance before it is deducted from social security payments and that the government should take account of previous 'clean break' settlements in creating a fairer system for absent parents.[12]

CSA successes and failures

From the mother's point of view:

> Kate Lister is an example of how the CSA was intended to work. Divorced six years ago, she says she received intermittent maintenance under a court order for her 10-year-old son Oliver and seven-year-old daughter Amy.
>
> The agency last year ordered her former husband to pay £78 a week which has left her £30 a week better off and enabled her to take a part-time job and come off income support. She says: 'For the first time in six years I have had some independence.'

Carol Pallister is typical of many women who feel the CSA is failing them. Although her former husband has his own company, he has been told he need pay no money towards their son, 13-year-old James.

Ms Pallister says her former husband left her six weeks before James was born. For the first eight weeks she had no idea of his whereabouts. She lives on income support after being made redundant last year.

Having received a 'nil' maintenance assessment, Ms Pallister is bitter at what she sees as the CSA's inability to deal with self-employed fathers. She says: 'The agency should not be targeting men who are honourably fulfilling their promises.'[13]

From the father's point of view:

Tony Walentowicz is an angry man. His marriage broke down. It was his wife's idea to split, but it was termed an amicable divorce.

They agreed the financial arrangements. Jenny McLean, his wife of seven years, kept their £60 000 home. He was to pay £120 a month towards the upkeep of their daughter, Amy, now six.

It has been a struggle for Mr Walentowicz, aged 41. He earns £19 000 a year as keeper of natural science with the council museums in Chelmsford, Essex. Mortgage payments on his new home are proving tough to meet.

The settlement . . . runs until 2004, when Amy will be 17. But last month the letter from the Child Support Agency arrived.

The agency says it will be reassessing what he pays each year. It will charge him £44 annually to do so . . .

He says: 'What I really object to is that they wrote to me as an absent father. That is really unfair. I've never ducked my responsibilities. I've always paid up. It's insulting to say that about me.

There are thousands of others in my position . . . We fully recognise our responsibilities. But it seems we are the ones who will be hit hardest, whilst those who have done a runner are quietly ignored.[14]

Activity 2.12

In groups of three or four, decide on policies which central government could implement to improve the position of single-parent families. Agree on a priority order for these issues.

2.6 Violence in the family

Violence against women

Newspaper and television reports are full of stories concerning violence on the streets. Yet many violent incidents take place within the home, between people who are close to each other: a woman has more cause to fear her husband than assault by a stranger. It is difficult to know the full extent of violence against wives, since it is probable that many incidents go unrecorded. This may occur because women feel shame or guilt about admitting that their marriage has gone wrong. Alternatively, they may fear that telling someone will lead to further attacks or that nothing can be done to help them. The following statistics provide no more than an indication of the extent of the problem. One study found that 25 per cent of all reported crime was domestic violence.[15] Other studies have estimated that there is severe and repeated violence in more than 1 in 100 marriages[16] and that in one in seven relationships there is violence at some point.[17] A survey of 1000 married women conducted by *World in Action* found that 28 per cent had been hit by their husbands and a further 5 per cent threatened with physical violence. Amongst women who had been separated or divorced the overall proportion of those either hit or threatened rose to 63 per cent.[18]

Violence in the family is most commonly directed against wives. One survey found 75.8 per cent of assaults involving family members were assaults on the wife; in only 1.1 per cent of cases were husbands the victims of marital violence.[19]

The particular form of violence inflicted on women by their husbands obviously varies, but is often of a very serious nature and results in severe injuries, and sometimes death. Here, one woman describes the results of an attack, which continued after she lost consciousness:

> He grabbed me from the chair, dragged me back into the sitting-room, to the hall, pulled me halfway up the stairs, then pulled me back down and started to kick and stand on me. And that was in front of his own mum. I was knocked out with the first couple of blows he gave me. He was hammering into something that was just like a cushion on the floor. I had a broken rib, broken leg on the right side, two front teeth knocked out, burst chin – I've still got the scar – I had five stitches, and a broken arm on the right side.[20]

Another woman describes her husband's threats to her life:

> He threatened to kill me no end of times. He used to put ropes round my neck and try to strangle me – he even once tried with wire – that's when I left. The worst time he locked me and the children in a bedroom, put a gaspipe underneath and turned the gas on – nailed the door up with 6 in. nails.[21]

Why does violence occur in marriage?

Activity 2.13 _____

Why do you think violence occurs in marriages? Make a list of possible causes.

Different ways of looking at this question will produce different sorts of answers. A survey which looked into immediate causes of violent episodes found several common themes. Sexual jealousy was frequently referred to, often flaring up simply as a result of a wife speaking to a neighbour who happened to be male, or where the husband imagined that something had happened. Another common source of conflict was housework. Some men considered it their right to set the standards for housework and for these standards to be met by their wives. Other explanations for violent episodes included disputes over money, the husband's drinking behaviour and the man's assumption that it was his right to have sex when he wanted.[22] At the time of the survey this last point was backed by law, since there was no legal concept of rape within marriage. More recently, a legal precedent has been set whereby a man who forces his wife to have sex can be found guilty of rape.

Violence tends to begin with marriage rather than earlier and men who assault their wives are not necessarily violent towards friends or other relatives. Bearing this in mind, explanations can be sought in marriage itself. Within marriage, the wife is vulnerable because she is dependent on her husband, and leaving means risking losing a home, breaking up a family and admitting to failure. The cause of wife-assault can be related to the way in which society sees a woman as the property of her husband, and subject to his control. The home is regarded as a private area in which people are allowed to behave as they wish. Linked to these points, there is a tendency for domestic violence to be seen as acceptable, trivialised, or treated as a joke, as in 'Punch and Judy' shows. The following quotation illustrates the acceptance of violence against women in marriage:

> There are times when a man is justified in using violence, hitting a woman. Yes. A man is justified when he has sufficient provocation. And there are many, many, many circumstances in which a man should react in this way.[23]

Help for battered wives

The discussion of the helping agencies which follows also demonstrates this acceptance of violence as a normal part of mariage.

___ **Activity 2.14** _____

Imagine that you discover that a neighbour is regularly beaten by her husband. She asks you for advice. Which agencies might be able to help her?

Many women feel trapped in a violent marriage because they do not know where to seek help, or because the people they have approached have proved unhelpful. There are several sources of help, although some are of limited use, primarily because of the sort of attitudes people have towards battered women.

Friends and relatives may be the first people to whom a woman turns, although some feel too ashamed to tell of their suffering and attempt to explain away visible injuries. Also, most people do not have big enough houses to take in a woman and her children, and therefore may be unable to offer more than advice and support. Women may be reluctant to put their friends or relatives at risk of repercussions from an angry husband. Neighbours are often aware of violence, but ideas about privacy, together with fear, result in their being reluctant to intervene in a violent situation.

The police

Battered women often contact the police in fear and desperation, but in the past have rarely been satisfied with the response they have received. The police called violence to wives a 'domestic dispute' and were often unwilling to get involved. One woman reports her attempt to seek help from the police in the following account.

> When we lived in Newark he hit me all over – I was black. I was very frightened. I ran out of the house to the phone box – I was really petrified. The police came and just sat me in the car outside and said 'Look, you've got a nice house, you're a young couple, kiss and make up. Be friends'.[24]

The police sometimes refused to believe the woman's story. Even if they turned up, it was rare for the man to be charged. There are several explanations for police conduct in cases of marital violence. They tend to see the home as a private area and distinguish between assaults in the home and the same behaviour in a street or public house. The police argue that women are unwilling to pursue a charge against their husbands. However, this may well be as a result of fear, since the woman will be expected to live with her attacker while awaiting a court hearing.

There is however some evidence that police attitudes are changing. A survey of 100 Women's Aid refuges in September 1992 found that in a number of areas, police officers are giving a higher priority to domestic violence, are giving out more information to women and are following up cases and generally showing more sympathy and understanding.[25] The survey also found that in some areas little had changed.

Where there have been changes in police behaviour, this is a result of changing policy guidelines. In 1987, the Metropolitan Police issued an order stating that domestic violence was a crime and should be treated as such. This was followed in 1990 by a circular from the Home Office to all police forces in England and Wales. This emphasised that violence which occurs within the home is 'no less serious than a violent assault by a stranger' and recommended that the widespread practice of 'no-criming' domestic assaults should cease. In response to this circular, many forces, particularly in London, set up domestic violence units to specialise in this area of work. Women's Aid Federation England (WAFE) welcomed these units but expressed some concerns also.

Whilst we give a cautious welcome to the setting up of specialist domestic violence units, we also have some concerns about this approach. It appears that many police forces have seen domestic violence units as 'the answer' to domestic violence, whilst at the same time failing to put sufficient resources into them. Most domestic violence units are staffed by one or two officers only. This means that any women calling the unit will invariably receive an answerphone message requesting her to leave her name and numbers to that an officer can get back to her. This is useless to women who have no phone or who are staying in Bed and Breakfast or other temporary accomodation, who feel unable to give out a refuge number or who are fearful that their abuser may intercept a call intended for them.[26]

Even in cases where the police press charges, the courts are unwilling to take effective action to protect the wife. The following account from a battered woman shows this:

He was charged with Actual Bodily Harm, common assault and unlawful assault. He got fined, bound over and was given a suspended sentence. It was useless because he wouldn't pay the fine and I had to. They threatened to take the furniture if I didn't. And it didn't stop him beating me.[27]

The courts
In theory the courts are a potential source of protection for women. Under the 1978 Domestic Proceedings and Magistrates' Court Act, married women can be granted a protection order by the magistrates court. This will state that the husband is not to use or threaten violence and can order him to leave the home. In some circumstances, powers of arrest can be attached to the protection order meaning that the police will arrest the man if he breaks the order. Under the 1976 Domestic Violence and Matrimonial Proceedings Act, the county court can offer protection to people living together as well as those who are married. The judge can order the man not to molest his wife – this includes violence, but also harassment such as verbal abuse or persistent telephoning. As in the magistrates' court, powers of arrest can be attached to the order and in some circumstances the man can be ordered to stay away from the house. In practice the usefulness of these orders is limited as they tend not be fully enforced.

The social services and doctors
The social services are another agency upon which battered women might call for help. The problem here is that social workers have a commitment to the family as a unit and attempt to dissuade the woman from leaving her husband. Like the police, social workers are reluctant to intervene in a marriage; also, they may be as afraid of a violent man as is his wife. Social services have limited ability to offer practical help and are felt by women to be more concerned about the risk to the children than with the plight of the woman.

General practitioners come into contact with victims of domestic violence. They tend to concentrate on treating the medical aspects of the problem and to solve any other difficulties by prescribing tranquillisers or anti-depressants. These drugs may inhibit the woman's ability to think through her situation and to take positive decisions. Doctors tend to be unaware of resources available to battered women, and are therefore not in a position to offer constructive advice.

Alternative housing

Women attempting to escape a violent marriage may approach the local authority housing department for help in finding alternative housing. Under the 1985 Housing (Homeless Persons) Act, women who cannot occupy their home because of violence should be treated as homeless. However, many local authorities have been slow to accept their responsibilities under the Act. Women have reported unhelpful attitudes on the part of housing officers, for example:

> They had no right to treat me as they did. I came out in tears many times. The housing officer says he hits his wife and vice versa – and that's the way of happy marriage.[28]

Even where local authorities accept battered women as homeless, the provision offered is often highly unsatisfactory, for example, in bed and breakfast accommodation.

Voluntary organisations

There are voluntary organisations which will offer assistance to battered women. Gingerbread, as we have seen, is one, although the group specifically concerned with marital violence is Women's Aid. Women's Aid has a national office and nearly 200 local groups offering safe, temporary accommodation in refuges, advice, support and help in finding permanent accommodation, if this is what the woman wants. Refuges are run by residents, support groups of volunteers and paid workers. Most refuges have little financial support and are often in poor physical condition. The pressure of demand means that many are overcrowded. An important aspect of refuges is that women regain confidence through meeting others who share their experiences and the women are able to help one another.

Activity 2.15

Find out if there is a refuge in your local town. It may not be in the telephone book, since it is important that violent men are not able to find their wives and children. The refuge can be contacted through the Samaritans, the Citizens Advice Bureau or the police. You may be able to arrange for people from the refuge to give a talk to the class.

The effects of violence

Men who are violent towards their wives are not necessarily child-abusers. Battered women are often reluctant to leave their husbands because they do not want to deprive their children of a father. On the other hand, others leave because they fear their children will be subjected to violence. Children can get involved through trying to protect their mothers. Even where children are not in physical danger themselves, they suffer the anxiety of seeing or hearing their mothers beaten up.

There is no real evidence to support the idea that children of violent fathers will be violent in their own adult relationships. Even where researchers have found that the father of a violent man was himself violent, this does not explain wife-battering, since not all the boys in the family have been shown to have been violent in their marriages. Being exposed to a violent marriage can have the effect of making boys determined not to behave in this way. Little is really known about the effects on children of violence between parents and it may be that individuals react in different ways.

This lack of understanding extends to other areas of the problem of marital violence and one of the tasks of Women's Aid is to help the public, the government, the police, doctors and social workers to gain a better understanding of the needs of victims of domestic violence.

Child abuse

The problem of cruelty to children in the family was first recognised in the 1960s. At that time the terms used was 'child battering', although this later changed to 'non-accidental injury' and, more recently, to 'child abuse'. The changes in name have reflected the way the issue has become broader in definition, now including physical injury, emotional damage, neglect and sexual abuse of children. Sexual abuse was rarely mentioned until the late 1970s, but recently has become an issue of major public and professional concern.

Since the 1960s, and especially in recent years, there has been a rapid increase in cases of child abuse. However, it seems likely that this does not mean there has been a real increase in cruelty, but rather an increase in public and professional awareness which means that more and more cases come to light.

The following case-studies from the National Society for the Prevention of Cruelty to Children (NSPCC) illustrate the nature of the problem.

When the NSPCC was called to Mark's home – after a serious row between his parents – [the] Inspector found a little boy, tiny for his two and a half years and very pale. He was suffering from what the experts call 'non-organic failure to thrive'. In other words, Mark's failure to grow and develop healthily was not due to a disease or medical condition but due to lack of loving care and nourishment.

Sarah was 15 and her young sister, Jo, 13 when the girls told their older brother, Michael, that their father had been sexually interfering with them . . . the girls had been sexually abused since they were very young. Their father fondled them, used sexually explicit language and, as they got older, had full sexual intercourse with them.

Six-year-old Kate was beaten by her mother. Thankfully she was not badly injured. But her mother felt terribly guilty. She contacted her family doctor and explained how she just couldn't cope with Kate and her four-year-old sister, Mandy.[29]

Agencies involved

Many different professionals are involved in cases of child abuse. These include doctors, both in general practice and in various hospital departments; other health workers such as health visitors and midwives; social workers and child guidance therapists; teachers and other school staff , educational welfare officers and educational psychologists; the police; workers in voluntary organisations such as the NSPCC and perhaps the church. Others who may be involved work in housing departments, the probation service and social security offices. A key issue in dealing with child abuse, often referred to in official reports, is effective liaison between so many people. The geography and the bureaucracy of the different departments often divides people and makes communication difficult. There are also different ways of seeing the issues and these can prevent people working together effectively. For example, the police may see the achieving of justice for the offending adult as their priority, the medical profession may prioritise clinical diagnosis and medical treatment, whilst social workers may be more concerned with a therapeutic approach to the whole family.

In 1988 the Butler-Sloss report was published following an inquiry into procedures for dealing with child sexual abuse in the country of Cleveland. The report said that there were three main reasons that things had gone wrong in Cleveland. First, the agencies involved failed to understand each other's function in relation to child abuse; secondly, they did not communicate sufficiently with each other; and thirdly, there were differences of view at middle management level which were not recognised by senior staff. Many local authorities have begun to develop multi-disciplinary teams for child abuse cases and joint training sessions for the different professions.

Protection of children at risk

Area Review Committees were set up in 1974 to co-ordinate multi-agency work on child abuse. These committees are responsible for keeping *At Risk registers* in their local area. These registers record names of children thought to be at risk of child abuse. They are sometimes managed by the NSPCC. In 1980 a government circular from the then DHSS now Department of Health tried to standardise the criteria for the registers across the country. The circular recommended that the criteria be broadened to include physical injuries where there is a suspicion of abuse, physical neglect, failure to thrive, emotional abuse and situations where a child is in a house with, or visited by, a person who has abused another child.

When a case of child abuse is discovered, the child can be admitted to hospital or removed to a safe place under an *emergency protection order*. Both of these actions can be taken very quickly. Then a case conference will be called, bringing together various professionals to decide on a course of action. The possibilities include returning the child to its home, with social work support for the parents or with supervision under a care order, or taking the child into the care of the local authority, either voluntarily or through care proceedings in the juvenile court. (These procedures are explained in Chapter 10 on children in trouble.)

Cases of child abuse can be particularly difficult for social workers as they can feel torn between their duty to protect children and their commitment to keeping families together and avoiding compulsory care orders where possible. There is a feeling that social workers will be condemned by the media and the public both for taking children into care and for not taking children into care. The public attention given to child abuse has tended to make this seem the most important aspect of social work and to lead to a draining of funds from other areas such as work with elderly people or people with disabilities.

Activity 2.16

There have been a number of official inquiries into deaths of children, from the Maria Colwell case in 1974 to that of Stephanie Fox in London in 1990. Find out about one of these cases. What went wrong – in the family and in the social service department? What could have prevented the death of the child? Could it happen again?

2.7 The family and the welfare state

In 1977, Patrick Jenkins, then Secretary of State for Social Services, warned of the dangers of the state taking over the responsibilities of the family. The extent to which this fear is based on reality is the subject of this section.

This chapter began by establishing the important role which the family plays in society. To summarise the aspects of this role, the family provides care and socialisation for children and meets many physical and emotional needs of both adults and children. However, we have seen that both the structure and the functions of the family have changed. For example, at one time, all education and training in skills for work was provided by the family. Similarly the family had sole responsibility for the care of the elderly, the sick and the disabled family members. Changes in the economy and the wider society have resulted in modifications in the family. Legislation and increased welfare provision mean that the family is no longer the sole provider of all education and care.

However, welfare provision has not taken over the responsibilities of the family in the sense of making the family redundant. The example of education demonstrates this point. It is compulsory for children to go to school from the age of five to sixteen. This does not mean that the state completely takes over all aspects of education. It was pointed out at the beginning of the chapter that children have learned a great deal by the time they go to school and they continue to learn, at home, as well as at school. Schools do not completely take over the care of children and tend to expect mothers to be at home on call during school hours. At a later stage, grants and loans for higher education are provided by the state, but parents are expected to contribute on a means-tested basis. In many ways, the state and the family have a joint role in educating children and young people.

Similarly, in the area of health care, the family plays a key role, but is supported by doctors and hospitals. It is women in the family who provide most basic health care. Social services see their main aim as being to support the family. It is only in unusual circumstances that social workers take over the care of children or the elderly. Relatives are, for most people, a major source of support in times of need. The current policy of care in the community means that the family is being increasingly relied upon to meet the needs of those who might previously have been cared for in residential institutions.

Taxation and social security policies have been geared to a traditional view of the family, viewing married women as dependants and carers. In writing the report (in 1942) which created the basis of the present social security system, Beveridge tended to think of the needs and life-patterns of working men and to regard married women not as earners or claimants in their own right, but as dependants of their husbands. He wrote, 'The attitude of the housewife to gainful employment outside the home is not and should not be the same as the single woman – she has other duties'.[30] This attitude continued long after the post-war years as the following quotation from the then DHSS shows:

> It is normal for a married woman in this country to be primarily supported by her husband, and she looks to him for support when not actually working, rather than to a social security benefit. Indeed, it continues to be a widespread view that a husband who is capable of work has a duty to society, as well as to his wife, to provide the primary support for his family.[31]

There have been a number of ways in which these ideas have affected rules concerning benefits and taxes. For example, it was not until 1986, as a result of a case won in the European Court, that married women could claim the Invalid Care Allowance when caring for a sick or disabled relative. Previously only men and single women could claim, since it was thought that caring for relatives was part of a married woman's role. Another example, unchanged until 1989, was that of the married man's tax allowance, based on the idea of a married man as head of a dependent household.

Although a number of reforms have been made to the social security and taxation systems it can be argued still that these reflect traditional ideas about the family and the role of women in the family.[32]

It would seem that there is little need to fear that welfare provision is making the family redundant. The family continues to be the primary source of care for most people and state provision exists to support, rather than threaten, the family. In spite of changes in family life, the family is a key part of society today.

Activity 2.17

Throughout this chapter, there have been many references to changes in the family. List and explain the changes you think most important.

— **Activity 2.18** ———————————————————

Make sure that you understand the following expressions, which have been used in this chapter. Check the glossary on p. 363 if you need to.

anti-depressant	monongamy
At Risk register	norm
case conference	nuclear family
Child Support Agency	polyandry
contact order	polygamy
contempt of court	polygyny
division of labour	prohibited steps order
divorce rate	reconstituted family
extended family	residence order
higher education	segregated roles
income support	socialisation
injunction	social security
invalid care allowance	specific issue order
joint roles	stigma
maintenance payments	tax relief
matrifocal family	tranquilliser
married man's tax allowance	voluntary organisation
means-tested	welfare provision
modified extended family	

Further reading

Most sociology textbooks contain useful sections on the sociology of the family. A collection of academic articles on various aspects of the family is found in R. N. Rapoport, M. P. Fogarty and R. Rapoport (eds), *Families in Britain* (London: Routledge & Kegan Paul, 1982).

Graham Allan, *Family Life* (Oxford: Blackwell, 1985) is a very useful review of issues relating to the family, including chapters on elderly people, unemployment and the family and the state.

Although more difficult than introductory reading, Nigel Parton's books on child abuse take an interesting sociological angle on the subject. These are *The Politics of Child Abuse* (London: Macmillan 1985) and *Governing the Family* (London: Macmillan 1991).

The Family Policy Studies Centre publishes up-to-date fact sheets on family life in Britain.

Detailed information on legal aspects relating to the family can be found in Hugh Brayne and Gerry Martin, *Law for Social Workers* (London: Blackstone Press), updated regularly.

Women's Aid Federation England (WAFE) are a useful source of information relating to domestic violence (for address, see below).

The NSPCC have information on child abuse (see below).

Useful addresses

WAFE: PO Box 391, Bristol BS99 7WS.
Helpline tel. 01179 633 542

The National Council for One Parent Families: 255 Kentish Town Road, London NW5 2LX
tel. 0171 267 1361

NSPCC : 42 Curtain Road, London EC2A 3NH
tel. 0171 825 2500

Family Policy Studies Centre: 231 Baker Street, London NW1 6XE
tel. 0171 486 8179 (for publications)

Gingerbread: 35 Wellington Street, London WC2E 7BN
tel. 0171 240 0953

National Council for One Parent Families: 225 Kentish Town Road, London NW5 2LX
tel. 0171 267 1361

Families Need Fathers: BM Families London WC1N 3XX
tel. 0181 886 0970

National Childminding Association: 8 Masons Hill, Bromley, Kent BR2 9EY
tel. 0181 464 6164

The Pre-School Playgroups Association: 61-63 King's Cross Road, London WC1X 9LL
tel. 0171 833 0991

National Society for the Prevention of Cruelty to Children (NSPCC): 67 Saffron Hill, London EC1N 8RS
tel. 0171 242 1626

National Foster Care Association: Leonard House, 5-7 Marshalsea Road, London SE1 1EP
tel. 0171 828 6266

Barnado's: Tanners Lane, Barkingside, Ilford, Essex 1G6 1QG
tel: 0181 550 8822

③ Poverty and welfare

'For you have the poor with you always', predicts the gospel of St John. In terms of the world economy, Britain is a wealthy country, yet this chapter will show that poverty is a continuing problem on a considerable scale. The chapter begins by looking at the difficulties in defining poverty and the extent of the problem, followed by an examination of explanations for the persistence of poverty (section 3.2). Sections 3.3–3.5 examine social policies designed to eradicate poverty.

3.1 Defining and measuring poverty

The first stumbling block in any discussion of poverty is the definition of the term. It is meaningless to say that so many people live in poverty, without first establishing the criteria for deciding who is 'poor'. The usual procedure involves calculating a weekly income which is required to meet the needs of an individual or family. This, in turn, means that needs have to be established. Activity exercise 3.1 illustrates the difficulty of this task.

Activity 3.1 _____

Make a list of the things you consider necessary for a family living in Britain. This means that you would consider a family who could not afford such items to be poor. Be precise giving details, rather than simply writing 'food' or 'clothes'. Compare your list with those of your fellow-students and attempt to reach agreement on items for inclusion in the list.

Poverty and society

People have quite different ideas about the standard of living below which people should be considered poor. This is a major element in the problem of defining poverty. For example, some people might consider a telephone or a car a necessity, whilst others may see these as signs of wealth. Alcohol can be considered a necessary part of social life or as a luxury item. In spite of these differences, few people would limit the list to the necessities for physical survival. It

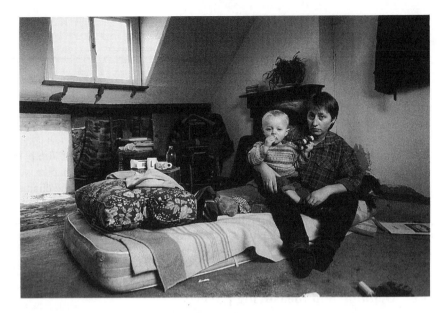

Source: Crispin Hughes, Photofusion
People in relative poverty lack the resources to obtain the living standards considered normal in the society in which they live

could be argued that anyone with the barest shelter, a few rags for clothing and a sack of potatoes could survive. However, a person living this way in Britain would certainly be considered to be living in poverty.

It will become clear that poverty is defined and experienced in the context of a particular society. A family which did not have a washing machine would not feel deprived in a society in which everyone washed by hand. Tea and coffee are not necessary to physical survival, but for many people, they are a key part of social life, such that a person who could afford neither tea nor coffee would experience hardship.

The idea that poverty is defined in relation to the society in which a person lives is expressed in the distinction made between *relative* and *absolute* poverty. Absolute poverty refers to the lack of basic necessities for life. Throughout the world, absolute poverty is a problem on an immense scale and there are many people who cannot survive because of lack of resources. In Britain, absolute poverty, although it does exist, is less common. This is primarily due to the existence of the welfare state. Discussion of poverty in this country is concerned with the second concept, that of relative poverty. This is poverty relative to the standard of living which is considered by most people to be normal. Such a standard varies from society to society, and changes over time. In any society with wide inequalities of wealth, there will be those who exist at a level below the accepted standards. These people are described as living in relative poverty. The following quotations illustrate the idea of relative poverty:

to have one bowl of rice in a society where all other people have half a bowl may well be a sign of achievement and intelligence . . . to have five bowls of rice in a society where the majority have a decent, balanced diet is a tragedy.[1]

Peter Townsend, in his classic study of poverty published in 1979, defined poverty in the following way:

Individuals, families and groups can be said to be in poverty when they lack the resources to obtain the types of diet, participate in the activities and have the living conditions and amenities which are customary, or at least widely encouraged or approved, in the societies to which they belong.[2]

Activity 3.2

In your own words, write a definition of 'relative poverty'.

Studies of poverty

The first studies of poverty in Britain were carried out around the turn of the century. These studies are important, both in their own right, and because of the continued influence of the ideas behind the research.

Joseph Rowntree

Probably the most famous poverty study was conducted in 1899 by Seebohm Rowntree.[3] The research was done in York where Rowntree's chocolate and cocoa factory was a major employer. Rowntree established the idea of a 'poverty line'. This is a concept, still in use, which sets a level of income, below which people are considered to be living in poverty.

Rowntree considered that people were poor if their income was so low that the resulting deprivation affected their health. For example, to calculate the amount of money required for food, Rowntree worked out the number of calories necessary for physical efficiency. He then found an inexpensive diet which provided the calorie requirement and established the cost. Rowntree admitted that the poverty line was based on an extremely austere scale and explained that he had designed it in this way to offset possible accusations of exaggeration. For example, no allowance was made for bus- or rail-fares, for newspapers or stamps to write to children living away from home. The poverty line excluded money for toys or sweets, tobacco or alcohol.

In considering poverty, Rowntree distinguished between 'primary' and 'secondary' poverty. Families were in primary poverty if their income was not sufficient to maintain their physical existence. Secondary poverty meant that the income would have been sufficient, were it not that some was spent on items not in the scale, whether useful or wasteful. Even on the basis of a far from generous definition of poverty, Rowntree found that 10 per cent of the population of York were living in primary poverty and a further 18 per cent in secondary poverty.

Rowntree conducted two later surveys, one in 1936 and one in 1950.[4] He changed his definition of poverty to some extent, recognising that poverty could not be defined simply as the lack of necessities for physical survival. This led to an acceptance of the social dimension of poverty, in terms of the inability to participate in the life of the community. As a result, the 1936 study included allowance for a radio, books, newspapers, beer, tobacco, presents and a holiday.

As mentioned earlier, Rowntree's work set a precedent for more recent research into poverty. It also influenced Beveridge in the design, in 1942, of the social security system. Rowntree himself was a member of a committee appointed to calculate the rates for Social Security benefits.

Breadline Britain

In 1983 a major survey on poverty in Britain was carried out for a London Weekend Television series called *Breadline Britain*. The results were written up in a book by Joanna Mack and Stewart Lansley called *Poor Britain*. In 1990 the survey was repeated to update it for the new decade.[5]

This survey defines poverty as 'an enforced lack of socially perceived necessities'.[6] In order to find out what were 'socially perceived necessities', the public were questioned using a set of cards with different items written on them. People were asked to place in one box the cards showing items felt to be necessary for all adults in Britain, and in another those which they did not feel were necessary. Table 3.1 shows the results of this first part of the survey, in 1983 and 1990.

Activity 3.3

Use the items in Table 3.1 to carry out your own small-scale survey. Compare your findings with those of the study.

In the earlier study in 1983, 26 out of a list of 35 items were considered to be necessities by a majority of the population. in 1991 there were 44 items on the list and 32 were classed as necessities by a majority of the people questioned.

The next step was to find out how many people lacked these necessities. In the second stage of the survey, respondents were asked which of the items they had. If they did not have an item, they were asked if this was by choice or not. Table 3.2 shows the proportions of people lacking each of the 44 items and the changes since the earlier study.[8]

One of the points that makes this survey better than previous attempts to measure poverty is that the survey took account of personal choice by asking people who lacked a particular item whether or not this was by choice. It is certainly true that there are quite well-off people who choose not to have carpets (scrubbed and varnished wooden floors are fashionable) or who prefer not to own

TABLE 3.1 **Proportions deeming items to be necessary, 1983 and 1990**

	1990 (%)	1983 (%)	Change (%, +/−)
A damp-free home	98	96	+2
An inside toilet (not shared with another household)	97	96	+1
Heating to warm living areas of home if it's cold	97	97	0
Beds for everyone in the household	95	94	+1
Bath, not shared with another household	95	94	+1
A decent state of decoration in the home[2]	92	–	–
Fridge	92	77	+15
Warm waterproof coat	91	87	+4
Three meals a day for children[1]	90	82	+8
Two meals a day (for adults)[4]	90	64	+26
Insurance[2]	88	–	–
Fresh fruit[2]	88	–	–
Toys for children e.g. dolls or models[1]	84	71	+13
Separate bedrooms for every child over 10 of different sexes[1]	82	77	+5
Carpets in living rooms and bedrooms in the home	78	70	+8
Meat or fish or vegetarian equivalent every other day[3]	77	63	+14
Celebrations on special occasions such as Christmas	74	69	+5
Two pairs of all-weather shoes	74	78	−4
Washing machine	73	67	+6
Presents for friends or family once a year	69	63	+6
Out of school activities, e.g. sports, orchestra, Scouts[1,2]	69	–	–
Regular savings of £10 a month for 'rainy days' or retirement[2]	68	–	–
Hobby or leisure activity	67	64	+3
New, not secondhand, clothes	65	64	+1
A roast joint or its vegetarian equivalent once a week[3]	64	67	−3
Leisure equipment for children e.g. sports equipment or bicycle[1]	61	57	+4
A television	58	51	+7
Telephone	56	43	+13
An annual week's holiday away, not with relatives	54	63	−9
A 'best outfit' for special occasions	54	48	+6
An outing for children once a week[1]	53	40	+13
Children's friends round for tea/snack fortnightly[1]	52	37	+15
A dressing gown	42	38	+4
A night out fortnightly	42	36	+6
Fares to visit friends in other parts of the country 4 times a year[2]	39	–	–
Special lessons such as music, dance or sport[1,2]	39	–	–
Friends/family for a meal monthly	37	32	+5
A car	26	22	+4
Pack of cigarettes every other day	18	14	+4
Restaurant meal monthly[2]	17	–	–
Holidays abroad annually[2]	17	–	–
A video[2]	13	–	–
A home computer[2]	5	–	–
A dishwasher	4	–	–

The descriptions of items have been abbreviated.
[1]For families with children.
[2]Not included in the 1983 survey.
[3]Vegetarian option added in 1990.
[4]Two hot meals in the 1983 survey.
Source: Joanna Mack and Stewart Lansley, *Poor Britain* (London: Allen & Unwin, 1985, 1991).

TABLE 3.2   Proportion of households lacking each of the items, 1983 and 1990

	1990 (%)	1983 (%)	Change (%, +/–)
A damp-free home	2	7	–5
An inside toilet (not shared with another household)	*	2	–2
Heating to warm living areas of home if it's cold	3	5	–2
Beds for everyone in the household	1	1	0
Bath, not shared with another household	*	2	–2
A decent state of decoration in the home[2]	15	–	–
Fridge	1	2	–1
Warm waterproof coat	4	7	–3
Three meals a day for children[1]	*	2	–2
Two meals a day (for adults)[4]	1	3	–2
Insurance[2]	10	–	–
Fresh fruit[2]	6	–	–
Toys for children e.g. dolls or models[1]	2	2	0
Separate bedrooms for every child over 10 of different sexes[1]	7	3	+4
Carpets in living rooms and bedrooms in the home	2	2	0
Meat or fish or vegetarian equivalent every other day[3]	4	8	–4
Celebrations on special occasions such as Christmas	4	4	0
Two pairs of all-weather shoes	5	9	–4
Washing machine	4	6	–2
Presents for friends or family once a year	5	5	0
Out of school activities, e.g. sports, orchestra, Scouts[1,2]	10	–	–
Regular savings of £10 a month for 'rainy days' or retirement[2]	30	–	–
Hobby or leisure activity	7	7	0
New, not secondhand, clothes	4	6	–2
A roast joint or its vegetarian equivalent once a week[3]	6	7	–1
Leisure equipment for children e.g. sports equipment or bicycle[1]	6	6	0
A television	1	*	+1
Telephone	7	11	–4
An annual week's holiday away, not with relatives	20	21	–1
A 'best outfit' for special occasions	8	10	–2
An outing for children once a week[1]	14	9	+5
Children's friends round for tea/snack fortnightly[1]	8	5	+3
A dressing gown	2	3	–1
A night out fortnightly	14	17	–3
Fares to visit friends in other parts of the country 4 times a year[2]	19	–	–
Special lessons such as music, dance or sport[1,2]	20	–	–
Friends/family for a meal monthly	10	11	–1
A car	18	22	–4
Pack of cigarettes every other day	5	6	–1
Restaurant meal monthly[2]	22	–	–
Holidays abroad annually[2]	32	–	–
A video[2]	10	–	–
A home computer[2]	16	–	–
A dishwasher	18	–	–

Items are listed in the order of Table 3.1, with necessities above the break.
The descriptions of items have been abbreviated to fit the page.
*Less than 0.5%.
[1]For families with children.
[2]Not included in the 1983 survey.
[3]Vegetarian option added in 1990.
[4]Two hot meals in the 1983 survey.
Source: Joanna Mack and Stewart Lansley, *Poor Britain* (London: Allen & Unwin, 1985, 1991)

a television. However, the question of choice is not as simple as it may appear. There are people who say they go without through choice, but for whom this does not really seem to be the case. The following example illustrates this point. Ernie is a 79-year-old pensioner living alone. He is unable to cook for himself and relies on meals-on-wheels. Instead of getting a lunch every day, he takes one every other day and eats half the main course at lunch time and half the sweet in the evening. He saves the rest for the next day. He tells the interviewer:

> I can't eat them. To be fair to myself, I know I haven't got the appetite I used to have. Therefore I just have enough to eat and then I have the rest the next day. It's an economic idea to have as much as you can afford. You can't go beyond your means. I mean, the point is I get the meals Mondays, Wednesdays and Fridays and that costs over a pound, £1.40 for that. I would have to pay twice that if I had it Tuesdays and Thursdays. See what I mean.[9]

The designers of the survey decided to take those who could not afford three or more of the items as an indication of the numbers of people in poverty. With this definition, the 1990 survey found 11 million people in Britain living in poverty (see Figure 3.1). This is one in five of the population.[10]

Measures of poverty

There is no official poverty line in Britain. However it is possible to use government statistics on income to create an unofficial measure of poverty. This is

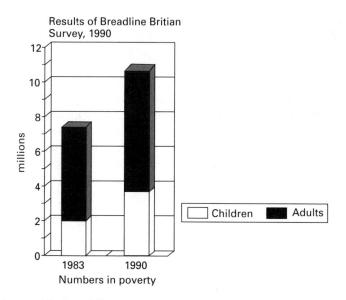

Source: Joanna Mack and Stewart Lansley, *Poor Britain* (London: Allen & Unwin, 1985, 1991).

Figure 3.1 Results of Breadline Britain survey, 1990

done by calculating the average income for the country, excluding housing costs, and halving the figure. Those people whose income falls below this point are considered to be living in poverty. Figures released by the government in 1994 showed there to be 13.9 million people living on below half of the average income. This is one in four of the population. Of these people 4.1 million are children, representing 31 per cent of all children. The figures show a big increase in poverty over the last 10 years.[11]

3.2   Understanding poverty

The poverty cycle

Measures of poverty such as that used in the *Breadline Britain* survey give a snapshot view of society, showing how many people are poor at a particular moment in time. These figures do not show the number of people who will experience poverty at some point during their lives. Rowntree was the first person to describe the poverty cycle, a process whereby people move in and out of poverty at different times in their lives.

Activity 3.4

Describe a typical life-cycle, indicating whether you would expect a person to be richer or poorer at each point.

The poverty cycle, as outlined by Rowntree, included five alternating periods of poverty and comparative prosperity. The first stage of early childhood would be spent in poverty, until the time when elder brothers and sisters began to earn money for the family. This more prosperous period would continue into young adulthood and the early years of marriage, until the arrival of children. Rowntree saw the following period of poverty as lasting about ten years until the children began to supplement the family income through employment. The fourth stage, when the children are older would be one of relative prosperity. The final period when the person was too old to work, would again be a period of poverty. Figure 3.2 is a diagrammatic representation of the idea of the cycle of poverty.

Activity 3.5

Consider the advantages of the concept of the poverty cycle as a means of understanding poverty.

Rowntree acknowledged that the poverty cycle was not relevant to everyone. There are many people who are never poor, having sufficient wealth and income

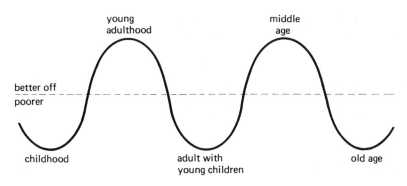

young
adulthood

middle
age

better off

poorer

childhood

adult with
young children

old age

Figure 3.2   The cycle of poverty

for the presence of dependent children, for example, to have no effect on their life-style. On the other hand, there are those who never escape poverty, perhaps because a disability prevents them from working or because they are low-paid workers. The poverty cycle does not *explain* why poverty exists – it is rather a *description* of the life-cycle of certain sections of the population.

The relative poverty or prosperity of families is affected by wider economic conditions as well as by individual circumstances. Unemployment is an example of such an economic factor. At the present time, the high rate of youth unemployment means that many young people cannot find work. They are therefore unable to help out financially when they leave school.

The poverty cycle is useful in understanding poverty in two respects. It indicates points to which state help might be best directed, for instance, to the old and to families with young children. It also gives an extra dimension to poverty statistics by showing that many people experience poverty at some stage in their lives.

The immediate causes of poverty

The causes of poverty in Britain can be stated quite simply. Either the wages people earn are insufficient to meet their needs or they are unable to work and the benefits they receive are inadequate. This does of course leave unanswered questions such as *why* people are paid low wages and *why* benefit rates are low. These political and economic questions are beyond the scope of this book. This section focuses on poverty at a more individual level, examining immediate causes of poverty. These immediate causes do not explain why people are poor, but show which groups are particularly vulnerable and illustrate changes over time.

Vulnerable groups: Rowntree's study

In the first York study, Rowntree found that for over 30 per cent of people who were living in poverty, the explanation was low wages. Other reasons he discovered were unemployment; old age; sickness, the death of the chief wage-earner in a family; and large numbers of children in a family. On the 1936 study, un-employment had increased in significance as a cause of poverty, although in-adequate wages were still a crucial factor.

Vulnerable groups: modern Britain

In Britain today, the groups most vulnerable are lone-parent families; unem-ployed people; people with badly-paid jobs; people who are sick or disabled and older people.

Government figures published in 1994 showed that 74 per cent of lone parents were living below the unofficial poverty line of half the average income.[12] Lack of childcare provision makes it difficult for many lone parents to work. Also most lone parents are women and, as we saw in Chapter 2, women's wages are lower than men's. A growing number of people are living in poverty due to unemployment. With long-term unemployment the effects of poverty deepen, as people have less and less resources to fall back on.

The figures also show an increase in the numbers of people who are working but living in poverty. Low pay tends to be concentrated in particular types of work and industries. These include catering; hairdressing; shop work; farm work; the textiles industry, and parts of the public sector such as nursing. In the past some of these areas of work were protected by wages councils and minimum wages. These however have now been abolished.

About a third of people with disabilities are living in poverty. Where people with disabilities are employed their incomes tend to be lower than those of able-bodied people. Many people with disabilities are unable to work or unable to save and therefore reliant on state benefits. Often disability creates extra costs. Older people make up a significant proportion of those living in poverty, although clearly not all elderly people are poor. Some continue to work beyond the state retirement age and are better off; others have more generous occupa-tional or other pensions. Elderly women are more likely to be living in poverty than elderly men – mainly due to men's better pensions. Some of these issues are dealt with in more detail in chapters 2, 13 and 14.

The culture of poverty

This concept is part of an attempt to explain the persistence of poverty, and the complexities of deprivation from a wider viewpoint than one which focuses entirely on financial aspects. An American writer, Oscar Lewis, is most closely associated with the idea of a culture of poverty.[13] He suggests that poor people form a separate group within wider societies. Poverty is associated with a dis-tinctive way of life which is passed from generation to generation. The features of the culture of poverty, as described by Lewis, cover most aspects of life from family relationships to attitudes towards money. For example, Lewis says that in many different countries the family life of poor people is characterised by freer sexual relationships and more frequent resort to violence, than is found in fam-ilies of the rest of society. Lewis argues that the culture of poverty instils a lack of interest in saving and a short-term, day-to-day attitude to money. On a more general level, the poor are unwilling to plan for the future and have a resigned and fatalistic attitude to life.

Lewis sees the culture of poverty as a positive attempt by poor people to cope with their situation and to defend themselves against the effects of deprivation. It also means that people are not psychologically equipped to take advantage of any improvements in opportunity. Further, the way in which aspects of deprivation are related to each other means that government attempts to solve problems one at a time are doomed to failure.

The cycle of deprivation

A similar theme is expressed in the idea of the cycle of deprivation, a concept popular in Britain in the late 1960s and early 1970s. Publicity was given to this notion by Sir Keith Joseph, when Secretary of State for Social Services, in a speech made in 1972. Joseph was looking at the problem of the persistence of deprivation. He suggested that there may be little-understood processes by which poverty continues in spite of relative prosperity and state intervention. These processes lead to the reproduction of the problems of one generation in the following one. The cycle of deprivation was seen as having four types of cause. These were economic factors such as unemployment; environmental factors such as poor housing; circumstances seen as personal such as illness and hereditary make-up; and, finally, child-rearing practices. Having outlined these four areas of concern, Sir Keith Joseph then ignored most of the issues and emphasised the need for government policies on family planning and preparation for parenthood.

Both the cycle of deprivation and the culture of poverty focus on the idea that people who are disadvantaged in childhood will be unable to break out of their situation and will become the parents of deprived families. Coates and Silburn considered the usefulness of these concepts in their study of a poor area of Nottingham in the 1960s.[14] They found that poverty did tend to lead to feelings of helplessness and despair over the possibility of any improvement. However, they did not find any evidence that poor people shared a separate culture, and concluded that poor people in Britain are not essentially different from anyone else.

Activity 3.6

List the advantages of using the concept of the culture of poverty as a means of explaining poverty.

Criticisms of culture and cycle theories

The idea of the culture of poverty has been criticised on several grounds. As already mentioned, there is little evidence that those living in poverty do not go along with the standard values in society. For example, in Britain, poor and non-poor alike believe in the Royal Family and share many other values. Lewis has also been criticised for confusing working-class culture with something associated with poverty. It is sometimes said that putting off pleasures for the future, for example by saving money, is a middle-class habit, and that working-class people live in a more day-to-day fashion. Many of the characteristics described by Lewis can also be seen simply as effects of lack of resources. Financial insecurity could lead to less permanent sexual relationships, if, for instance, people are unable to afford to set up house together, or have to move around in search of work.

Both the cycle of deprivation and the culture of poverty focus on the characteristics of the poor. This carries the implication that poverty is the *fault* of poor people. Such an approach can be used by governments as an excuse for their inability or unwillingness to tackle problems of poverty.

However, the ideas are useful to the extent that they illustrate the complexity of the issues. The concepts show that poverty is not simply one problem, but a multiplicity of interrelated problems. This understanding means that governments are less likely to propose simple solutions, expecting to end the problem. For example, the elimination of poverty will not mean the end of the culture of poverty. The style of life based on apathy and despair starts from a situation of economic deprivation but becomes in itself, a much more complex problem. Lewis's approach is also important in that it sees positive aspects of poverty and explains ways in which the poor cope with their situation.

A dependency culture

This is an idea which dates back to the nineteenth century (see section 3.4) but which has more recently attracted attention, especially from right-wing politicians. The idea of the dependency culture is that people on benefits become reliant on the state and as a result have no interest in trying to find work or in living as economically as possible.

A survey of low-income families in five inner-city areas found no evidence of the dependency culture among the people interviewed.[15] One of the authors of the study said:

> There is no culture of dependency that people prefer to stay on benefits rather than work. What they wanted above all else was work. Men wanted to earn their living and women wanted part-time jobs which they could combine with looking after children. They did not want increased benefits, even if that was politically feasible.[16]

The distribution of wealth

A different way of looking at the problem of poverty is to see it as a problem of wealth. Perhaps it would be more useful for people concerned about poverty to focus their attention on rich, rather than poor, people.

In this country, there is considerable inequality in the distribution of wealth, as shown in government figures. These statistics reveal that, in 1991, 18 per cent of the country's wealth was owned by 1 per cent of the population. The most wealthy 10 per cent owned 50 per cent of the wealth. Looking at the situation from the other end of the scale, the least wealthy 50 per cent of the population owned only 8 per cent of the wealth.[17] This distribution has remained relatively unchanged, over time, in spite of different taxation policies. The only change which has occurred is between the wealthiest groups, where there has been a redistribution of wealth from the very rich to the rich. The proportion of wealth owned by the majority of people has changed very little.

Activity 3.7

Figure 3.3 shows the ranking of some of the wealthiest people in the country.[18] How do you get your wealth (a job, by being left money when a relative died) and how does your wealth compare with theirs?

The distribution of income

The situation is similar, if less dramatic, in the case of the distribution of income. Figures published in 1994 revealed that the top 10 per cent of people in the country received 25 per cent of the total incomes. The bottom 10 per cent received only 3 per cent. The last 30 years have seen a widening of the gap between those with the very highest and those with the very lowest incomes.[19]

3.3 The effects of poverty

Poverty has effects for individuals, communities and the whole of society. It is hard to describe the full effects of poverty on an individual family or person. CPAG reports this comment from someone living on state benefits.

> Sometimes I don't have enough money for food for my kids. Sometimes I go without. It makes me feel like a pauper . . . It makes me feel cross, I feel hurt because I cannot give my children proper nourishing meals.[20]

Poverty means going without and constantly thinking about money. It leads to humiliation, shame and feelings of failure. People trying to live on low incomes suffer from mental and physical health problems. The frustration and anxiety experienced as a result of poverty can lead to family violence or cause people to resort to alcohol or drugs like valium. Poverty leads to feelings of powerlessness and a real inability to participate fully in society.

Poor communities become run-down physically and are characterised by general feelings of despair. Crime and juvenile delinquency are related to

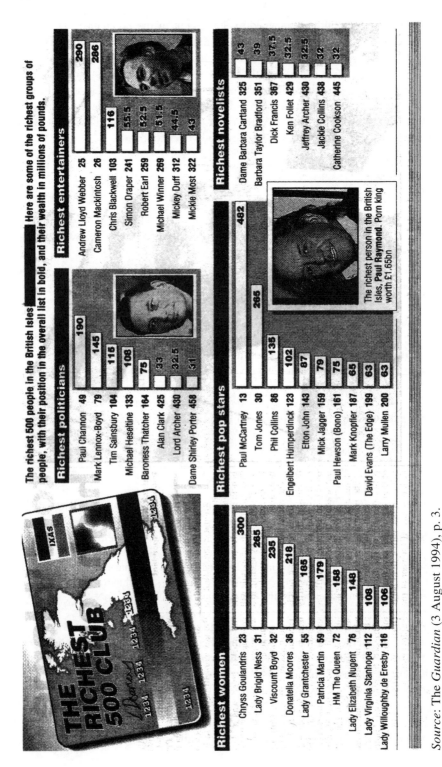

Source: The Guardian (3 August 1994), p. 3.

Figure 3.3 The richest 500 club

poverty and lack of employment. This, in turn, causes problems for poor communities and society in general.

Activity 3.8

Write an essay, imagining you are a child or an adult living in poverty, saying how you cope with poverty and describing the obstacles you have to overcome.

Activity 3.9

Examine each of the following statements. Write about a paragraph arguing for or against the view expressed in the statement.
1 Few people in Britain will experience poverty through much of their lives.
2 More people could get off benefits if they weren't so choosy about the jobs they were willing to take or the level of pay.
3 With Child Benefit people can afford to have more children.
4 Unemployed people can live comfortably on the money they receive from the state.
5 With state pensions, there is no need for anyone to fear poverty in old age.

3.4   The relief of poverty

The Poor Law

By looking back in history it is possible to see different attitudes to poverty and to trace the development of the present system. The first law about poverty was the Elizabethan Poor Law in 1601 which allowed officials in each village or parish to collect money known as the poor rate from each household and distribute help to those in need. The help given would take various forms, depending on the individual needs of the family. Sick or elderly people might be taken into places known as almshouses; others would be given work to do in return for money; widows might be given a small pension or have bills paid. The following account, based on records kept at the time, shows how varied the help could be.

> In 1775 the Collins family was subsidised during the illness of Mrs Collins to the amount of £18 11s 1d. The children were boarded at the blacksmith's; they were shod and the boy breeched. Fuel, soap and meat were provided. Mrs Collins had a nurse . . . wine and brandy [eighteenth-century invalid foods] and oatmeal. Evidently she died, for her funeral cost £1 – after which Mr Collins was removed to another parish.[21]

This system was run on a local basis and people could not be helped if they were not settled in the parish. Help was classified as *outdoor relief* or *indoor relief.* With outdoor relief the family received help in their own home; indoor relief meant moving into an institution of some sort.

Activity 3.10 _____

Find out from history books what sort of society Britain was in the eighteenth century. Where did people live? What did they do? What changes occurred in society between 1700 and 1900?

Speenhamland and other local systems

As time went on, this system of poor relief became increasingly impractical. Parishes were very small and whilst this did not matter in country areas with small populations, it was a problem when towns began to develop. The laws of settlement whereby newcomers would not be helped, but returned to their original parish, also created problems. The rules were complicated and could be very harsh. The laws were also thought to deter people from seeking jobs in other areas.

Towards the end of the eighteenth century conditions in Britain began to change very dramatically, bringing new needs, new ideas and demands for change in the poor law. There were wars, especially with France, which meant that food could not be imported to compensate for a bad harvest. This resulted in very high food prices so that people could not afford to buy bread, even when they had work. Several parishes began to develop schemes such as that tried in Speenhamland in Berkshire. The Speenhamland system gave allowances from the parish based on the price of bread and the number of children in the family. This meant that people would be working and receiving poor relief. It was criticised for a number of reasons: it allowed employers to pay low wages, knowing their workers would be subsidised; it demoralised workers, making them rely on the parish even when in work; it was said to encourage large families and deter people from seeking better-paid work, perhaps in the towns. Another change was enclosure, which meant that poor people could no longer keep animals or grow food. Finally and probably most importantly, the population was increasing very fast. From 1781 it rose from nearly nine million people to twenty million people in 1851.

As a result of all these factors the poor rate began to rise rapidly and people became reluctant to pay it. Attitudes towards the poor began to change. People became less sympathetic and began to blame poor people for their situation.

1832 Royal Commission

In 1832 a Royal Commission was set up to investigate the workings of the poor law. Twenty-six commissioners travelled the country, visiting 3000 parishes. It seems however that the Commissioners had decided what to say in the report before they completed the research. The report was critical of a number of aspects of the poor law and made strong recommendations for change. Firstly, they suggested that a central board be set up to make sure that the same system existed throughout the country. Secondly, parishes would join together to provide workhouses for the poor. It should be illegal for anyone who was physically able to work to be helped other than in the workhouse. The Commissioners believed that conditions in the workhouse must be worse than the living conditions of the poorest person in work. This was known as the *principle of less eligibility.* It was thought that this would deter people from coming to the parishes for relief and make them find work. The following extract explains this idea in the Commissioners' own words:

> Every penny bestowed, that tends to render the condition of the pauper more eligible than that of the independent labourer, is a bounty on indolence and vice. But once the condition of the pauper is made more uncomfortable than that of the independent labourer then new life, new energy, is infused into the constitution of the pauper; he is aroused like one from sleep, his relation with his neighbours high and low is changed; he surveys his former employers with new eyes. He begs a job – he will not take a denial, he discovers that everyone wants something done.[22]

Unions and workhouses

There were many things wrong with the ideas of the Royal Commission of 1832, but since it was likely to cut the poor rate it was popular with better-off people and its ideas became law in the Poor Law Amendment Act of 1834. This act set up a central commission of three Commissioners and nine assistants. It called for parishes to group into Unions and to elect Boards of Guardians to oversee a workhouse. Outdoor relief would only be available for those who were sick or disabled and all others would be offered relief only in the workhouse. The Commissioners would set the standards for the workhouses.

Within a few years of the law being passed, most parishes had formed Unions and set up workhouses.

Activity 3.11

Find out if there were workhouses locally. Quite often, these are still standing, converted into hospitals or flats. It may be possible to visit one. Ask older members of the community if they remember the workhouse. Ask them what it was like and how people felt about it.

The new commissioners supervised the task of building new workhouses and adapting already existing ones to their way of thinking – in the words of one commissioner, to make them 'wholesomely repulsive'.[23] The furniture in the workhouse was basic with people sharing beds, packed into rooms, with coarse and uncomfortable bedding. Inmates had to wear uniforms which were uncomfortable and marked them out as being in the workhouse. The food was dull and tasteless, consisting mostly of gruel and bread and cheese. The routine of the day was boring and the work which inmates had to do was deliberately made very hard and uninteresting.

The following poem was written by John Withers Reynolds who spent some time in Newmarket workhouse in 1846.[24]

Since I cannot, dear sister, with you hold communion,
I'll give you a sketch of our life in the union.
But how to begin I don't know, I declare;
Let me see: well, the first is our grand bill of fare.
We've skilly for breakfast; at night bread and cheese,
And we eat it and then go to bed if you please.
Two days in the week we have puddings for dinner.
And two, we have broth, so like water but thinner;
Two, meat and potatoes, of this none to spare;
One day, bread and cheese – and this is our fare.

And now then my clothes I will try to portray;
They're made of coarse cloth and the colour is grey,
My jacket and waistcoat don't fit me at all;
My shirt is too short, or I am too tall;
My shoes are not pairs, although of course I have two,
They are down at the heel and my stockings are blue . . .
A sort of Scotch bonnet we wear on our heads,
And I sleep in a room where there are just fourteen beds.
Some are sleeping, some are snoring, some talking, some playing,
Some fighting, some swearing, but very few praying.

Here are nine at a time who work on the mill;
We take it in turns so it never stands still;
A half hour each gang, so 'tis not very hard,
And when we are off we can walk in the yard . . .

I sometimes look up to a bit of blue sky
High over my head, with a tear in my eye.
Surrounded by walls that are too high to climb,
Confined like a felon without any crime;
Not a field nor a house nor a hedge can I see -
Not a plant, not a flower, nor a bush nor a tree . . .
But I'm getting I find, too pathetic by half,
And my object was only to cause you to laugh;
So my love to yourself, your husband and daughter,
I'll drink to your health in a tin of cold water:

Of course, we've no wine nor porter nor beer,
So you see that we all are teetotallers here.

Break-up of the Poor Law

The 1834 Poor Law Amendment Act was in some ways a success. People's fear and hatred of the workhouse was so great that they would do everything in their power to avoid it. Therefore in some parts of the country at least the poor rate was reduced as people starved rather than enter the dreaded workhouse. However things began to go wrong very quickly and the so-called *break-up of the poor law* began almost as soon as the act was passed. (Although the system was not completely abolished until after the Second World War, and some people would say that remnants of it still exist today.) Many scandals occurred and attracted bad publicity, such as that at Andover where men working on crushing bones were found to be eating bits of rotten meat and gristle left on the bones. Different groups of people were mixed together in some workhouses, so that children shared rooms with adults who were mentally ill or handicapped. There was confusion over the application of the principle of less eligibility: were elderly people to be included on the basis that they should have saved for their old age? Most importantly, the system was based on the false idea that poverty is the fault of the poor.

There was a great deal of opposition to the workhouses. Riots occurred in some areas; petitions were sent to parliament. Some areas refused to elect guardians, others broke the rules and continued to give outdoor relief. The poor law was gradually eroded over the hundred years that followed its passing. Several administrative changes were made until finally in 1948 the relief of poverty was taken over entirely by central government (see below). Social inquiries, such as that done by Rowntree, showed poverty not to be the fault of the poor. Several Royal Commissions, especially that of 1905, gave support to those opposed to the poor law. Economic depressions in the 1880s and 1930s showed that poverty and unemployment were not caused by the laziness of the poor, but by economic factors.

Changing government attitudes

Attitudes to the role of government in helping people began to change. Previously, the attitude had been one of *laissez-faire*, that the government should not interfere in the workings of the economy. Increasingly, in the first half of the twentieth century, it was believed that the government should take a more active role. Finally, the poor law was eroded as other forms of help developed and fewer and fewer people depended on it for help. These other forms included self-help groups, such as friendly societies, charities, employment-based insurance schemes. Also, alternatives were introduced by the government at the beginning of the twentieth century.

Significant reforms were brought in by a *Liberal government* which came to power in 1905. In terms of the relief of poverty, the acts were the ones that brought in old age pensions and sickness and unemployment insurance. In 1909 a pension of 5 shillings (25p) was given to people over 70 whose income was not more than 10 shillings (50p) a week. A couple received seven shillings and six-pence (37$\frac{1}{2}$p). The 1911 National Insurance Act covered health and unemploy-ment benefits. Workers earning less than £160 a year were provided with free medical attention, free medicine and sick pay of seven shillings (35 pence) a week. They and their employers had to pay contributions towards these benefits. The treatment was available for the worker only and did not include his wife or children. Contributions were also made to receive unemployment benefit of seven shillings (35p) to cover fifteen weeks in any year. At first this did not apply to all workers but only those in industries likely to experience intermittent unemployment.

Activity 3.12

Interview a person who can remember times before the introduction of the welfare state after the Second World War. This means they will have been born around 1920. Find out what life was like, for example what happened when someone was ill, when someone was unemployed, if a child was orphaned, or an elderly person unable to look after themselves.

The following account comes from an interview carried out and written up by Val Derrett, a student on the In-Service Course in Social Care at Colchester Institute in 1987–8.

Alf is a tall, active, grey-haired man aged 81 years. He is slightly hard-of-hearing but has a keen brain and a good memory.

Alf's Dad worked on the railway, he and his wife had six children. He died young leaving his wife to bring up the children, all under ten, on a widow's pension. She was unable to cope financially and applied to the Board of Guardians to get assistance and had to undergo a means test to get 'parish money'. The two eldest children were sent to the Railway Servants orphanage in Derby, a crippled sister was sent to a home for the physically handicapped in Winchmore Hill, London.

'They only came home once a year at Christmas', said Alf, 'so we didn't get to know each other very well'.

Alf and his two brothers attended a Charity School in Currier's Lane, Ipswich. Each child had a well-to-do sponsor who bought a suit of clothes and a pair of shoes per year for their child. The uniform was very distinctive and they stood out as 'charity boys' and they felt looked down upon. The children had to attend church every day and three times on Sundays and had to doff their caps to the Vicar and to the teacher. Once a year, at Easter, they had to pay a visit to their sponsor dressed up in their school uniform. There was also Ipswich Ragged School for children too poor or deprived to be suitable for the ordinary charity schools.

Alf started work at 14 with the railway in Ipswich and received a boy's pay until he was 21. He belonged to the NUR (National Union of Railwaymen) and came out on strike in 1926 in sympathy with the NUM (National Union of Mineworkers). He received only strike pay for over a year and 'times were hard'.

At the age of 21 he met his wife Mary, aged 23. They were courting for six years before they married as they had to save up from Alf's small wage of £2.4s.0d [£2.20p] and Mary's £1.5s.0d [£1.25p] as a machinist at a clothing factory. They rented a six-roomed house (no bathroom or central heating) for nine shillings a week which was a big part of their income, especially when Mary left work because she was expecting their first baby.

Alf changed his job to work at a tent-maker's in town. It was better hours and not such dirty work as at the railway. He was never unemployed as such but knew plenty who were. If a job was offered, a man had to take it or lose the dole. Many families suffered terribly, he remembered an account in the newspaper of a man who cut his throat because he could not bear to see his children starve. Unemployed men were sent to the 'spike' (workhouse) to do menial work such as chopping wood and stone picking.

Alf said there was a system of insurance whereby a small deduction was made from his pay towards sickness benefit, but there were no paid holidays. They also paid twopence a week to a doctor's club and a friendly society, because at that time if you called out or attended a doctor, you had to pay him.. Old folk had a small old age pension and managed as best they could. Some went to live with their children, others ended up in a hospital or workhouse. Orphans and other children from destitute homes were cared for by charitable bodies such as Dr Barnado's or the Church of England Children's Society. Children from the same family were often split up when they were adopted and many ended up in different countries such as Canada and Australia. Mentally and physically handicapped people were largely cared for by their parents and relatives, if not they ended up in an asylum or workhouse.

Activity 3.13

Look back over the history of welfare before the Second World War. Note things which have changed and things which remain the same. Look especially for evidence of ideas which continue, although perhaps in a different form.

The Welfare State

The Beveridge report

In 1942, William Beveridge wrote the report which formed the basis of the present welfare system.[25] Beveridge said that there were five 'giants' which had to be slain by government in the post-war period. These were Want (poverty), Disease (ill-health), Squalor (poor housing), Idleness (unemployment), and Ignorance (lack of education). His report was concerned with the abolition of want. He saw poverty as having two causes; loss of income due to old age, unemployment, sickness, etc., and the costs of children.

To help families with the costs of children, Beveridge proposed that children's allowances be paid to meet the full subsistence costs of all children except the first in each family. To replace lost earnings, Beveridge proposed a system of social insurance. The idea was that people would qualify, on the basis of contributions made, for payments when they could not work. All people in work would pay a set sum per week and receive, as of right, a set payment in times of need. These benefits would be contributory, non-means-tested benefits since people received them on the basis of having contributed and without being questioned about their means. Beveridge believed that most cases of need could be met by the insurance benefits but he recognised that there would be some people not covered. This is because benefits would be payable only to those who have contributed, and there will always be people, for reasons of disability for example, who cannot contribute. Therefore a safety net was added, termed national assistance. This would be subject to a means-test.

The Social Security System

Beveridge's report was very well received by the public and several acts were passed to implement his ideas. The 1945 Family Allowance Act brought in allowances for all children except the first in each family of five shillings (25p) a week. This was not, as Beveridge had suggested, the full basic cost of keeping a child. The 1946 National Insurance and 1946 National Insurance (Industrial Injuries) Acts provided a system of flat-rate contributions and benefits to provide for unemployment, retirement, sickness, disability, widowhood, maternity and funeral costs. The levels of the benefits were lower than Beveridge had intended and unemployment benefit was to be payable for 180 days only. The 1948 National Assistance Act brought in a non-contributory, means-tested benefit for those not covered by national insurance.

Many piecemeal changes have been made to the social security system set up after the war, but the basic structure remains. National Insurance still exists, but its importance has been eroded and the significance of means-tested and other benefits increased. Contributions are no longer flat-rate but are earnings-related. Beveridge believed that for most cases of loss of income, the working population could earn its own cover through insurance. Theoretically, the social security system could therefore pay for itself. This has not worked for two main reasons. First, there is no-one who has yet paid into the system for the whole of his or her working life. Second, Beveridge allowed for 8 per cent unemployment, which proved to be too low a figure. Because of these factors, national insurance benefits are financed partly out of weekly contributions from employees and employers and partly from general taxation. The contributions paid include a token payment towards the health service and a payment towards the Redundancy Fund. National Assistance came to be highly stigmatised and its name was changed in 1965 to supplementary benefit. Further changes came as a result of the 1986 Social Security Act and supplementary benefit was replaced by income support. In 1976, the family allowance system was changed, and the new 'child benefit' is payable in respect of all children. Child benefit is non-contributory and non-means-tested. Changes in taxation accompanied the increased payments. Before 1976, the fourth sector of the social security system was tax relief for dependent children. This was abolished so that the only people who can now get tax relief for children are single parents.

Social security benefits

The main social security benefits are described in the following section. It is important to note that the rules concerning benefits are extremely complicated and this book does not provide a comprehensive guide to welfare rights.[26] The benefit rates given are correct from April 1994 and are revised each April by the government. The benefits are arranged, as far as possible, on the basis of entitlement.

Contributory, non-means-tested benefits

- National insurance *retirement pensions* are currently paid to men over 65 and women over 60 who have paid sufficient contributions. The government has announced that the retirement age for women is to be increased to 65 between 2010 and 2020. The change will affect women born after 5 April 1950. The standard rate is £57.60 for the claimant, £34.50 for an adult dependant and £11.00 for a child. In 1978, a new system of earnings-related pensions was introduced. This is described in Chapter 13 which looks at provision for older people.
- *Unemployment benefit* is a short-term benefit payable for one year only. Entitlement is based on the person's contribution record and availability for work. People who have left work voluntarily or who have been sacked for gross misconduct are disqualified for up to 26 weeks. The current rate is £57.60 a week plus £28.05 for an adult dependant. The government has announced that in 1996 unemployment benefit (and income support for those out of work) will be abolished and replaced by a benefit to be called *job-seeker's allowance*. Claimants are required to sign an agreement that they will take certain steps to look for work. For people who have paid contributions the benefit will not be means-tested, but this will apply for six months only.
- *Statutory sickness benefit* is paid by employers for 28 weeks. For employees earning over £195 a week the amount payable is £52.50. For people earnings less than this but over £56.00 a week the statutory sick pay is £47.80. People who earn less than £56.00 a week are not entitled to statutory sick pay. Many employers pay a higher amount of sick pay. After 28 weeks, *invalidity benefit* replaces statutory sick pay. The weekly rates are £57.60, £34.50 for an adult dependant and £11.00 for a child. *Invalidity allowances* are extra payments which vary according to age.
- *Statutory maternity pay* is paid by employers for a maximum of 18 weeks.
- A woman whose husband dies will receive certain benefits if he paid sufficient contributions before his death. Widows under 60 whose husbands have paid contributions receive a *widow's payment* of £1000. This is a one-

off lump sum. Widows with children receive a *widowed mother's allowance* of £57.00 until the children have grown up. For middle-aged women there is a *widow's pension* also of £57.60 a week.

Non-contributory, non-means-tested benefits

As is indicated by the title, these benefits are not based on contributions or a means-test.

- A *severe disablement allowance* of £34.80 for the claimant, £20.70 for an adult dependant and £11.00 for a child is payable to people who have been incapable of work for 28 weeks and who have not paid enough contributions to qualify for invalidity benefit. People over 20 must also be categorised as severely disabled.

  There are separate benefits with different rules of entitlement for those injured at work. *Disablement benefit* is paid at a weekly rate which varies depending on the extent of the disability. Another benefit exclusively for people disabled due to an industrial accident or illness is constant attendance allowance (see below).

- The *disability living allowance* (DLA) is for people who are disabled and need help with extra costs for personal care or getting about. (This benefit replaced the mobility allowance and the attendance allowance in 1992.) For the *mobility component* the claimant must be over five and under 66 when first claiming. There are two rates of payment depending on the extent of the disability: a higher rate of £31.95 a week and a lower rate of £12.15 a week. The *care component* of DLA has three rates of payment, depending on the amount of help needed. These are £12.15; £30.55 and £45.70. The *attendance allowance* is still paid to those who began to need care after the age of 65. There is also a *constant attendance allowance* for people severely injured at work. The highest rate for this benefit is £74.80 although the amount depends on the extent of the disability and the need for care.

- *Invalid care allowance* is to people of working age who spend at least 35 hours a week caring for a person receiving a benefit for people with disabilities needing care. The weekly rate is £34.80, plus the standard increases for dependants.

- A £10 Christmas bonus is payable to people receiving certain contributory and non-contributory benefits. The benefits which entitle people to the bonus include the retirement pension, the invalid care allowance, the widowed mother's allowance, and the attendance allowance.

- *Child benefit* to payable to all those responsible for a child under 16 or aged 16–19 and in full-time education. The rate is £10.20 for an only child or the eldest child and £8.25 for other children in the family. Lone parents receive an additional payment of £6.15 a week.

Several benefits are now subject to tax. Unemployment benefit is taxable. The effect of this change is that a refund of tax is not made when a person becomes unemployed, but when unemployment benefit stops, or at the end of the tax year, whichever comes first. The calculation of the refund includes the benefit paid.

Other taxable benefits are pensions, the invalid care allowance and the widowed mother's allowance.

Means-tested benefits

- *Income support* is the benefit which people often, wrongly, refer to as 'social security'. It can be claimed by anyone who is not in full-time work or education and whose means fall below a level set by Parliament. The age limit is 18; although there are some exceptions, whereby benefit can be paid at 16. People are not eligible for income support if they have savings worth more than £8000. To calculate the amount of income support received it is necessary to work out the person's or family's needs and to subtract their income from this, the amount remaining is the amount of income support to be received. Table 3.3 shows the personal allowances for different people and the premiums. These, plus housing costs, equal needs.
- There is insufficient space here for all the details of how people quality for premiums. A single-parent family in which the child was disabled would be eligible for three premiums: the family premium, the lone-parent premium and the disabled child premium, in addition to their personal allowances. From the figure for needs must be subtracted any income such as child benefit, maintenance payments and earnings, although a small part of earnings is not counted.
- Family credit is a benefit for low-income families in work. The qualifications are that there be a dependent child and the claimant be in paid work for at least 16 hours a week. Family credit is not paid to people with more than £8000 savings and capital of between £3000 and £8000 will be treated as equal to a weekly income of £1 for each £250. The amount payable is the difference between the person's income and the appropriate maximum family credit. The maximum family credit is calculated by taking £44.30 for the adult(s) and adding £11.20 for the children younger than 11, £18.55 for children between 11 and 16, £23.05 for those 16–18 and £32.20 for those 18–19. If a family's net income is at or below the threshold level (71.70 in 1994) they receive the full family credit for their family. If the income is higher than the threshold, the family credit paid is reduced by 70 per cent of the excess income. As an example, family with three children aged three, six and nine with an income of about £120 would receive about £49 in family credit.

  Family credit and income support are sometimes described as *'passport'* *benefits*. This means that they automatically entitle recipients to certain other benefits. These include free prescriptions and free dental treatment. Income support, but not family credit, entitles people to free milk and vitamins for expectant mothers and children under five and free school meals.
- *Housing benefit* is paid by local councils and helps low-income families and individuals with rent. People on income support receive the maximum amount which is all of the rent. Others receive an amount which is calculated using the same needs allowances as for income support. *Council tax benefit* works in a similar way and can be claimed by anyone liable for council tax. The maximum benefit is all the tax due.

TABLE 3.3   Income support rates, January 1994

Personal Allowances	£
Single	
– under age 18 (usual rate)	27.50
– under age 18 (in certain circumstances)	36.15
– aged 18–24	36.15
– aged 25 or over	45.70
Single parent	
– under 18 (usual rate)	27.50
– under 18 (in certain circumstances)	36.15
– aged 18 or over	45.70
Couple	
– both under 18	54.55
– one/both over 18	71.70
Dependent children	
– under 11	15.65
– aged 11–15	23.00
– aged 16–17	27.50
– aged 18	36.15
Premiums	
Family	10.05
Lone Parent	5.10
Pensioner	
– single	18.25
– couple	27.55
Enhanced pensioner	
– single	20.35
– couple	30.40
Higher pensioner	
– single	24.70
– couple	35.30
Disability	
– single	19.45
– couple	27.80
Severe disability	
– single	34.30
– couple (if one qualifies)	34.30
– couple (if both qualify)	68.60
Disabled child	19.45
Carer's	12.40

- *Disability working allowance* is a tax-free benefit paid to people entitled to other disability benefits who are working more than 16 hours a week. The benefit is means-tested and is intended to top up the income of people in low-paid jobs. People with savings of more than £16 000 are disqualified from claiming.

The social fund

The 1986 Social Security Act set up the social fund. The fund has two parts. The first provides grants for funerals, maternity needs and cold weather fuel allowances. People are entitled to these grants when they meet the conditions agreed by Parliament. The maternity expenses payment is paid to people receiving income support or family credit and is £100. People on income support, disability working allowance and family credit are entitled to the grant, although the amount is reduced if people have savings over £500. *Funeral payments* from the social fund are designed to meet reasonable funeral costs for people on low incomes who are responsible for a funeral. These are payable to people on income support, family credit, housing benefit and the disability working allowance.

The second part of the social fund is made up of payments made at the discretion of the social fund officers and must come out of a set budget available to each social fund office. There are three categories of discretionary payments. The first category consists of non-repayable *community care grants*. These are for vulnerable people such as those with learning difficulties moving into the community from an institution, but also can be paid to help with exceptional pressures on families or with certain essential travelling expenses. *Budgeting loans* are interest-free loans for people on income support who need help with exceptional expenses. An example might be the purchase of a bed or a cooker. These loans are paid back through deductions from benefit. Finally, *crisis loans* are payable to anyone who has no other means of avoiding damage to their health or safety.

The social fund has been criticised on a number of points. The fact that it is discretionary may mean that different people are treated differently by local officers. There is no procedure for appeal against a decision which seems unfair. The fund is cash-limited which may mean that people in desperate need at the end of the financial year cannot be helped if the money has run out. Also it will be very difficult for people on income support to pay back loans. Attempting to do so will push them below the poverty line.

Activity 3.14

Select a social fund benefit and find out the details of entitlement and the current rates. The local benefits office will provide leaflets which contain this information. Report your findings to the class.

Activity 3.15

The social security system is very complicated and not even officials or advice workers are expected to know all the details off by heart. The following questions will help you check your understanding of the main benefits.

1   Ms Nixon has been deserted by her husband. She has two children of school age. She lives in a council house and works 30 hours a week. Which benefits should she apply for?

2   Mike is eighteen has just finished a training scheme and is unable to find a job. To which benefit is he entitled?

3   Mr Ruprah has been made redundant after working for 10 years. In addition to redundancy pay, what can he claim?

4   Ms Andrews stays at home to look after her severely disabled mother who receives a disability living allowance. To which benefit could Ms Andrews be entitled?

5   Ben has a disability and is receiving benefits. He has just been offered a job. Although the pay is low he will gain valuable experience. Is there a benefit to help him manage?

6   Janice is a single parent. She has been receiving income support for some time. She is about to be rehoused from a furnished flat into a council house. She has no money for furniture. What help might be available?

7   Mrs Bal's husband has died. Before his death he was employed and she stayed at home to care for their three young children. She is worried that she will now have to go out to work. Which benefit can she claim?

8   Richard is 7 and severely handicapped. He requires assistance with feeding, going to the toilet and cannot be left alone. Which benefits can be claimed for him?

9   Marvia and Gerry have been told by an advice worker that they qualify for family credit. They are wondering whether to bother to claim since the amount they will receive is not a great deal. What else will they receive for themselves and their children if they claim family credit?

10   Mr Jones is about to be discharged from a psychiatric hospital to live in the community. What help will he be entitled to?

3.5   Issues in welfare

Take-up of benefits

Despite all the fuss made about 'welfare scroungers' in the popular press, many people do not claim benefits for which they are eligible. 'Take-up' is defined as the percentage of people eligible for a benefit who successfully claim it. The benefits with the lowest take-up rates are the means-tested benefits. A government report published in 1994 estimated that take-up of family credit was between 62 and 68 per cent. Around £1300 million was unclaimed in income support benefits and £320 million in housing benefits.[27]

___ **Activity 3.16** ___

List all the reasons you can think of why people might not receive benefits to which they are entitled. What could be done to improve their situation?

There are many possible explanations for low take-up rates. Social security benefits are very complicated and not widely understood. Many people will not have heard of benefits such as family credit, let alone realise that they are eligible to claim. There is a feeling, especially common among the elderly, that benefits are a form of charity. Pride can therefore prevent people who are aware of benefits from claiming.

Explanations for the problem of low take-up rates can be sought by comparing the rates for different benefits. The means-tested benefits have the worst records probably because the means test carries a stigma. People may feel that to claim family credit, for example, labels them as 'poor' or 'inadequate', setting them apart from other people. Many people find it humiliating to be questioned about their income and resources. These points can be illustrated by considering the difference between child benefit and other benefits. Child benefit is paid in respect of all children and therefore has no means-test and no associated stigma.

Although the funding for child benefit comes from the Department of Social Security, people have never had to go to benefits offices to apply for child benefit or to collect their money. Instead, this has been done through post offices. Explanations for low take-up rates must consider the treatment which claimants receive at the local benefits office. People can be put off claiming benefits by their experience or by rumours they have heard.

There are families in need who do not claim free school meals because of the stigma attached and the treatment by schools of children receiving this benefit. CPAG produced a report on the subject, quoting from letters they had received. One parent wrote

> I know Matthew is entitled to free school dinners but I have never accepted this for him as some children can be so cruel about these things and I do not want Matthew to have to face that so my earnings pay for his dinner.[28]

It would be possible to improve take-up rates, if the government was committed to this. However, it is possible that the expense concerned is too great. The benefit system could be simplified, although the trend has been for it to become more complex. Benefits could be better publicised, in ways which ensured that the information reached people. More advice workers could be provided to inform individuals of their rights and to initiate publicity campaigns. Education could not only inform but attempt to change attitudes, so that people understand that social security benefits are a right, not a form of charity.

Stigma could be reduced by a move away from means-tested benefits, towards benefits for categories of people. For example, instead of single parents relying on income support, they could receive a non-means-tested benefit. Procedures could be simplified and improved, officials could be encouraged to see claimants as people claiming their rights. In the specific case of free school meals, it is possible for the procedures to be organised in such a way that no-one knows which children receive free dinners. This is already done in some schools.

These measures are all possible but they do require a level of commitment from the government not at present found. Also, any campaigns to change attitudes are working against the powerful influence of the popular press, with their stories of 'scroungers' falsely claiming massive amounts of social security money.

The poverty trap

The term 'poverty trap' is used to describe situations in which people attempt to improve their position but end up no better off. The poverty trap discourages some people from seeking work and leads to increased feelings of hopelessness and despair. The poverty trap occurs as a result of the system of taxation, contributions and benefits. A person may begin work or receive an increase in wages but lose entitlement to benefits, while paying more in tax and national insurance.

Efforts have been made by governments to improve the situation for people in low-paid work. Entitlement to family credit means that a family with low-paid job should not be worse off than on income support. The disability working allowance protects people with disabilities in a similar way. People in work can continue to claim housing benefit if their income is low. However the poverty trap can still affect childless people who are only entitled to claim housing benefit and who may find themselves no longer entitled to free prescriptions or dental care. Single parents have long complained that the high costs of child care mean they cannot afford to work.

'Deserving' and 'undeserving' poor

The idea that people can be categorised as 'deserving' and 'undeserving' poor dates back to the Victorian era. Yet this way of seeing poverty continues and is built into the welfare system. Certain groups living in poverty attract more public sympathy than others. This tends to be reflected in benefit levels. For example, the child of an unmarried mother is forced to live at a lower level of poverty than a child whose mother is a widow. The payment of the Christmas bonus highlights this situation, with beneficiaries of certain benefits included and others excluded.

The idea of deserving and undeserving poor is also behind the different sorts of treatment different categories of claimants receive. People entitled to contributory benefits are treated more as people claiming their rights than are those applying for income support, for example.

The expectation of the social security system was that it would bring an end to poverty. It fails in this aim in two basic ways. First, there continue to be large numbers of people living below the poverty line. Second, those who live at income support level experience hardship which is tantamount to poverty in the context of today's society. Fundamental problems exist in the over-worked social security system which is attempting to do a job far larger than that for which it was designed. To some extent, the system has been weakened, rather than strengthened by the piecemeal reforms which have been made.

This chapter emphasised the complexity of the problem of poverty. It is not a problem which can be solved easily. Solutions require a commitment from the government and the public which is not present at this time. A full understanding of the complexities and the interrelationships of the problem is also necessary as a basis for real change. In the meantime, people continue to suffer.

Activity 3.17

Make sure that you understand the following expressions, used in this chapter. Check the glossary on p. 363 if you need to.

absolute poverty	poverty trap
dependency culture	primary poverty
deprivation	redistribution of wealth
earnings-related	relative poverty
eligibility	secondary poverty
less eligibility	social security
means-tested	stigma
National Insurance contributions	take-up
passport benefit	welfare state
poverty line	workhouse
poverty cycle	

Further reading

The best source of information on poverty and welfare benefits is the *Child Poverty Action Group* (CPAG) which publishes results of surveys, statistical information and a regular journal. The organisation also produces comprehensive guides to benefits which are updated each year. Joanna Mack and Stewart Lansley, *Poor Britain* (London: Allen & Unwin, 1985) is a readable and comprehensive study of poverty in Britain.

A useful summary of statistical and other information relating to poverty can be found in Carey Oppenheim, *Poverty: The Facts* (CPAG, 1993).

Useful addresses

CPAG: 1–5 Bath Street, London EC1V 9PY
Tel. 0171 253 3406

National Claimants Federation: PO Box 21, Plymouth PL1 1QS

Leaflets on social security benefits:
Health Publications Unit, Storage and Distribution Centre, Heywood Stores, Manchester Road, Heywood, Lancashire OL10 2P2

Freefone line, social security
Tel. 0800 666 555

4 Unemployment

Unemployment causes suffering to people who are made redundant or who cannot find a job on leaving school or college. The families of these people also experience financial difficulties, anxiety and stress. In areas where a high proportion of people are out of work, communities become demoralised and depressed. High unemployment means that even people in work suffer, through reduced opportunities to change jobs, and the feeling of vulnerability which spreads throughout society. The costs of unemployment are borne by the society as a whole, both in terms of financial and social factors. Increased demands are made on social workers, doctors and other caring workers as they are called upon to deal with the effects of unemployment on the physical and mental health of individuals, families and communities. Unemployment is thus an issue of individual and national concern.

4.1 Types of unemployment

Economists have distinguished several types of unemployment, related to particular causes. First, *structural unemployment* is caused by changes in the industrial structure, for example, the decline in manufacturing industry or the introduction of new technologies which reduce the need for labour. The second type is *cyclical unemployment*, which is caused by a tendency for the economy to go through periods of boom and recession in demand and production. Third, *frictional unemployment* results from people being unemployed between jobs or before they start work. Finally, there is *voluntary unemployment*, where people choose not to work, perhaps because wages are too low to provide an incentive.

Activity 4.1

Which of these definitions of unemployment seems most appropriate to describe Britain's situation in the 1990s?

4.2 New patterns of employment

Continuing high rates of unemployment in the 1990s have led commentators to talk of a new kind of society: one in which full-time, permanent jobs will be rare, and people will instead be employed in several part-time jobs on a more casual basis. This pattern of employment has of course always been common for women. The 1980s and 1990s saw a decrease in the types of jobs traditionally done by men; where new jobs were created, many were of the type traditionally done by women. These trends suggest changes ahead for men as they increasingly find themselves either unemployed whilst their partners are in work or working in situations previously associated with women.

4.3   The numbers of unemployed people

In January 1994 government figures showed there to be 2 889 300 people unemployed and claiming benefits. This was more than 400 000 down on the post-war record figure, recorded in January 1986.[1] There is however considerable disagreement as to whether or not these figures give true indications of the numbers unemployed.

Activity 4.2

Why might the official statistics not be a real measure of the extent of unemployment?

Source: Crispin Hughes, Photofusion
There are more unemployed people than job vacancies

Calculating the number of unemployed people requires a definition of unemployment and an accurate method of counting. Recent years have seen around 20 changes in the way the government calculates the figure. In 1982 a major change was introduced when the figure stopped being those registered as 'unemployed' and became those 'claiming benefits'. The Unemployment Unit has estimated that use of the old criteria would increase the figure by some 400 000.[2] The new measure excludes those who have been unemployed too long to qualify for unemployment benefit and whose spouses are working and earing too much for income support to be claimed. Also not counted are men aged 60–64. Similarly, the figure does not include people on training schemes. Some argue that people in part-time work who want full-time work should be included in the figures, especially since some two thirds of the jobs created in recent years are part-time jobs. From a different point of view the International Labour Organisation (ILO) carried out a survey in 1986 with a narrower definition of unemployment. This required that a person must be without a paid job, be available to start work within a fortnight, and have looked for work in the last four weeks or be waiting to start work. This definition reduces the figures by 200 000. Taking the whole range of definitions of unemployment, estimates have ranged between 1 and 5 million people without work.[3]

The current acceptance of some 3 million unemployed people is hard to understand but perhaps is partly explained in terms of the prevalence of myths about unemployment. These myths include the idea that the existence of the system of benefits for people out of work means that unemployment does not cause suffering. There are also people who believe that no-one is unemployed for very long and that it is quite nice to have a period off work, living on welfare benefits. Finally, despite the high level of unemployment, there are those who argue that there is no genuine unemployment and that people could get a job if they wanted to.

Activity 4.3

Discuss with your fellow students the following statements, which represent some people's view on unemployment. Draw on your experience or that of friends or relatives, and information you might have from reading newspapers or books.

1   There are jobs available if people really want to work.
2   Benefits are high enough that people don't feel the need to look seriously for work.
3   Some people are better off on benefits than in work.
4   People who are made redundant will find another job in a few weeks.
5   Many people manage to cheat the system by working on the side whilst claiming unemployment benefits.

4.4 The distribution of unemployment

In a period of high unemployment, work becomes a scarce resource, and like most scarce resources, is not shared out equally. If unemployment was divided equally among the whole working population, each person would be unemployed every six years or so – about eight times in their working life.[4] This is not the case, many people are never unemployed, while other more vulnerable groups are unemployed for long periods and at frequent intervals.

Activity 4.4

Which groups of people might be more vulnerable to unemployment? Why?

Regional inequalities

Throughout the 1980s there were large variations in the unemployment rates of the different regions in the UK. In 1989 the highest rate of unemployment, in Northern Ireland, was five times that of the lowest region, East Anglia. Other areas of particularly high unemployment were the North, the North-West and Scotland. The south of England generally had low rates of unemployment. The 1990s saw striking changes in patterns of unemployment with massive job losses occurring in areas previously experiencing little unemployment. In 1993 the rate for Northern Ireland, although still the highest, had actually fallen to 12.5 per cent; whereas figures for the South and East Anglia rose almost to a par with those for the North. The ordering of the regions has remained pretty much the same, but the differences are much smaller than they were. Within regions unemployment is often concentrated in particular areas, leading to particularly high rates in particular towns or parts of the regions.[5]

The reasons for regional inequalities are complex, but one explanation lies in the concentration of particular industries in particular areas. The large variations in the 1970s and 1980s were partly caused by the decline of older industries such as ship-building, engineering and metal-manufacturing. These industries were concentrated in the North and in Scotland. Unemployment in the South in the 1990s has resulted from cutting back of staff in many different areas of work such as banking, the public sector, telecommunications as well as closures of firms in newer industries.

Vulnerable groups

Young people are vulnerable in times of high unemployment. Statistics show that youth unemployment rises faster than overall unemployment, although it

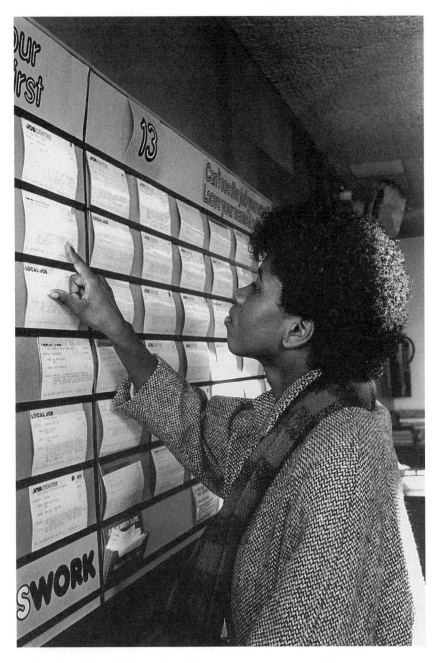

Source: Janis Austin, Photofusion
Some people are more vulnerable to unemployment than others

also falls more quickly as unemployment decreases.[6] This is because, in a recession, employers do not take on new workers. About a third of those unemployed in January 1994 were between the ages of 18 and 24.[7]

Older people who are made redundant find it difficult to find a new job, as employers tend to think that people over 50 or so are unable to adapt to a new situation. In 1994 466 000 people 50 and over were recorded as unemployed.[8]

Women are also vulnerable to unemployment, although the fact that married women may not be eligible for benefit makes it difficult to estimate the extent of female unemployment and the figures from the government show relatively low levels. Many women work part-time and a firm wishing to reduce its workforce may dismiss the part-time workers first, since their conditions of service offer less protection and more limited rights to redundancy pay.

Research shows that ethnic minorities are more likely to be unemployed than white people. Department of Employment figures for 1993 show black people as being around three times more likely to be unemployed (see Figure 4.1).[9]

Discrimination by employers is illegal under the 1976 Race Relations Act (as we saw in Chapter 1), but continues on a very significant scale. This has

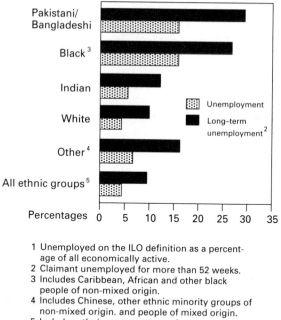

1 Unemployed on the ILO definition as a percentage of all economically active.
2 Claimant unemployed for more than 52 weeks.
3 Includes Caribbean, African and other black people of non-mixed origin.
4 Includes Chinese, other ethnic minority groups of non-mixed origin. and people of mixed origin.
5 Includes ethnic group not stated.

Source: Employment Department

Source: *Social Trends 1994*, 24 (London: HMSO, 1994, © Crown copyright), p. 63.

Figure 4.1   Unemployment rates[1], by ethnic group, Great Britain, Spring 1993

been shown in research using black and white actors matched for qualifications and experience. In these tests, Asian and West Indian applicants were discriminated against in 46 per cent of cases.[10] In the same research project, written applications for jobs were sent, making it clear that some applicants were not white.

The letters received from employers clearly demonstrate the existence of racial discrimination. In one case, the white applicant is invited to arrange an interview, while the other is told the vacancy no longer exists as a result of the fuel crisis of the time. In another case, a married woman is invited to telephone for an appointment, while another is told that 'we have a policy in the office not to employ married women'.[11]

People without skills or qualifications find it more difficult to secure employment, since many of the vacancies which exist are for skilled workers. Related to this, manual workers are more likely to be unemployed than non-manual workers. Finally, people who are discriminated against by employers are less likely to find work when there is a high level of unemployment. These people include those with a learning disability or physical disability and people coming out of prison or psychiatric hospital.

4.5   The effects and costs of unemployment

___ Activity 4.5 _____

What might be the effects of unemployment on an individual or a family? Do you think that the experience of unemployment is different for some people than for others, for example, for a school-leaver as opposed to a parent?

Effects of unemployment

We live in a society in which work plays a major part in people's lives. People who are in work may complain about it and say they only work for money, but the experience of unemployment highlights the fact that work provides more than just an income. Employment is a source of status and gives people a role in society, as well as structuring the day, week and year. People who are without work dread being asked what they do, and there is no pleasure in Friday evening, the weekend or bank holidays when all the days are the same.

Personal
The following section includes several quotations from people who are unemployed, to show how they feel about their situation. These illustrations of

people's experiences are taken from research carried out by Jeremy Seabrook in various parts of the country.

When people are first unemployed, they may experience a certain elation, especially those who receive redundancy money. A man from Sunderland tells how, at first, he:

> felt like a millionaire. At first, great, you don't have to get up in the morning. That goes on for a few weeks. Then you have a twinge of anxiety. You think 'Next week I'll look for a job'. You put it off for a week or two. Then you have a casual look round, and the thing that strikes you is the shortage of work. You get more anxious; you see your money dwindle.[12]

With or without redundancy money, being unemployed gets worse as time goes on. Many people tell how at first they enjoy the change and the opportunity to catch up on decorating and other jobs around the home. Gradually, feelings change as jobs are completed or the motivation goes. Long-term and recurrent unemployment are both becoming more and more significant. Nearly one in two unemployed men have been unemployed for more than a year.[13]

People's feelings about unemployment vary, and for some people the experience is one of shock that redundancy could happen to them. This initial feeling changes as lethargy and boredom set in. The same man quoted above goes on to say.

> You don't realise just how much your life was parcelled out to fit the needs of the company you worked for. You're not used to constructing it for yourself; and when you get to a certain age it becomes harder.[14]

This problem of structuring the day without work leads many people to stay in bed late and to spend hours watching television. It is easy to put things off when endless days stretch ahead.

Common themes in people's accounts of unemployment are feelings of shame and uselessness. People start to feel that they are on the scrap-heap of society and that they have nothing to offer, or that society has no need of their talents and abilities. The woman speaking in this quotation has just heard that a neighbour, out of work for fifteen months, has committed suicide.

> Of course, I've no evidence that it was anything to do with his being out of work, but I could understand if it was. If you're able-bodied you've got to have a reason for living; and for most people, their job is the main reason for living. If you can't do that, you feel you're on the scrap-heap; you feel a burden to society.[15]

Unemployment is a source of stigma and leads to feelings of shame and failure. People with children are ashamed that they cannot provide them with everything they need and want. Many people feel that they are a failure in the eyes of their children. People who are out of work also feel isolated, missing the social life at work and avoiding people out of embarrassment. It is difficult for someone to go out for a drink knowing they cannot afford to buy a round if they meet their friends. People fear the charity and pity of those still working, or, perhaps worse still, criticisms of the way they spend their money or the fact that they are unable to find work.

Unemployment can also have a brutalising effect and, in Seabrook's book there are accounts of young people who turn to violence, racism and brutalised sexual fantasy to escape the boredom and meaninglessness of their days.

Unemployment can also affect health. A government-sponsored report in 1987 found that unemployed people had much poorer health than those in work.[16] Another study, based on official statistics, found that unemployed men were more than twice as likely to commit suicide as the rest of the population. The author of the study argues that stress is probably the cause of the increased rate of illness amongst unemployed men.[17]

Financial

Little has been said so far about the financial aspects of unemployment. Unemployment is a major factor in explaining poverty and leads to considerable anxiety over money. Only people on very low wages with large families do not experience a significant drop in income on becoming unemployed. Benefit rates, as set out in Chapter 3 on poverty and welfare, are well below the national average income. For a single person, unemployment benefit is about a quarter of the average net wage; for a family with four children, it is about half. Many people who are unemployed have problems with debts and difficulty in paying for basic needs like heating and housing. A survey carried out by the National Association of Citizens' Advice Bureaux found that nearly 50 per cent of CAB clients in debt were not in full-time employment.[18]

A further factor in understanding the stigma and humiliation felt by people without work is the treatment people receive when claiming benefits. Many people feel that they are subjected to unnecessary rudeness and tactless questioning when claiming benefits to which they have a right.

Family problems

The effects of unemployment reach further than just those individuals without work. Whole families suffer from poverty and the anxiety of having a member out of work. Problems occur in a variety of different situations and anxiety is expressed in different ways. In this society, it is considered to be normal for a man to go out to work and be the main source of financial support for the family. Families who exchange roles with the woman working and the man looking after the home, often find this situation stressful, especially if it is not voluntarily chosen, but a result of external factors, such as unemployment. However, there can also be problems when both partners are at home. Women who are used to being alone to get on with the housework may resent the continual presence of their husbands. Men may feel that there is nothing for them to do in the home and that they are in the way.

There is a tendency for people to take out feelings of frustration on people close to them. Stress can cause family quarrels and ultimately marital breakdown. There is also the risk of violence when frustration and resentment builds up. In the account given below, a man living in Newcastle-upon-Tyne tells how he came to leave his family in Scotland, after a long period of unemployment.

> I couldn't stand the pressure. I hated being at home. I felt useless. I was no good to them. They're better off without me. I've four kids, the eldest is nine now. But when I was there, I was shouting at them all the time. I never spoke to them in a normal tone of voice. One night I got that mad, the baby wouldn't stop crying, I went to pick her up, but I knew if I did, that would be it. I'd've broken her like a doll. That was it. I had to get out. It makes me feel bad, what I did. But I don't know what I would have done if I'd stayed there. It's best for all of us.[19]

Up to this point, the emphasis has been on negative aspects of unemployment. This is representative of most people's experiences, although there are those who manage to cope with their situation without being demoralised. As the man quoted next explains, feelings about unemployment are related to the importance which society attaches to work. This man was a joiner and his wife does not work because she suffers from angina.

> I don't feel I've been destroyed by not having a job. I've had a set-back, yes; time hangs heavy sometimes. But my purpose now is the same as it's ever been – to look after the kids and now I've got the added job of looking after my wife as well. That isn't unworthy of a man. Quite the opposite. Being out of work is an attack on dignity and self-respect, but maybe that's because we set too much store on things that don't matter – dignity and self-respect should come through your relationship.[20]

There are also people who make use of their time and gain satisfaction and self-esteem through involvement in community work or political activity.

Community and social problems

Unemployment causes problems for communities and for society as a whole as well as for individuals and families.

___ **Activity 4.6** ___

Consider ways in which unemployment has implications for a local community, and for the whole of society.

Communities become demoralised when a high proportion of people are out of work and no employment is available. Poverty also leads to physical deterioration of properties and empty factories or warehouses give a feeling of decay to an area. High unemployment leads to a deterioration in services as health visitors, doctors and social workers attempt to cope with the increased pressure. Commercial and shopping facilities are also affected and big supermarkets are reluctant to open branches in areas where people have no money to spend.

The level of crime and vandalism in poor districts may be caused by unemployment, although this relationship is difficult to prove conclusively. Jeremy

Seabrook's book contains several accounts of young people who take to crime, either as a source of money or to relieve boredom and create excitement. In this account, a woman who was trained as a nursery teacher, tells how her feelings of frustration gave her an understanding of vandalism.

> one day when I came out of the Jobcentre, I was so pent-up, I felt a sudden overwhelming desire to smash every window in the street. It was quite overpowering. I just stood there and said 'Calm yourself down, this isn't going to get you anywhere'. But I felt I suddenly got a great insight into vandalism and violence because there it was in myself.[21]

Unemployment can lead to an increase in crime in that people feel that they have nothing to lose. Someone who is unemployed already need not fear losing their job. Unemployed people cannot pay large fines, although obviously they can still be fined. For some young people, there is even a feeling that being sent to prison would not make much difference to their lives. Communities already suffering the effects of unemployment are also victims of high crime rates and a high level of vandalism.

Trade unions also suffer in periods of high unemployment and are the main pressure group campaigning for a policy of full employment. Trade unions lose members and funds as a result of unemployment and are placed in a weak position for bargaining when jobs are few and far between. The Trade Union Congress has been involved in establishing centres for the unemployed to help people without work. The loss of strength of trade unions in a period of high unemployment extends to the whole of the working class who become demoralised and less able to make demands for improved pay and working conditions.

Cost of unemployment

Increased pressure on health and social services and on the police means increased costs for society as a whole. The riots which took place in the summer of 1981 are considered by most people to have been related to unemployment. The cost to society of such events is immeasurable although more direct costs of unemployment can be calculated. The most obvious cost of unemployment is in terms of benefits and special employment measures, paid for by the state, through taxation and national insurance contributions. The price of these is measured in billions of pounds. The social security bill for unemployed people is £9 billion.[22] The cost of benefits for unemployed people plus the loss in taxes they are no longer paying is £24 billion.[23]

4.6   Government programmes on unemployment

Activity 4.7 _____

List any government schemes for advice and training for the unemployed of which you have heard or have experienced.

Unemployment is an issue of national concern and over the years a number of initiatives and programmes have been devised by successive governments. There have been many changes to these programmes and this is quite a complicated area with a lot of different acronyms (words made up of initials) being used.

Programmes for unemployed people are the responsibility of the Department of Employment. However the running of many of the schemes is increasingly in the hands of local organisations. In England and Wales, 82 *Training and Enterprise Councils (TECs)* have been set up. These are led by employers and have a budget set by the government and performance targets which they are expected to achieve. In Scotland 22 *Local Enterprise Council (LECs)* fulfil a similar role but have slightly different responsibilities.

Advice

Advice and information services are run by the government through the Employment Service, which is part of the Department of Employment. The Employment Service provides:

- local offices with information about jobs
- advice and guidance
- a range of special programmes.

The Employment Service has over 1300 jobcentres and unemployment benefit offices. In the early 1990s it was announced that jobcentres and unemployment benefit offices would be combined into single buildings and this is gradually being implemented. There is a Jobseeker's Charter which sets standards for the service.

Services provided by the Employment Service include *new client advisors* who interview people when they first claim benefit. As well as sorting out the benefit, they work with the claimant to agree a *Back to Work plan* which sets out plans for finding a job.

Programmes available

Restart

Restart began in 1986 and is a scheme whereby everyone who has been unemployed for six months is invited to attend an interview with a claimant advisor. The interviews are compulsory and anyone who does not attend risks losing benefit. The interview may be followed with the offer of a place on one of the following:

- *Jobclubs*
  These provide training and advice on skills in looking for work and access to facilities such as a telephone and newspapers.

- *Restart courses*
  These are intended to rebuild confidence and motivation and include help with finding a job.
- *Jobplan workshops*
  These began in 1993–4 and are for people who have been unemployed for a year. The workshops involve assessment of skills and qualities and planning for training needs.

The Employment Service also helps people with disabilities to find work. All the programmes available for unemployed people are open to people with disabilities. *Placing Assessment and Counselling Teams (PACTS)* provide specialist advisory services for people with disabilities and there are nine regional Ability Development Centres. These carry out training and development work as well as providing an advice service for employers. PACTs provide a wide range of services, including sheltered employment schemes for more severely disabled people. There is more detail of these schemes in chapter 14.

Youth Training

Youth Training (YT) has developed from a series of other schemes, starting in the 1970s with the Youth Opportunities Programme (YOP). In 1981, the government announced a massive Youth Training Scheme (YTS) which was to provide training and work experience for all 16-year-olds not in full-time education or work. The scheme was initially for one year but was extended to two years in 1985. YTS was originally run by the Manpower Services commission but in 1988 this organisation was replaced by a Training Agency within the Department of Employment.

YTS was replaced in 1990 with Youth Training (YT). This is run by the local Training and Enterprise Councils (TECs). All young people aged 16 and 17 are eligible for YT and the government have guaranteed that a place is available for all who want one. The training is not limited to one or two years but gives the opportunity to train to National Vocational Qualification (NVQ) Level 2. Trainees receive a weekly allowance of £29.50 which increases to £35 on their seventeenth birthday. This can be topped up by the employer.

It is estimated that 71 per cent of young people leaving school to enter the labour market go into Youth Training.[24]

The various youth training schemes have been criticised for a number of reasons. In the beginning it was said that the schemes would not be made compulsory but in 1988 income support was withdrawn from 16- and 17-year-olds. Thus the training scheme effectively became compulsory. There is no guarantee of employment at the end of a training scheme and many young people have resented the idea of working for such low pay. Also schemes have varied in quality a great deal. Some are very good, offering high-quality training and valuable work experience; others do not meet this standard and offer routine and boring work with little training. Indeed, not all jobs require training or experience. In these cases, trainees feel they are being used as a source of cheap labour. The scheme has provoked accusations of substitution, whereby employers have used trainees instead of workers on full pay. To the extent that this is the case, the scheme serves to increase, rather than decrease, unemployment. Figures from 1987 showed that just over half of young people on YTS found a job after training. The details were as follows.[25]

- 28 per cent found a full-time job with the employer with whom they had trained
- 25 per cent found a full-time job with another employer
- 4 per cent found a part-time job
- 3 per cent went on to a full-time course
- 6 per cent went on to another training scheme
- 6 per cent did something else
- 28 per cent were unemployed.

The unemployment figures for young people (see section 4.4) do not indicate any great improvement since 1987.

Youth credits

This scheme operates in a similar way to YT. The idea is that young people receive credits for training. The credits have a money value and can be exchanged with an employer or trainer in return for training. The pilot projects for this scheme started in 1991 and youth credits will be available to all young people by 1996. The aim of the government is that this scheme should eventually replace YT.

Training for work

This is a programme introduced in 1993, replacing Employment Training and Employment Action (which in turn replaced earlier schemes such as the Community Programme and the Job Training Scheme). The Training for Work scheme is also operated locally by the TECs. The scheme is available for people who have been unemployed for six months, aged between 18 and 59. Priority is given to those who have been out of work for a longer period and people with disabilities can join without having been unemployed for six months. There is an initial assessment and the programme might involve work-related training, work towards NVQs, work preparation or temporary work to update skills. Like its predecessor Employment Training (ET–known to some as Extra Tenner!) people on a Training for Work programme receive their usual benefit plus £10. It also may be possible to get help with travel expenses, costs of lodgings and child-care costs. In 1993 – 4, 150 000 places were made available.

Learning for work

This scheme was announced by the government in 1993. It is for long-term unemployed people and allows them to attend education courses relevant to work.

Career development loans

These are operated by the Department of Employment in partnership with three banks. The loans are for people to pay for their own training. Loans of between £200 and £5000 are available to pay for 80 per cent of the costs of course fees and other expenses such as books. The loan can be for a course lasting up to a year or for the first year of a longer course. No repayments need to be made during the course or for the first three months. During this time the interest is paid by the Employment Department or the local TEC. Afterwards the repayments must be made with interest.

Business start-up allowances

The enterprise allowance scheme was a national scheme providing a weekly sum for people wanting to become self-employed. Now the local TECs are responsible for business start-up schemes and rules and requirements vary from area to area. People who have been unemployed for at least six weeks can apply and the TEC may provide an allowance of between £20 and £90 a week for a period of between 26 and 66 weeks.

Problems with government schemes

Although it is undoubtedly true that people have been helped with by the programmes provided by the government there are problems with the various schemes.

One of the most obvious criticisms lies in the confusion caused by constant changes of names and rules and the bewildering numbers of acronyms used. Even the staff working in this area are said to have difficulty in keeping up to date with the changes and certainly this is the case for unemployed people, employers and the general public. There is also confusion over who is responsible for what scheme and sometimes a lack of co-ordination between trainers, colleges, TECs, the Employment Service and careers advisors.

It has been argued that schemes such as Restart were more concerned with reducing numbers of people on unemployment benefit that with helping long-term unemployed people. Many unemployed people found the letters they received worrying and felt anxious that the purpose of the interview was to somehow catch them out and withdraw their benefit. Certainly it is the case that along with these measures the government has introduced a number of methods to check on people's 'availability for work' and therefore entitlement to benefits.

Schemes such as the Jobclubs and Restart courses imply that people could get jobs if they were better at looking for work. With more and more redundancies being announced each month, this seems a rather unfair blaming of unemployed people for a situation which is beyond their control. At best many unemployed people feel these courses are a pointless waste of time.

As with YT, there is a feeling that schemes such as Training for Work are compulsory insofar as refusing might mean loss of benefits. Also, as with YT, there is no guarantee of a job at the end of the training, and schemes involving work experience can feel like hard work for very low rewards.

Activity 4.8

Find out more about these and other schemes concerned with unemployment. The local Jobcentre will have information and literature.

Activity 4.9

In groups of three or four, think of policies which the government could implement in an attempt to solve the problem of unemployment. Note down arguments for and against each idea.

Work-sharing and job creation

The initiatives which have been described do little to solve the problem of there being more people wanting work than there is work available. There are proposals for more radical policies which would have a greater impact on unemployment. One such suggestion is for work-sharing. Work-sharing is not the same as job-sharing. Job-sharing refers to a situation where more than one person does a job. Work-sharing would mean adjusting working patterns of the whole society to fit the amount of work which is available. This has happened before in the sense that working hours have been reduced from the time when people worked an 80-hour, six-day week. Work-sharing could be achieved by reducing the working week to 35 hours with a statutory limit on overtime. This would be a way of allowing everyone to work for a shorter period, rather than having some people not working at all, whilst others work 40 hours and often more with overtime.

Another way of tackling unemployment was put forward by the Labour Party. Labour argued that government money should be used to create jobs in the public sector as a means of reducing unemployment. It is certainly true that although there is a shortage of jobs, many needs are not being met. Old people's homes and hospitals are two examples of areas of provision with a desperate need for more staff. Obviously, both the proposals outlined here cost money, but then so does unemployment.

Activity 4.10

Make sure that you understand the following expressions, used in this chapter. Check the glossary on p. 363 if you need to.

acronym

cyclical unemployment

ethnic minority

frictional unemployment

National Vocational Qualification (NVQ)

Placement Assessment and Counselling
  Teams (PACTs)

pressure group

Restart

status

stigma

structural unemployment

Training and Enterprise
  Councils (TECs)

voluntary organisation

work-sharing

Further reading

As mentioned in Chapter 3, the Child Poverty Action Group produces up-to-date and interesting articles and information on unemployment. In addition, a readable, if somewhat depressing book is Jeremy Seabrook, *Unemployment* (London: Granada, 1982).

Details of schemes for unemployed people can be found in the leaflets produced by the Department of Employment.

⬡5 Housing and homelessness

People need shelter from the environment in the same way as they need food, as a condition for survival. Housing is also a precondition for many other aspects of life, such as raising children. Housing is a political issue in that it reflects ideas about the way society should be organised. For example, housing can be seen as a social service, provided by the state, or as an area of life to be left to private individuals and free enterprise. Houses can be owned communally, by individuals or by various social groups. The size of buildings reflects ideas about ideal social groupings. For instance, in this society at this time most housing is designed for occupation by a man, a woman and a small number of children.

Activity 5.1

Whilst there is a certain level of agreement on housing ideals, individual preferences do vary. Imagine you are looking for a home and think about the factors which are most important to you. Would you prefer to share with others or live alone? Would you rather rent or buy? Is your ideal location in a city, the country or a suburb? Would you like to live at the top of a high-rise block of flats or in a cottage with a garden? Compare your ideas with those of the rest of the group.

5.1 Social policy and housing

Since housing is so important and has political dimensions, it is not surprising that there is considerable state intervention. This began in the nineteenth century and takes many forms, including central and local government subsidies, control of planning, building of council houses and regulation of relations between landlords and tenants.

Housing is an extremely complex area of social policy. Housing shortages can only be prevented by anticipation of future housing needs. This is difficult to achieve since needs alter as society changes. It is not sufficient to predict changes in the population, since the number of households can also vary independently. For example, an increase in the number of single-parent families creates a demand for more housing, as does a tendency for young people to live apart from their parents. The prevention of problems associated with housing also requires coordination of planning, building and the availability of money

113

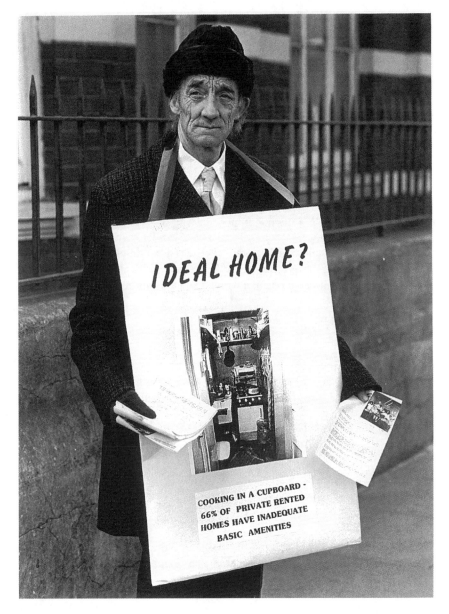

Source: Martin Mayer, Network Photographers
A protest outside the Ideal Home Exhibition

for housing. A number of agencies are involved in housing. Central government, through the Department of the Environment, is responsible for establishing housing policies. Local authorities are involved in the implementation of these policies. Building societies and banks largely control the availability of mortgages, which affect house prices. Architects and builders are also involved, as, of course, are ordinary people as 'consumers' of housing.

In Britain, at present, there is what is called a 'crude surplus' of housing. This means that there are more dwellings than households, by which is meant individuals or people living as separate units. In 1986, the numbers of dwellings exceeded the number of households by approximately 1 million. Figure 5.1 shows the trend from 1951 to 1986.[1]

Updating these figures from the 1991 census does not change the situation. The census found the total number of dwellings in Great Britain to be 23 000 473 and the total number of households to be 21 897 322.[2] Still a surplus of just over 1 million.

The fact that there is a crude surplus of housing does not however mean that there are no housing problems.

Activity 5.2

Make a list of reasons why it is possible for there to be both a crude surplus of housing and a housing shortage, at the same time.

There are several explanations for this seemingly contradictory situation. Housing is of little use if it is in the wrong place, for example where there is no

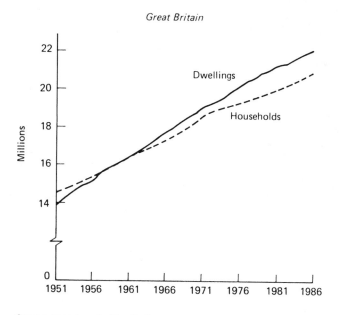

Source: Department of the Environment

Source: Department of the Environment.

Figure 5.1   Households and dwellings, 1951–86

employment. The dwellings may be unsuitable, too big or too small, unfit, or too expensive for people to be able to afford. A number of people own more than one house, and a number of properties are used for holiday lets. Also, the number of households may be misleading, in that some people live with others because they cannot find separate accommodation, for example, people who have to live with their parents.

5.2   Types of housing tenure

Housing can be seen as being made up of different sectors or types of *tenure*. Tenure describes the way in which houses are occupied. Most people live in homes which are privately rented, rented from the council or which they own. These are the three main types of tenure. These will be examined separately, although it should be remembered that they are not entirely distinct, in the sense that changes in one sector will have implications for the other two. Figure 5.2 shows the changes in tenure since the beginning of the century.[3] Figure 5.3 updates this showing the numbers of dwellings with the three types of tenures from 1961 to 1992.[4]

__ Activity 5.3 _____

Carry out a local survey of availability and costs of housing in each of the three sectors. In order to make a comparison, it is best to decide on a particular sort of property, for example a three-bedroomed estate house. Consult newspapers, the council, estate agents and letting agencies for information.

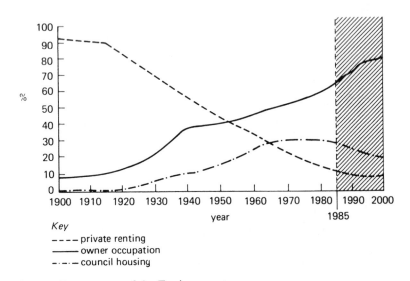

Key

---- private renting
——— owner occupation
-·--·- council housing

Source: Department of the Environment.

Figures 5.2   Changes in housing tenure, 1900–2000

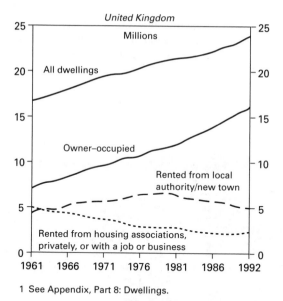

United Kingdom

Millions

All dwellings

Owner-occupied

Rented from local
authority/new town

Rented from housing associations,
privately, or with a job or business

1961   1966   1971   1976   1981   1986   1992

1 See Appendix, Part 8: Dwellings.

Source: Department of the Environment

Source: *Social Trends 1994*, 24 (London: HMSO, 1994, © Crown copyright),
p. 110.

Figure 5.3   Stock of dwellings by tenure, UK, 1961–92

Privately-rented accommodation

Declining housing sector

At the time of the Second World War, the majority of homes were privately
rented. The trend has been for this sector of housing to decline. This has
happened as a result of several factors. At one time, buying or building
property to rent was a good investment. Changes in taxation policies, and in
interest rates for other forms of investment, now mean that rented property
brings a comparatively low level of return on money invested. Inflation has
also resulted in increased maintenance and repair costs. A number of rented
properties were lost in the 1950s and 1960s as a result of slum-clearance
programmes. The availability of improvement grants encouraged landlords to
improve property and there was a tendency for such property then to be sold
for owner-occupation. Tax relief on mortgages increased the possibility and
desirability of home-ownership. An important factor was also the introduction
of legislation giving tenants security of tenure and controlling rents. For all
these reasons, the decline in private renting has been such that, while in 1951,
52 per cent of homes were rented, only 7 per cent were privately rented
in 1990.[5]

Least-favoured tenants

In Britain today, the worst-quality housing is concentrated in the privately-rented sector. There is a high proportion of accommodation which is old, lacking in basic amenities such as baths and inside toilets, and in a poor state of repair.

A roof, but is it a home for a family?

The people who rent from private landlords can be seen as falling into two groups, short-stay and long-stay tenants. Many short-stay tenants are students, newly-married couples, single people and those who move around with their work. These groups live temporarily in rented housing and, for some, it is a stepping-stone on the way to owner-occupation. Long-stay tenants tend to be those who are trapped in this sector, because they cannot get a mortgage, or a council house. Such people would include those on a low income or who are unemployed.

Private tenants are the least-favoured group in current housing policy. Not only do they occupy the worst housing, they also receive no automatic subsidy from the state. The only subsidy to private tenants is through the means-tested housing benefits. Unlike tax relief on mortgages and council house subsidies, housing benefit has to be claimed, and consequently many people – eligible for benefit – do not receive it. In 1994 it was announced that the government intended to introduce restrictions on housing benefit.

Rent control and housing legislation

The market for rented property has always been characterised by scarcity. This leads to unequal relations between landlords and tenants. Attempts have been made by governments to redress the balance and since the Second World War, rents have been controlled and de-controlled in a zig-zag fashion. The first period after the war was a period of rent control. In legislation passed in 1954 and 1957, the Conservative government removed rent controls. Some properties were to be decontrolled as tenants left and this led to cases of harrassment and eviction of tenants by landlords. This phase ended in 1965, when tenants of unfurnished accommodation were given security of tenure, which meant they could not be evicted at the whim of the landlord. At the same time, the concept of a '*fair rent*' was introduced. This is a rent assessed on the basis of all aspects of the property, except scarcity value. The 1974 Housing Act extended security tenure to furnished properties.

In 1980 a measure of decontrol was introduced by the Conservatives with the introduction of *shorthold* and *assured tenancies*. Shorthold tenancies are for a fixed period of between one and five years. Initially they had to be assessed for a fair rent by the rent officer, but this requirement was dropped. Assured tenancies were given to approved landlords on newly-built properties. They exist outside the Rent Acts and tenants can be charged any rent and have no security of tenure. The rent is agreed by the landlord and tenant at the beginning of a term, which can be any period. The tenancy automatically continues at the end of the term, unless either party gives notice for the tenancy to be ended or renewed on a new basis.

In 1988 controls were reduced further. Under this legislation, effective from 1989, all new tenancies are to be either shorthold or assured tenancies. This did not affect existing tenants. At the same time the laws against harassment were strengthened.

___ **Activity 5.4** _____

Do you think that relations between landlords and tenants should be
regulated by law? Give reasons for your answer.

Landlords are in a more powerful position than tenants and the laws exist to
correct the balance. Whilst the landlord is the owner of the property, it is important to remember that it is the tenant's home. People cannot enjoy their home if
they can be evicted at any moment, or if the rent can suddenly increase to a level
which means that they have to leave. Existing legislation does, however, have
disadvantages. Many landlords exploit loopholes in the law, leaving tenants with
no rights whatsoever. It is also the case that requests for a rent assessment often
result in rents being increased. Legislation designed to help tenants can also work
to their disadvantage, in that landlords are deterred from renting out property. It is
also interesting to note that the decrease in controls on landlords have contributed
to the huge rise in the cost to the government of *housing benefit*, since many
tenants of private landlords are claiming benefits. This forced the government to
introduce restrictions on housing benefit (announced in 1994).

Housing societies and housing associations
A proportion of rented property is available from organisations within the voluntary housing movement, which operate on a non-profit-making basis. Voluntary
housing has a long history in terms of small-scale provision of rented accommodation for the homeless, the elderly and the disabled. However, in the 1950s, the
decline in private rented property caused Conservative politicians to be concerned about the dominant role being assumed by local authority housing, a
concern based on a belief that council tenants voted Labour. The Conservatives
saw housing societies as an alternative form of housing in this situation.

Housing societies and housing associations had been similar sorts of organisations up to this point. Following the 1961 Housing Act, housing societies were
defined as organisations which built new houses and let them at cost-rents. The
Act gave the societies access to low-interest government loans for this purpose.
Since cost rents would be relatively high, this form of housing was only available to those with a higher than average income. In 1964 the loan provision was
extended and the Housing Corporation set up to act as a clearing-house for government funds. However, by the 1970s, high interest rates meant that it was no
longer feasible to charge cost-rents on new houses. This prevented any further
expansion in the role of housing societies.

The 1974 Housing Act allowed housing associations, as well as housing societies, to receive money through the Housing Corporation. Housing-association
priorities were outlined as being to improve housing, increase the amount of
property available for rent and help people in special need such as people with
disabilities. Following this legislation, housing societies increased in importance. They have been particularly active in buying up older, inner-city property,
improving it and letting it to existing tenants and people in need.

The role of housing associations changed again and expanded as a result of legislation in 1988. This encouraged housing associations to set up housing schemes with half the funds coming from the Housing Corporation and half raised from the private sector. The rents charged have to be high enough to pay back the loan from the private sector.

The government made it clear that from 1988 onwards housing associations would be the major providers of new social housing – the role previously of the local authorities. As a result, the housing association sector is expanding rapidly. Housing associations own, manage and maintain over 600 000 homes and some 55 000 hostel bed-spaces in England and in 1992–93 60 000 new homes were provided by housing associations.[6]

In England and Wales the rights of housing association tenants are protected under *Tenant's Guarantees* which are issued by the Housing Corporation. These set out the terms of the tenancy and the principles for deciding the rent.

The recent expansion of the role of housing associations has led to some concern that housing associations will inherit the problems traditionally associated with council housing: the bad image which attached to some council estates may now be transferred to housing association developments.

Local authority housing

In Britain, the state has played an active part in providing housing for rent. However, since the Second World War, there have been changes, both in terms of the priority given to public housing and the role allocated to such provision. In the period immediately after the war, providing council-housing was an important part of housing policy. The aim was to build good quality houses available at rents which people could afford. The houses were to be for any citizen and not restricted to the poor or those living in slums. Later, council housing came to be seen as a second-class alternative for disadvantaged people. The subsidy to council housing is perceived as a 'hand-out', unlike the subsidy to owner-occupiers, and, in times of financial stringency, is vulnerable to cuts. Council tenants currently receive about one fifth as much subsidy as do owner-occupiers.[7]

Eligibility

The fact that the demand for council housing is greater than the supply has resulted in provision being limited to certain categories of people. People eligible for housing are those needing to be rehoused as a result of redevelopment, those in need and homeless people. Homelessness is defined in the 1985 Housing (Homeless Persons) Act, which is discussed later in this chapter. Need is usually decided on the basis of a points system, taking into account factors such as length of residence in the area, existing housing, the size of the household and health problems. Most councils have long waiting lists, on which applicants are placed according to the urgency of their need for housing.

___ **Activity 5.5** _____

Find out from your local council the policy for selection of tenants, and the number of people on the waiting list.

_____

Responsibilities and allocation

Council housing is administered by local authority housing departments. Since these are controlled by councillors, there is considerable regional variation, according to the political composition of the council. For example, Labour-controlled councils tend to be more committed to providing public housing and keeping rents as low as possible. Housing departments have a variety of responsibilities. These include the designing and building of houses and flats. The housing department also decides the rents to be charged. However, local authorities are restricted by central government regulations and limits imposed on expenditure.

Allocation of council housing is also the responsibility of the housing department. The way in which properties are allocated is important as council housing varies considerably in quality and desirability. Properties include high-rise flats, pre-war estates and newer estates of high quality houses. Councils have a tendency to give the best houses to certain types of tenants, believing them to be somehow more deserving and more likely to take care of the property. The following quotations from local authority housing visitors illustrate this point:

'Poor type, will need supervision – suitable for old property . . . seems to have taken over the tenancy of this house and sat back until rehoused';
a good type of applicant – this is not a long-haired person. Suitable for a post-war re-let.[8]

Tenant's Charter

In 1992, the government introduced a Tenant's charter for council tenants, setting out their rights. This covers areas such as allocation of housing, security of tenure and repairs.

Sale of council houses

The most important issue in public housing has been the sale of council houses. Legislation was passed in 1957 which allowed councils to sell off property. As a result, some councils, mainly those with a Conservative majority, did pursue this policy. The 1980 Housing Act established the 'right to buy'. Under this clause of the Act, tenants can buy their homes with discounts of 33 per cent for those who have been tenants for three years, rising to 50 per cent for tenants of thirty years' occupancy. In 1983, the qualifying period was reduced from three to two years. People who wish to take up this option are also entitled to a mortgage which covers 100 per cent of the cost of the property and the legal fees involved.

In 1986 a new scale of discounts was introduced for flats. The discount starts at 44 per cent for a tenant of two years standing and goes up to 70 per cent for a tenant who has been with the council for 15 years or more. It has been Conservative policy to encourage tenants to buy in two ways, first, through the discount scheme, and second, by increasing rents. In the period 1979–80, council rents rose by 117 per cent.[9] Some Labour-controlled authorities have attempted to resist the right-to-buy policy, but in 1982, it was ruled in court that one such council must speed up its sales process or have its housing department taken over by central government. Between April 1979 and the end of 1991 some 1.8 million council, housing association and new town homes were sold in Great Britain.[10] In 1993 new legislation introduced a Rent-to-Mortgage Scheme whereby local authority tenants can buy their homes by initially paying only the amount they would have been paying in rent.

Activity 5.6

What are the advantages, and the disadvantages, of giving council tenants the right to buy their home at a discount price?

The question of council house sales can be looked at in two ways, from the point of view of the tenant wishing to buy and from an approach taking into account the interests of others. Home-ownership is seen as desirable and there-fore individual tenants benefit from being able to realise this ideal, with the help of generous discounts and mortgage provision. People who buy have greater freedom to carry out repairs and to 'personalise' their homes. However, home-ownership can become a burden and a liability. There is the fear of not being able to keep up with mortgage repayments and consequent court orders, with ultimate repossession of the property by the lender. There is also the responsibil-ity of repairs which can be an unforeseen cost. Balancing these factors, the majority of council tenants who buy their home probably do benefit from the transaction.

The disadvantages become clearer when the issue is looked at from a more general point of view. Council housing was introduced in order to provide decent homes at rents which people could afford. Once houses are sold, they are no longer available for future tenants. This will lead to problems where little council housing is available and local authorities are required to house victims of redevelopment schemes and other homeless people. In financial terms, it has been calculated that the sale of council houses means a long-term, net loss to the state.[11]

The properties which are being sold are the better council houses. Few people would consider buying a high-rise flat, or a low-quality house on a disreputable estate. Also, the allocation policies described above mean that the better-off tenants, those most likely to be in a position to buy, have the best housing. This situation has several consequences. It means that government discounts are available to those least in need, many of whom could afford to buy on the open market if they so wished. Councils are left with older, less desirable properties in which to house needy families. This increases the already-present stigma attached to local authority housing. Finally, council tenants in low-quality accommodation have less chance of moving into better housing. However, it is possible that a revised policy could avoid these disadvantages of selling rented properties.

Changing government policy

Government policy in the 1980s and 1990s has been to reduce the role of local authorities as providers of housing. It is argued that local authorities should rather work with housing associations and the private sector, allowing them to take over the role of providing rented property. The 'right to buy' is an aspect of this policy. Also, in 1988, legislation was passed to give council tenants the right to choose their landlord. If a new landlord – perhaps a housing association or a private development company – is interested in taking over an estate, tenants will be able to vote for a transfer to that landlord. The new landlord will be approved by the Housing Corporation and the tenants will be offered assured tenancies. Tenants cannot transfer back to the local authority even in the event of the estate being sold on. This has not proved a popular idea and the government has instead concentrated on boosting the role of housing associations in providing new properties and in encouraging private landlords by reducing controls on rented property (see p. 119 above).

Owner-occupation

Since the war, there has been a considerable increase in the proportion of people who own their homes. In 1951, for example, only 30 per cent were owner-occupiers, while in 1992 the figure was 67 per cent.[12]

Activity 5.7 _____

Why might people want to own a home of their own?

Incentives to buy

Government papers in the 1970s suggested that the desire to own property is natural.[13] Yet it is a recent phenomenon and can be seen as resulting from several political and economic factors. Government policies resulted in strong financial incentives to buy. Tax relief is at present given on mortgage-interest payments and housing is free from capital gains tax. (In both cases, this applies up to a certain amount only.) Also, inflation in the 1980s meant that home-ownership was a wise investment, since repayments remained the same, while wages and the value of the property increased (see below). Some people buy a house because there is no other alternative. Privately-rented property is scarce, expensive, and does not provide security of tenure. Council accommodation is rarely available to those without children. Other advantages of owner-occupation are the degree of choice and freedom from restrictions, both of which are greater than in the other two housing sectors. There is also considerable social status attached to home-ownership.

It is important to understand that the trend towards home-ownership has been encouraged by government policies. The ideal of owner-occupation is an integral part of Conservative party policy. Labour governments are less committed to the philosophy of home-ownership, but conscious of the numbers of people who own, or want to own, a house, and mindful of the potential vote-loss involved in withdrawing the privileges attached to owning property.

Government funds have been channelled into building societies and the tax relief on private housing constitutes a major subsidy. In 1990–1 the cost to the government of mortgage interest tax relief was £8.3 billion.[14] This figure dropped in 1992 as interest rates fell and the government reduced the amount of relief allowed. Costs can be expected to continue to fall after a further cut in relief in 1995. These changes, although perhaps not liked by home-owners, have been welcomed by housing policy experts who have long criticised the unfair subsidy to home-owners. In the past this was especially unfair, as those in owner-occupation were generally much better off than people in rented accommodation. Also the larger the house, and therefore mortgage, people had, the larger the subsidy they received. (As house prices overtook the limit of the tax relief, this second point no longer applied.) Mortgage tax relief was therefore an example of a *regressive subsidy* – one which benefited the better-off and least in need of state support – and this is why it was criticised.

Mortgages and loans for housing

An indication of Labour party support for home-ownership is shown in the fact that it was a Labour government who introduced the *option mortgage scheme*. People with option mortgages pay lower rates of interest instead of receiving tax relief. The extra interest is paid by the government. Option mortgages benefit those whose income is too low for them to receive tax relief. Approximately one fifth of mortgages are option mortgages.

Few people can afford to buy a house outright, and therefore most have to obtain a loan. There are several ways of raising a mortgage, which is simply a type of loan, whereby the lender owns the property until the money owed is paid off. The four most common sources of funds are building societies, banks and insurance companies. Building societies have a long history and currently play the largest part in providing mortgages. They were originally literally building societies, in which skilled workers clubbed together to build houses. The role of building societies has changed to the extent that today they do not build properties, but provide investment and lending facilities.

Building societies are reluctant to take risks with the money available to them. This means that they will only lend to people who meet certain conditions, and who want to buy particular sorts of properties. They usually lend an amount equal to two and a half times the borrower's income, and look more favourably on young people with secure salaries. In terms of property, the societies are conscious that, in the event of non-repayment of the loan, they will have to be able to sell the house or flat. The ideal property is seen as being a family-sized, modern house in a residential suburb and better terms are available for such properties.

In the 1970s, it was discovered that building societies were operating a policy which came to be known as 'red-lining'. The term originates from the idea of lines marked on a map of a town and the implication is that societies will not provide money for properties in certain areas. The way in which this policy works is demonstrated in the following quotation from Short's research on housing.

> During an interview with a branch manager of a major building society the term redlining came up. The manager stated categorically, 'we do not red-line'. Later in the discussion he pointed to the St Paul's district of Bristol on the map and said that 'there are certain areas in the city, however, where we won't lend'.[15]

The significance of red-lining is that the building societies, despite their benevolent image, are contributing to the circular process of inner-city decay.

Building societies are conservative institutions, slow to accept change. Gradually, they are beginning to lend money to people who do not conform to the ideal of a nuclear family in a new house on a suburban estate. Recent competition from banks in providing mortgages may accelerate this process of change.

Repossession, mortgage arrears and 'negative equity'

The extension of owner-occupation to people who are not so well off as previously has begun to create problems for some. The 1980s saw a rapid rise in the numbers of repossessions of houses by building societies for non-payment of mortgages. In the 1980s, 3000 properties were repossessed and 13 000 loans were in arrears by between 6 and 12 months. At the end of 1993 the number of households with mortgage arrears in excess of a year was 152 000 and a further 164 000 households had 6 to 12 months' arrears.[16] The level of repossessions in 1993 was 60 000.

In 1991, the government announced measures to prevent repossessions in cases of arrears. These include provisions for benefits to be paid direct to lenders and encouragements to banks and building societies to develop schemes to allow people to remain in their homes. For the first time since 1984 there was a drop in the number of repossessions in 1992.

A new problem for home-owners in the 1990s has been that of 'negative equity'. For a long time it was believed that house prices could only go up and that housing was always a good investment. Massive price rises in the early 1980s created a rush to buy and many people, particularly in the South, bought at hugely inflated prices. This period was however followed by one in which house prices, again particularly in the South, fell rapidly. People who bought at the peak of the rise are now left with properties worth less than the price they paid and therefore loans higher than the value of the property. Figures from the Bank of England revealed that, in 1993, 1.3 million owners were in this situation, known as 'negative equity'.[17] This creates anxiety for people wanting to move or needing to sell for other reasons. It also means that people who have houses repossessed will still owe money on their mortgage after the house has been sold.

Lenders have introduced schemes to alleviate this situation but these are not well publicised. Negative Equity Mortgage Schemes allow people to move, transferring the negative equity to their new house.

5.3   Housing and race

When black people came to Britain in the 1950s, work was available, but not housing. As a result of discrimination and existing housing problems, ethnic minorities became concentrated in areas of poor housing and general deprivation. Ironically, some sections of the white population then argued that the blacks created poor housing conditions, and for some reason liked to live in slums. However, in the words of the Community Relations Council:

> All the evidence shows that there are no differences between black and white households in the quality of housing they aspire to. Inadequate space standards and poor conditions are largely the result of the weak position of minority households in the housing market.[18]

Statistics show there to be a number of differences between black and white people in terms of housing. Indian people are the group most likely to own their own home with four out of five (80 per cent) doing so. This compares to 67 per cent of white people, but only 47 per cent of black Caribbeans.[19] The unusually high incidence of owner-occupation amongst Asians is explained by the existence of direct and indirect discrimination in other sectors of housing. Private landlords have discriminated against black people, although it is of course against the law. A black actor tested accommodation agencies for a survey carried out by the Commission for Racial Equality. He was shocked when the white tester who went in after him came out with more addresses in the same area and the same price range. 'I'd never have known', said the black tester, 'She was so friendly and helpful'.[20]

In the public sector there is evidence of some direct discrimination together with indirect discrimination in the form of clauses stating that applicants must have been resident in the area for a certain period of time. The Commission for Racial Equality found that in Liverpool ethnic minority families had to wait longer for a council home, and had far less chance than white people of getting a house with central heating and a garden.[21] It is also the case that the type of local authority housing available does not meet the needs of Asian families.

In all racial groups, the majority of people borrowed money from building societies for purchase of a house, but other forms of finance are more common for Asian and West Indians than for whites.[22] A relatively large proportions of Asians have loans from a bank. This reflects the difficulties they have experienced when seeking property they can afford which is large enough for their households. Such properties are often in inner-city areas not popular with building societies or in need of too much repair.

Estate agents have been found to be illegally discriminating against ethnic minorities. An estate agent told white people in a survey carried out by the Commission for Racial Equality they would not want to live in certain areas 'because of the Asians'. They did not tell this to Asian people.[23] This discrimination has the effect of segregating people by race and also makes it harder for Asians to sell houses as fewer people are sent to view and forces prices down for Asian owners.

The overall trend in housing is that the best-quality housing is that which is owner-occupied. In spite of this and the fact that a high proportion of black people own their own homes, a higher percentage of black than white households live in poor-quality homes. Black home-owners are more likely than whites to be sharing, to be overcrowded and to live in houses which lack basic amenities such as inside toilets. Members of ethnic minorities are concentrated in older housing in inner city areas. Similarly those members of ethnic groups who are in council housing are allocated to less desirable properties, and are again more likely to be sharing, to be overcrowded and to lack basic facilities.[24]

5.4   Homelessness

Who is 'homeless'?

Despite the surplus of housing referred to at the beginning of this chapter, there are people in Britain without a home. Understanding of this problem is hindered by the lack of statistics showing the full extent of the situation. The official statistics on homelessness are restricted to the number of people accepted by local authorities as homeless. These statistics have several limitations. Homelessness is defined in the narrow sense of 'being without accommodation'. People who are homeless may not approach the council or may be turned away. The voluntary organisation most concerned with homelessness, Shelter, argues that the definition should be broadened to include those who do not have a home, rather than simply counting the number of people without a roof over their heads.

Activity 5.8

Think about what is implied by the term 'home'. Write a full definition of what it means to have a home. Discuss your ideas with the rest of the class.

Empty houses, yet homeless families

In its definition of homelessness, Shelter includes people who have accommodation which is insecure, overcrowded, dangerous, damp or lacking in basic amenities. People who are 'squatting' are considered homeless, as are those living with relatives, for example, married couples living with their parents.

In 1992 167 000 households were accepted as homeless by local authorities in Great Britain. The number of people homeless in terms of a wider definition is unknown.[25]

Causes of homelessness

The causes of homelessness can be looked at in several ways. At one level, homelessness is caused by a national shortage of adequate and suitable housing in the right places and available at the right price. It is also possible to examine

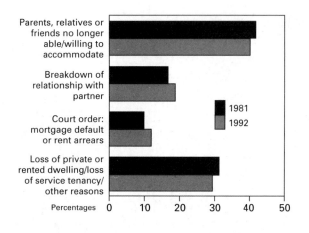

1 Households for whom local authorities accepted
responsibility to secure permanent accommodation under
the Housing (Homeless Persons) Act 1977 and the Housing
Act 1985, which defines 'priority need'.
2 Categories in Wales differ slightly from those in England so
cases have been allocated to the closest English category.
Data for Wales includes priority cases given advice and
assistance.

Source: Department of the Environment;
Welsh Office; Scottish Office

Source: *Social Trends 1994*, 24 (London: HMSO, 1994, © Crown copyright),
p. 110.

**Figure 5.4   Homeless households[1] found accommodation by local
authorities, by reason,[2] for homelessness, Great Britain, 1981 and 1992**

immediate reasons for particular cases of homelessness. Figure 5.4 shows the
reasons given by people accepted as homeless by local authorities in 1981 and
1992.[26]

It should be borne in mind however that statistics do not necessarily tell the
whole story, since a breakdown in a relationship for example could be caused by
poverty or over-crowding.

A third way to think about the causes of homelessness involves considering
groups of people who are excluded from access to particular types of housing.
People who are low-paid or unemployed find it difficult to get mortgages – this
would include many single-parent families. Black people have, as we have
seen, suffered from discrimination by building societies, estate agents and
private landlords. Local authority housing policies have also indirectly discriminated against immigrants through residence clauses. Landlords are sometimes reluctant to let to people with children and usually demand references
which can be a problem for people who have been in prison and other institutions. Local authority policies operate to the disadvantage of single and childless people.

___ **Activity 5.9** _____

People leaving community homes and psychiatric hospitals often experience particular housing difficulties. Find out from your local social services department if any special help is given to such people in your area.

Consequences and help available

Homelessness has severe consequences for the individuals concerned and for society. It can lead to unemployment and to the break-up of families and can result in children being taken into care. The psychological effects are also serious. It is likely that homelessness will increase in future years. This is mainly because there has been a decrease in the building of new houses. In 1980, a start was made on 152 000 houses – the lowest figure in peace-time since the 1920s[27] The number has risen a little since this time, but is still much lower than in previous decades.

Local authorities have a duty to help homeless people. Between 1948 and 1977, the legal basis for this was Part III of the 1948 National Assistance Act. This stated that local authorities had to provide temporary accommodation for people in urgent need. The provision came to be known as Part III accommodation. Local authority temporary housing was often in a poor state of repair and characterised by restrictive rules, for example, banning husbands (housing women and their children only and not allowing men to stay with their families, even overnight). The demand for Part III accommodation increased in the 1950s as a result of the decline in privately-rented property. This pressure on temporary housing continued to increase in the 1960s and 1970s.

Bed-and-breakfast accommodation

In response, local authorities in London began to use bed-and-breakfast accommodation as a solution to the problem. This policy has since spread to other areas of the country, reaching a peak in 1991 with 12 200 families in bed and breakfast.[28]

The unsatisfactory nature of bed-and-breakfast provision for homeless families is illustrated in the following description.

Life in such places was awful. Often a whole family would live in one room, with nowhere to cook – meals had to be bought in a local cafe. Facilities for washing clothes would often be non-existent. In many places families were required to leave the guest-house after breakfast and walk the streets all day, until they were allowed back in the evening. Families with babies would often have to smuggle in electric kettles or small stoves in order to be able to heat up bottles. As one family told me, 'We do our ironing on a tiny coffee table or on the floor. The only meal you can get here is breakfast and you can't cook so we either live on sandwiches or fish and chips. The kids have to sit on the beds and eat their chips. We haven't had a Sunday dinner for nearly a year'. In short, bed-and-breakfast is no 'holiday on the rates' – rather it makes normal family life impossible.[29]

Source: Crispin Hughes, Photofusion
Life in 'bed and breakfast' accommodation

Despite the inadequacy of guest-house accommodation for homeless family, it costs local authorities considerable sums of money. The cost in 1986 to the London boroughs alone was £63 million.[30] More recent figures calculated by shelter show that the annual cost of building a new home would be less than councils pay to keep people in bed and breakfast.[31]

Some hotels have been set up specifically to exploit the situation and good profits are to be made. A report in a newspaper in 1987 told of a group of three London hotels who were found to be charging more than twice their usual rate to the council to provide fewer facilities. Tourists paid £8 to £15 a night whilst council tenants paid £17.50 to £34. Up to six people shared one room.[32]

Activity 5.10

Find out from your local housing department what provision is made for homeless people in your area.

'Intentional' homelessness

The duty of local authorities to help homeless people is now set out in the 1985 Housing (Homeless Persons) Act. As mentioned earlier, the Act defines people as homeless if they have no accommodation which they are entitled to occupy.

Battered women can be considered homeless if they cannot occupy their home because of violence or the threat of violence. While the Housing Act was passed as a result of pressure put on the government by groups concerned with homelessness and is an improvement on the previous situation, problems remain. The Act contains a clause freeing local authorities from responsibility for those who are considered to have 'intentionally' made themselves homeless. The interpretation of this clause can cause problems for homeless people. For example, people who accept advice from bank managers to sell their homes to pay off debts can be argued to be intentionally homeless. Similarly, eviction following rent arrears can be looked at in this way. The clause on intentional homelessness can also be used against people who, not understanding their rights, leave rented property when told to do so by the landlord.

The following extract from a Shelter report shows how the intentional homelessness clause can be used:

> Mr and Mrs H and their two children rented a flat from a landlord who later fell into arrears with the mortgage on it. Repossession was on the cards, which would mean the tenants would be evicted at the same time. The H family decided to move out before the inevitable happened, and accepted an offer from Mr H's employer to put them up in a caravan. But as there was no planning permission for the site the Council forced the employer to put the family out. The Council then declared them 'intentionally' homeless because they had given up their initial accommodation, which the Council regarded as 'secure'. The Council discharged its responsibility to the family by finding them accommodation in a hotel at their own expense.[33] Stricter rules regarding 'intentional homelessness' are planned.

Priority need

Another problem with the legislation on homelessness is that the Act only requires local authorities to house homeless people who are defined as being in 'priority need'. Priority need groups include households with dependent children or pregnant women, the elderly and people with health problems. In 1994 the government announced proposals to change the system of allocation of council houses, reducing the obligation on local authorities to provide permanent housing for homeless people.

Living on the streets and squatting

The system of priority need ignores the problems faced by single homeless people. As a result of this and other policies such as the withdrawal of benefit for 16- and 17- year-olds, increased numbers of people began sleeping rough. Considerable publicity was given to people living on the streets in towns like London. The 1991 Census recorded 2674 people sleeping rough in England. Shelter however argue that the figure is much higher, estimating there are 8600 people sleeping rough.[34] There are a number of shelters and hostels run by voluntary organisations such as Centrepoint in London. In 1990–1 the government introduced the *Rough Sleepers' Initiative* to provide additional beds in hostels and other temporary accommodation. Some £96 million was spent in three years and surveys have shown a drop in the number of people living on the streets.

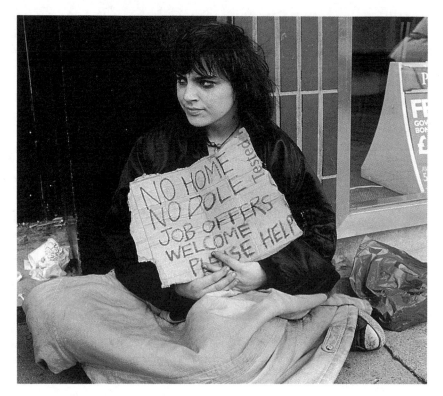

Source: J. Southworth, Photofusion
Changes to benefit rules in 1988 caused some young people to become
homeless and destitute

Homelessness, combined with the existence of a large number of empty properties, led to an increase in squatting in the late 1960s and early 1970s. This attracted
considerable attention from the media, focusing mainly on mythical cases of
squatters moving into houses while the owners were on holiday. An important
consequence of the actions of squatters was that, in 1969, the government issued a
circular urging local authorities to use their empty property as short-life housing.
Such housing was let, on a temporary basis, to licensed tenants or turned over for
management by housing associations. Surveys have suggested that in 1990 there
were some 30 000 squatters in London and about 50 000 in the UK as a whole.[35]

In 1977, squatting was made into a criminal offence instead of a civil offence,
as previously. As a result, squatters can be arrested by the police and, if convicted, fined £1000 or given a six-month prison sentence. In 1994 new measures
were brought in to speed up removal of squatters.

Activity 5.11 _____

Should homeless people have a right to occupy empty houses? Discuss this
with the rest of the class.

5.5   Bad housing and rehabilitation

Housing standards have risen this century and Britain is one of the best-housed countries in the world. However, there remains a significant proportion of housing which is unfit or without basic amenities. The 1991 Housing Condition Survey found 1.7 million houses in Britain which are unfit for human habitation and another 3.8 million in need of urgent repair.[36]

Social effects

The effects of poor housing on those who live in such conditions are considerable. Damp or dangerous houses are a risk to health. When houses are in a poor state of repair, attempts at improving or maintaining living conditions often produce little result. For example, decorating quickly becomes a pointless exercise if damp means that wallpaper will not stay on the wall. Old, poorly-maintained houses are difficult to keep clean. These factors have a morale-reducing effect on people trying to maintain a home in such conditions. The risk of marital breakdown or domestic violence is present if partners blame each other for their situation or express their frustration through violence. Poor housing can result in children being taken into the care of the local authority. Young people living in inadequate housing may spend more time on the streets and risk getting into trouble with the police. These problems are of concern to society as well as to the individuals concerned.

Possible solutions: rehouse or rehabilitate?

There are several possible solutions to the problem of bad housing. In the period following the Second World War, local authorities were encouraged to demolish older properties and build new estates, often in the form of tower blocks. Some twenty years later, disillusionment with such policies led to increased interest in the rehabilitation of housing.

Changing government thinking
The following extract demonstrates the shift in government thinking.

> The Government believes that, in the majority of cases, it is no longer preferable to attempt to solve the problems arising from bad housing by schemes of widespread, comprehensive redevelopment. Such an approach often involves massive and unacceptable disruption of communities and leaves vast areas of our cities standing derelict and devastated for far too long. Regardless of the financial compensation they receive, many people suffer distress when their homes are compulsorily acquired. Increasing local opposition to redevelopment proposals is largely attributable to people's understandable preference for the familiar and, in many ways, more convenient environment in which they have lived for years. Large-scale redevelopment frequently diminishes rather than widens the choice available to people in terms of style of houses, their form of tenure, and their price.[37]

Activity 5.12

List as many advantages as you can think of for rehabilitation rather than demolition of older properties.

It has been increasingly recognised that redevelopment has costs and disadvantages. In purely financial terms it is cheaper to improve existing properties than to build new ones. In 1969, it was estimated that it would cost £600 million per annum to construct 200 000 council houses, while the same number of properties could be rehabilitated for £115 million.[38] While costs of building fluctuate, it is probably still cheaper to renovate old houses than to pull them down and build new ones.

The social costs of breaking up established communities are now acknowledged. This can be seen in the following quotation from Peter Walker, when Secretary of State for the Environment.

> New homes are not enough. We need many more new houses, but it should be remembered that whilst new homes take a matter of months to build, it takes much longer to build a new community . . . We have established communities with their local churches, their local schools, their local pubs and their local football teams, where the inhabitants are friends and neighbours of each other. It is important that where possible, instead of using the bulldozer we retain the community and improve the quality of the housing and the environment.[39]

Dangers of community break-up

Whilst there is a danger of becoming too romantic about the virtues of areas of older housing, research such as that carried out by Young and Willmott demonstrated the existence of extended families and community network.[40] Breaking up such communities can have far-reaching and unforeseen effects. It can mean the loss of support for people such as young mothers and the elderly, resulting in increased pressure on social services departments. In long-established communities, the inhabitants know one another and this can constitute a form of self-policing. For example, a stranger entering a property will be noticed or young people getting into trouble reported to their parents. Many of the newer estates are characterised by a high level of crime and vandalism.

Demolition often meant that people were moved out of city areas to estates on the edge of the town. This could lead to isolation and increased costs for travel to work or to visit friends and relatives. The policy of moving people into high-rise flats is now acknowledged as having created many new problems. It is difficult for inhabitants of such housing to feel a sense of territory, either as individuals or as a community. There is a feeling of being cut off from social contact, especially for people remaining at home during the day. Practical problems also arise – for example, parents cannot allow children to play out alone. Many of the tower blocks were shoddily constructed and not maintained adequately. Commonly, lifts break down, and there is a high level of vandalism to the buildings. High-rise flats are not necessarily always unsuitable as places to live, but they cause problems for families with young children and elderly people.

Finally, re-housing people who already have homes adversely affects those on council waiting-lists, delaying the possibility of their being offered housing.

Improvement policy
There has been legislation allowing local authorities to improve housing for some fifty years. However, little was done as a result of early legislation, as the impetus was towards redevelopment, rather than rehabilitation. From 1959, local authorities were required to make grants available to owners installing basic amenities such as baths. In 1964, local authorities were given the power to compel owners to renovate properties in designated improvement areas. This provision was extended in 1969 through legislation which followed the publication of the government paper, 'Old Houses into New Homes'. The following extract from the paper describes local authority's new powers to create General Improvement Areas.

> Local authorities should have power to declare General Improvement Areas. The aim in these areas would be to help and persuade owners to improve their houses and to help them also by improving the environment. Authorities would be able to buy land and buildings and carry out work for this purpose. They would also have power to buy houses for improvement and conversion and to buy any houses which were unfit and which stood in the way of improvement of the whole area.[41]

The General Improvement Areas were introduced in the 1969 Housing Act as small areas of approximately 300 houses. As a result of this legislation, the number of grants allocated increased considerably. In 1974, Housing Action Areas (HAAs) were introduced. These were also small areas and were to be characterised by social factors such as overcrowding, the proportion of large families and elderly people. In these areas, local authorities could work directly on improvement, and housing associations were encouraged to acquire and manage property.

As is often the case in social policy, even with well-intentioned proposals, the laws did not always work to the advantage of those intended to benefit. Problems arose as landlords improved properties with the assistance of grants, only to sell the property or evict poor tenants and bring in better off people who could afford higher rents. People were thus pushed out of the improved areas, and forced to move into other run-down properties. Restrictions were introduced in an attempt to prevent this process, but they were inadequate and came too late to be fully effective.

In the 1990s, the government's emphasis has been on improving existing housing stock, rather than demolition.

For council housing the government plans to introduce a *'homesteading scheme'* which will allow people in housing need to restore council properties for a reduced rent or to buy at a reduced price. There is also the *Estate Action Programme* which began in 1985 and which provides local authorities with extra resources to regenerate run-down estates. The 1988 housing legislation introduced more radical measures for the rehabilitation of run-down council estates. Estates would be taken out of the control of the local authorities and run by *Housing Action Trusts (HATs)*. The HATs improve the estate with money from central government and then sell them to a new landlord within 5 years. The first batch of estates, 18 in six inner-city areas was announced for a programme starting in 1988 with a budget of £125 million. As a result of protests by tenants a House of Lords' amendment allowed tenants to vote on their change of landlord. The idea of HATs has not so far proved popular with tenants and by 1993 only three HATs had been established.

The 1989 Local Government and Housing Act allowed local authorities to declare renewal areas according to certain criteria set down by the government. This gives the local authority extra powers to purchase land and extra funding for improvement of properties.

Grants to enable owner-occupiers to improve their houses have been cut. The 1989 Local Government and Housing Act allows grants to be given only to the poorest people living in the worst houses. There are mandatory grants to pay for work to make property fit for human habitation; discretionary grants can be given by the local authority for improvements beyond this standard. There are also grants available for special facilities for people with disabilities. All grants are, however, means-tested.

The role of housing in society

The politics of grants for owner-occupiers raises wider issues about the role of housing in society and who should take responsibility for housing. For some housing is a social issue – the effects of bad housing spread wider than the individual and the nation should take responsibility for maintaining the housing stock of the country. In a report looking at the results of the 1991 Housing Condition Survey, the National Housing Forum argued that poor housing had a bad effect on the whole nation's well-being. The chairperson of the Forum added that:

> Neglecting housing makes no sense in economic terms because the public purse has to bear the costs of the increased health and social care which results from poor quality housing. There is also the cost of ultimately demolishing homes which are in the most serious disrepair.

The government take a different line, with a spokesperson for the Department of Environment saying that:

> The primary responsibility for repairing a home is the owner's. Public resources to help private owners are necessarily limited and are therefore targeted on the needy.[42]

___ **Activity 5.13** _____

Most parts of the country have areas of housing problems, whether they be old council estates, newer high-rise blocks or inner-city slums. As a class, decide where such areas are located locally. What policies could the local council implement to improve these areas?

This chapter has attempted to demonstrate the complexity of housing issues. It can be seen that many of the current problems have their origins in history. Housing policies have failed to take an overall view of the issues, but rather have tended to deal with single aspects of problems as they become apparent. Partly because of this, policies have rarely provided solutions, and in some cases, have then created new problems. Inequalities in housing persist, and some policies, such as the sale of council houses, increase the polarisation of different people into different types of tenure and into good and bad housing.

___ **Activity 5.14** _____

At the beginning of this chapter the political nature of housing policy was mentioned. This is reflected in the different approaches followed by Labour and Conservative governments, although there are points of overlap. Table 5.1 gives a summary of the main aspects of post-war legislation on housing. Using this list and information found in this chapter, work out the main themes of Labour and Conservative policy. (Do not expect to find totally clear-cut distinctions.)

TABLE 5.1   Housing legislation after 1945

Government	Date	Name of Act	Summary
Labour	1946	Housing Act	Encouraged council house building by increasing subsidies and allowing local authorities to borrow money at low interest rates
	1949	Housing Act	Local authorities allowed to provide housing for all, not just working-class people
Conservative	1952	Housing Act	Stimulated all house building, increased subsidies to local authorities
	1954	Housing Repairs and Rent Act	Rent increases allowed in private rented sector after improvements
	1956	Housing Subsidies Act	Reduction in subsidies to local authorities, larger subsidies given for high-rise building
	1957	Rent Act	Partial decontrol of rents in private sector
	1957	Housing Act	Allowed sales of council houses
	1961	Housing Act	Subsidies reintroduced for housing; low-interest loans available for housing societies
	1964	Housing Act	Extended housing society support; set up Housing Corporation Local authorities could compel landlords to improve property

TABLE 5.1   *Continued*

Government	Date	Name of Act	Summary
Labour	1965	Rent Act	Security of tenure for unfurnished accommodation tenants. Introduction of fair rents
	1967	Housing Subsidies Act	Subsidy to local authorities to help with increased interest rates. Introduction of option mortgages
	1969	Housing Act	Increased improvement grants. Introduction of General Improvement Areas
Conservative	1972	Housing Finance Act	Reduced subsidies to local authorities; increased council rents
Labour	1974	Housing Act	Increased improvement grants; expanded role of housing associations Introduction of Housing Action Areas; removed 1972 Housing Finance Act Security of tenure to tenants of furnished rented property
	1975	Housing Rent and Subsidies Act	Increased subsidies to local authorities
	1977	Housing (Homeless Persons) Act	Gave local authorities a duty to house homeless persons
Conservative	1980	Housing Act	Increased control of local authority spending, introduction of shorthold tenancies in private renting, increased rents in private and public sector, introduction of right to buy for council tenants
	1984	Housing and Building Control Act	Gave more rights to council tenants
	1988	Housing Act	Reduced control on rents in private rented properties; allowed housing associations to use private loans; allowed council tenants to choose a new landlord; introduced Housing Action Trusts to renovate council estates
	1989	Local Government and Housing Act	New finance arrangements for local authorities new system of grants for improvements; allowed for renewal areas
	1993	Leasehold Reform, Development Act	Introduced Rent-to-Housing and Urban Mortgage Scheme

---

Activity 5.15

In small groups, discuss the following statements:
1   Housing is a basic right and should be provided for all.
2   People should not be allowed to live in houses which are larger than they need.

3 Houses should not be individually-owned, but allocated to people and re-allocated in the event of death.
4 There should be no state involvement in housing and no subsidies. People should simply buy or rent privately homes they can afford.

Activity on language

___ **Activity 5.16** _____

Make sure that you understand the following expressions used in this chapter.

bureaucratic	Part III accommodation
fair rent	paternalistic
General Improvement Area	'red-lining'
Housing Action Area	redevelopment
Housing Action Trust (HAT)	regressive subsidy
housing association	rehabilitation
Housing Corporation	rent arrears
interest rate	security of tenure
mortgage	short-life property
mortgage default	shorthold tenancy
negative equity	squatting
	tenure

Further reading

Shelter is the best source of up-to-date information on homelessness, housing needs and housing policy on which the organisation publishes a number of booklets.

Useful addresses

Shelter: 88 Old Street, London ECIV 9HU
tel. 0171 253 0202

CHAR (Housing Campaign for Single People): 5–15 Cromer Street, London WC1H 8LS
tel. 0171 833 2071

The National Federation of Housing Associations (NFHA):
175 Gray's Inn Road, London WC1X 8UP
tel. 0171 278 6571

The Housing Corporation: 149 Tottenham Court Road, London W1P 0BN
tel. 0171 387 9466

The Department of the Environment, which is responsible for government policies on housing, has various regional offices.
Their national office is at: 2 Marsham Street, London SW1P 3EB
tel. 0171 276 3000

The address for information on the Tenant's Charter is:
The Council Tenant's Charter, FREEPOST, Department 7 DT
Newcastle Upon Tyne X, NE85 1BR

⑥ Living in cities

Most of Britain's population lives in urban areas. This chapter looks briefly at the implications of urban life for social services and then focuses on problems of the inner-city areas. This is followed by a discussion of policies relating to improvement of the inner-city environment.

6.1   Urban and rural societies

Within sociology, attempts have been made to draw distinctions between urban and rural societies.[1] Typically, urban societies are said to consist of larger communities, in contrast to the small communities found in rural areas. This is believed to result in different types of relationships between people. In a small community, it is possible for everyone to know everyone else and for people to have a strong sense of belonging to a group. Both these factors lead to informal social control by the community. For example, in a close-knit community, people will be controlled by local gossip. Similarly, a person doing something wrong, perhaps committing an act of vandalism, will be recognised and may have his or her act reported to parents or dealt with on the spot. In contrast, in urban areas, day-to-day life is seen as consisting of many social encounters with strangers. Relationships between people are superficial and urban dwellers have little sense of belonging to a community with shared values.

Activity 6.1

To what extent, in your experience, is this view of urban and rural life accurate? If this is a true picture of urban life, what implications might this have for social services?

In areas where people are strangers to each other, or have only superficial relationship, more demands will be made upon local social services. There will be a lack of support for people such as parents of young children, the elderly or people with disabilities living at home. Such people will feel isolated and lonely. The lack of informal social control can lead to increased levels of crime and vandalism as well as other forms of anti-social behaviour. Sociologists have argued that people who have no sense of belonging to a group are more vulnerable to mental illness and more likely to contemplate suicide. The current trend towards a policy of care in the community is unlikely to be successful in areas where no community exists to give support to those in need. The implications of this are discussed further in chapter 9.

However, it has been argued that the features described above are not necessarily part of urban life, although they may exist in areas with a large number of new arrivals or where people live temporarily before moving on. Young and Willmott's study of Bethnal Green, in London's East End, conducted in the 1950s (see chapter 5), found a strong sense of community in this urban area. Within a small locality, people were surrounded by relatives and close friends, providing mutual support for one another.

It may be that both these conflicting views of urban life are true and that it is not possible to generalise any further. Within large cities, there are small local communities, such as that found in Bethnal Green, and areas where people are strangers and which provide no sense of belonging and no community support. These features are of course attractive to many people and experienced as a freedom from interference and social convention. People whose life-style might result in condemnation from a rural community find the anonymity of city life allows them the freedom to live in the way they wish.

6.2 Britain's inner-cities

The inner-city problem has attracted considerable publicity over the years, culminating in the riots of the summer of 1981 in many inner-city areas. There have been a series of government policies aimed at improving the environment and quality of life in these areas. The relative lack of success of these policies is in part related to the difficulty in pin-pointing the nature and origin of deprivation. The best way of conceptualising the inner-city problem is through the term 'multiple deprivation'. This emphasises the fact that the urban problem is not a single problem but one of the concentration of a number of problems in one area, which added together lead to a situation of deprivation.

Activity 6.2

Make a list of the sort of problems which add up to multiple deprivation.

Loss of population

As has been said, most of Britain's population live in urban areas, yet the inner-cities have suffered a loss of population. The introduction of cheap transport and the desire for gardens and clean air led people to move from the urban centres to the suburbs of towns and cities. This emigration was initially sup-

The inner-city

ported by government policies. These included the funding priority given to the new towns developed under the 1947 New Towns Act, grants for 'overspill' estates on the edges of towns, and money for housing and industrial development in 'expanded towns' such as King's Lynn in Norfolk. There was also pressure on people to move as commercial development in the cities led to rapidly rising land values. Some commercial developers, anxious to make a quick profit, used harassment to shift tenants from these areas. The city centres experienced a sharp drop in population, beginning in the 1950s and accelerating in the 1960s. However, not everyone was in a position to move, and those who did so tended to be young and to be skilled or professional workers. As a result, the populations of the inner-cities because unbalanced with a high proportion of elderly people and people living on a low income. This trend, whereby people have moved out of large urban areas into more rural areas has continued: in the period 1971–81 government statistics showed that populations in all metropolitan areas fell as people moved from cities such as London to more rural areas like East Anglia. After 1981 the trend continued, although to a lesser extent, particularly in Greater London where the population remained more or less the same.[2]

Loss of industry and employment

There has also been a loss of industry from the urban areas, caused by a general decline in manufacturing and relocation of industry, encouraged by generous government grants. To the extent that industry has been replaced, it has been replaced by commercial enterprises and warehousing, which do not tend to provide employment opportunities for unskilled manual workers. There has been an overall loss of employment in the urban centres–for example, in Liverpool, the number of jobs for men fell by 18 per cent between 1966 and 1971.[3] The jobs lost were mainly unskilled manual work, such as in building, engineering and on the docks.

Environment and housing

Environmentally, inner-cities have suffered in a variety of ways. Commercial development often occurred as a result of a slow process whereby developers gradually bought up areas, boarding up empty properties and spreading a general sense of decay. High-rise office buildings dwarf many urban centres, creating impersonal environments in which few people can feel at home. Local authorities have also played a part in the deterioration of inner-cities through 'planning blight'. There was a tendency for councils to plan over-ambitious renewal schemes. They would purchase properties compulsorily, only to delay or reverse their plans. This contributed to the decay of the physical environment and led to uncertainty and a run-down of local facilities.

Inner-city areas are characterised by housing stress, with long council waiting-lists and a high incidence of overcrowding. Environmental and economic problems of unemployment and poverty lead in turn to social problems.

Many inner-city areas have high numbers of people suffering from physical and mental illnesses and handicaps and an unusually large number of children in the care of the local authority. All these factors mean that there is a great deal of demand on already over-stretched local authority budgets. The urban problem is not a simple one, but rather the sum of a variety of problems with complex causes. Multiple deprivation refers to the interaction of all these environmental, social and economic problems.

'Gentrification'

This section has so far focused on negative aspects of life in Britain's inner-cities. Although a government-sponsored survey of Lambeth in South London found that 42 per cent of people surveyed wanted to move out, there are people who live in urban centres by choice.[4] Such people are attracted by the proximity to facilities such as theatres and the excitement and pace of city life. Recent years have seen a process which has been termed 'gentrification' describing the

Source: Gina Glover, Photofusion
Isolation in the inner-city

fashion amongst professional people for renovating old properties in inner-city areas. This process has been aided by the systems of generous improvement grants described in chapter 5. Gentrification tended to mean that poorer people were pushed out of areas as more middle-class buyers moved in, pushing up house prices. The two-sided nature of this trend is illustrated in the following quotation:

> Many inner residential areas in the major cities now became in fashionable demand, and very nice they looked with bright new paint, shining brass and cheerful plants in tubs and window-boxes. The only snag to this happy burst of environment improvement was the question of the previous tenants, who had been moved out of their rented homes so that lawyers, architects, advertising executives, teachers, university and polytechnic lecturers and such like could move in.[5]

Many urban centres have fashionable streets inhabited by comparatively wealthy people neighbouring on areas of poverty and deprivation. The huge price rises in all areas of London in the 1980s accelerated this trend to the extent that it is common for so-called 'yuppies' to live next door to longer-standing working-class residents. The mix of characters in the BBC TV series *East Enders* reflects this trend.

Activity 6.3

Make a list of areas of the country where you might expect to find multiple deprivation.

Measuring and comparing deprivation

It is important to establish the location of areas of deprivation for the allocation of funds available from central government. It is, however, very difficult to establish criteria for the evaluation of need. Figure 6.1 (p. 155) shows the areas which receive preferential treatment under the latest policies for the regeneration of the inner-cities. However, there are suggestions that these may not be the areas with the greatest problems.

Multiple deprivation means that areas are seen as falling into decline as a result of a combination of factors such as unemployment, overcrowding and unbalanced populations, for example, consisting of a high proportion of elderly and poorer people. To measure and compare deprivation, indicators have to be established. These are factors which are not necessarily problems in themselves, but which indicate deprivation. Department of the Environment statisticians used census information to produce a list of the most deprived areas in Britain. They used eight factors as indicators of deprivation – unemployment, overcrowding, single-parent households, households without sole use of basic facilities such as toilets, numbers of pensioners living alone, population change, mortality rate and the number of households in which the head of the household was born in the New Commonwealth or Pakistan.[6]

Using these indicators as a basis for statistical analysis, the most deprived local authority areas outside London turned out to be (in order) Manchester; Leicester; Wolverhampton; Liverpool; Coventry; Sandwell; Nottingham; Blackburn; Knowsley (Merseyside); Middlesbrough; Slough; Preston; Scunthorpe; Hull; Bradford; Corby and Rochdale. The deprivation scores of boroughs inside London are worse than those anywhere else. Areas of deprivation were (again in order) Hackney; Newham; Tower Hamlets; Lambeth; Hammersmith; Haringey; Islington; Brent; Wandsworth; Southwark and Camden.

Activity 6.4

Consider the indicators of deprivation used by the Department of the Environment. Could any other factors be more relevant in comparing different areas? Bear in mind that social indicators are not intended to be problems in themselves, but rather a way of measuring a problem.

6.3   Inner-city case studies

This section illustrates the problems of inner-city areas by looking at a particular area.

Brixton

The information used here is taken from the Scarman report, written in response to the 1981 riots.[7] Brixton is part of the London borough of Lambeth in South London. It is an inner-city environment with a mixture of residential, industrial and commercial premises. In the late nineteenth century and early twentieth century, Brixton was a prosperous area. It was inhabited by professional people who enjoyed the easy access into the centre of London, and others for whom there were good local employment opportunities.

The economic decline of Brixton began after the First World War, continuing to the present day. The physical appearance and standard of amenities in Brixton are typical of inner-cities areas. These has been a decline in shopping facilities and the physical environment has been affected by indecision in planning. For example, the Railton and Mayall Road area was to be redeveloped until the plans were overruled by central government, leaving boarded-up sites at the junction of Railton and Mayall roads.

Brixton is an area of housing stress. In 1977 a Housing Action Area was declared and some areas have been improved as a result. There is a housing shortage, although there are also empty properties, into which squatters have moved. Some households are overcrowded and some of the housing is below standard. The newer council estates of high-rise flats also have problems. The housing problems combined with the deterioration in the physical environment give a sense of decay to the area. Brixton has few leisure and recreational facilities, especially for young people in the area. This is in spite of the availability of funding under the schemes described in section 6.4 of this chapter.

The population of Brixton is falling as people, in particular those aged between 25 and 60, move away. There is a high rate of population movement, with a net loss of professional and unskilled workers. Brixton has a high proportion of children in care and a high level of mental illness and disability. There are also a large proportion of families with only one parent. All these factors, together with high unemployment and a large number of low-income families, lead to high expenditure on social services.

Brixton in common with some, but not all, inner-city areas, has a relatively large black population, although white people make up the majority. Many Asian and West Indian people came to Britain in the 1950s around the same time as people were moving from the inner-cities to the suburbs. As has been noted in chapter 5, the immigrants found work easily but housing was more of a problem. As newcomers, they had to accept any available housing and many were pushed into the privately-rented sector in the cities. Since then, many have become owner-occupiers although they have continued to be restricted to less desirable properties. Although black people have been blamed for the problems of the inner-city areas, it is important to note that these problems already existed before they arrived.

Hackney

The information in this section is taken from Paul Harrison's 1983 book on Hackney.[8] Harrison suggests, probably rightly, that the London borough of Hackney, with low-paid employment, unemployment, poverty, poor housing, dereliction, educational failure and a high crime rate, is 'one of two or three contenders for the title of the Most Awful Place in Britain'.[9] Like many inner-city areas Hackney was once a pleasant residential area housing the rich. The turning-point came towards the end of the nineteenth century when a development boom led to rapid building of poor-quality housing. The local economy, based on clothes manufacture, was notorious for its poor working conditions and low pay. These two factors created a vicious circle of deteriorating conditions. The bad housing could be rented cheaply by unskilled workers on low incomes. The resulting lack of skills in the population affected the type of employment attracted to the area. The circle continues as poverty leads to further decline when people are too poor to maintain and repair properties.

The industries of Hackney have been those particularly vulnerable to recession and the move of manufacture from Britain to Third World countries. This has obviously led to redundancies and cuts in wages as the remaining firms try to compete and stay in business. Even people who have work struggle to survive on low wages with frequent periods of lay-off. The inner-city problem results from the combined effect of several problems and Hackney has all the typical inner-city problems. In the following extract a woman who is relatively well-off in so far as her husband has work and they do not live on the worst estate, describes the problems of life in a high-rise flat.

> I didn't want to move in . . . but they said we had only one choice, and we had nowhere else to go. I don't like heights, I feel closed in, I get very depressed. I hate this area. I know everywhere is rough these days, but Hackney is *really* rough. I hate the thought of my kids going to school here. I got attacked in the lift once . . . I have a terrible fear of getting stuck in the lift. If our lift (serving 'odd' floors) is broken, we have to use the other (serving 'even' floors) and walk down from the twelfth floor. Andrew carries the kids and I carry the double-buggy. You shouldn't have to do that sort of thing just to get in at your own front door. My gran who's 77, she came one day when both lifts were broke, she had to walk up twenty-six flights of stairs. There's glue-sniffers using the top of the staircases and there's people who dirty in the lifts, they go to the toilet in there.[10]

Poor areas like Hackney have the greatest need for health and social services provision yet have the worst facilities for providing care. Such areas lack populations of middle-class people involved in voluntary organisations and campaigning for improvements in services. Poor housing and schools and unattractive environments mean that doctors and teachers do not want to live and work in such areas. Those who do are over-stretched and risk disillusionment as problems overwhelm them.

Inner London's educational record is poor and Hackney has a high level of educational failure. Schools are unable to compensate for the poverty of the children's home-life. Children come from overcrowded homes where tension and conflict are part of the normal environment. Few houses have decent gardens, yet play areas are lacking or in states of disrepair because of the pressure on land, the high density population, vandalism and the local authority's lack of money for facilities. Children are forced to play on roads and other unsafe areas, risking injury. The following list was taken from a survey of playgrounds in Hackney:

Somerford Gardens   A dismal little playground that local parents find too dangerous for children to use.
Clissold Park   Umbrella immobilised since April; see-saw chained up since July, playground unchanged since Victorian days. If dangerous equipment is removed little remains.
Springfield Park   Paddling-pool empty for a year; sandpit fouled by cats and dogs; swing chained up; never seems to be open.
Millfields   Roundabout has exposed nails and rotten board seats; sand has broken glass in it.
Hackney Downs   Rocking-horse removed; slide irreparable, must be removed immediately; dogs a problem.[11]

Parents face the choice of cooping up their children, depriving them of the opportunity to explore, have adventures and mix with other children, or allowing them to risk accidents and the possibility of getting into trouble with the police.

The high crime rate in Hackney includes crimes committed for money or to fund a drug habit and acts which provide no benefit to anyone, except perhaps a release of frustration. The effects of crime are felt by people who live in fear or lose their few possessions, as well as by the community as a whole. Shops and businesses suffer as insurance premiums are increased or as areas become uninsurable. These effects are passed on to the community in price-rises or when firms move out of the area. No types of facility are immune from crime and vandalism, even when they are provided by residents for the benefit of the local community. For example, a tenants' association attempting to improve the quality of life on a particularly bleak estate was victim to the following setbacks:

in July 1981, an old people's party had to be cancelled because the food and drink had been stolen. In August the social club had to close for a time after two burglaries had cleaned them out of bar stock worth £300. And in January 1982 the disco equipment was stolen from the community centre – for the second time.[12]

The list of problems in Hackney is long and the combination of poverty, crime and the inner-city environment lead to low morale and feelings of hopelessness which cause further deterioration in a circle difficult to break.

Activity 6.5

Find out about a local inner-city area. The local authority or the Department of the Environment as well as libraries will be able to provide information.

6.4 Inner-city policies

The policies described here are those dating from the 1960s to the present. There have been government schemes for specific areas for longer than this but the programmes discussed are distinctive in that they are concerned with the problems characterised in terms of social and economic factors.

1960s

The first measure to use this approach was included in Section 11 of the 1966 Local Government Act. This allowed special aid for areas with a concentration of Commonwealth immigrants. Local authorities could claim a 75 per cent grant from central government for approved expenditure in areas such as education, child care or maternity services. In practice, however, most of the money was spent on education. This source of funding is still available.

The second programme to combat deprivation followed the Plowden Report in 1967. This established Educational Priority Areas (EPAs) which are described in detail in chapter 7. The thinking behind EPAs was based on the theory of the culture of poverty and the cycle of deprivation, discussed in Chapter 3. EPAs were to be given extra resources and to be designated on the basis of social indicators, although the factors to be used were never clearly established. The criteria suggested by Plowden were: the occupation of the head of household; size of families; the extent of overcrowding and sharing of basic facilities; the number of people relying on welfare benefits; poor attendance at school; the proportion of children with disabilities; the number of 'incomplete' families and the number of pupils unable to speak English.

In 1968, the Urban Programme was set up, which continues in a revised form. This resulted from a speech by Enoch Powell which caused great alarm at the time, predicting social unrest caused by urban deprivation and concentration of immigrants in cities. The Urban Programme was based on the idea that there existed small localised pockets of deprivation, defined in terms of social factors such as overcrowding; large families; unemployment; poor environments, immigrant populations and large proportions of children in the care of the local authority. As was the case with the EPAs, these factors were never quantified. Under the Urban Programme, central government would provide 75 per cent of funds for projects expected to produce quick results. Initially, these projects were mainly concerned with the provision of nursery facilities. Later the scheme diversified and expanded. It is now linked to the Partnership and Programme Area schemes and described as the Traditional Urban Programme. It takes up a small part of the larger budget and consists of a variety of community projects.

In 1969, the Home Office set up the Community Development Project (CDP). The emphasis was on raising local people from a position of 'fatalistic dependence' on local authorities to self-sufficiency and independence. Twelve local terms were employed to work with local communities in deprived areas, with a research team to monitor the results. The assumptions in the CDP plan were that it was the 'deprived' who were the cause of deprivation and that the problem could be overcome by tackling apathy in communities. The CDP teams soon ran into trouble with local authorities and central government as they began to criticise policies and the approach they were expected to take to their work. In the words of a CDP report:

A few months' field-work in areas suffering long-term economic decline and high unemployment was enough to provoke the first teams of CDP workers to question the Home Office's original assumptions. There might certainly be in these areas a high proportion of the sick and the elderly for whom a better co-ordination of services would undoubtedly be helpful, but the vast majority were ordinary working-class men and women who, through forces outside their control, happened to be living in areas where bad housing conditions, redundancies, lay-offs, and low wages were commonplace.[13]

This criticism of a small-scale localised approach to the problem of deprivation led to the development of a different analysis, focusing on structual problems in society. The following quotation from the Newcastle CDP team demonstrates the approach taken:

> The team had moved away from the original assumptions of the CDP programme that the causes of deprivation are to be found in the local community, and in the shortcomings of local policies and services. Our experience in Benwell convinces us that much of the disadvantage to be observed arises from structural causes. In other words, we would argue that the workings of the general economic and associated political system are inherently liable to create wide inequalities between groups in society.[14]

1970s

As a result of this switch in approach, the CDP programme was abruptly ended in 1976. In 1974, Comprehensive Community Programmes (CCPs) were set up as a more acceptable substitute for the CDPs. The new project analysed problems and put forward recommendations, although they had little overall impact. The Community Development Project was successful in challenging the assumptions behind inner-city policies and a change in approach was to come in later schemes.

The Housing Action Areas, set up in 1974, and discussed in Chapter 5 were another attempt to deal with small areas of deprivation. Briefly the idea was to provide special levels of grants for owner-occupiers and landlords in small areas of older housing. The scheme intended that improvement of housing would lead to an upgrading of whole areas. The programme achieved little success for several reasons. Cuts in expenditure were introduced shortly after the introduction of the scheme which seriously curtailed the efforts at improvement. Some local authorities were not enthusiastic about the programme since funds were inadequate, the improvements did not have to conform to traditional standards and there was a fear that the establishment of Housing Action Areas would divert attention from other areas of need. These factors contributed to the failure of the programme to make any great impact on the urban problem. However, it has been argued that even if these problems had not existed, the limited scope of the policy would have meant that it had little effect where problems were caused by poverty and lack of investment in inner-city areas.

The change in emphasis in urban policy began with the Inner Area Studies. These were studies carried out by consultant architects for the Department of the Environment between 1972 and 1977. The brief was to look at the problems of a small area, taking a wide approach to the task. The Inner Area Studies suggested the need for economic regeneration, the need for sensitivity towards local people, the need for improved housing and – perhaps most importantly – the need for an overall approach to inner-city problems, taking account of social and economic factors.

The Inner Area Studies resulted in a government White Paper, 'Policies for the Inner City', published in 1977. In line with the new approach, the White Paper placed the emphasis on economic rather than social problems, and economic solutions to deprivation.

The Act which followed–the Inner Urban Areas Act 1978 – continued the policy of area-based positive discrimination with a social-services orientation, but with a new focus on economic revival. The new policy for the inner-cities included a specific commitment to urban centres which was a reversal of earlier policies for economic and demographic dispersal. The aim was to work on three fronts outlined as economic, environmental and social aspects of deprivation. Inner cities were to be given a priority second only to the assisted areas in the provision of grants for industry. Local authorities were empowered to make loans for up to 90 per cent for land purchase,and could declare Industrial Improvement Areas, providing help with the cost of site preparation. The act retained the traditional Urban Programme and expanded this provision. Finally, Partnerships were set up between local and central government in seven areas, Liverpool, Birmingham, Glasgow, Manchester/Salford, the London boroughs of Lambeth and Islington/Hackney, and the London docklands. Each partnership had a team to analyse the needs of the area and to draw up a programme for regeneration. The map in Figure 6.1 shows the areas coverd by these policies.[15]

Figure 6.1   Inner-city authorities in England

The following sections give an idea of the scope of the Urban programme by describing four examples from over 5000 projects. The projects are selected from a Department of the Environment document.[16]

In *Lambeth*, a craft workshop for people with learning disabilities received funding under the Urban Programme. It is a branch of *L'Arche* which is a national association of communities for people with a learning disability. People are referred from the local social services department and are involved in working on contracts for industry or making craft items for sale. The second example comes from *Manchester*, where a group received £15 000 for an anti-vandalism campaign. The scheme involves local residents and the activities include publicity, making repairs following acts of vandalism, and organising activities like football in the hope of preventing vandalism.

A very different project on *Merseyside* received £110 000 for a maritime museum on a derelict site in the city. The museum is in the Canning Dock area and includes restored quaysides with horse-drawn wagons and steam lorries on display. The final example was of an industrial project in the Derwenthaugh Industrial Improvement Area in *Gateshead* in the North East of England. This was a five-year project with an annual grant of £300 000. The task was the improvement and development of run-down industrial land, aiming to revitalise existing industry and to attract new industry to the areas. The borough was involved in improving the site in the hope that firms would take up the initiative to improve their own premises.

1980s

The Inner Urban Areas Act was passed by a Labour government. When the Conservatives came into power in 1979 they retained the commitment to the inner-city areas whilst shifting the emphasis of the policies. The Partnerships were to remain, although the rate-support grants which had been increased for urban local authorities were reduced and cash limits were imposed on local-authority spending. The focus of policies moved further from social aspects of deprivation to economic factors. Two other trends in the Conservative approach were a transfer of power away from the local authorities and an emphasis on encouraging private enterprise in urban regeneration. Figure 6.2 shows how the balance of funding has shifted towards assisting private companies.[17]

The Conservative government introduced Urban Development Corporations (UDCs), the first two being set up to take over the work on London and Liverpool docklands. UDCs are financed by central government, bypassing local government, and their task is to reclaim land, with a comprehensive building plan, and to financially assist private development. The best known scheme is that of the London Docklands Development Corporation which cost £385 million in government funds and attracted £3 billion in private investment to develop housing and industry on London's docklands. The Docklands development has been a huge financial success for the investors,

Changes in urban expenditure are helping private investment. Urban Programme, Development, Regeneration and Derelict Land Grants, and UDC expenditure is shown here.

This represents a real terms increase of 58%

■ Spending to assist private investment

□ Spending on social and community projects

£593m

£472m

£207m

£138m

£118m

£109m

1979/80   1983/84   1988/89

Figure 6.2   Shifting the balance of urban group programmes, 1979/80–1988/89

mainly due to the closeness of the area to the City. These developments are not always popular with local authorities since they mean a loss of control and can be criticised for being undemocratic. John Banham, director-general of the CBI, has also criticised the way that UDCs cut across the work of local councils and can spoil good relationships between industry and local government. He said,

> Local authorities cannot be by-passed – they are there and in many respects they are efficient and effective . . . We're not going to get there by depriving them of resources . . . penalising them by spending money they ought to be spending . . . or worse still, holding them up to public ridicule.[18]

In 1987, several further UDCs were set up, including those in the Black Country (West Midlands), Tyne and Wear and Teesside.

The Conservative government also introduced Enterprise Zones (in 1981) which are areas free from planning and other controls and where industries pay no rates. Enterprise Zones have been subjected to criticism on the basis that they do little to create employment since it is often existing firms who benefit from reduced costs or those who make short-distance relocations to cut cost. A report by an independent urban research centre, the Centre for Environmental Studies, concludes

> EZs have not resulted in a net job gain to either the local or the national economy. Although they have strongly influenced the choice of location within an area, almost all establishments and jobs would have been created anyway.[19]

It is argued that the greatest benefit from the zones is to industrial and commercial development companies, especially in the context of the recent extension of the scheme to areas like North Kent and Wellingborough, which cannot be described as deprived inner-city areas.

In 1985, five City Action Teams (CATs) were set up to encourage co-ordination in their areas. They aim to bring together civil servants from the three departments concerned with inner city policies. These are the Department of the Environment, the Department of Employment and the Department of Trade and Industry. There are also 16 Task Forces which operate more at a local level to bring together people from industry and government. Urban Development Grants and Urban Regeneration Grants are schemes whereby government money is available in some areas of the country for private companies to use in plans to develop run-down and derelict sites.

These policies achieved only limited success, for when Mrs Thatcher took office for her third term she announced that a central priority for the government that term would be the improvement of the inner cities. A year later, in 1988, a glossy document called *Action for Cities* was published by the government setting out the various policies for the inner cities. These include the following:

- An increased number of Urban Development Corporations
- Additional City Action Teams
- Replacing the Urban Development Grant and Urban Regeneration Grant with a simplified City Grant.
- Continuation of Inner Area Partnerships and other earlier schemes.
- A series of breakfast meetings around the country, costing £450 000, where business people can discuss plans over breakfast with government officials.

1990s

The early 1990s saw a continuation of the trend for involving the private sector in initiatives to improve inner-city areas.[20]

By 1994 the number of CATs had increased to eight. These work on co-ordinating government activities in their areas and encouraging participation from the private sector and other organisations. Each has a small budget for this work and can give grants to local authorities, businesses, local community groups and voluntary organisations working in or moving to an inner city area.

Task forces were first set up in 1986 and are small teams of civil servants and others which work in the most deprived urban areas. They concentrate on improving employment propects for local people by supporting training and education and other projects aimed at removing barriers to employment. They also promote local enterprises in business and community initiatives to solve local problems. The idea is that a Task Force will exist only as long as necessary and once local organisations are strengthened the Task Force will be closed down. In 1994 there were 16 Task Forces.

The Urban Programme is one of the longest established initiatives, although it has gone through a number of changes as political ideas have changed. In 1994 the Urban Programme was concentrated on 57 target areas with the greatest problems and the most severe deprivation. As was stated on p. 153, the Urban Programme provides grants for projects with 75 per cent of the funding coming from central government and the remainder from the local authority. From 1993–4 there were no new projects supported through the Urban programme, although previously approved projects will continue to be funded.

A new scheme announced in 1991 was the City Challenge. Under this scheme local authorities, in partnership with private and voluntary organisations, local communities and government agencies are invited to offer imaginative and comprehensive plans for improving local deprived areas. The best of the proposals receive government funding over a period of five years.

Urban Development Corporations (UDCs) have been mentioned already. By 1994 there were 13 UDCs. The initial ones were in London's Docklands and Merseyside. Additional UDCs have now been established in: Birmingham Heartlands, Bristol, Leeds, Central Manchester, Plymouth, Sheffield, Trafford Park (Greater Manchester) and Cardiff.

Action for Cities (1988) (see p. 158) included the establishment of City Grants. These exist to encourage private development in inner cities. By May 1993, 330 schemes had been approved.

The Enterprise Zones established in 1981 as already described ran for 10 years. The early ones have therefore now ended. In 1994 there were 10 Enterprise Zones, although five ended in that year. Three new zones were designated in 1994 in areas affected by job losses in the mining industry. Apart from this there are no plans to extend the scheme. A related idea is that of Simplified Planning Zones (SPZs) which also last for 10 years. These allow planning permission for certain types of development. In 1993 there were six SPZs.

EC funding

Money is available from the European Community (EC, now known as European Union, EU) for inner-cities. This can come from the European Regional Development Fund and the European Social Fund. These, together with the Agricultural Guidance and Guarantee Fund, are know as the European Structural Fund. The funding is focused on the following objectives:

(1) to assist those regions whose development is lagging behind
(2) to revitalise regions affected by serious industrial decline
(3) to combat long-term unemployment
(4) to integrate young people into the job market.

(There is a fifth objective relating to rural areas, but this is not relevant in this context.)

Areas of England which are eligible for assistance are Merseyside (under objective (1)) and parts of the North-West, North-East, Yorkshire and Humberside and the Midlands, Plymouth, Thanet in Kent and parts of London (under objective (2)).

Figure 6.3   Urban policy initiatives
Source: Central Statistical Office, *Britain 1994: an official handbook* (London: HMSO, 1994, © Crown copyright).

Figure 6.3 summarises the inner-city initiatives currently in operation.

It is difficult to evaluate the success or failure of the various urban policies outlined in this chapter. Certainly, the earlier programmes tackling specific aspects such as housing or education in small areas had a limited impact on the overall problem of multiple deprivation. The newer policies are perhaps too new to comment on, but the early signs are that they are having little effect on the unemployment in poorer areas which is a major factor in deprivation.

___ **Activity 6.6** _____

Make sure that you understand the following expressions, used in this
chapter. Check the glossary on p. 363 if you need to.

cash limit	informal social control
community care	multiple deprivation
culture of poverty	planning blight
cycle of deprivation	positive discrimination
economic regeneration	rate support grant
gentrification	social indicator

Further reading

Paul Harrison *Inside the Inner City* (Harmondsworth. Penguin, 1983) is a readable study of Hackney in London, argued to be one of the most deprived areas in
the country. Up-to-date information on inner city initiatives can be obtained
from the Department of the Environment or from a very useful reference book
called (in 1994) *Britain 1994*. This book is produced each year by the government and covers all aspects of life in Britain.

Useful addresses

The Department of the Environment, which is responsible for government policies on inner cities, has various regional offices. Their national office is at: 2
Marsham Street, London SW1P 3EB
tel. 0171 276 3000

7 Schooling in Britain

Education is an important aspect of society from the point of view of the whole society and of the individual. In terms of society, education is a major consumer of public expenditure. In the year 1991–2 total government expenditure on education was £29 482 million.[1]

To some extent, education determines the future of society, providing the next generation of adults with abilities and skills. The significance of education to individuals is demonstrated by the strength of even older people's memories of their school-days. Education is also linked to the kind of work a person can do, and therefore has an effect on an individual's income and life-style.

This chapter examines some of the important issues in education. It begins by describing educational provision, making a distinction between private and state education. Education is further categorised into pre-school, primary, secondary, further and higher education sectors. There is also special education provided for children with learning disabilities. The chapter also covers provision related to education such as educational welfare benefits and careers guidance. Education, perhaps more than any other aspect of the welfare state, has been subject to a great deal of research and debate. The final part of the chapter examines some issues of continuing concern in education.

In spite of the importance now attached to education, compulsory education is a relatively recent phenomenon. It was only in 1870 that education was made compulsory, and then only for children up to the age of 10. Over the following 30 years the school-leaving age was gradually raised to 13. In 1918, legislation made it compulsory for children to remain in school until they were 14. The 1944 Education Act, of which more is said later, raised the school-leaving age to 15. Today, as a result of legislation passed in 1972, young people are required to be in school until they are 16.

7.1 The education system

This section is given the title, 'The education system', yet it will quickly become apparent that education in this country is not so much a system but is better described as including several different systems, varying considerably from area to area. There are several reasons for this diversity of provision, the main one being the complex and changing relationship between central government and the local education authorities. The Department for Education is the government department in charge of education, responsible for overall policies and legislation. Some aspects of education are governed by legislation passed through Parliament and are therefore the same throughout the whole country. For example, the school-leaving age is 16 for all children, whether they live in Devon, Sheffield or Newcastle. The 1980s and 1990s saw an increase in national control of education, particularly with the introduction of the national curriculum and standardised testing of children (discussed in more detail later in Section 7.2).

Local education authorities (LEAs) have traditionally been responsible for the actual provision of state education: building schools and colleges, employing teachers and other staff, and exercising considerable control of the organisation of education in their areas. This changed in the late 1980s and 1990s: first, because of the introduction of the national curriculum which, as mentioned above, set national standards and reduced local decision-making; and secondly as a result of schools being allowed to opt out of LEA control. Both of these changes were introduced by the 1988 Education Reform Act.

In 1994 the majority of schools were still provided and funded by the local authorities. In these cases the LEA allocates funds to the school, largely on the basis of the number of pupils attending. In 1994 the government required all school governing bodies to be responsible for managing this budget – paying staff, buying equipment, etc. As mentioned earlier the 1988 Education Reform allowed schools to become independent of the local education authority and by 1994 some 15 per cent of schools had done so. A vote of parents of children currently in the school is required before a school can become self-governing, or 'grant maintained', as they are termed. Grant-maintained schools are funded from central government. The governing body of the school, which includes parents, teachers and people from the community, is responsible for all aspects of the management of the school. Reducing the powers of the local authorities is part of Conservative party philosophy, and the Conservative government is keen that more schools should become grant-maintained.

The 1993 Education Act set up a new statutory body, the Funding Agency for Schools, to calculate and pay grants and to monitor finances for self-governing schools. When 10 per cent of either primary or secondary pupils in the area are in such schools, then the Funding Agency will work with the LEA in providing school places in the area. If this is the case for 75 per cent of pupils, the Agency will take over responsibility for providing all school places.

Colleges of further education are now self-governing with funds allocated through further education funding councils. Similarly there is another funding council to allocate central government money to universities.

Activity 7.1

What was your experience of the education system? Begin with any preschool education, including the kind of secondary school you attended, and whether or not you had to take an examination before you went there. Compare your experience with that of the rest of the class.

7.2   Provision of schooling in Britain

Several variations can be expected in the educational experiences of a group of people. Some will have attended a private nursery school, others a nursery class attached to a primary school, whilst others will have had no pre-school education. From the age of 5, members of the group may have gone to an ordinary state school, a school run by the Church or an independent school. In terms of secondary schooling, many areas have comprehensive schools, while others retain some grammar schools. Some people will have had to sit an examination before transferring to a secondary school. Some members of the group may have changed schools at the age of 11 whilst others may have attended middle schools and moved into secondary education at 12 years of age.

Pre-school education

In Britain, there is no systematic nursery provision, although the 1944 Education Act stated that local education authorities should provide nursery education. This was clarified in the 1980 Education Act, where provision for the under-5s is stated to be at the discretion of the local authorities. During the war, when women were required to work, nursery provision expanded, but the trend was reversed in the period after the war and government money was withdrawn. By the 1960s, only 5 per cent of children could be given nursery education.

During the 1960s, there was increasing concern over the lack of child care and nursery facilities. In 1967, the report of the Plowden Committee, 'Children and their Primary Schools', was published, recommending the expansion of nursery provision. In 1969, as we saw in Chapter 6, the government established the Urban Aid Programme which provided financial resources for areas of the country thought to be in particular need. In the initial years of the Urban Programme, much of the money was spent on day-care for children. The Conservative government, in 1972, promised to expand nursery provision, but this plan fell victim to public expenditure cuts after 1973.

Provision of pre-school education is limited and varies across the country. This limited and patchy state provision has resulted in the development of private and voluntary nurseries and playgroups. The various types of pre-school education and day-care are now described.

Local authority day nurseries

In 1992, approximately 23 800 children had places in day nurseries provided by local authorities.[2] Within this overall figure there is considerable local variation. London boroughs, for example, tend to have a higher ratio of places than rural areas.

Local authority day nurseries are provided by social service departments and take children from a few months old to the age of 5. They are open up to 10 hours a day, including school holidays. Places are mainly reserved for children thought to be in special need, such as children at risk of non-accidental injury or

Source: Gina Glover, Photofusion
Should nursery places be made available for all children?

those living in areas with no play facilities. Nurseries are staffed by trained nursery nurses. The demand for places far exceeds the availability and long waiting-lists are common. Fees are charged, on a sliding scale, depending on the income of the parents.

Nursery schools and classes

Nursery schools and classes are provided by local education authorities, opening for school hours in term-time. In England in 1992, there were 53 093 children in nursery schools.[3] The majority of these children attended on a part-time basis and many places were taken up by children coming up to their fifth birthday. Since nurseries take children for short hours during term-time only, they are of little help to working parents. As a result, it may be that the children who would most benefit from pre-school education are most likely to be those deprived of it. Local education authority nurseries are staffed by nursery teachers and emphasise the development of the child by means of stimulating play. Nurseries are free, but in common with local authority day nurseries, the demand for places outstrips availability.

Playgroups

Playgroups are usually run by voluntary organisations, the most successful being the Pre-school Playgroups Association. This organisation was started in 1961, in response to the lack of pre-school provision at the time. The movement expanded rapidly and in 1992 there were 409 800 places in playgroups.[4]

Playgroups emphasise the importance of play and education activities for young children. They usually take children over 3 years of age, and involve parents in the running of groups. Pre-school playgroups are not evenly spread throughout the country and can be criticised for being predominantly middle-class in appeal. A survey carried out in the 1980s by the Pre-School Playgroups Association found that only 10 per cent of groups were in inner-city urban areas, whilst 38 per cent were in villages. The Pre-School Playgroups Association receives a grant from the government and, whilst they are successful and popular, it is likely that they are encouraged by the government because they provide a cheap means of meeting a need.

Private nurseries
Private nurseries have to be registered with the local authority social services department and must comply with regulations concerning staffing and facilities. It is difficult for a private nursery to run successfully without charging fees which most parents would be unable to afford. As a result, there are only a few private nurseries.

Education and work-place nurseries
There are a small number of nurseries attached to places of work and colleges of further and higher education. This type of provision is most useful to parents who want to work or study, happy in the knowledge that their children are safe and close-by.

Child-minders
The lack of availability of places in nursery schools and day centres means that many parents leave their young children with private child-minders. Child-minders are required to register with the local authority who ensure that certain standards are met. It is probable that there are unregistered child-minders operating illegally. In 1992, 254 300 children (under 8) were cared for in the UK by registered child-minders.[5] Child-minders work long hours and receive little money.

Figure 7.1 summarises the situation regarding daycare and education for children under five.[6]

_ Activity 7.2 _____

What facilities for children under 5 exist in your area? Are they privately-or state-funded.

In the extract below, Helen Penn – an expert on education – makes strong criticisms of Britain treatment of under-5s:

We have a crazy system which offers 25 per cent of children nursery education in shifts, shoves four-year-olds into school before they can cope with it, segregates

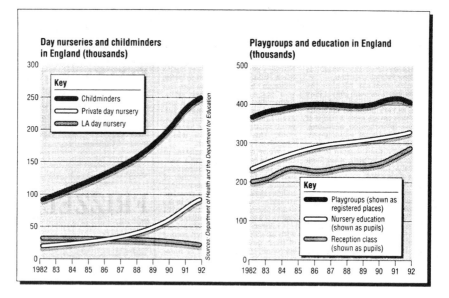

Source: *Guardian Education* (7 December 1993), p. 4.

Figure 7.1   Daycare and education for children under 5, 1982–92

depressed and forlorn children into a different and temporary system in social services, family centres and day nurseries, and considers children of working parents best catered for in the private pay-as-(or if)-you-earn sector. We refuse to listen to the evidence about parents' views, and if we have no idea how much we spend or what on, nor will we contemplate any more expenditure. We have a Children Act and an Education Reform Act, and national and local economic and employment initiatives concerning young children; but each of them ignores the other, and none of them takes early years' education into account.

Children beginning formal school at five have already experienced very different levels of intervention. Should we continue to believe, as the Government does, that we have a system which offers 'choice' or would it be more apt to call our system unjust wasteful and very nearly pointless?[7]

For many years successive governments have acknowledged the need for expansion in pre-school education to provide sufficient places for all children whose parents want their child to attend. This is often, however, made dependent on availability of resources and as a result the promised expansion does not materialise. In 1993 Prime Minister John Major stated that nursery education was the government's top spending priority in education and that he wanted to see universal nursery education. He refused, however, to set a date for this expansion and said that the government did not have resources for it. Three months later he said,

As and when resources are available we shall move towards further nursery education, towards universal nursery education.[8]

What are the advantages of making state provision of nursery education available to all 3–5-year-olds?

There are several advantages for children, parents and the wider society in state provision of pre-school day-care. Nurseries prepare children for school, helping them to adjust not only to leaving their parents but also to school routines. This preparation means that children will settle in quickly at school and that schools can get on with the task of teaching. Nursery classes in schools and nursery schools attached to infant schools are especially useful in this respect, introducing the child gradually to school. Children aged 3–5 are at a stage in their development when they are eager and willing to learn. The trained teacher or nursery nurse can make use of this, and provide an environment to stimulate learning. Play facilities provided by nurseries are of a better standard and less restrictive than those available in most homes. For children from poor or overcrowded homes, or those living in high-rise flats, the nursery may provide the only opportunity for creative play.

Pre-school education teaches children to socialise and to mix with other children, which is particularly important for children from families where there are no other small children. Nursery schools can be involved in preventative work, in that the staff watch for signs of health or development difficulties in children. Early recognition of problems, whilst of benefit to the child, could also save money for the health or educational services. Also, children who are at risk of abuse can be recognised at an early point.

Providing facilities for disadvantaged children only (as do many local authorities at present) groups together and isolates such children. Full-scale provision would avoid the problems inherent in putting all these children together, separate from others. Looking at the present situation from another point of view, much of the provision is more readily available to middle-class families. Comprehensive state provision would lead to greater equality in access to pre-school education.

Nursery schools give greater freedom to parents of children aged 3–5, allowing them to work, develop their own interests or devote time to younger children in the family.

Finally, state provision might ensure that day-care for under-5s was of an adequate and uniform standard. The present lack of facilities means that parents have to use private child-minders, where the care provided may not be satisfactory.

Primary and secondary education

Primary and secondary education is provided for all children from the age of 5 to 16. There are several different types of schools.

- *County (or maintained) schools* are owned and maintained by the LEA.
- *Voluntary schools*, usually set up by religious organisations, are also maintained by the LEA, but some of the costs for the buildings might be paid for by the Church for example.
- *Grant maintained schools*, as mentioned earlier, are funded directly from central government and all decisions are the responsibility of the governing body.
- *Independent schools* are privately run and parents pay fees for their children to attend. They benefit from tax exemptions – as a result of their status as charities.

Standards in schools

Standards in schools are monitored by the Office for Standards in Education (OFSTED). OFSTED visit schools at least every four years and produce a report – a summary of this is sent to all parents. A parents' charter was produced by the government in 1991 and updated in 1994. This sets out national targets for education and parents' rights concerning their children's education.

The national curriculum

In 1988, the government introduced the *national curriculum* for all maintained primary and secondary schools in the country. This has been introduced gradually: by 1996–7 the whole of the national curriculum will be taught to all pupils. The national curriculum consists of three core subjects: English, mathematics and science, as well as foundation subjects of history, geography, technology, music, art, physical education and, for secondary schools, a modern foreign language. In each subject there are *statutory attainment targets* setting what children should know and be able to do at the *key stages* of age 7, 11, 14 and 16. Standard tests and assessments are required at these ages with results made available to parents.

Aspects of the national curriculum have proved very controversial, particularly with teachers. The conflict which arose between teachers and the government reached a head in 1993 with a successful boycott of tests by teachers. Teachers basically objected to the amount of extra work involved in teaching to the national curriculum, the amount of material to be covered, the time taken up with the testing procedures, and the lack of freedom for teachers to plan their own teaching – for example English teachers objected to the mandatory lists of authors to be covered. In 1993 Sir Ron Dearing was asked to review the national curriculum and make recommendations for change. The Dearing Report introduced a slimming down of the national curriculum to make it more manageable and to allow time for schools to offer other options. Dearing also recommended that the tests and gradings be simplified and no further changes to the curriculum be introduced in the short-term future. In the summer of 1994 the government also announced that teachers would not be expected to mark tests as part of their ordinary workload and outside examiners would be paid to do so.

7.3   Primary and secondary education

Primary education

Children must attend school from the age of 5, although some begin before their fifth birthday. Primary education is usually organised into infant and junior schools, taking children from 5 to 7, and 7 to 11 respectively.

Changes in philosophy of learning

There have been many changes in primary education over the years, mainly in terms of the methods of teaching and learning. In the 1950s, children learnt in classrooms like those in secondary schools with popular teaching techniques requiring the whole class to chant multiplication tables and to memorise spellings. In the 1960s the philosophy of primary education changed and the development of the individual child was seen as more important than learning a great deal of factual information. Schools reorganised their buildings to allow open plan classrooms in which several teachers might work with children sitting in small groups. Much primary teaching was based on projects covering many skills rather than separate subjects, as in secondary school. Classes were mixed ability without any attempt to grade children into ability groups and children

Source: Gina Glover, Photofusion
Most children attend state schools

were encouraged to work at their own pace on individualised learning schemes. Also at this time there were a number of experiments with new ways of learning reading and mathematics. In 1987 the national curriculum (described above) was introduced, encouraging a return to a more structured approach to assessment of learning in primary school.

The Plowden Report
In 1967, as mentioned in the previous section, a major government report on primary education – the Plowden Report – was published, containing many recommendations. These included the idea that parents should be more involved with their children's education. Plowden was also in favour of middle schools, for children from 8 to 12 years of age. The most important recommendation, however, of the Plowden report, was that Educational Priority Areas (EPAs) be established. This idea was based on a conclusion of the report that poorer areas tended to have poor schools, and that positive discrimination was necessary to bring these schools up to the standards of the best in the country. The policy of positive discrimination meant that schools in deprived areas would qualify for additional resources. The money would be spent on more buildings and materials, extra pay for teachers, the provision of teachers' assistants and better ratios of teachers to pupils.

The government has never actually designated EPAs, but in 1967, local authorities were invited to submit claims for government money. The money was available for areas of multiple deprivation (see Chapter 6), characterised by factors such as overcrowding, a high incidence of families needing financial support from the state and a rapid turnover of teachers. The money available was a comparatively small sum, insufficient to meet the need. In 1968, it was agreed that teachers in schools in deprived areas should receive an extra £75 year. Again the criteria suggested for designating deprived areas were vague. The factors to be considered were: the social class of parents in the area, the incidence of homes without basic amenities and the numbers of children receiving free school meals. By the end of 1968, approximately 2.5 per cent of maintained primary schools received some form of special help.

Considerable hope was raised by the Plowden Report and the subsequent government proposals. However, the implementation of the policies has achieved little, for a variety of reasons. The means of deciding the areas in need of extra resources has never been satisfactorily settled. The amount of help provided has been inadequate to deal with the massive problems of poor areas. Also, there is less acceptance now of the idea that improvements in educational provision can effect wider problems in society, such as poverty and deprivation.

Secondary education

Secondary education was made compulsory by the 1944 Education Act, sometimes known as the Butler Act. The act was based on a report produced in 1943, by the Norwood Committee. The Norwood Committee believed that there are three types of children; first those who enjoy learning for its own sake, can grasp ideas and are interested in finding out why things happen; second, those whose abilities lie in applied sciences and arts; and finally those who are not interested in ideas, but in practical work.

The 1944 Educational Act introduced *universal secondary education* which most local authorities provided in the form of a tripartite system, under which there would be grammar schools for academic pupils, technical schools for vocationally-oriented pupils, and secondary modern schools to provide a general education for the remainder of children. It was believed that the 11-plus examination could determine which type of education was most suitable for each child. In practice, few technical schools were established and so there were mainly two types of schools, grammar schools for about 20 per cent of children, and secondary modern schools for the rest. The grammar schools prepared children for examinations which led into higher education. Secondary modern schools did not offer any examinations until 1965, when the Certificate of Secondary Education was introduced. In theory, the different types of schools were equal, although providing different sorts of education. They were to have 'parity of esteem' which means equal status. In practice, however, there was a hierarchy, with grammar schools having more status than secondary modern schools.

The Crowther Report
Two important reports concerned with secondary education were published following the 1944 Act. The first was the Crowther Report, in 1959, which focused on young people aged 15–18. The report looked for reasons why many children failed to progress in school, and why working-class children tended to leave school at the earliest possible date. The Crowther Report found a relationship between home background, and success at school, and indicated that educational attainment was more closely linked with social class than with ability.

The Crowther Report contained many recommendations, including the suggestions that the school-leaving age be raised to 16; an examination be provided for secondary modern pupils and that education in schools should be more orientated to technology. The report recommended an expansion in all forms of further education, and the establishment of county colleges for sixth-form students. Little was done by the government in immediate response to the report, although many of the recommendations were taken up in later years.

The Newsom Report
The Crowther Report was followed in 1963 by the Newsom Report, entitled 'Half Our Future', meaning that the less privileged 50 per cent of children with whom the report was concerned, would, in time, be half the country's citizens, workers and parents. The report found that many secondary modern schools were deficient and argued that the less privileged 50 per cent of children did not receive their fair share of resources. The Newsom Report found wide differences in educational attainment between one school and another, and in different parts of the country. The Report supported the idea that it was social factors which held children back and argued that this led to a waste of talent and ability, which was not in the interest of the economic development of the nation.

The Newsom Report recommended that the school-leaving age be raised to 16 and that the school day be lengthened. Newsom sought to establish a government working party to look at the social and educational problems of slum areas. The Report further suggested that schools should provide learning more closely related to the everyday lives of the pupils. In common with the Crowther Report, little was done by the government at the time of the publication of the report, although some of the recommendations were implemented at a later date.

Comprehensive education

Both the Crowther Report and the Newsom Report supported the tripartite system of education, but in 1965 a major change was initiated. All local authorities were sent a central government circular, known as Circular 10/65, asking them to submit plans to abolish selective secondary education and introduce a comprehensive system. The circular described various ways in which local authorities might effect this change. Circular 10/65 came as a result of many years of debate by politicians, educationalists and others over the merits and problems of selective schools.

Activity 7.4

What are the advantages, and the disadvantages, of comprehensive schools? Discuss the points you have listed with the rest of the class.

Many different points have been put forward in the long debate over selective and non-selective schooling. Sometimes the same argument is used by both sides, each believing that it proves their case. For example, those in favour of comprehensive schools argue that such schools improve educational standards while those against comprehensive schools claim that they mean a reduction in standards.

In favour   Several of the criticisms of the tripartite system concerned the process of selecting children for different schools. The 11-plus examination has been attacked on several grounds. A child, for reasons of sickness or nervousness, could produce results on the day of the examination which would not be an accurate reflection of his or her ability. It has been increasingly recognised that some children are 'late developers' and that assessment at the age of 11 does not provide an indication of their future ability. It was possible for children to change schools after the age of 11, but in practice, this rarely happened.

It was argued that 'failing' the 11-plus examination had an adverse effect on children, although strictly it is not possible to fail an IQ test, since it simply measures and compares certain sorts of ability. The IQ test was criticised for being biased in favour of middle-class children, enabling a greater proportion of them to gain access to grammar schools. Both Crowther and Newsom found children wrongly placed as a result of errors in the test.

Other arguments for comprehensive schools included the fact that such a system would eliminate regional variation, which meant that some children had a better chance of going to a grammar school because they lived in an area where there were more grammar-school places. In addition, the fact that comprehensive schools would be bigger than selective schools would mean they could provide better facilities with a wider range of subject options. Finally, those in favour of comprehensive schools argue that selective schools increase social divisions in society and that comprehensive schools promote greater equality.

Against   On the other side of the debate, there are those who argue that large schools are impersonal institutions. It is said that comprehensive schools hold back brighter pupils to benefit the less able ones. Dividing pupils within one school into streams or sets according to ability is argued by some to create greater divisions between children than existed in the selective system. Finally, proponents of grammar schools argue that they had developed fine traditions, worthy of conservation.

The extent to which the proposals in Circular 10/65 were implemented varied throughout the country. This was because local education is controlled by local authorities in the absence of legislation. In 1976, legislation was introduced to make comprehensive schools compulsory, but this was repealed in 1979. In the five years following the issue of Circular 10/65, 35 per cent of schools turned comprehensive, and by late 1980s over 85 per cent of all children were educated in comprehensive schools.[9] However, for two reasons, many comprehensive schools are not fully 'comprehensive'. The first involves the continued existence of voluntary and independent schools, which select pupils. As a result, comprehensive schools do not take all the children in a particular area. Second, most comprehensive schools stream or set pupils in some way, on the basis of the school's perception of their ability. Recent years have seen a further drift away from the idea of comprehensive education as schools opt out and some move towards selection for entry, and with the development of City Technology Colleges (described below).

Changes in the curriculum
Other developments in secondary education concern the curriculum and its assessment. In the summer of 1988, the first students took the GCSE examinations which replaced the old GCE 'O' levels and CSEs. This meant that all students entered the same examination, instead of there being two types of exam. Most GCSEs included coursework assessment in addition to more traditional examinations. Although most teachers and students were pleased with this broader form of assessment, the change meant a lot of work for both teaching staff and students. The principle behind GCSEs is that they should be *criteria-referenced*, that is that students' work should be measured against a set of criteria stated in advance, rather than against the overall standard of the work. In the early 1990s the School Curriculum and Assessment Authority (SCAA) became

responsible for approving GCSEs and all other aspects of the curriculum. From 1994 GCSEs have been used to test pupils on the national curriculum (see above) at age 16. The structure of the exams is being adapted in line with the requirements of the national curriculum.

'League tables' of results

Schools are required by law to publish their results and all secondary schools have to be included in the 'league tables' which provide information about truancy rates and examination results.

Vocational initiatives

In 1983, the government established the Technical and Vocational Education Initiative (TVEI). This initiative sets out to change the curriculum for 14–18 year olds, making it more relevant to work. By 1987, many local education authorities were running pilot schemes in schools and colleges, with funding from the Manpower Services Commission (now Training Agency). The national extension of TVEI was announced in 1986, extending the initiative to all LEAs. All courses must adapt to meet the criteria of TVEI. These criteria include a practical, problem-solving approach to learning, the use of new technology, avoidance of sex-stereotyping, and the development of links with industry with various schemes for work experience and work shadowing. TVEI continues to be funded and administered by the Training Agency within the Department of Employment.

Education Business Partnerships consist of representatives from industry, education and the community. They are funded by TECs and LEAs and aim to link education and industry and make sure that the right attitudes and skills are taught in schools to make pupils attractive to employers. Under this scheme, teachers have spent time in business settings to update their knowledge of the world of work and improve the careers they pass on to pupils. *Compacts* are schemes which involve employers and others in encouraging pupils to achieve more at school and continue in education beyond the minimum leaving age. Under these schemes young people agree to work towards certain goals – perhaps in terms of attendance and punctuality, or staying on another year – and in return employers offer incentives, including in some areas, jobs with training.

City Technology Colleges

The 1988 Education Act also proposed the establishment of 20 *City Technology Colleges (CTCs)*. These were originally to be located in deprived inner-city areas. CTCs are independent schools taking children from 11–18 and charging no fees. Children are selected on the basis of their interest in technology and CTCs offer a broad education with a special bias to technology. They should have better science and technology facilities, more specialised staff and close links with industry. In the words of the government, they should be 'beacons of excellence'.

The original plan was that the CTCs would be set up with money from industry and the running costs met by grants from the government. However, industrial sponsors have not shown the interest the government hoped for. Most have preferred to continue with existing schemes spread over a wider number of schools and potentially benefiting more children. In response the government was forced to put in more money than was originally intended. By 1993 15 CTCs had been established around the country.

In 1993 the CTC idea took a new direction when it was announced that voluntary or grant-maintained secondary schools could apply to become CTCs. Schools had to raise a sum of money from industry and would then receive up to £250 000 in extra funding from the government. However, again sponsors from industry have been hard to find. Many of the larger firms are already involved with schemes such as Compacts (outlined above). The head of educational services at BT, Peter Thompson, commented :

> We would prefer to maintain our consistent relationship with a significant number of schools in the way we have done rather than select one or two of them for substantial funding.[10]

7.4   Further and higher education

The 1944 Education Act states that local authorities have a duty to provide education up to the age of 19 for all those who want it.

Organisation of provision

The way in which education for the post-16 age-group is organised varies from area to area. The traditional pattern was for young people wishing to take 'A' levels to remain at school in the sixth form, and for others wanting more vocational courses to attend a college of further education. In some areas this system continues. Many schools have however widened their provision for people staying on and offer courses other than 'A' levels, perhaps working in partnership with the local college. In other areas there are sixth form colleges which take students from the local schools and provide 'A' level, GCSE and possibly other courses. The college will continue to provide vocational courses. A third variation is a tertiary college which provides all education for those over 16, in one establishment.

Colleges of further education usually provide some GCSE and 'A' level courses for people re-sitting examinations, or for those who wish to continue their studies, but do not want to remain in a school environment. Colleges also offer full-time courses related to specific areas of work such as nursery nursing, hairdressing and secretarial work. In addition, colleges provide day-release courses for local employees, varying to suit the needs of local industry. Finally, colleges provide part-time recreational classes in such subjects as modern languages and crafts. Since 1993 colleges are self-governing, independent from the

LEAs, and are funded by further education funding councils. In 1990s charters were produced for students, parents and employers – these set out the standards of service and complaints procedures.

The National Council for Vocational Qualifications (NCVQ) has been set up to provide an overall structure for the many different courses and qualifications offered in further education. Levels of achievement are set so that the different courses can be compared with each other more easily. There are also General National Vocational Qualifications (GNVQs) which are mainly for young people in full-time education. They replace BTEC and some other qualifications and are in subjects such as Art and Design, Business and Health and Social Care. They prepare people for a range of jobs in a particular vocational area and, at advanced level, are equivalent to 'A' levels and a route into higher education.

Numbers staying on

Recent years have seen an expansion of the numbers of young people entering colleges for full-time courses. In 1993 a record 7 out of 10 young people stayed on beyond the age of 16. This compares with 1989, when only 5 out of 10 young people stayed on.[11] This is partly a reflection of government policy which is to encourage young people to stay on in education or training. By the mid-1990s the government hopes that all 16- and 17-year-olds will be in education or training, encouraged by the offer of Youth Credits (see chapter 4) which enable young people to buy training at an establishment of their choice. The expansion in numbers of young people staying on is however also a reflection of the lack of choice available at 16. There have been few job openings for young people and their rights to benefits have been cut.

There has also been an expansion in the number of mature students attending further education courses. *Access* courses have proved especially popular, offering an alternative route into higher education and some areas of professional training. These include study skills training, counselling and guidance as well as academic study at advanced level and are usually assessed through coursework, rather than examinations.

Although there are increased numbers of full-time students, there has been a reduction in day-release students, as fewer young people have been taken on by employers.

Grants for students attending further education courses are discretionary and therefore vary from area to area, depending on the policy adopted by the local education authority. Discretionary grants are means-tested and paid to parents or mature students on low incomes. Fees are free to all full-time students under 19 and in some circumstances LEAs provide grants for fees for mature students as well.

Adult education

Adult education refers to non-vocational study ranging from subjects such as philosophy to recreational classes in pottery or art appreciation. Classes are run by local education authorities in colleges of further education and by the Workers Education Association (WEA). In 1973, the Russell Report recommended expansion in this area of educational provision but provision has decreased and cuts have resulted in increases in fees for classes.

Higher education

Higher education consists of degree and degree-equivalent courses taught in universities and colleges of higher education. Colleges of further education have also increasingly began to offer degree and degree-level courses, and there has been an expansion of vocational courses which lead to a degree. Examples of these are in nursing and occupational therapy.

Until 1992 there was a *binary system* within higher education – with polytechnics and universities offering broadly similar provision. Universities tended to have a higher status in people's minds than did the polytechnics. In 1992 polytechnics and some colleges of higher education were allowed to become universities and most did so.

Numbers in higher education

In 1963, the Robbins Report reviewed higher education. The Report recommended expansion in its provision to allow all qualified young people access to higher education. At the time of the report, 8 per cent of young people entered universities and the report recommended that this should increase to 17 per cent of the age group by the 1980s. The Robbins report was remarkably successful and almost immediately the government allocated a large sum of money for the expansion of higher education. The number of universities increased again in 1992 when the polytechnics were allowed to become universities. In 1994 there were 83 universities, including the Open University. The proportion of 18-year-olds in higher education increased in the late 1980s and early 1990s, reaching almost one in three in 1993.[12] There has also been an expansion in the numbers of mature students going to university and in 1991 some 30 per cent of first year undergraduates were over 21.[13]

Universities are self-governing and are funded by higher education funding councils, with the exception of Buckingham University, which is a private university.

Students on first degree courses are eligible for mandatory grants from their local education authorities. (There are also discretionary grants for non-designated courses.) These are assessed according to parents' or spouse's income. The grant covers fees and a maintenance allowance to live on. Grants have not been increased in line with inflation and students are eligible to apply for loans to help pay their living expenses. The idea of the loan system is for students to share in the cost of their education. The loans are not means-tested and repayments start in the April following the end of the course and are linked to inflation. The loans are administered by the Student Loans Company in Glasgow.

7.5   Private education

In January 1994 466 105 pupils between 2 and 19 were in private schools. This is about 7 per cent of the school population. The proportion of children in private schools rose through the 1980s but fell in the early years of the 1990s.[14] The majority of these pupils come from middle-class homes. A MORI poll in 1994 showed that 54 per cent of parents sending their children to private schools earned more than £40 000 a year.[15] Children who have attended private schools are most likely to gain places at the high-status universities, for examples, Oxford and Cambridge. A large number of the people who occupy powerful and well-paid positions in society attended private schools.

Changes 1968–80

In 1968, the Public Schools Commission was set up to look into public schools and consider their integration into the state system. Two reports were published, one in 1968 and one in 1970. The 1968 report focused on the small number of schools classified as public schools. The report recommended a number of changes such as the inclusion of girls in public schools and the abolition of certain traditional features such as the beating of boys, and 'fagging' (a system whereby younger boys acted as unpaid personal servants to older boys.) The second report concentrated on independent day schools and direct grant schools.

Source: Bob Watkins, Photofusion
A minority of children attend private schools and even fewer go to public schools such as Eton

The direct grant schools received a grant from central government, on condition that they reserved 25 per cent of places free for children educated for at least two years in maintained schools. The 1970 report recommended that the direct grant system be ended.

These reports caused a great deal of controversy, although little was done at the time of their publication. In 1975, however, the government announced that the direct grant system would stop. As a result, many of the direct grant schools changed their status to that of independent schools. The 1980 Education Act established the Assisted Places Scheme to enable children who would not normally have been able to attend independent schools to receive assistance from public funds to do so. Schools can apply to participate in this scheme and, if accepted, will take a number of pupils free, or for reduced fees. There are 37 000 places available under the assisted places scheme.

Should there be private schools?

Activity 7.5

Some people believe that private schools should be abolished. What are the arguments for and against this proposal in your view?

There are several arguments against the existence of private schools alongside the state education system. First, the very existence of private schools means that comprehensive schools cannot be said to be truly comprehensive, since some children in a particular area will go to a separate school. Second, state education is based on the idea of equal opportunity for all children. Private education operates against this principle, in that richer parents can buy a private education for their children. Whilst it is difficult and probably impossible to evaluate and compare in the field of education, most private schools have smaller classes than state schools and are more successful in terms of examination results. Third, private schools are said to perpetuate an elitist system. This means that people in the most privileged group in society are able to buy a separate education for their children, which leads into positions of power and prestige. This has the effect of dividing society into distinct and separate groups. It also means that people in positions of power are not necessarily those with the greatest ability. Finally, private education is state-subsidised through tax relief. Private schools have charitable status which gives exemption from income tax, corporation tax and capital gains tax on income or profits. Gifts to private schools are also partly exempt from capital gains tax and private schools benefit from a 50 per cent reduction in rates. The sum of money lost to the government has been estimated to be around £38.5 million.[16]

The arguments presented in favour of private education include the belief that parents who choose to educate their children privately, should be able to do so.

Also, some important educational innovation and experimentation has taken place within the private sector, for example at the school set up by A. S. Neill at Summerfield, where children were given much greater freedom and choice about their education, including the right to choose whether or not to attend classes.

7.6   Special education

The 1944 Education Act required local authorities to make provision for children with special educational needs. Such children were to include those with disabilities and those who were confined to bed, either at home or in hospital. One of the continuing problems of special education has been the difficulty of defining the children in need of special help. In 1959, the categories of children with special needs were legally defined in regulations issued by the government. The groups listed were: the blind; the partially-sighted; the deaf; the partially-hearing; the delicate; the educationally sub-normal; epileptic children; maladjusted children; the physically handicapped and those with speech defects. In 1971, the list was extended to include severely subnormal children, children who are both blind and deaf, those with autism and other psychoses and those suffering from acute dyslexia. In 1991–2, 111 000 children received full-time education in special schools in the UK.[17]

The Warnock Report

In 1978, the Warnock Report on children with special educational needs was published. The report attempted to move away from the idea of special categories of children, since the categorisation of needs had come to be seen as a restriction on provision. The report saw children with special needs as making up some 20 per cent of the school population, as distinct from the 2 per cent receiving education in special schools.

The Warnock report stated that a range of provision was required to meet varying needs. Some children would require extra help and support whilst remaining in ordinary classes. For others the best way of meeting their needs would be to provide for some periods of withdrawal to special classes. For children placed in special classes, some would benefit from periods in ordinary classes, others would need social contact with the rest of the school. Children in special schools might have some classes in an ordinary school or might participate in social activities. The report also said that there was a need for long- and short-term provision of education in hospitals and other institutions. Finally, some children would require home tuition.

Priority areas indicated in the Warnock report were: provision for the under-5s, further education and the need for teachers to be trained to meet special educational needs.

1981 Education Act and 'statementing'

The 1981 Education Act is based on the recommendations of the Warnock report, although no government money was made available to improve special education. The 1981 Act defines special educational needs as

'learning difficulties, greater than those experienced by the majority of children, or which hinder the child in benefiting from education'.

The Act states that as far as possible the local education authority must educate children with learning disabilities in ordinary schools, whilst taking into account the views of parents, the needs of the child, the needs of other children and the efficient use of resources.

It is a requirement of the Act that, in the case of a minority of children, the authority carries out a formal assessment, consulting parents as well as medical, psychological and educational experts. The parents must be told that the child is to be assessed, allowed to give evidence and informed of the authority's plans for the child. This process has come to be known as 'statementing'. In addition parents must be given the name of a local authority officer from whom they can obtain information.

Although the 1981 legislation improved parents' rights with regard to special education some problems have remained. One has concerned the distinction which has arisen from so-called 'statemented children' and others with learning disabilities. Around 2 per cent of children have statements and a further 18 per cent are thought to have some degree of learning disability. The effect of the statementing procedure has been to concentrate resources and attention on 'statemented' children and for the needs of the rest to slip into the background. Also processes have been very slow. In the worst cases children have moved on to a different stage in their education by the time the authority has made a decision. Many parents have felt they have had to fight every inch of the way to get a satisfactory deal for their child. Such a system works very much to the disadvantage to those who are less articulate, less confident and less knowledgeable about how to get things done.

1993 Education Act

As a result of concerns over the working of the 1981 legislation, a new law was passed. The 1993 Education Act requires that:

- The local education authority carries out procedures for assessments and statements within a set statutory time limit
- The education authority fits in with the parents' choice of school unless this is not appropriate for the child or involves an inefficient use of resources
- There is an independent tribunal for appeals against decisions by the education authority.

The law also now states that a state school named in a statement must take a child. There is a code of practice for schools in identifying and assessing special needs. Finally, schools must give details of their policies for treating children with special educational needs who are not 'statemented'.

Current problems

Activity 7.6 ─────────────────────

The 1981 Act says that where possible children with learning disabilities should be provided for in ordinary schools. What advantages can you see in this policy?

There are advantages both to children with learning difficulties, and to other children, in educating the largest possible number of children in mainstream education. From the point of view of ordinary children, the removal of handicapped children does not encourage young people to learn to accept those who are in some way different.

Local authorities cannot afford to provide a large number of special schools, for example there may be only one school for blind children for the whole area. This means that many children are unable to travel daily and are obliged to attend school as boarders. The standard of academic education in some special schools is not as high as that provided in ordinary schools. As a result, children may become educationally disadvantaged as well as handicapped. The segregation of children may have the effect of increasing any social difficulties they experience (see also chapters 11, 12 and 14).

Problems with children's learning and behaviour at school can be difficult to assess and there can be unfair biases in assessment. Cultural biases can operate against working-class and black children, especially in cases where the child's use of language is different from that of the teacher. In 1969, Haringey Education Committee admitted that errors had been made when it was discovered that 50 per cent of children in the borough's special schools were black, compared with 18 per cent of the local population. Whilst this problem has now been recognised, there are people who believe that the biases persist. The organisation MIND, reports a case of a 13-year-old West Indian boy who had been in a car accident in which his uncle was killed. As a result he was emotionally disturbed and the misinterpretation of his behaviour led to his being wrongly placed in a school for children with learning difficulties.[18]

The advantages of special schools are that they can provide specialised aids, equipment and teachers who fully understand the problems of children with a particular disability. Also they shield disabled children from the cruelty of other children.

Fears have been voiced that the requirement for secondary schools to be measured against each other in performance or 'league tables' will discourage schools from taking children with learning disabilities, worrying that these children will do less well in examinations.

7.7   Education and welfare

Special services

Local authorities employ Careers Officers who interview young people and provide advice and information on employment and opportunities for further education. In 1993, the government began a gradual programme of competitive tendering to provide careers services. The winning contractors came under the control of the Department of Employment. Youth workers are also appointed by local authorities to make contact with young people in their areas and to organise social activities.

Child guidance clinics are usually run by the education authority and the health service. They are staffed by a multi-disciplinary team of psychologists, psychiatrists and social workers. Referrals to the clinic may come from the school or other sources. The team make a study of the child and the family and look at the child's school record. Various recommendations can follow and the clinic can provide long-or short-term therapy to work on emotional problems.

Education welfare officers visit schools and families to investigate non-attendance and entitlement to benefits. They also work with families with problems.

Educational welfare benefits

School meals
Until 1980, local authorities were obliged by the 1944 Education Act to provide meals at a standard price and of a prescribed nutritional standard for all children, and free for some children. Entitlement to free school meals was later defined in terms of low income or receipt of family income supplement (now family credit) or supplementary benefit (now income support). The 1980 Education Act changed this, allowing local authorities to provide school meals, but not requiring them to do so. Education authorities had to make some provision, the nature of which was left to them to decide, for those children whose parents received family credit or income support. When the social security benefits were reformed in 1988, family credit no longer entitled children to free schools meals. So it is now only income support which is a passport to free school meals. In grant-maintained schools, it is the school rather than the local authority which has the duty to provide the meals.

After the 1980 Act prices of school meals rose in most areas. The numbers of children eligible for free meals fell, since parents on a low income, but not claiming benefits, are not automatically entitled to free meals for their children. A further result of the new legislation is that provision of school meals varies considerably throughout the country. Some local authorities only provide a cold snack at mid-day for those children claiming free meals.

School milk
Since 1971, school milk has been limited to children under 8, or attending special schools. The 1980 Education Act allows authorities to provide milk for any category of children and to charge for it, if they wish. As a result, some authorities do not provide milk for children under 8, whilst others continue to do so.

Discretionary grants
Grants can be made to allow pupils to participate in educational activities. This means that local authorities can help parents in paying for school outings, holidays and extra lessons.

Uniform and clothing grants
Most local authorities have schemes for providing clothing for school to less well-off families. Again, there is regional variation, as it is for the authorities to decide what they will provide.

Transport
Local education authorities are bound by law to provide transport for children under 8 whose school is more than 2 miles from home, and children over 8 who travel more than 3 miles to school. The authority can provide free transport or give a grant to cover the cost of fares. It is left to the discretion of authorities to provide more than this – that is, to shorten the distances or help low-income families even if their children live nearer to the school.

Maintenance allowances
Local education authorities pay allowances to some young people who continue their education beyond the age of 16. This is a discretionary allowance, normally decided on the basis of the income of the parents.

Higher education allowances
All students on degree and other recognised courses are paid a grant by the local authority. These grants are therefore known as *mandatory awards*. For students who are under 25, or who have not supported themselves for three years, the grant is based on a parental means-test, although a minimum amount is paid to all students. Grants have now been frozen, and are being progressively reduced, and a system of loans introduced for students to top up their income (see section 7.4 above on higher education).

7.8   Inequality in education

Equality in education is believed to be important, both as a goal in itself and because society cannot afford to waste talent. Therefore an important aim in education has been to discover and develop abilities in every individual, regardless of their background. A considerable amount of research has focused on the extent to which this has been achieved.

The early research in this area focused on inequalities relating to social class. More recent work has examined the achievement and treatment of ethnic minorities and of girls and women.

Education and social class

A great deal of research has investigated social class and educational achievement. The evidence produced shows that social class is more significant than ability in determining educational attainment. At each stage in their educational careers, children from middle-class homes are more successful than working-class children.

Statistics show that it is children from the upper social groups who are more likely to benefit from education before they are 5.[19] Reasons for this were given earlier in this chapter, in section 7.2 on pre-school education. A major research project, known as the National Child Development Study,[20] demonstrated significant differences in attainment, according to class, in children in infant schools. The study found that, by the age of 7, the chances of an unskilled manual worker's child being a poor reader were six times as great as those of a child of a professional worker.

Douglas, in 1964, found that children from upper middle-class homes were five times as likely to go to a grammar school as children with working-class parents. Success in 'O' levels was also found to be related to class, rather than ability. Several studies have found that early leaving is statistically linked to class.[21] The Robbins Report found that few working-class students entered universities.

It was partly as a result of such research findings that comprehensive schools were introduced. Many people believed that the abolition of selection at 11 would lead to greater equality of opportunity. However, more recent research shows that policies intended to reduce inequality have had little effect. Two studies published in the 1980s found that class-related inequalities were as great as in the period before the war.[22]

Several explanations have been put forward for inequalities in education success.

- The child's progress in school may be affected by the home environment. Overcrowding, for example, will make it difficult for a child to find a quiet space in which to do homework. The presence of books in a middle-class home perhaps encourages a child to want to learn to read. Money may also be a significant factor, in that children from poorer homes might be encouraged to leave school and bring home a wage.
- Other explanations concentrate on different attitudes to education. It is believed that the amounts of interest parents take in their child's education is important. Some studies have found that working-class parents are less keen to visit their child's school.[23] This may not be because of lack of interest, but rather that the parents are more easily intimidated by the school.

Middle-class parents may feel more at ease with teachers, since they are themselves middle-class. Research carried out in the 1950s discovered a feeling among working class people that the grammar schools were not really for 'people like them'.[24] It may still be the case that working-class parents do not put as much value on education and do not expect their children to stay on at school and go to university.

- More recent studies suggest that the values of school are middle-class and cause conflict in working-class children. An example of this might be the idea that it is better to stay in and do homework than to go out having fun, because sacrifice now will produce rewards later. The values of the school, including examination results and further education are rejected by some working-class children.

- Another approach to the same problem argues that middle-class and working-class people use language in a different way.[25] Two mothers might mean the same thing, when one says, 'Shut up', and the other says, 'I'd rather you made less noise, darling'. This does not matter, except that the language of school-teachers is middle-class. The working-class child has to translate what the teacher says in order to make sense of it. There may be cases where the child is not able to translate what is being said, and will be left feeling puzzled.

- Finally, it is suggested that teachers and pupils can be involved in a self-fulfilling prophesy. The way this works is that the teacher believes that certain children are more intelligent and will be more successful. The teacher then treats the children as if they are more intelligent and communicates to them his or her belief in their abilities. As a result, the children believe in themselves and do better. Teachers do not expect working-class and black children to succeed at school, and, as a result of this expectation, they do not. This could also be relevant in explaining why boys do better than girls in science subjects, for example.

Activity 7.7

Which of these ideas make the most sense to you? Try to think of any other reasons why social factors such as class, gender and race may affect educational achievement.

Girls' education

There are differences in the educational achievement of boys and girls. Girls are less likely than boys to leave school with GCSEs in Science and Mathematics, but more likely to leave with English GCSE. At advanced level, a higher proportion of boys than girls leave school with two or more 'A' levels. The differences in attainment continue into higher education. More males than females go to University and men very much outnumber women on courses in the sciences and engineering.[26] These differences, especially in achievement, are narrowing, although still remain at the highest levels. For example, in 1991 –2, at undergraduate level (first degree) there were 107 000 women and 144 000 men and at postgraduate level (further degrees) there were 17 000 women and 21 000 men.[27]

Why are there differences?
There are various factors which could explain these differences, although there has been little work done in this area until recently. The situation is complicated by the relationships which exist between education and other areas of society, such as industry. For example, girls may choose not to study scientific and technical subjects, believing that they have little chance of gaining employment in these areas. This will, in itself, mean that careers in science and engineering remain restricted to males, since females lack the necessary qualifications for entry.

It is only relatively recently that girls have been allowed to take certain subjects. A report on comprehensive schools found that at least 50 per cent of schools limited some subjects to boys only.

The 1975 Sex Discrimination Act made it illegal to restrict educational opportunities by sex but more subtle factors still intervened to limit choice. Subjects were often blocked together on a timetable in such a way as to prevent pupils combining arts or science or offering the choice between domestic science or technical drawing. This had the effect of continuing to push boys and girls into stereotyped choices. Teachers and friends may have been influential in persuading girls that arts subjects were more appropriate – perhaps more 'feminine' – than sciences and engineering. The fact that science teachers have tended to be male discouraged girls from seeing science as a female interest. The influence of the home may also be of relevance, giving girls less familiarity and interest in technical matters.

It is interesting to note that research has found that in single-sex schools, girls are more likely to opt for mathematics and science subjects than are girls in co-educational schools.[28] This indicates the influence of social factors on girls' choice of subjects for study. The national curriculum requires all children to cover certain subjects in school (fully implemented in 1996). The national curriculum means that boys and girls will study pretty much the same subjects up until age 16. It will be interesting to compare results at GCSE level and beyond to measure the effect of this change.

The reasons why fewer girls than boys enter higher education may be related to lingering attitudes holding that girls only need a basic education since they are expected to marry and spend their lives as housewives. Teachers may be influenced by this kind of approach to girls' education. Surveys have found that in mixed classes, boys receive more attention than girls from teachers.[29] This is partly because boys' behaviour is noisier and more potentially disruptive, also girls in a mixed group are less assertive in asking questions and seeking help.

— Activity 7.8 ———————————————————————————

Think about your own school education. Were some subjects available only to one sex? Were they any influences which led to girls being discouraged to succeed in some areas? Compare your experience with that of the rest of the class.

Differences in treatment at school

Recent studies have documented not only the differences between boys and girls in educational achievement but also the way girls are treated in school. A study of three comprehensive schools pointed to a number of ways in which girls were made to feel uncomfortable and out-of-place at school.[30] Boys tended to monopolise space in classrooms and in play-grounds. They made girls feel they should not speak out in class. One girl in the fifth year reports,

> They put their pens down – you know – time for a break. If she carries on they fold their arms, lean back in their chair and – sort of – look deliberately bored.

Another girl, in the third year, says

> The boys always look bored whenever a girl says anything in class. It doesn't matter what she says, she's soon drowned down with groaning and sighing.[31]

Outside the classroom the harassment continued. The author reports,

> Sexually appraising looks, many types of threatening gesture, boys holding their noses when girls passed in the corridor and pretending to talk about them in a very obvious way, imitating their steps and mock fighting to impress, all had their counterparts in girls avoiding groups of boys whenever possible, sometimes without realising they were doing so.[32]

The book reports girls being asked to list names they knew boys used about them. In half an hour, one group collected 72 and another group over 80 words. Not all the names overlapped, the words were

> appallingly graphic and foul, creating images of woman's bodies that were no less than pornographic.[33]

Verbal abuse was accompanied by physical harassment:

> boys grabbing girls' breasts, dropping things down their blouses and pinging their bra straps, looking and slipping their hands up girls' skirts and boys exposing themselves.[34]

> __ **Activity 7.9** _____
>
> What are the advantages and disadvantages of single-sex schools for boys and for girls? Do you think they might be more beneficial to one sex than to the other?

Race and education

Disadvantage and bias

Black children have been disadvantaged in school in several ways. The Commission for Racial Equality found:

- In one school in the North, fewer Asian children were entered for GCSEs than white pupils. More Asian children were put in the lowest set and they weren't moved up, even when their grades were as good as those of pupils in higher sets.
- Black children are more likely to be encouraged to do 'soft', less academic subjects – and sport – and are scoffed at when they want an academic career.
- In some schools Afro-Caribbean children were four times more likely to be suspended than white children, and often for the same sort of behaviour.[35]

Other problems occur for children whose first language is not English. Knowing another language should be seen as a skill but children have been categorised as having learning difficulties and placed in special groups. In the following quotation a Pakistani girl talks about how she felt about this:

> On starting school we were put into the 'immigrant' class along with other Asian children for the first year. We had special reading sessions with the headmaster a few times a week, for which the group was termed 'backward readers'. A few years later I can remember feeling resentment at having been called a 'backward reader'.[36]

There is also racism built into the content of lessons, which affects the way black and white children view the world.

> __ **Activity 7.10** _____
>
> How do you think a school curriculum could be biased in terms of race? Discuss your own experience at school with other members of the class.

Many of the lessons in school contain an implicit message that white people are superior and other cultures are of less value. European culture predominates and children are not taught about achievements of black people. History tends to be biased in the sense of presenting only a 'British' point of view, for example in teaching about the time of the British empire. In 1990 Mrs Thatcher made this bias very clear, saying

> From our perspective today, surely what strikes us most is our common experience, for instance, how Europeans explored and colonised and yes – without apology – civilised much of the world.[37]

In geography, there is a tendency for countries like Africa to be shown as primitive jungle-lands, whereas in fact there are large cities very like those of Europe. Cookery lessons ignore different cultures and religious instruction assumes the superiority of Christianity. Also schools, even in areas with large Asian populations, ignore the bi-lingual abilities of many children.

Black children also face racism from other pupils and sometimes from teachers. This operates in many different ways: from making a child feel odd and different, as the extract below describes, to bullying and violence in some schools. In the extract Rifat Malik explains why her 11-year-old brother does not want to go to the same predominantly white school as she attends

> Like countless Asian children before him, he fears being treated like some kind of alien life-form. He fears he will be ridiculed for silly things, such as his name being deemed unpronounceable. Then of course there is the aggravating fact that he dares to have six siblings! This is undoubtedly a capital offence in a society where it is *de rigeur* to have 2.2 children.[38]

As a result of all the factors described above, many black children underachieve at school.

The Swann Report, published in 1985, collected statistics on educational achievement.[39] Although these have been criticised, they appear to show that West Indians in particular under-achieve throughout their educational careers.

Activity 7.11

What measures are schools or local education authorities in your area taking to improve the situation for black and white children, leading to greater equality and a recognition that Britain is a multi-racial society?

Multi-cultural understanding

There have been several initiatives by local education authorities to introduce what is termed *multi-cultural education*. Multi-cultural education involves a recognition of different cultures in the content of lessons and in the school environment. These moves have, however, been criticised for not going far enough to combat racism. An anti-racist policy in a school involves a commitment to opposing racism in pupils and teachers and in the running of the school. It also means greater involvement of black parents and of the community as a whole.

The Swann Report argued that society was faced with a dual problem: eradicating discriminatory attitudes of the white majority and evolving an educational system which ensures that all pupils achieve their full potential. The title of the report was *Education for All*, meaning that the problem for schools is not how to educate children of ethnic minorities, but how to educate *all* children. The report argues that:[40]

- Britain is a multi-racial and multi-cultural society and all pupils must be enabled to understand what this means.
- This challenge cannot be left to the independent initiatives of education authorities and schools: only those with experience of substantial numbers of ethnic minority pupils have attempted to tackle it, though the issue affects all schools and all pupils.
- Education has to be something more than the reinforcement of the beliefs, values and identity which each child brings to the school.
- It is necessary to combat racism, to attack inherited myths and stereotypes and the ways in which they are embodied in institutional practice.
- Multi-cultural understanding has also to permeate all aspects of a school's work. It is not a separate topic that can be welded on to existing practices.

The Report also made a large number of specific recommendations for implementation of 'education for all'. These include the need for more language teaching, although not in separate centres; the need for teacher training to include experience in teaching in multi-racial classrooms; and the need for more black teachers in schools.

Activity 7.12

Several government reports have been mentioned in this chapter. Find out about *one* of the reports listed below, including the recommendations, and what happened as a result. Report your findings to the class.
Government Reports on Education:
The Early Leaving Report (1954)
The Crowther Report, *15–18* (1959)
The Newsom Report, *Half Our Future* (1963)
The Robbins Report, *Higher Education* (1963)
The Plowden Report, *Children and their Primary Schools* (1967)
Public Schools Commission (1968, 1970)
The James Report, *Teacher Education and Training* (1972)
The Bullock Report, *A Language for Life* (1975)
The Taylor Report, *A New Partnership for Our Schools* (1977)
The Warnock Report, *Special Educational Needs* (1978)
The Swann Report, *Educational for All* (1985)

The Elton Report, *Discipline in Schools* (1989)
The Dearing Report, *The National Curriculum and its Assessment* (1993)
Note: Two books will help in this exercise: A. Corbett, *Much to do about Education*, 4th edn (London: Macmillan, 1978) and R. Rogers, *Crowther to Warnock* (London: Heinemann, 1980).
For more recent reports see the summaries provided in the Education Yearbook, which is published annually by Longman Community Education, or contact the Department for Education.

--- **Activity 7.13** ---

The Department for Education has told your local education authority that there is some money to spend on education locally. In groups of three or four, decide how the money should be spent, explaining why such an area is a priority.

--- **Activity 7.14** ---

Make sure that you understand the following expressions, used in this chapter. Check the glossary on p. 363 if you need to.

binary system
central government
City Technology Colleges (CTCs)
comprehensive school
curriculum
direct grant school
discretionary
dyslexia
education welfare officer
elite
equality of opportunity
General National Vocational
    Qualification (GNVQ)
grant-maintained school
independent school
IQ
local authority
mainstream education
maintained school
mandatory

national curriculum
non-accidental injury
parity of esteem
positive discrimination
pre-school education
psychiatrist
psychologist
public school
segregation
selective education
special school
speech therapy clinic
'statementing'
tripartite system
tertiary college
therapist
tripartite system
universal
voluntary school

Further reading

There is a vast literature on education, which makes it difficult to choose one or two books to list. The Department for Education is a useful source of statistical information, although not always in a very digestible form. Most Sociology text-books contain useful sections on education and inequality.

Useful addresses

Department for Education: DFE Publications Centre, P O Box 2193, London E15 2EU
tel. 0181 533 2000

The Pre-School Playgroups Association: 61–63 King's Cross Road, London WC1X 9LL
tel. 0171 833 0991

8 Personal social services

This chapter looks at the origins and work of the local authority personal social services department. This work has taken a new direction as a result of the NHS and Community Care Act in 1990. Community care is the subject of the next chapter and therefore the two chapters go together to some extent. The following five chapters are also relevant since they focus on the needs of groups with whom social workers are likely to be involved.

8.1   The origins of social service departments

Nineteenth-century services

The present system whereby each local authority has a social services department has only existed since 1970. The origins of social work can however be traced back to the nineteenth century. Services were originally concerned only with poor people and the only government run provision was the workhouse for the destitute set up under the 1834 Poor Law (see chapter 3). There were also a number of charitable organisations to help people in poverty and need and it was fashionable in the nineteenth century for middle- and upper-class women to visit and help the poor. Some women took this further and were more systematic in their attempts to work with needy people. One such was Octavia Hill who renovated and built housing for poor people in the slum areas of London. She developed a kind of casework approach to her tenants, offering advice and support as well as a home to rent. She trained her rent-collectors, mostly young women, in the same skills and approach. Although these activities can be considered as the origins of present-day social work, the help was often given in a very condescending and patronising way.

1920s–1960s

The next important development came at the beginning of the twentieth century when hospitals began to employ 'almoners' or social workers. These were initially concerned only with assessing whether the patient deserved and needed free treatment, but soon widened their role. Training courses were set up and in 1920 the Institute of Almoners was established.

After the Second World War, at the time that the Welfare State was being established, local authorities began to provide welfare services for some groups of people. In 1948 Children's Departments were set up to provide services for children deprived of a normal home life. The work of these departments was the most professional of local authority social work. The 1946 National Health Service Act gave the local authorities the responsibility for maternity and baby welfare, for the after-care of mentally ill people, and for home services for elderly people and some other groups. The 1948 National Assistance Act required that local authorities provide accommodation and some other services for elderly people, handicapped people and homeless families. Although all these services were provided by the local authorities they were not organised in a coherent way, but were fragmented.

These fragmented services and divided responsibilities were thought to be unsatisfactory for a variety of reasons. The focus on particular client groups such as the mentally ill had the effect of isolating people in need from their families and the community. There were both gaps and overlaps in provision and a confusion over responsibility for meeting needs. Also, the services operated primarily on a casualty basis, only becoming involved when problems arose. The need for preventative help was increasingly recognised, as was the need for community alternatives to residential care.

Seebohm Committee (1968) and afterwards

As a result of these misgivings over existing provision, the Seebohm Committee was set up by the government to look into local social services. The Report of this committee was published in 1968, recommending that a *unified* and *family-orientated* service be established. The report argued for:

> a new local authority department, providing a community based and family orientated service, which will be available to all. This new department will, we believe, reach far beyond the discovery and rescue of social casualties; it will enable the greatest number of individuals to act reciprocally giving and receiving service for the well-being of the whole community.[1]

The proposals of the Seebohm Committee were incorporated into the Local Authority Social Services Act 1970, which came into force on 1 April 1971. The 1970 Act required local authorities to appoint a Director of Social Services and set up Social Services Committees. The new social services departments would be responsible for the welfare of all sections of the community. This was the beginning of *generic social work*, whereby social workers deal with all kinds of people and problems, instead of specialising in one area, such as mental illness or deprived children. The training of the new generic social workers was to be the responsibility of the Central Council of Education and Training in Social Work (CCETSW) which was set up in 1971. The central government department to which local authority social workers are responsible is the Department of Health.

8.2   Social work

There is no clear and simple definition for the term *'social* work'. It is often used in a broad sense, for example by people working in education or the police force, who may see their work as including aspects of social work. In this chapter, social work is discussed in the more limited context of people employed by the local authority as social workers.

Activity 8.1 _____

Use library resources to collect a number of different definitions of social work. Decide on the definition which seems most appropriate to you.

Social workers are involved in a broad area of work, although there is a tendency of caseloads to concentrate on problems such as old age, disabilities of various kinds, low income and family relationships. Working with children also takes up a large part of social-work time and this is dealt with separately in chapter 10, in conjunction with a description of the role of the courts involved with young people. Some of the duties of the local authority social services department are statutory, that is, services required by legislation. Other provision is at the discretion of the local authority and therefore varies from area to area.

Activity 8.2 _____

What services do you think are provided by the local authority social services department?

This summary of services is divided in terms of the different client groups with which social workers are involved.

Children

Statutory responsibilities for children include those for children who have got into trouble with the police as well as those for children whose parents are thought to be unable to provide adequate care. The legal responsibilities of social services towards children are set out in the 1989 Children Act which is looked at in chapter 10. Social workers organise foster-parents and provide supervision for children living at home. Where residential care is needed, it may be provided in social services-run homes. Alternatively social services place children in privately-run homes or those provided by voluntary organisations. These homes are inspected by social services and placements are monitored and reviewed.

Other local authority duties concerned with children include acting as an adoption agency and registering child-minders in the area. Day-care is also provided for children in need as described in chapter 7. The Children Act also requires that social services monitor all day care for children up to the age of 8.

There is a tendency for work with children to dominate field social work. This is partly because of the number of statutory responsibilities which personal social services departments have for children. There has also been a rise in the number of child sexual abuse cases since the publicity given to this issue. The various enquiries involving children and social workers have also caused a great deal of anxiety, and meant other areas of social work have tended to be seen as less pressing. (See also chapters 2 and 10.)

Older people

Social workers are also involved with the needs of older people in a variety of ways. Social workers may be needed as care managers sorting out a package of care for older people living at home. The package of care might include meals-on-wheels, home helps or home carers and the provision of adaptations for homes, ranging from small items such as kitchen equipment to help people with severe arthritis to stairlifts for those unable to get upstairs. Some of these services are organised within social services departments and others are provided by outside agencies, with social services monitoring and reviewing the services. There will be charges for these services in many cases, although services are usually free for the very poorest people. Day centres for older people are sometimes provided by social services, offering recreational and social facilities. Social services can also intervene to help older people who are unable to remain at home. Increasingly however residential care is in private or voluntary homes rather than in homes run by the social services department. Private homes are inspected and registered by social services.

Disabled people

Social services departments also have responsibilities to people who are sick or disabled. Sheltered workshops are run to provide opportunities for rehabilitation for people with disabilities, through employment and recreation. In these and other areas of work, social workers work in conjunction with voluntary organisations. Social workers are also based in psychiatric and general hospitals, providing advice and working with therapists.

Families

Social work with families involves providing counselling, putting people in touch with other agencies, both statutory and voluntary and guiding people through the complexities of housing or social security provisions.

Activity 8.3

What skills and personal qualities do you think are required for social work?

8.3   Social workers

Very different sorts of people can be successful in social work, so different qualities can be useful in different ways. However, at a general level, social workers need a considerable degree of self-awareness, including an understanding of their own motives in their work. They should be people who are able to get along with a wide variety of other people without falling back on stereotyped notions. Understanding and sympathy are important qualities for social work, as is patience. Social workers need to be able to cope with conflict and to be able to make difficult decisions, perhaps against the will of their clients. At the same time, where possible social workers should allow clients to make their own decisions and encourage self-determination.

Social workers need skills in assessing situations and needs. They need to be organised in record-keeping and filing information. Finally, social workers need knowledge of resources which may be useful to clients and an understanding of the working of society and individual psychology.

Training for social work aims to develop skills and abilities in all these areas, through development of personal skills and the teaching of psychology, sociology and social administration. Pre-service training combines theoretical knowledge with supervised practice in a variety of placements. As mentioned earlier, social work training is organised by the Central Council in Education and Training in Social Work (CCETSW). CCETSW validates courses of social work training in universities and colleges. The basis professional qualification for social workers is the Diploma in Social Work (DipSW). Since this is quite a recent development, many social workers currently working have other qualifications. In the past social workers working in the community trained for a Certificate of Qualification in Social Work (CQSW) while those in residential work qualified with a Certificate of Social Service (CSS). Now the two qualifications are combined and all social workers whatever their area of work train for the same diploma. CCETSW also runs courses for qualified social workers to update or further develop their knowledge and skills.

The social-work profession is made up of field-workers and residential and day-care workers. Field-workers are involved primarily with families and individuals in the community. Family and individual casework involves providing information and counselling and support to help people to understand and cope with their problems. Field-workers may be involved in a combination of individual and family casework, and group work and community work. Residential workers are employed in the various types of residential accommodation provided by the local authority. The Barclay Report on social work, published in

1982, saw residential social work as the 'Cinderella service' within social work. Residential workers suffer low pay and the stigma attached to institutions. Demoralisation results from the tendency for residential care to be seen as 'undesirable' and only to be used 'as a last resort'.

8.4   Organisation of social services departments

Generic approach

Social services departments vary in the way the work is organised. The Seebohm Report recommended that all social work take a generic approach. In the early days most social services departments were divided into teams covering a geographical area. Each social worker in the team would have a generic caseload, including all types of clients. However, there was a trend towards specialisations within the teams. For example intake workers would deal with all new inquiries and referrals, before passing them on to other social workers. Social workers began to specialise in particular areas such as welfare rights or the needs of older people. Now it is common for departments to be organised into teams, dealing with different types of work or clients.

--- Activity 8.4 _____

List what you think are the advantages and disadvantages of generic social work. How will a department decide what policy to adopt on this issue?

Frustrations and satisfactions

There is some feeling among social workers themselves against the generic approach, as is illustrated in the view of this social worker.

> Why we can't have social workers for people with disabilities, people with a learning disability, and so on, I don't know. I think it will come. If you are going to work under stress, you should work in a field you know something about.[2]

There are obviously arguments on both sides of this debate and it may be that the best situation is that which exists at the present time, where teams have a generic approach, whilst allowing individual social workers a degree of specialisation.

Social workers have a very difficult and demanding job which can put them under considerable stress. Whilst the work has many satisfactions, it can also be depressing as the comments of this social worker demonstrate:

> I sometimes get depressed when I think of all the things I'd like to do for my clients but can't. I've worked with some of them for the last two years and, with some, it's the

same sort of situation now as it was then – particularly with adolescents in trouble. You don't see results like you do other jobs. If you do ever finish a case there's always another one to take over. A lot of the time you're physically tired, and there's always the paperwork.[3]

Many social workers express frustration over the hierarchical organisation of social work. Promotion takes workers away from the job for which they were trained and into a management role. There is little opportunity for experienced social workers who wish both to further their career and to retain contact with clients. Many social workers experience feelings of demoralisation in the face of the difficulties of their work, criticisms from outside and cuts in expenditure.

Barclay (1982) and Griffiths (1988) Reports

In 1982, the Barclay Report was published, following the establishment of a committee by the government to examine the role of social work. The report emphasises the importance of the role of local people in providing care in the community. In this context, the report recommends that social work develops in the role of providing support for carers in a community-orientated service. The report itself contains criticisms of this approach to social work and is intended as a guide to ideas and possibilities rather than as a blueprint on which to base legislation, requiring local authorities to follow particular policies.

Partly as a result of the Barclay Report, some social services departments have developed a 'patch system'. This means that small groups of social workers move out of the area office and set up in a house, shop or Portakabin in the neighbourhood in which they are working. This way it is hoped that they can have better links with the community and develop local resources.

In 1988 the Griffiths Report on community care was published. This is discussed in detail in chapter 9 on community care. The Report criticised the lack of organisation between all the different agencies and people involved in providing community care services. The Report recommended that the position of local authorities be strengthened to allow them to take a lead role in organising and overseeing community care provision. These recommendations of the Griffiths Report were accepted by the government and became law in the 1990 NHS and Community Care Act. This was finally implemented in 1993. The changes broaden the range of social work to include working with some people who were previously the responsibility of the health services (such as people with mental illnesses leaving psychiatric hospitals). It has also meant a change in role, further towards managing services provided by other agencies, for example in the private and voluntary sectors (see chapter 9 for more detail on this).

Criticisms of social work

Considerable criticism of social work is made by social workers themselves, by clients and by academic writers.

— **Activity 8.5** —

> How would you criticise social work in the light of recent press reports
> about the handling of child abuse cases, etc.?

Seeing people as clients

Social workers have a tendency to see people as *clients*. Clients are then thought
of as people who are unable to take rational decisions and live independently of
social workers. Being seen as a client has a stigmatising effect and can lead to
resistance on the part of the person who needs help, or an acceptance of the
label, resulting in increased feelings of inadequacy and dependency. The social
worker–client relationship rarely includes any notion of mutual needs and
support. For this reason, many people feel that they gain more from the support
of friends, or of self-help groups, as described in chapter 16. This stereotyping
of people as clients probably helps social workers to cope with the pain and
demands of their work and is common also to the nursing and teaching professions, where people are seen not as whole people, but as *patients* or *pupils*.

Counselling not practical help

Social workers are also subjected to criticism because they are often unable to
provide practical solutions to problems. Many clients see their problems as
essentially practical, such as the need for a job, extra money or better housing.
Social workers have very limited power to solve these problems and instead
offer counselling and social work support. Both clients and social workers experience frustration as a result. Clients may reject counselling in situations where
they feel they should be given practical help.

Role conflict

The job of social workers involves several roles which can come into conflict.
On the one hand, they are expected to befriend clients, whereas at other times
they have to carry out statutory duties without the agreement of the client. This
conflict can be particularly acute when social workers have to take children into
care against the wishes of the child or the parent. In situations such as this, many
people come to see the social workers' role as being more like that of the police
than that of friends.

In the 1960s and 1970s, there was a move towards *community work*, instead
of individual casework. Community workers aim to encourage and help groups
of people in the community to get together to solve their own problems.
Community work sometimes leads social workers into difficulties over loyalties
and obligations, in situations where the community groups oppose the decisions
of the local authority. This dilemma also arises in other forms of social work and
many social workers experience conflict between their commitment to the
people they are supposed to help and that to their employers. Community work
tends to be vulnerable in times of cuts in expenditure and increasing demand.

The following quotation from a social worker illustrates one view about the role of social work in society and the feeling of frustration over the limitations of casework:

> It's all very depressing if you come to think about it. Society uses social workers to appease its conscience about the poor. . . I was idealistic when I started but it's brought home to you with a jolt how it really is when you have to say to someone, 'Sorry there's nothing we can do for you except, perhaps, take the children away'. We are not caring for the community, helping a community to cope with its own problems. We're dealing with individuals, and have no time to invest in community projects.[4]

Social control and individual failure

Radical criticisms of social work focus on two related aspects, social control and the emphasis on individual problems and casework. Expressed very briefly, those who see social work as a form of social control look at the way in which social workers, as state employees, go into people's homes, criticising and keeping records on life-style and activities. Social workers have the power to take away children if the way people are living their lives is thought to be unsatisfactory. In this way, social workers, mainly middle-class themselves, impose standards of behaviour and family life on their working-class clients. The second line of attack emphasises the way in which social work is a way of individualising problems, which are social and economic in origin. Many clients are poor and living in bad housing conditions. Individual casework can do nothing to solve these problems. By treating the victims of problems in society as people with personality problems, social workers help to maintain the status quo and distract attention away from the wider issues. People are thus encouraged to see structural problems in society in terms of individual failure.

8.5   Race and social work

In recent years attention has been paid to the issue of race in the context of social work. Problems have been noted such as the lack of black people in social work professions, lack of knowledge of social workers of black cultures, and inadequate understanding of the nature of racism in social work and in society. The following extract makes a number of proposals for improving social work practice in this area. It is written by a social worker in children's home in London.[5]

> Many of the black people and those of other ethnic communities living in this country were born here, and are second or third generation. Notwithstanding, we are providing a home to many people for whom the English language is a second one. Social services departments could channel communication skills into producing a range of leaflets about provision for elderly, mentally and physically handicapped people, or children and families, written in various languages, reflecting and recognising the needs of certain ethnic groups within an area.
>
> Included in the information provided could be details about sheltered housing, home help and other domiciliary services. In a leaflet about child care, information

could be included about the juvenile court system and the way care orders are awarded, explaining at the same time clarification about parental rights regarding access and appeal. A list of useful addresses could be included, indicating details of lawyers experienced in handling complex child care law. Where appropriate for example, a Turkish Cypriot social worker in an area team, or a Nigerian Yoruba-speaking home help, could be in some way identified, so that people could seek appropriate help or even interpretation.

Field and residential social workers need to be aware of different cultural values, and should not make judgements on people's parenting skills for example, based on what is an acceptable norm in our white European society.

There is a need to recognise that Afro-Caribbean families are usually very close and there is a large extended network within them. It is quite natural for an African child to be looked after by older more responsible siblings and these children can be brought up by any number of different relatives while the natural parents continue their education or undertake some commercial business.

When receiving black or other children from ethnic groups into care, social workers need to be aware of these extended family networks, and of the need to explore other members of the family if possible, before taking a child away from its natural family, and putting a child into an unnatural environment of foster-parents or a residential care home.

Regarding qualifying training there could be changes on the horizon, but a dipstick survey carried out on students who are taking part in a CQSW [now DipSW] course or who have just completed one, reveals that many students feel that their courses are not equipping them for working in a trans-cultural society.

One student said that she had spent only half a day on her CQSW [now DipSW] course looking at cultural issues. It would be unfair to blandly accuse the course of not covering cultural issues sufficiently, as already too much has to be crammed into the [social work] courses. . . .

Again if change is to be truly effective, wider representation from ethnic groups is needed on bodies like the Central Council for Training and Education in Social Work, and at the [Department of Health]. This is not to undervalue the work of sitting members, but unless there are more people from ethnic groups involved, such an important body is not in a position to truly reflect the needs of the various communities.

Two more practice issues are relevant, firstly in terms of adopting an acceptable anti-racist dialogue within social work. We need to get rid of redundant and often offensive terminology. As a fundamental basic it is offensive to refer to black or brown people as 'coloured'. They are black or brown people and are proud of that fact and as a matter of courtesy should be referred to likewise. Equally, children born of black and white parents should never be referred to as of 'mixed-race'. This again is quite offensive and these children should be addressed as being 'mixed-parentage'.

The second practice issue is in terms of placement of children, and some of these comments apply equally to all children who are placed away from their respective community and links. For some inner-city children being placed away from home in some country area can be a tremendous shock. It cannot be doubted however that for some children a period away from the inner-city can prove a valuable experience. However in general for black and other children from ethnic groups, this has led to some appalling experiences.

Living away from their families and their natural culture only serves to further isolate many of these young people. Most of the towns outside major urban areas are in predominantly all white areas. Here the young people lose touch with their cultural identity, and for many it is only in their late teens that they come into contact with their own black community.

We should think really hard before condemning a black or other ethnic child to cultural isolation, and instead concentrate on seeking a placement either directly in the individual's own locality or in the immediate surrounding area.

The role of professional associations to support and direct moves within social services towards trans-cultural provision is enormous. The record of some of these bodies on this issue has not always been good. Some years ago many black social workers formed their own professional association, and they may need persuading that these organisations are relevant to their needs.

8.6   Home help services

This chapter has focused on field social workers but the work of others in social services departments is also very important. Home helps in particular provide a service much valued by clients but somewhat unrewarded in terms of pay and status. The work of the home help service extends far beyond the traditional image of housework and cleaning. Home helps offer support and counselling as well as practical services. In some areas they have become known as 'family aids' to stress their changing role. The policy of care in the community care has placed great pressure on the home help services as more elderly and disabled people are maintained in the community instead of in residential care.

Source: Sam Tanner, Photofusion
Services are available to enable people to remain in their own home

---

Activity 8.6

Contact a home help organiser in your area. Is it possible to interview a home help or to accompany them during their work to find out what the job involves?

Activity 8.7

Make sure that you understand the following expressions which have been used in this chapter. Check the glossary on p. 363 if you need to.

care manager	care package
'Cinderella' service	community care
community work	domiciliary service
field social worker	foster-parent
generic social work	patch system
personal social services	self-help group
statutory duty	stereotype
stigma	voluntary organisation

Further Reading

Community Care is a useful source of up-to-date articles on issues relating to social work. Details of careers and training in the personal social services can be obtained from the CCETSW Information Service (See below) A very detailed and useful source of information on legal aspects of social work is Hugh Brayne and Gerry Martin, *Law for Social Workers* (3rd ed) (London: Blackstone Press, 1993).

Vivienne Coombe and Alan Little (eds), *Race and Social Work* (London: Tavistock, 1986) also has many useful articles concerning race.

Useful addresses

CCETSW Information Service: Desbyshire House, St Chad's Street, London WCIH 8AD
tel. 0171 278 2455

British Association of Social Workers (BASW): 16 Kent Street, Birmingham, B5 6RD
tel 0121 622 3911

Social Care Association: 23A Victoria Road, Surbiton Surrey, KT6 4JZ
tel. 0181 390 6831

9 Community care

In 1990 the NHS and Community Care Act was passed. This introduced a radically new system of care for many different types of people : older people; people with disabilities; people with a learning disability and those with mental illnesses. Since the legislation, changes are continuing to be made to the system and will no doubt continue as new problems and solutions emerge. This chapter describes the history of the idea of community care, outlines the procedures introduced by the 1990 Act and looks at some of the problems being encountered. The chapters on mental illness, disability, old age, learning disability and children in trouble also cover aspects of community care in relation these groups. (See also chapter 2 on the family.)

9.1   What is 'community care'?

The term 'community care' is notoriously difficult to define. As will be described later, it has gone through a series of changes in use and is still used differently by different people in different contexts. The idea behind community care is that it is better (and perhaps cheaper – although this is debatable) for people to live in their own homes than in institutions. Nowadays community care is generally taken to mean the provision of services for those needing some support to live independently.

Key aspects of community care

Aspects of community care include the following:

- The closure of large psychiatric and (to use the old-fashioned name) 'mental handicap' hospitals.
- The development of new jobs for people working with clients or patients in the community, for example community psychiatric nurses or home carers (different terms are used in different areas).
- The development of services to support informal carers (relatives or perhaps neighbours).
- The development of smaller-scale residential units.

Enablers and service 'packages'

The NHS and Community Care Act encourages local authority social services departments to take the role of 'enabler' or 'manager' of services rather than that of provider. This means that the local authority will be less likely to own and run their own homes, day-centres and other services and more likely to refer people to services run by voluntary or private organisations (the independent sector). Social services are responsible for providing a 'package' of such services and for inspection and monitoring of homes. This change in the role of the social services is not necessarily a part of the philosophy of community care. It reflects a wider desire by the Conservative government to privatise services, widen choice and reduce the role of local authorities. Because the two ideas have co-incided, private provision of services is inextricably bound up with the development of community care in the 1990s.

9.2 The history of community care development

Problems of total institutions

Community care first began to be talked about in relation to people with mental illnesses. The traditional treatment was in large hospitals built in the nineteenth century on the outskirts of most towns. Patients who went into these hospitals often did not come out again. In the 1950s and 1960s people began to question whether this was the best way to deal with mental illness. It was however to be nearly 40 years until a real response was made.

Living their whole lives within the institution led to patients becoming 'institutionalised'. People's original symptoms may have disappeared but they had become dependent on the routines and ways of the hospital and could no longer function outside its walls. The majority of the population would be unlikely to enter their local hospital but everyone was aware of the large brick-built buildings in spacious grounds. Lack of knowledge and fear led to stigmatising of the hospitals and this extended to anyone who had been a patient. The stigma of having been in the hospital created further difficulties for a patient seeking to re-integrate into the community.

Concern over these issues led to a search for alternatives. Community care was first mentioned in the 1954–7 Royal Commission on Mental Illness and Deficiency. The Commission recommended a 'general orientation away from institutional care in its present form and towards community care'. Then, in 1961, Enoch Powell, then Minister for Health, announced the run-down of the mental hospitals. At the conference at which Powell made his speech it was argued that the motives for this change were primarily in terms of saving money and that there was no commitment to building up community resources in place of hospitals. This was a comment which was to echo throughout the next 35 years (and probably beyond). The community care policy was developed further in the 1963 government publication, 'Health and Welfare: the Development of Community Care' known as the 'Community Care Blue Book'.

The arguments for community care were strengthened by sociological critiques of institutions. Goffman's book *'Asylums'*, published in 1961, introduced the concept of a *total institution*. Total institutions included mental hospitals, army barracks and prisons and were characterised by several features. In a total institution the barriers usual in our society between areas of work, play and sleep are broken down,

> all aspects of life are lived in the same place, under the same authority and with a number of others, all doing the same things. The activities are subject to routines and schedules, designed by the authorities.

Finally, according to Goffman,

> the various enforced activities are brought together into a single rational plan purportedly designed to fulfil the official aims of the institution.[1]

Other characteristics of total institutions are the split between the 'managed' group and the staff, who have stereotyped views of each other and between whom there is no social mobility. This means that a member of staff could not become an inmate and an inmate could not become a member of staff. There is also a barrier on information and inmates are discouraged from finding out why decisions are made. Other distinguishing factors include the role of work (for which incentives for work outside do not exist) and the lack of any notion of family life.

Activity 9.1

Try to visit a local institution, for example a home for older people. To what extent did you find it a 'total institution'?

Other writers looked at other areas of care, providing further evidence of institutionalisation. In 1962 Peter Townsend carried out a survey of homes for old people.[2] He found that many of the residents did not really need to be in a home and were there for reasons of poverty or homelessness or because they had no relatives. He also found that people were isolated and lacked freedom of choice and power over their own lives. In 1969 Pauline Morris looked at the 'mental subnormality hospitals' as they were then known.[3] She had found a similar situation to that reported by Townsend : many of the residents did not need to be there and they were poorly cared for by an inadequate number of staff.

In the late 1960s and 1970s publicity was given to a series of scandals concerning cruelty and neglect in institutions. Reports followed on these and a series of government White Papers suggested improvements in services for people with mental illnesses and learning disabilities (then known as mental handicaps). The reports argued for services to be provided to support people in their own homes or in smaller residential settings in the community. Still, however, progress was slow.

Moves toward community care

The 1980s saw greater impetus towards community care with the closure of many residential institutions and the encouragement of community care for all groups previously thought to need residential care. However there was a tendency for the development of services in the community to lag drastically behind the closure of institutions. This meant that ex-patients were often isolated and uncared for in bed-and-breakfast accommodation or that great strain was placed upon relatives. Existing community services, such as home helps, were stretched to breaking point, without any expansion in resources to meet the need. Increasingly publicity began to be given to these issues and there was growing public awareness that something needed to be done.

One of the problems with the development of community care concerned funding arrangements. Hospitals are part of the national health service (NHS) and the NHS is funded from national government with tax payers' money. Social services, however, are part of local government and therefore financed by the council, mainly with money from rates in the past, and now from council tax. The closure of hospitals in effect meant a saving for the NHS but an increased cost to the more limited budgets of the social services departments and the councils who became responsible for people in the community.

In 1976 a system was set up to allow joint-funding of projects by the health authority and the local authority. An example of a joint-funded scheme is the Neighbourhood Resource Centre at Elm Tree Close in Frinton, Essex. Elm Tree Close is an Elderly Persons' Home with the Neighbourhood Resource Centre attached. The work of the centre is as follows:[4]

> This will be a joint venture between Social Services and the North-East Essex Health Authority. Elm Tree Close will provide the centre from which a team of Health and Social Services Department staff will support elderly people in the Community. The tasks of that team will be to identify those people 'at risk' in the surrounding area, to design and deliver 'packages of care' for such vulnerable clients, including the provision of relief for carers, and to determine which elderly people need to live in Elm Tree Close on a permanent basis. The team will include a Social Worker, a Home Help Organiser, a Health Visitor, a Nurse, an Occupational Therapist and some Physiotherapy treatment. The Neighbourhood Resource Centre will have its own tail-lift vehicle and driver. We will be able to provide maximum planned support for elderly people to remain in their own home, but if and when the time comes that there is no alternative to permanent admission to an Elderly Persons' Home, the Home will not be strange and alarming, but a known and trusted environment.

The Audit Commission – an organisation which monitors local government and health – produced an important report on community care in 1986. The report pointed out other financial anomalies. In the case of elderly people, the system of financial support was working against the development of community care. Social security payments were available for residential care (up to a certain amount) but there was no equivalent to pay for care in the community. Social services were therefore likely to want to place people in homes rather than providing expensive services for them to remain in the community.

The Griffiths Report

Following this report, the government asked Sir Roy Griffiths to look into community care and make recommendations for change. The Griffiths Report, *Community Care : Agenda for Action* was published in 1988.[5] This became the blueprint for the White Paper which followed and the resulting 1990 legislation. The terms of reference for Griffiths were:

> to review the way in which public funds are used to support community care policy and to advise on the options for action that would improve the use of these funds as a contribution to more effective community care.

The Report argued that the system whereby community care was shared between the health authorities, the local authorities, voluntary and private organisations and informal carers with no overall lead given was ineffective. Griffiths believed that an overall responsibility should lie with the local authorities as 'arrangers and purchasers – not monopoly providers' of community care services. This would require some clarification and strengthening of local authority powers. The report also recommended that the government should appoint a Minister with overall responsibility to set standards and to oversee provision. This Minister would also distribute central government grants to help local authorities with about half the costs of community care projects.

The Wagner Report

In the same year as the Griffiths Report, the Wagner report on residential care was published. This Report argued that residential care should be seen as a positive choice. People should not have to go into a residential home purely in order to receive the level of care they needed. This should be provided for people at home by the local authority. Gillian Wagner made many recommendations to improve care for various different groups of people. The underlying philosophy she set out in five principles – five Cs. [6]

The Wagner Report – five Cs to improve residential care

- Caring
  This should be personal and residents should feel valued, safe and secure.
- Choice
  Each resident's right to exercise choice over their daily life should be respected.

- Continuity
  This includes both consistency of care from staff, and the maintenance of links with a resident's previous life.
- Change
  For residents, the opportunity for continued development; for staff, a commitment to respond to changing needs.
- Common values
  Ensuring that practice is based on a shared philosophy and values.

Caring for People

Nearly two years after the Griffiths Report the government published the White Paper *Caring for People*. This adopted many, but not all, of Griffiths' recommendations. Instead of social security payments only for residential homes social services would receive additional money to use for care – either in a residential home, or in the community.

The White Paper set out six key objectives:

- Services should be targeted on those in most need
- Carers should be supported
- There should be assessment of need and good care management
- Authorities should make use of the independent sector
- It should be clear who was responsible for what
- The social security money previously used to pay for homes should transfer to social services.

The 1990 legislation and afterwards

The 1990 NHS and Community Care Act gave local authorities the duty to draw up a plan for community care, to assess people's needs and to inspect all provision of community and residential services. The implementation of the Act was delayed and the date for the beginning of community care was finally April 1993.

As from April 1993 the system of community care works as follows:

- The local authority has lead (but not sole) responsibility for care.
- The local authority has the duty to plan the overall *pattern of care* in the area. The plans must be publicised and available for people to see.
- People who appear to need community care services are *assessed*. How exactly this is done varies according to the situation and different procedures adopted in different areas of the country.
- A *care plan* for the individual is drawn up, taking into account their wishes and needs and those of their relatives.
- For more complex cases, a *care manager* is allocated to supervise, monitor and review the care.

- Services provided include those of the independent sector (voluntary or private organisations) to provide a wider choice.
- The local authority is accountable for the services they provide and there is a complaints procedure.

In 1994 the Health Secretary announced the introduction of *charters for community care*. These are locally prepared documents to allow for variations in areas, but all include standards for the speed and quality of services and set out which services must be paid for by users.

In a book on community care, written for Age Concern Barbara Meredith gives the following example of a community care package.[7]

> Mr O'Malley has tripped on the sill of the back door and fractured his hip. He is in hospital recovering, learning to walk with a frame, and contemplating returning home.
>
> His family live 200 miles away. They are concerned that he might fall again and feel guilty that they can't visit more frequently. They feel that he might be safer in a care home.
>
> But Mr O'Malley is determined to remain at home, if necessary moving the bed downstairs. An assessment is arranged in the hospital, to sort out his care needs. The social worker, physiotherapist, occupational therapist and doctor all agree on the services which will help him remain at home, and a care manager takes responsibility for arranging this support.
>
> An arrangement is made with a neighbour to shop and do other errands for him. Mr O'Malley will contribute to the cost of this service. A home from hospital scheme will help with other care in the first few weeks. A physiotherapist and home gardening scheme will also offer support.
>
> From time to time Mr O'Malley's 'care package' will be reassessed. If his needs have changed or increased, he and the care manager may need to readjust it.
>
> Mr O'Malley reassures his family that he would rather be at slight risk of another fall than move to a care home, away from his friends and neighbours.

Activity 9.2

Get a copy of your local community care plan (you could write to the county council or to the local social services office). Study it carefully and try to identify the following:
- The process of consultation with local people.
- Examples of use of the independent sector to provide services.

Select a particular group and look at the provision for them. What is available? Where are the gaps? What is planned for the future?

9.3   Can community care work?

Most people agree that community care is a 'good thing' and there has been a remarkable level of agreement among the politicians on this issue. There have, however, been problems with the implementation of the policy and a number of criticisms of the basic thinking and of the practice of community care have emerged.

The nature of communities

Through the development of the idea of community care there has been a continued ambiguity over the role of the 'community'. Some writers have argued that there are two different ideas : care *by* the community and care *in* the community. Government documents have varied in their emphasis. The quotation below from the 1981 White Paper *Growing Older* shows how the government of the time expected the community itself to provide care:

> Whatever level of public expenditure proves practicable, and however it is distributed, the primary sources of support and care are informal and voluntary. These spring from the personal ties of kinship, friendship and neighbourhood. They are irreplaceable. It is the role of public authorities to sustain and, where necessary, develop – but never to displace – such support and care. Care *in* the community must increasingly mean care *by* the community.[8]

Expectations of care *by* the community contain a number of assumptions. The word 'community' has itself a tendency to mislead. It a cosy, romantic sort of word: one that conjures up images of friendliness and caring. Perhaps it makes you think of villages in the countryside where everyone knows everyone else and people are constantly popping in and out of each other's houses, borrowing sugar and offering lifts to town. Or maybe of the sort of communities portrayed in television soap operas: in *East Enders* they may not always get along but people of different races and classes all mix together, spending time in the local pub, all knowing each other's business. There has been very little research carried out on modern-day communities but it seems unlikely that many of us live in the type of communities imagined above or shown in television fiction.

Activity 9.3 _____

Think about where you live. What sort of contact do you and your family have with others in the locality? What kind of favours could you ask of your neighbours, and what do you do for them? Compare your experience with those of others in the group. What factors could explain any differences and similarities?

For most people the idea of 'community' has little meaning. In an article on community care, Nigel Derricourt argues that increased social mobility has meant that people are less likely to have links with others in their immediate area. Instead people are likely to have various networks of relationships through work, hobbies and interests and family members. Some of these will be in the neighbourhood and some not.[9] Within social networks, some relationships will be more limited than others: some will be based on a particular area of life only; some will be very superficial. For many people, relationships with immediate neighbours are not close. Most of us live in 'communities of limited liability': we can ask our neighbours to feed the cat when we go on holiday or to take in a parcel, but this is just about the limit of 'community caring'. Also it is very important to note that some people will have very limited networks – if any at all – and these may well be the people with the greatest needs.

Activity 9.4

1   Make a list of all your relationships with people. Categorise these in the following way:
   - *Near/distant*, depending on the geographical distance between you – your grandmother, for example, may live far away.
   - *Strong/weak*, depending on the strength of the relationship. You probably have stronger relationships with your immediate family and a few close friends than with your neighbours.
   - *Specific/general*, depending on the nature of the relationship. You may know people through a sports club with whom you share an interest. Perhaps you could ask them favours related to this – a lift to a competition maybe – but the relationship does not extend beyond your shared interest. You may have a similar type of relationship with people at work, or work-based friendships may have developed further.

2   Attempt to draw a diagram to show your networks of relationships.

3   How effective would your support be if you or someone in your family were seriously ill or disabled and needed a lot of help? How many of these people would be able and willing to support you, and in what ways?

Of course it is true that, in some areas, a real sense of community does exist and members do support each other. This is more likely to be the case in rural areas where communities are smaller. Also the population is often more stable with families staying on the same farms for several generations although increasingly young people move away to find work and cheaper housing as richer commuters move into rural areas. Another factor which makes a difference is the number of women at home. Where women are working outside the home, it is unlikely for strong community relationships to develop. Areas with predominantly young families – such as new estates – commonly provide mutual support for parents caring for small children. The school may provide a meeting point as parents drop and pick up their children. However such communities are not necessarily willing to extend their support to others more needy and less able to offer anything in return. In fact communities such as these are more likely to oppose housing for people with learning disabilities or mental illnesses. More anonymous city areas where people are at work all day and out pursuing interests in the evenings and week-ends are also more tolerant.

Activity 9.5

Discussion question: Is community care possible in this society? To what extent are people prepared to tolerate and give to others who may be able to offer little in return and whose behaviour and appearance may be different?

The role of families

Despite romantic ideas of caring communities, research has found that most care is provided by family members, and within the family it is usually women who provide care. In 1982 the Equal Opportunities Commission stated :

> A growing body of evidence suggests that 'community care' has in reality meant care by individuals on an unpaid and often unaided basis in the home. . . They will often find themselves badly supported by statutory services and without any real choice as to whether they will care or not. Far from the community carrying the costs, the allocation of caring responsibilities has major implications in financial, social, and emotional terms for the individuals involved.[10]

The idea of the family taking a greater role in caring as the welfare state shrinks is at the centre of the Conservative Party's philosophy.

There is an assumption that family members are willing and able to care for relatives. But at the same time as the family has come under increasingly pressure to provide care, changes in both the structure of the family and the wider society have made this increasingly difficult. These changes include:

- increasing numbers of women in paid employment
- increasing trend to cohabitation instead of marriage
- higher divorce rate
- increasing re-marriage and step-parenting
- increased number of single parents
- a tendency for families to move apart in search of work
- smaller numbers of children.

Trends such as cohabitation, divorce and re-marriage may serve to weaken ties between people. Janet Finch has researched the role of the family in caring and she found that one of the things people think about is what they *ought* to do in a particular situation.[11] It may be that people are less likely to feel they ought to care for a parent who left as a result of divorce, or for a step-parent. Where people do not marry they feel not feel the same sense of obligation to their partner's parents.

Also it cannot be assumed that everyone has relatives. A significant proportion of people in residential care do not have relatives at all. There are also cases where people have no desire for contact with their relatives.

Carers

The term 'carers' did not exist in the 1980s. Now it has come to describe people who care for a relative or friend, without pay. Since the 1980s there has been a growing interest in carers – both in research and government statements. Janet Finch's research on carers found the following :

- few people care for non-relatives
- single, never-married women are the traditional carers, but there are a few of these. They do however provide a disproportionate amount of care
- men care for wives, but women care for husbands, parents, children and other relatives
- carers receive little support from other family members
- caring often dominates the carer's life.[12]

Carers face a variety of problems. All situations are different but several common themes emerge from accounts by carers. Many feel isolated and lonely. Many carers are themselves elderly or have a disability and may find the physical work involved in caring very difficult. For anyone, caring is exhausting. The hours are long and there are no week-ends or holidays. For some the personal care aspect is embarrassing and difficult – perhaps especially so if you are caring for a parent. The symptoms of Alzheimer's disease can be particularly difficult to cope with. The disease involves loss of memory, often to the point that the sufferer will not know his or her own relatives and people in the later stages of the disease are likely to develop bizarre, anti-social, and distressing habits. Spending long periods of time with someone with Alzheimer's disease tests the patience and good nature of even the most tolerant and caring nurse. Many carers feel guilty. There is the guilt of feeling sometimes cross and tired, perhaps even of wishing at times that the person would die. There is guilt if a carer feels he or she is neglecting others – especially children. Of course it is not all gloom and doom and there are many sources of satisfaction in caring, but most carers report themselves to be very tired and many experience periods of depression.

In many cases people want to care for their relatives but want some support to enable them to do so. This might include respite care which gives the carer a break for perhaps a week-end or longer, or a sitting or day-care service to allow people to shop or enjoy some time alone. A common theme in research on carers is that such help has not been available. A study sponsored by the National Institute for Social Work on people looking after a confused relative found that

45 per cent of heavily incontinent people were never visited by a community nurse and lacked other support services. They had never been offered the services. 83 per cent would have liked short-term respite care.

Activity 9.6

Imagine you are a carer. Write a letter to a newspaper describing your situation and the sort of help and support you need to receive, and how far local provision is likely to help you.

The 1990 NHS and Community Care Act makes a commitment to supporting carers and social services departments have emphasised this in their plans for community care. But the help still does not seem to be reaching the people who need it. The Carers' National Association (Carers) is a voluntary self-help group for carers. In a survey of 426 carers in touch with a voluntary organisation they found that one in four carers had not even heard of the system of community care introduced in 1993. Almost three in four of the carers had had no assessment carried out on the person they cared for. 79 per cent said the new law had made no difference to them and 8 per cent believed that services had in fact got worse.[13] Below is the 10-point plan drawn up in 1994 by a group of organisations involved in caring.

Carers' needs: a 10-point plan for carers

A group of organisations involved in caring, including Age Concern, the Alzheimer's Disease Society and the Carers' National Association have produced the following list of carers' needs

1. Recognition of their contribution and of their needs as individuals in their own right
2. Services tailored to their own individual circumstances, needs and views, through discussions at the time help is being planned
3. Services which reflect an awareness of differing racial, cultural and religious backgrounds and values, equally accessible to carers of every race and ethnic origin
4. Opportunities for a break, both for short spells (an afternoon) and for longer periods (a week or more) to relax and have time to themselves
5. Practical help to lighten the tasks of caring, including domestic help, home adaptations, incontinence services, and help with transport
6. Someone to talk to about their own emotional needs, at the outset of caring, while they are caring, and when the caring task is over
7. Information about the available benefits and services, as well as how to cope with the particular condition of the person being cared for

8. An income which covers the costs of caring and which does not preclude carers taking employment or sharing care with someone else
9. Opportunities to explore alternatives to family care, both for the immediate and long-term future
10. Services designed through consultation with carers, at all levels of policy planning.

(*King's Fund Informal Programme*)

Life in the community or life in a hospital or home?

It is not possible to make any general or conclusive statements about the best form of care. Individual needs and desires have to be taken into account and everyone's situation is different. It is also important to note that none of points made below about residential care are bound to be the case. The problems with institutions in the past could have been tackled within institutions and changes made. To some extent this has happened and much more flexible and sensitive practices have been adopted. It is also true that many of the problems of community care are not intrinsic to community care. Better resources and facilities

Source: Debbie Humphry, Photofusion
Hostels provide some support whilst allowing people to lead independent lives

could vastly improve people's lives in the community. Education could shift public attitudes.

The section below sums up this chapter by considering some of the pros and cons of residential care and community for the people most directly affected. The focus here is on people with mental illnesses : some of the points are relevant to other situations; some are not. These issues are also covered in the chapters in mental illness, disability, learning disability and old age.

If we take the situation of people with mental illnesses, it is undoubtedly true that many people were in hospital who did not need to be there. Many people stayed much longer than necessary and it became impossible for them to leave. (Nowadays this would not happen and people are treated and then leave – only returning if things get worse.) Within institutions, there is a strong tendency for the needs of the organisation to take precedence over the needs of the individual. In one large hospital in the 1970s it was the practice for everyone to be got up by the night staff who went off duty at 7.30 a.m. This meant that patients were woken around 6 a.m. The day staff would have everyone in bed before they went off duty – this was at 8.30 p.m. and patients would start going to be bed around 7 p.m. The day was built around other rigid routines with everyone having drinks, baths and meals at set times – even going to the toilet at particular times in the day. There was no choice over food and little choice over clothes for most people.[14] Institutions have a tendency to be authoritarian in these sorts of ways, minimising choice, freedom and power over one's own life. Residents feel inferior, lose confidence in their abilities and become dependent. Many of the buildings were unsuitable: too large and too old. It is probable that acts of cruelty did occur and quite commonly – either in deliberate acts of violence and deprivation or in the form of insensitivity to suffering. Residential care takes people away from the community and usual patterns of living and carries a stigma.

On the other hand the hospital is a safe environment for people in trouble. There are no responsibilites to worry about and bizarre behaviour is tolerated. The community can be a cruel place for people who do not fit it. Large psychiatric hospitals formed communities in themselves in which people with mental illnesses had a social life – visiting the cafe, attending occupational and other therapy centres, going to organised social events and outings, visiting other wards and roaming in large grounds. Many people with mental illnesses have left hospital only to be lonely and isolated in bed and breakfast accommodation with none of the social facilities they had in hospital.

Activity 9.7

Think about each of the following situations. Imagine that you are the person or that he or she is a close relative. Would community or residential care be best? In each case explain your reasons, thinking through the pros and cons of each.

- May is 80 and living alone. She has a large house which she lived in with her husband (now dead) and her family. She has become frail and cannot move about very well. She is unable to shop or cook and feels insecure – worrying that she will be burgled or robbed or worse.

- Sue is 25 and has quite severe Downs Syndrome. She has lived most of her life in institutions.
- John has schizophrenia. He is 40 and has long lost touch with his relatives. For quite long periods he feels fine. Every so often however he is tormented by voices. Sometimes the voices tell him to hurt himself.
- Balwinder is 18 and is unable to walk following a riding accident. She has been living at home but does not get on very well with her parents.
- Andrew is 50 and has multiple sclerosis. Gradually his condition has deteriorated, affecting all movements and balance. He is a widower and his daughter lives some 200 miles away. He is lonely and increasingly unable to look after himself.

__ Activity 9.8 _____

1   *Discussion question*: What is needed to make community care work?
2   Write a report setting out a strategy for a policy of community care for people with mental illnesses in your area.

__ Activity 9.9 _____

Make sure that you understand the following expressions used in this chapter. Check in the glossary on p. 363 if you need to.

Audit Commission	independent sector
care manager	informal carers
care package	institutionalisation
care plan	joint-funding
carer	learning disability
charter	respite care
cohabitation	stigma
community care	targeting
community psychiatric nurse	total institution
enabler	voluntary organisation
home carers	White Paper

Further reading

There are a number of government reports and White Papers in this area: most make for dry and difficult reading. An exception to this is the Wagner Report on residential care – its full title being *Residential Care: A positive choice* (London: HMSO, 1988). This was written to be helpful to staff working in this area and it is full of information and ideas for all types of residential care. Barbara Meredith, *The Community Care Handbook* (London: Age Concern, 1993) is a useful guide to community care for older people and includes much general information as well. A lot of useful articles are included in Joanna Bornat, Charmaine Pereira, David Pilgrim and Fiona Williams (eds) *Community Care: a reader* (London: Macmillan, 1993). Finally it should not be difficult to get local documents on community care: try the council or social services departments.

Useful addresses

Carers' National Association: 29 Chilworth Mews, London W3 3RG
tel. 0171 724 7776

King's Fund: 126 Albert Street, London NW1 7NF
tel. 0171 267 6111

⬡ 10 Children in trouble

Chapter 2 on the family has already looked at the growing problem of child abuse. This chapter focuses on procedures by which children come into the care of the local authority, perhaps because they have been abused, but also because their parents cannot look after them either temporarily or permanently, or because they have broken the law in a serious way. Child-care law is very complicated and only an indication of the main points can be given here, together with a discussion of some of the key policy issues. The chapter finishes by examining the various way in which young offenders are dealt with by the courts and social services.

10.1 The historical background

Young offenders were treated in exactly the same way as adults until the beginning of the nineteenth century and punishments for even trivial crimes tended to be very harsh. In 1838 a prison was opened to deal specially with children, so that they would not be locked up with adults. Then in 1854 Reform Schools were started as an alternative to imprisonment. Also around this time, in 1847, magistrates were allowed to deal with children for some offences instead of sending them to a trial with a jury. Over time, it became the custom for magistrates to hold separate sessions for juvenile offenders and in 1908 an Act was passed saying that such cases must be heard in separate sessions. The same Act abolished imprisonment for children under the age of 14. The 1920 Juvenile Courts (Metropolis) Act stated that only specially selected magistrates could work in the children's courts.

Children without parents or whose parents could not or would not look after them were looked after under the Poor Law in institutions or boarded out with families. In both cases life could be very hard and families usually expected a child to work hard in return for food and a roof. Charities such as Dr Barnado's also ran orphanages and boarding-out schemes. Here the treatment was usually of a higher standard. The attitude taken towards deprived children at this time was less that they needed love and a caring family, as it is now, than that they would best be helped by being offered training to enable them to find independent employment. Some charities paid fares so that older children could go out to Australia and Canada to work.

The 1933 Children and Young Persons Act gave magistrates in the juvenile courts the power to remove children believed to be in need of care and protection from their parents. They would then be looked after in foster-homes or in children's homes run under the Poor Law.

The Curtis Report on child care was published in 1945 and its recommendations became law in the 1948 Children's Act. This important Act attempted to bring together all the responsibilities for homeless children. Local authorities were to employ Children's Officers who would draw on expert knowledge and be managed by a Children's Committee of the local authority. Local authorities would receive children into care voluntarily if the parents were unfit or unable to provide adequate care. They would supervise children who were boarded-out and register adoption societies. The Children's Department would also provide magistrates with information and be responsible for children sent to remand homes, committed to the care of the local authority by the courts or sent to approved schools. The act stated that local authorities must seek to return the child home wherever possible and to try to board-out children who could not be returned home. Reception centres were to be set up to assess the child's needs on coming into care.

As mentioned in Chapter 8, the work of the Children's Officers was highly professional and set the scene for the future development of family casework in the Social Service Departments created in 1970.

10.2   Care and protection of children

In 1991, the 1989 Children Act was implemented. The Act pulled together lots of older Acts and aimed to simplify the law. Under the Act, local authorities have a duty to protect children in their area. This duty is carried out by the social workers in the social services departments. Although the law does not say how local authorities must organise their service, they are bound to provide services which prevent children from being the victims of ill-treatment or neglect. If it is suspected that a child may be in danger, the local authority is bound, under law, to investigate the situation.

The main principles of the Act are that:

- The welfare of the child must come first
- Children are best looked after by their own families and should only be removed if absolutely necessary
- Decisions must be made quickly and without the courts if possible
- Local authorities must work in partnership with children and their parents
- Parents have a right to have a say in decisions about their children
- Parents keep responsibility for their children, even if someone else is looking after them
- Families must be helped to keep in contact with their children
- Services to children and families must take account of race, religion, culture, language and any disability.

The law provides for a number of different court orders which give social workers powers to intervene in families. Cases involving children are dealt with in the Family Proceedings Court. Magistrates in these courts have special training in children's cases. The courts are more informal than others and no-one wears a wig or a gown. The public are not allowed into the Family Proceedings Court.

In a situation where social workers are concerned for the welfare of a child, they do not have to take the child into care. The social worker may feel that it is damaging for a child to be taken from his or her home. If the child is not felt to be in danger, he or she may be left at home. Social services can provide support in the home – perhaps the services of a family home help, or the support of a social worker. They can also provide money if this will help the situation. The law also provides that help – perhaps in the form of different housing – could be given to someone else in the household, for example someone who is suspected of abusing the child. But these decisions must always be made with the child's interests and safety as the main consideration.

Child assessment order

If the social workers feel that a child is at risk in their home they must investigate the situation. They must then apply for one of court orders available or decide to review the situation at a later date. There have been situations in the past where social workers have not been able to get access to examine a child they were worried about. To stop this happening again, there is now a *Child assessment order*. The court will give this order if they feel that there a suspicion of significant harm to the child, but no immediate emergency. A child assessment order lasts for 7 days. It can include the child being taken from the home for examination if this is thought to be necessary.

Emergency protection order

An *Emergency protection order* can be granted if the court feels that the child is likely to suffer significant harm if he or she is left at home or allowed to go home. It lasts for 7 days and can be extended for a further 7 days. The police have the power to remove a child straightaway, but they must then inform the local authority. This is for a period of 72 hours and the parents must be allowed to see the child.

Care order

Care orders bring the child into the care of the local authority. A care order gives parental responsibility for the child to the local authority. With a care order the child would normally be removed from home to live with foster parents or in a community home run by the local authority or a voluntary organisation. The fact that the local authority has parental responsibility does not remove responsibility from the parents (or people looking after the child). It is *prime* responsibility only that goes to the local authority. The law encourages parents to continue to be involved with the child and local authorities are expected to look for ways to share responsibility. The grounds for a care order are:

- that the child is suffering or is likely to suffer significant harm, and
- that the harm is because either,
  - (i) the care given by the parents is not what it is reasonable to expect, or
  - (ii) the child is beyond the control of the parents.

Supervision order

With a *supervision order*, the child remains at home and has a social worker whose role is to advise, help and befriend. The child and the parent must make sure the social worker is aware of any moves of house, and can meet the child. It may be that the child is required to live at a particular place or has to join in some organised activities. The grounds for a supervision order are the same as those for a care order.

Interim care order

It is also possible for an *interim care order* to be made, if the full hearing cannot take place for some reason. This lasts for up to 8 weeks but a second one can only last for 4 weeks.

Guardian ad litem

There is a system whereby an adult is appointed to represent the interests of the child in court. This person is called a *guardian ad litem*. It is the duty of the court to appoint such a person unless the court is satisfied that it is not necessary to do so. The guardian *ad litem* carries out an investigation, interviewing various people such as the child him or herself, social workers, parents and relatives. A report is then presented to the court which tries to state what actions are in the best interests of the child.

Case conferences

As was mentioned earlier, the law does not state how the social services depart-ments must act to prevent child abuse. The usual system is through multi-disci-plinary committees and case conferences. These bring together all the different people who might be involved with a particular child. Knowledge is shared and a decision made as to the best course of action. The people involved are likely to include social workers, police officers, a member of staff from the school, GPs and other health care workers such as health visitors. There may also be workers from the National Society for Prevention of Cruelty to Children (NSPCC), if they are also involved with the case.

'At risk' registers

All areas keep a register of children who have been abused or who are suspected of having been abused. This is either looked after by the local authority or by the NSPCC.

Children looked after by the local authority

It is possible for a child to be looked after by the local authority without being in care. This happens in situations where the local authority is providing a home for a child without there being a court order. Social services must provide for children who have no-one to look after them, who are lost or abandoned, or whose carer is unable – temporarily or permanently – to provide care. The child's wishes in such a situation should be considered and the parents are allowed to take the child back without any notice. The local authority have a duty to help there to be contact between the parents and the child. This can include paying the costs of visits to the child. There must also be regular reviews of the situations of all children being looked after by the local authority.

The numbers of children looked after by local authorities (previously described as being in care) have gone down through the 1980s and 1990s. In 1980, 95 300 children were in care. In 1992 the figure for children being looked after was 55 000.[1]

Practical problems

Although the 1989 Children Act has done a great deal to improve the legal situation and to extend more rights to parents and children, problems remain. The section below looks at some of problems which researches have identified.

Rochdale Area Child Protection Committee commissioned a research study to look at parental participation in case conferences. The study found that many parents left feeling confused. Reporting on the study in the *guardian*, Kathy Batt writes:

> You are sitting at a table, surrounded by a dozen people. You know the health visitor and the teacher. You recognise the social worker, just. She was the one that came to the door a fortnight ago to tell you that your child's welfare was 'causing concern'. But there are other people you have never seen before – health managers, psychologists, social service managers and a policeman. They are all there to talk about your family and to decide whether your child is 'at risk'. You are now taking part in a Child Protection Case Conference.
>
> Everyone says they 'want to work in partnership with you'. That's all right then. A partner is an equal and if you don't agree with their decision you can say so and they will have to change their mind. Won't they?
>
> Well, no. Most local authorities now invite parents to case conferences, where a skilful chairperson will ensure that the parental viewpoint is given due consideration.

But if parents disagree with the conference's recommendations, there is not a lot they can do about it. No wonder so many parents leave the conference feeling confused.[2]

The survey also found that 25 per cent of parents did not turn up. This was due to many factors. Sometimes the problems were practical, such as difficulties to do with work, child care or transport. Sometimes however it was their feelings about the system which stopped them attending. Some parents felt too angry. Others felt too much of an outsider from the powerful system that was making decisions about their lives. In other cases parents were simply terrified. Parents who did attend the meeting felt they were inadequately prepared. They did not fully understand who was who and what was going on. The majority of parents were however glad they had been able to attend, even if they left feeling somewhat angry or bewildered.[3]

Problems of liaison and co-ordination

A common theme in the reports which have been published on child abuse has, as we have seen, been the lack of communication and co-ordination between the various services involved. These can include: social services; schools; doctors; health visitors; the police; voluntary organisations; nurseries; hospitals; child guidance clinics and educational welfare officers. Many reports have recommended closer links between the various agencies. In 1991 a government document, *Working Together Under the Children Act 1989*, stated that Child Protection Committees should be organised in each area to set up, monitor and review procedures to ensure inter-agency communication. These committees have been established. However a report commissioned by the National Children's Bureau argues that these sort of strategies have a very limited effect. Setting up new structures and new committees is not an effective method of making children the primary concern. The organisations involved with children – the police, social services, the health services, etc. – have too many other issues to deal with. Children are not 'centre stage' among all the various concerns of the organisations. What is needed, the report argues, is a small team of various professionals solely concerned with children's needs.[4]

To intervene or not?

Whatever new laws are brought in, whatever procedures are set up, it seems that social workers face an impossible task in protecting children. They carry an enormous and unrealistic burden of responsibility for the safety of children. They work with the fear of public exposure hanging over them: knowing they will be damned by the press and the public if a child is hurt, but similarly damned if children are taken into care wrongly. It is not surprising that social workers cannot usually work very long in this type of work before they 'burn out'.

Research in Britain and Australia has demonstrated the impossibility of predicting which parents will hurt their children and which will not. The research shows that the families in which children die are just like any others. Yet social workers have often been trained to look for key factors which singly or in combination indicate a risk of abuse. The Australian study found that social workers were too influenced by moral standards on how families should live – focusing their attentions on families whose houses were dirty, parents whose children were not clean or well-dressed and those who had unusual life-styles. Families under investigation were more likely to be poor, headed by lone parents or Aboriginal. In Britain the emphasis was on families with a history of violence of some sort. The head of the research in Britain, Jane Gibbons, agreed that the child protection system cannot identity children at risk. She said,

> It is probably quite impossible to pick out children who are going to be killed or seriously injured. Common sense may tell us that a child living with a man with a conviction for violence is at greater risk, but we don't actually know that.[5]

A sociologist, Nigel Parton,[6] believes that child abuse demonstrates the impossible situation in which social workers are expected to work. On the one hand society expects that social workers will protect children and intervene in families. But on the other hand the family is seen as a very private area. We believe that parents should have the responsibility for bringing up their own children and no-one should interfere with this. Therefore it is only when things go wrong that social workers can legitimately intervene. By which time it may be too late and the social services department will get the blame. In other words the social worker involved with children is always treading a very fine line between interfering too much and not doing enough.

10.3   Provision for children and young people

Foster-parents

At the present time the trend is away from residential care for children, to care in the community. Two explanations for this lie in the fact that care in the community is cheaper and in the widespread belief that children benefit from a family home. Whilst there is much to be said for these points of view, there are dangers in the situation. For example, there is a tendency for residential homes to close before sufficient resources in the community have been established. Second, some disturbed children, especially adolescents, have difficulty coping with the emotional pressure of family life and benefit from the less demanding atmosphere of an institution.

The following quotations from a young person illustrate the danger of assuming that foster-parents provide the best care for all children. The first extract recalls experience of being fostered:

> The most striking feature of the boarding out was the loneliness – I was one child, a stranger with a family. The family had been going on for years and could not really be expected to adapt itself to me, and yet I was not old enough to adapt myself to people –

not really. It was rather like a tug-of-war and in turn they expected that, 'I am doing so much for you, surely I deserve something in return!' and that something in return always seemed to be far more than I could give.[7]

The same young person goes on to compare fostering and life in a children's home:

I can't think why there is so much controversy about foster-parents versus Children's Homes, institutions versus foster-parents – there is no comparison. In a Children's Home there is nothing except good behaviour demanded of a child – no loyalty and they don't have to fight their way into the circle – it is accepted on its terms. There is no fighting inside the family circle, because each child is there on its own merits. No one has more right than another, there is no feeling that you have to be loyal to the houseparent and forsake your own. It is a neutral sort of place where you can go and recover from whatever has happened to you, or get ready for the next step.[8]

Social workers spend a lot of time looking at the suitability of people to foster children in need. In spite of this, breakdowns are common. Often as described above, the foster-parents expect too much of the young person and of themselves. Fostering is a cheap way of providing care for children as the majority of foster-parents are not paid, but given an allowance towards the cost of the child. There is however a move towards paying 'professional' foster-parents, who take older and more difficult young people into their homes.

Activity 10.1

Discussion questions on fostering:
1 What are the advantages and disadvantages of foster-parents, as opposed to institutional care, for children and young people?
2 Should foster-parents be paid?
3 Should single men and women, or those who are lesbian or gay, be allowed to foster children?

Publicity has recently been given to the needs of black children in foster-care. It has been argued that children must be placed with parents of the same race and living in black communities. There are two basic reasons for this viewpoint. First, it is believed that black or mixed race children brought up by white parents in white areas will grow up confused about their identity and will tend to deny that they are black. Secondly, it is argued that black people need to grow up in black communities and to have the support of each other in order to cope with the racism they will experience in British society. In other words of John Small, assistant director of social services in Hackney:

Black and ethnic people need to develop survival skills, and this means not denying their racial origin. There are many white liberals around who don't accept that we have racial problems in Britain today.[9]

The following two cases studies illustrate the problems faced by black children raised in white foster-homes in white communities.

Harry

Harry is the illegitimate West Indian child of a brief alliance between a widow who already has six children of her own and her deceased husband's brother who is also married with six children. Harry had never been accepted by either of his parents who freely expressed their hatred of him. The situation reached a peak following the birth of the mother's latest baby while Harry was living with her. In her over-wrought condition she threatened to kill Harry and the Social Services department had no choice but to take him into care for his own safety. He was placed with the only foster-mother available. This foster-mother happens to be white and lives in an all-white neighbourhood. There are only about two or three other black children at the school Harry attends, but he shows no particular affinity with them. Harry has never expressed any desire to see any member of either side of his family and for a time called the foster-mother 'mummy'. He is very concerned about the difference in the colour of her skin and often asks why he can't be white like her. Occasionally he makes secretive attempts at whitening himself. For some time, for example, the foster-mother has been finding white powder on the bathroom floor, only to discover later that Harry was rubbing Harpic on his skin. There is no doubt that Harry has received more love from his foster-parent than he has ever received from his own parents. However, the foster-mother is worried that this may still not be sufficient to help him later in life, after he has passed the stage of childhood.[10]

Perlita

Perlita Harris went into care at birth, and was later fostered then adopted by the same couple. Her parents were Christian and specified Christian foster parents.

Her foster parents, however, are white. Perlita is Pakistani. Growing up in Gloucestershire she never saw another black face. She was the only black child in her primary school and she didn't meet an Indian until her natural father tracked her down when she was 17.

He introduced her to her Pakistani family, but her grandmother didn't speak a word of English, and Perlita spoke no Urdu.

It left her with an irreparable feeling of disorientation. She studies sociology and anthropology at university and has since chosen to live within the black community where her feminist views cause conflict with her Pakistani family, exacerbated by the cultural differences which she was totally unprepared for, and which she feels is a common experience of black children in care. 'White people see you as black, treat you as black, black people want to know why you behave so white. You're always answerable to somebody.'[11]

A problem in the past has been the lack of black people to foster black children. As a result, many local authorities have mounted special campaigns to attract black and mixed race foster parents.

Residential care

Social services provision includes small family group homes, community homes and specialised provision such as observation and assessment centres. Some homes are run privately with the aim of making a profit and some are run by charitable organisations. Social services pay to send children to these private and voluntary institutions.

Community homes vary a great deal in the sort of atmosphere and regime provided for children and young people. Homes with a high reputation often maintain this by operating a selection policy and only taking young people whom it is argued will benefit from a stay in the home. The inclusion of offenders along with other children leads to a situation where many community homes treat children as in need of treatment of some sort. There is also a tendency for people to think of children in community homes as delinquents. In the words of one young person:

> People think that if you're in care you must have done something wrong. The first question they ask is 'What did you do?' It's not just teachers and other kids at school but it's the kids and staff in children's homes. When you go to a new place, before you've got your feet in the door they say 'Hey, what are you in for?[12]

There is undoubtedly a stigma attached to being in care, no matter how good the provision is. There have been various scandals regarding children's homes. These have sometimes involved cruel and unacceptable systems of discipline and sometimes abuse of children by members of staff. There are now stricter national regulations regarding what is allowed in children's homes and more attempt is made to inform children of their rights. The following is an extract from a booklet written for children and published by the Department of Health.

> Some kinds of punishment are not allowed in children's homes. You should not be punished in any of the ways listed below:
>
> - Hit, slapped, pinched, squeezed, shaken, dealt with roughly or have things thrown at you.
> - Stopped from having food or drink.
> - Stopped from seeing your parents, family or friends, stopped from getting or sending letters or from getting or making phone calls.
> - Stopped from getting in touch with your social worker, guardian *ad litem* or solicitor.
> - Made to wear clothes that draw attention to yourself, things like punishment badges or pyjamas during the day time.
> - Stopped from having your usual medicines or from going to the doctor or dentist when you need to.
> - Given any other form of medicine, such as drugs to keep you quiet, or given medical or dental treatment when you do not need it.
> - Deliberately stopped from going to sleep.
> - Made to pay a fine (unless it is a court fine) but up to two thirds of your pocket money can be kept from you.[13]

Social services must hold review meetings to make plans for children in care. The first review must be 4 weeks after the child is placed in care, the second after 3 months and then reviews must continue every 6 months. Children do not have a right to go the review but will often be invited for some or all of the meeting. Exclusion is sometimes resented, as is shown by the view of a young person who says,

> What happens, you see, they talk about you, what you are trying to think. Well, how do they know what you are thinking if you are not there?[14]

Another issue concerned with care involves the use of secure units in residential accommodation. Authorities have had the discretion to lock up the children who commit offences or who are difficult to control, although some have rejected this approach and have no secure accommodation. Since April 1983, local authorities are no longer allowed to lock up young people for more than 72 hours without a court hearing. Under the Children Act children under the age of 13 must never be locked up in secure units in children's home unless special permission is first given by the government. In all other cases children cannot be locked up unless they have a history of running away or are likely to hurt themselves or someone else.

Leaving residential care

A major problem with care comes when young people are expected to leave and suddenly adjust to looking after themselves, having been used to living in an institution. Some local authorities attempt to help with this problem by providing rehabilitation programmes, perhaps in a self-contained flat within the home. These policies are not always successful as is demonstrated in the following example, taken from a placement report written by Heather Roberts on her experiences as a student on a Preliminary Course in Social Care. The community home had a programme to prepare young people for leaving care. In spite of this, one ex-resident had a habit of visiting the home at meal-times, obviously wanting to be fed. When the staff limited the times of the visits, other residents began to pass food out of the window to the boy. Heather identifies two reasons for the seeming failure of the home to prepare the young people for independence. The first is related to institutionalisation and the second to the often unrealistically high standards set by social services. She says:

> a person who seems unwilling to be independent at de Bouvoir House [not the real name] and so is assumed to be incapable could simply be quite prepared to let someone else do things for him while they are there to do it but is more than able to cope on his own. Added to this is the difference between the standards set at de Bouvoir House, 'ideal' standards, and those by which many of the young people will live. Ideal standards of cleanliness, tidiness and diet are actually achieved by only a minority of people – especially people living alone. So if a person doesn't seem to be up to expected standards at de Bouvoir House it could quite possibly be irrelevant as he would not live by those standards anyway.

In addition to these factors in explaining the 'failure' to achieve independence, it should be said that many young people who have left their parents' home return for food, washing of clothes, loans and other forms of support. Leaving home is rarely an abrupt cut-off from sources of help. This issue is particularly important if the situation is to be avoided where being in care is the beginning of a life in institutions. In the words of a young person with experience of care:

> For the first time in your life you are making real decisions about yourself, and as you are not used to this, it is truly survival of the fittest. It's easy to see why so many of us get into trouble with society. We can very easily become lost souls.[15]

The 1989 Children Act attempted to improve the situation for young people leaving care. When a young person of 16 or over stops being 'looked after' by the local authority, he or she is entitled to help up to the age of 21.

The social services department have a duty to befriend and advise and may provide financial or other practical help. However since the implementation of the Children Act young people leaving care are still have difficulties in making their way in the outside world. A national survey published in 1994 found the safety net for young people to be 'small and full of holes'. Problems were found in benefits, grants and training and in the social services implementation of their duty to befriend and advise. Although not all young people leaving care get into trouble, more than 40 per cent of homeless teenagers in London have been in care and many end up in trouble with the police. The report says

> Young people who have been in care are amongst the most vulnerable people in the country . . . But they need support and encouragement to achieve.[16]

The following account describes how young people's needs are not receiving the priority they require:

> Owen has spent his early years in care, experiencing that nomadic existence which sadly characterises young people caught up in the care system. He vaguely remembers eight children's homes and two sets of foster parents and now waits until he can move into independent living. But he has been failed by the education system, has a number of medical problems which have never been satisfactorily resolved because of his constant moves, and is now not regarded as a high priority by the local housing department. Despite the clear responsibilities which the 1989 Children Act puts on all the local authority departments – rather than solely upon social services departments – where Owen lives little provision is made for young people leaving care and needing accommodation.[17]

Charter of rights for young people in care

The following is a charter of rights drawn up by a group of young people in care and reproduced in the book *Who Cares?*[18] It was written before the Children

Act extended the rights of young people in care, but it is still relevant even after the implementation of the Act.

> We have drawn up this charter for 'young people' because we feel it is the responsibility of the residential worker and social worker to make sure that younger kids get a good deal.
>
> 1   The right to be accepted and treated as an individual member of society. Also the right to be treated with the same respect given to any other valid member of the human race.
> 2   The right to know who we are. To know our parents and brothers and sisters. To have factual information about our family origins and backgrounds.
> 3   The right to be able to make our own decisions and to have real influence over those decisions we are sometimes considered too thick to participate in.
> 4   The right to privacy. We understand that in care it is not always possible to choose who we are going to live and share our lives with. But we are still human beings and are still entitled to the essential amount of privacy needed before cracking up.
> 5   The right to be given an insight into the use of money by handling it, using it and paying the consequences if we misuse it, for example, being given the money in our hand to buy the clothes our clothing allowance will allow.
> 6   The right to choose those who will represent us whether it be legally or otherwise, for example, social workers. Also the right to choose who we wish to confide in.
> 7   Finally, the right to be as much a part of the society as the next person and not to be labelled in any way. In short, to live.
>
> These rights can be interpreted how you like. But don't misuse them or distort them for your own devices.

Activity 10.2

Do you agree that young people in care should have the rights listed in this charter? Are there any other rights which could be included? What specific rights should people in care have – for example, should they be allowed to attend reviews, to have visitors, to have access to contraception on the same basis as other young people?

Activity 10.3

In small groups, design a residential institution for children or young people. Think about how many residents there should be, and of what age. Consider the physical lay-out, the staffing, the rules and obligations for residents and workers. Discuss your ideas with the whole class.

Workshops on children in care

A conference was held to discuss issues relating to black children in care. Some of the participants were social workers, but the majority were young black people in care or recently out of care. Five workshops were held, producing the following resolution for the future.[19]

Workshop on culture, health, hair and skin
(a) Social workers should learn about black health and the needs of black children and young people for hair oils and skin creams in relation to hair treatment and skin care.
(b) Young black people should be educated about and tested for sickle cell anaemia.

Workshop on mixed parentage
(a) Social workers must not use the term 'half caste' and 'half breed', etc. when addressing young people from mixed parentage families. Instead the term 'mixed parentage' must be used.

Workshop on racism in the care system
(a) Disciplinary action must be taken on those social workers who make racist remarks or comments to young people.
(b) Young black people should be provided with references to their cultural history and backgrounds.
(c) Funds should be made available for young people to visit their origins.
(d) Black people should be encouraged to take residential and field social work posts.
(e) Black people should not be split up when going into care – they must be kept together.
(f) Young black people should be placed in the black community and not sent out to areas where there are no black people.

Workshop on fostering
(a) Young black people and parents must have a say as to whether they are fostered in a black or white family.
(b) At least one black person must be involved in fostering procedures when a black child is to be fostered.
(c) More foster homes should be found within the black community.

Workshop on leaving care
Young black people should be prepared for leaving care and returning to the black community, through social services ensuring that they experience their own culture in care – e.g. through weekly 'black activities' courses, positive black image books, posters, videos and cooking experiences in the home. Also encouraging contacts in the black community would help.

10.4 Treatment or punishment for young offenders?

For a long time there has been uncertainty in society and in social policy as to how best to deal with young offenders. Are young offenders to be seen as unfortunate victims of their backgrounds, needing help and support, or are they to be held responsible for their actions and punished accordingly? Social workers have tended to take the first approach – seeing the causes of crime in terms of social and emotional deprivation and offering support to young offenders. The police tend to take a more punitive approach, believing that crimes must be punished. Through punishment it is hoped that offenders will be put off from offending again. (The evidence does not, however, show this to be the case, especially when young people are sent away in detention.) The popular press and the majority of the public seems generally to line up with the view that young offenders should be severely punished for serious offences. Sometimes the motive here is a desire for revenge rather than a belief that any good will be done to the criminal.

The James Bulger Case

The tragic case of the two 11-year-old boys who, in 1993, killed the toddler James Bulger, illustrates these points very clearly. The boys, John and Robert, were brought up in an inner-city area of Liverpool characterised by poor housing and poverty. The unemployment rate in the area was twice the national average and both boys' fathers were out of work. Both John and Robert had experienced their parents' separation. Both families were poor and Robert in particular was always conscious of the pressures of poverty. Neither child was successful at school and Robert was a persistent truant. The children regularly watched horror videos.

Opinions on the case varied. The policeman who headed the investigation was not impressed by theories of the effects of inner-city deprivation. He believed the children were 'evil'. Another policeman, a religious man, said, 'you could look into the eyes of Robert and know you were looking at evil'. Others explained their behaviour in terms of the absence of an adult male role model. A psychotherapist said,

> I think it has something to do with a hatred of vulnerability and babyness in themselves which they projected onto this toddler. If, in their own lives, they have had it so extremely tough and been bullied and neglected and abused then they end up having to prove themselves to be extremely tough and invulnerable . . . In this state it is quite painful to see a normal relationship between mother and child. There is hatred and envy directed at the baby – a wish to see it suffer in the same way they have suffered. They probably weren't out to kill someone, but they were probably out to ruin someone else's happiness.[20]

The international press told the story to its fullest extent and generally the public bayed for blood. Public opinion was that the boys should be locked up for a long time and should suffer for what they had done.

Discussion questions:
1 At what age are children aware of right and wrong?
2 At what age should children be held responsible for their behaviour?
3 Are criminals born or made?
4 Do children who break the law need help or punishment?

10.5 Provision for young offenders

The various forms of provision for young offenders reflect the uncertainty which exists as to the best way to deal with juvenile crime. The idea that young and adult offenders should be dealt with separately has been accepted for some time, as has the notion of reform. However, the ways of achieving, or attempting to achieve, reform are varied and at different times, some approaches have been more popular than others. There have been a confusing number of changes in recent years to the juvenile justice system. This reflects the highly political nature of this issue. Politicians, especially from the Conservative Party, often liven up their party conferences with promises to 'crack-down on crime'. The policies which then follow are often re-hashes of previous policies. This section will describe some of the types of provision available for offenders, bearing in mind the debate between principles of punishment and treatment. As has been remarked earlier, this debate is confused and often measures which are designed to treat rather than punish may be seen as punishment by the young people concerned.

Youth custody

Criminal proceedings cannot be brought against children below the age of 10 years old. A child between 10 and 14 cannot be convicted of a crime unless it is first proved to the court that the child knew he or she was doing wrong.

A new law, the Criminal Justice Act, was passed in 1991, affecting children over 10. Children up to the age of 17 are dealt with in *youth courts* (previously known as juvenile courts and taking children up to 16). The magistrates are especially selected for these courts and must include a woman. For young people aged 10 to 15, parents must attend the court. Parents can be bound over by the court to exercise proper control over their child and their financial circumstances are looked at in making decisions about fines.

In the case of very serious crimes or, more commonly, repeated crime, young people can be sent away to a detention centre (see below). Over the last 15 years or so, there have been a series of name changes and changes in regulations regarding lengths of sentences and age limits. This section traces some of the changing ideas on youth custody.

Detention centres

Detention centres used to take young people age 14 to 21 for a short period, reduced under the 1982 Criminal Justice Act from a minimum of 3 months to a minimum of 3 weeks. Detention centres aimed to give young people a 'short, sharp shock' to deter them from committing further crimes. The regime was one of strict discipline, involving highly structured routines and physically demanding activities. A typical day involved rising at 6.30 a.m. with physical training on the parade ground, cleaning cells and dormitories, inspection, work from 8.00 a.m. to 4.30 p.m., more physical education, and in the evenings, classes in subjects like English and time for reading and writing letters.

Detention centres provided a punishing routine and it is interesting to note that when the Conservative Party sought to increase the deterrent effect of detention, most of their proposals for a hard system were already in existence. In terms of preventing crime, detention centres were not particularly successful, since many people who had been in a centre committed further crimes. The reasons for this are not fully understood and certainly not agreed by everyone working in the area of juvenile crime and justice. One possible explanation for the failure of detention centres to provide a deterrent is provided in the following quotation from an ex-inmate:

> Three months' detention was a shock. However, all of us began to adapt very quickly to this, and it was no time at all before the shock became routine frustration. Any treatment of this kind is moderately successful in breaking habits and behaviour, but in replacing the offender in his environment, with no change in him or that environment, it seems to defeat what would be the real object.[21]

In addition to this explanation of continued criminal activity which focuses on the inability of detention to change the young person or the environment, other reasons might be the way in which detention leads a young person to identify with the criminal way of life and to learn from others in this situation. Also, the chances of securing employment are reduced by a period in a detention centre.

Youth custody orders

From May 1983, magistrates were able to impose a youth custody order on boys and girls over 15 and under 21, under the Criminal Justice Act of 1982. The youth custody order replaced Borstal training. The Criminal Justice Act stated specifically that youth custody orders were only to be used as a last resort, although 6 months after the introduction of the sentence, concern was being expressed at the numbers of young people serving such sentences. This reflected a tendency for magistrates to make use of any sentence available and to fail to reserve them for use as a last resort. Most of the youth custody centres were old Borstals and there was pressure on the Home Office to establish new centres, possibly by making use of detention centres. Youth custody centres aimed to reform young people through discipline and training. The daily life was similar to that described for detention centres. Reconviction rates show that they achieved little in terms of reform. The discipline and structured life can make it more difficult for young people to cope with life outside an institution, rather than showing them a better way to live.

Young offender institutions

Following the 1988 Criminal Justice Act the terms detention centre and youth custody centre are no longer in use and the law simply refers to young offender institutions. For a young people aged 17 or under, detention may be in a secure local authority residential unit (as was the case in the boys convicted in the James Bulger case), a centre managed by the Youth Treatment Service or a young offender institution (for those over 18). Offenders aged 18–20 are sent to a young offender institution. The 1991 Criminal Justice Act again tried to ensure that young people are only sentenced to custody for very serious offences. A young person can only be put in custody if the offence will result in imprisonment for an adult and one of the following conditions apply:

- The offence is violent or sexual and only a custodial sentence will protect the public from serious harm
- The crime is so serious that an alternative cannot be justified.

The minimum period for custody is now 2 months. The idea of this is to stop the courts from using a sentences of a few weeks for less serious reasons.

Secure training orders

The 1993 Criminal Justice and Public Order Act introduced secure training orders. These are to be in units providing 'high standards of care and discipline' for 12- to 14-year-olds who are seen as persistent offenders. 'Persistent offenders' are defined as children who have been found guilty of three or more imprisonable offences or who have re-offended during a supervision order or broken the rules of a supervision order. The secure training order is for a maximum of 2 years, half of which is spent in custody and half under supervision in the community. The Act provides for five new secure training centres, each with 40 places. The institutions can be provided by public, voluntary or private organisations and the government hopes that in fact the centres will be provided by the private sector.

A study by the independent Policy Studies Institute has questioned the logic of this approach. Many imprisonable offences are in fact quite petty and the three offences could have been committed at the same time. It is not easy to decide who is a 'persistent offender' and who is not, in any way which is fair and objective. The study could not identify a group of children committing a large number of offences over a period of time. To put some children into secure units will not have a noticeable effect on crime rates. According to a report of this study in the *Guardian:*

The study paints a detailed portrait of seven frequent re-offenders, in which their lives and early backgrounds emerge as chaotic, peppered with school failure, home break-down and children's home admission. John, aged 12 at the beginning of 1992, had 15 known offences on his record for that year, including theft from shops, causing actual bodily harm and criminal damage. He was shuttled from one children's home to another, to his father, back to a children's home, then another, then to his mother and back to his father. At 13, he escaped from one home and spent three and a half months living rough on the streets. The interviewer commented: 'He looked to have the world's sadness in his eyes . . . I wish I knew what had happened to cause such pain'.

Yet most of the youngsters stressed the importance of family members, particularly mothers, in helping them break out of the cycle of offending. Placing such children in five isolated centres without regional catchment areas, up to 250 miles from their home base, is hardly designed to strengthen their perceived reliance on what remains of their fragile families.[22]

Attendance centres and orders on young people

Alternatives to sending young offenders away include making them report to *attendance centres*. These are run by the police, usually on a Saturday morning and take people aged 12–21. The sessions commonly include drill and some form of craft work. The police see themselves as impressing on people that their activities will lead them into further trouble. Since the 1982 Criminal Justice Act, *community service orders* can be made on offenders aged 16, whereas previously the age limit had been 17. Community service orders are intended to be an alternative to custody and require the offender to do a specified amount of supervised community work, such as gardening or working in an old people's home. In 1989 minimum national standards were set to, in the words of the Home Office Minister, 'toughen up' community service orders. At least 21 hours of manual work must be done and a weekly report of the work compiled. The intention of the 1991 Criminal Justice Act was to further make sure that community options for sentencing of offenders were tough and thought of as a punishment.

Supervision orders can be made on children aged 10–17. This puts the young person under the supervision of the local authority social services department or the probation office. Various requirements can be added by the court to a supervision order. These include:

- Living in local authority accommodation (a number of circumstances must apply for this be to required, more usually a young person under a supervision order would live at home)
- Living with a particular person
- Taking part in supervised activities
- Reporting to the supervisor at certain times (maybe Saturday afternoons if the offence was connected with a football match)
- A curfew, meaning that the offender must not be out at certain times in the evening or night

- Attending school or college
- Agreeing to requirements set by the supervisor, for example participating in certain activities.

Probation orders can be made on young people over 16. The involves supervision by a probation officer and again requirements may be attached to the order.

Curfew orders are for between 2 and 12 hours a day for up to 6 months. They were introduced by the 1991 Act and are to be enforced by the probation office (who are not at all keen on the idea).

Therapy schemes

Various other schemes exist for offenders and include group therapy sessions to enable people to gain insight into themselves and others, and recently-devised schemes for offenders to meet victims and make some repayment by doing tasks such as repairs.

The following report from the *Guardian* illustrates an innovative community-based scheme for children under 17 found guilty of taking and driving away cars. The treatment is designed to fit the needs of the young people.[23]

> Normally those under 17 convicted of joyriding – taking and driving away in police-speak – will be sentenced to custody, but recently the Home Office has been experimenting with alternative community-based schemes. One – the first of its type – is the Inderton Road Motor Project in Deptford, South London.
>
> At IMP ex-joyriders are encouraged to get old cars ready for banger racing. Every evening in a chilly warehouse 20 boys can be found hard at work on rusty Cortinas and Datsuns – all generously donated by a local scrap dealer. The boys (and one girl, who recently left the project) rip out seats; insulate the petrol tank to lessen the chances of explosion if the car crashes during a race; fix steel rods through the middle to act as a support in case of somersaults; and paint the exterior in jazzy designs.
>
> Everyone at IMP must attend at least two nights a week. Then, if they keep out of trouble with the police the boys are allowed to race against professionals at a local banger track.
>
> Inderton Road may not sound like punishment but, as project leader Peter West argues, 'prison does not work for joyriders. Here we actually confront the reasons why people steal cars in the first place.'
>
> The results so far support his argument. Very few attenders at IMP leave and reoffend. Mark, 21, has 'done a couple of turns in prison for driving without a licence' and says that before coming to the project he was always in trouble.
>
> Now, he believes, 'I'm on the right track.'

In some areas juvenile justice centres have been set up to provide alternatives to custody for young offenders. Essex County Council has set up a number of such centres. They describe the work of the staff in the centre as follows:[24]

> Staff within the Centres will be responsible for the provision of a range of programmes suitable for juveniles subject to Supervision Orders. Programmes will be made known to the Courts in social enquiry reports, with the agreement of the offender and the

offender's parents being sought to the recommendations made. Programmes will include intensive contact between the offender and supervising staff and introduction to additional constructive activities in order to deter further offending. For example, where an offender has broken into a house, repair of damage and apology to house occupier in certain circumstances may be the correct course to pursue. Involvement in group work to improve life and social skills, a requirement to give service to the community or the opportunity for the individual juvenile offender to consider how he or she can use their time and energy usefully may be offered. It will be expected that the offender subject to such a programme would have already been cautioned, conditionally discharged or fined and be at serious risk of removal from home to care or custody. *A wilful failure to comply with the conditions attached to a Supervision Order would result in the juvenile being brought back before the Court.*

Centre staff will keep local Courts fully informed of the range of facilities available for juvenile offenders and an annual report will be published. Local support from volunteer helpers will be encouraged and it is anticipated that measures aimed at crime prevention and deterrence will be developed.

__ **Activity 10.5** _____

What are the arguments for and against taking young offenders into custody? Make a list of points and decide what sort of approach you think is most useful.

It is difficult to reach a conclusion on the best way to deal with young offenders, since the issues are complex and the evidence conflicting. Arguments that punitive measures such as detention centres act as a deterrent and prevent crime are not valid as re-conviction rates are high. Whilst the more liberal methods of dealing with young offenders cannot be conclusively shown to be more successful, they are certainly no worse. At a purely practical level, community-based schemes are cheaper than custodial provision. There is also the argument that crime is predominantly a young person's activity which will be grown out of unless the person is locked up and begins to identify with the criminal world. It does however seem to be true that society seeks revenge for crime and wants people to be punished. This can be seen in the popular press's calls for harsher punishment and longer sentences. The balancing of these views by the government has, at times, as much to do with politics and votes, as with looking at evidence on the effectiveness of various measures and at the needs of young people.

__ **Activity 10.6** _____

Working in pairs, write a brief account of an imaginary young offender. Describe the offence, the history of offending and any punishment, and give brief details of the home environment. Pass this on for the next pair to decide what action they think the youth court should take if the person was found guilty. Use the summary of possible actions given below, some of which have been described in more detail in the preceding section.

Bind over – the person agrees, on a sum of money specified by the court, to keep the peace for a certain period. Parents can be bound over to exercise proper control.

Absolute discharge – no action at all.

Conditional discharge – if a further offence is committed within a certain period, the person may be punished for the original offence.

Deferred sentence – no action for a period of up to 6 months whereupon the person reappears in court and the decision will depend on the person's behaviour during the period of time.

Fine – if the person is under 17 the parents are ordered to pay a fine.

Compensation order – up to £1000 can be ordered to be paid to the victim.

Disqualification – young people charged with motoring offences can have their licence endorsed or be banned from driving when they reach 17.

Attendance centre (10–21 years).

Supervision order – can have conditions attached such as participation in activities or a night restriction condition, whereby the young person must remain in a certain place, usually at home, between 6 p.m. and 6 a.m. for up to 30 days. Other conditions can be made such as an order to refrain from attending football matches or to undertake particular activities devised by the local authority or probation service.

Community service orders (16 years and over).

Detention in a young offender institution (15–21).

Activity 10.7

This chapter has included a lot of terms which may be unfamiliar. Make sure that you understand the following expressions, used in this chapter. Check in the glossary on p. 363 if you need to.

at risk register	group therapy
attendance centre	guardian *ad litem*
bind over	institutionalisation
Borstal training	legal aid
care order	multi-disciplinary
care proceedings	probation officer
case conference	rehabilitation
community home	secure unit
community service order	social inquiry report
detention centre	supervision order
foster-parent	

Further reading

There are a number of guides to the 1989 Children Act available. One is Nick Allen, *Making Sense of the Children Act*, 2nd ed (London: Longman, 1992). This is detailed and covers all aspects of the Act. At a much simpler level the Department of Health have published guides written for children and young people. These are available from BAPS (see below).

Useful addresses

BAPS: Health Publication Unit, Storage and Distribution Centre, Heywood Stores, Manchester Road, Heywood, Lancashire OL10 2PZ.
Tel 01706 366287

NSPCC: 42 Curtain Road, London EC2A 3NH
Tel. 0171 825 2500
Childline: 0800 1111

National Association of Young People in Care (NAYPIC)
8A Stucley Place, London NW1 8NJ

Barnado's: Tanner Lane, Barkingside, Ilford, Essex IG6 1QG
tel. 0181 550 8822

National Children's Bureau: 8 Wakley Street, London EC1V 7QE
tel. 0171 843 6000

⬡11 Mental illness

This chapter, together with the three which follow, concentrates on the needs of a particular group of people and the welfare provision which exists to meet these needs. People suffering from mental illnesses are the subject of this chapter, while the following three look at learning disability, old age and physical disabilities. In many ways there is nothing special about the nature of the needs of these people. For example, the need to be accepted and to have a place in society are needs shared by all human beings. Similarly, everyone needs suitable housing, an income and care in times of ill-health. However, there are people for whom meeting these needs requires additional help. The problems which may be experienced by groups like those who are elderly and those with a disability are problems for the whole of society, since it is not so much old age or learning disability which is a problem, but society's attitude to people who are old or have some disability.

There are several problems in discussing this area of social need and social policy. First, there is a danger of implying neat distinctions, which do not exist in reality. For example, there are no clear-cut definitions for terms like learning disability and physical disability and categories often overlap: many elderly people also suffer from disabilities. Finally it should be emphasised that many people who are physically disabled, elderly, mentally ill or have a learning disability manage their lives without needing any special provision.

11.1   Attitudes to mental illness

There is considerable misunderstanding about mental illness. Many people have stereotyped, prejudiced or old-fashioned ideas.

Activity 11.1

Note down any thoughts which come into your head about mental illness. Start with some statements like: 'If someone is mentally ill, it means that . . .' Working in small groups, compare your ideas and feelings. Try to sort out which are true and which are not. Check out your ideas with those in the rest of this chapter. Compare them with those of anyone in the group who has had a relative or a friend suffer from a mental illness.

A survey carried out by the Department of Health found that nearly a third of the people surveyed believed it was a simple task to spot the difference between someone with a mental illness and a 'normal' person. Only 19 per cent would allow a woman who had been in a mental hospital to babysit for them. However, on the positive side, most believed that society should adopt a more positive attitude, would be happy to live next door to someone with a mental illness and backed the policy of caring for people with mental illnesses in the community.[1]

Mental illness is a complex area, difficult to define, and definitions of normal and abnormal behaviour vary over time, from society to society and in different contexts. Mental illness is much more common than people usually realise with 1 in 10 people experiencing it. In 1990–1, some 91 million working days were lost due to mental illness, compared with 800 000 days lost due to strikes.[2] Even though mental illness is so common, it carries a stigma. Glyn Jones, who suffers from depression writes,

> Depression should have a blacker name. It is a disease which shrinks the spirit and sucks the colour from life. I know because I am a depressive, now mercifully stabilised with drugs, one of the 11 million people in Britain who will experience some kind of serious mood disorder in their lifetime.
>
>   Not that it is wise – save in really enlightened circles – to admit publicly that you are a sufferer. You might become known as a bad risk. There is no limit to the social stigma. However frequently depression strikes, society still winces and walks away.[3]

Many people are reluctant to believe that a person who has been mentally ill can ever be fully recovered. The stigma is probably greatest for those who have been in hospital and to admit this can cause problems with employers, landlords and credit agencies.

Activity 11.2

Consider the following list of activities and decide if you would consider a person doing such a thing to be mentally ill.

1   Going for a walk in a thunderstorm.
2   Joining a demonstration against nuclear arms.
3   Parading London with a sign warning of the end of the world.
4   Checking the door is locked three times before leaving the house.
5   Having three baths every day.
6   Being a Communist.
7   Wearing a Nazi uniform.
8   Betting £1000 on a horse.
9   Having hair dyed pink with green stripes.
10   Living in a commune.
11   Becoming pregnant without being married.
12   Being scared of spiders.
13   Getting anxious before an examination.
14   Writing an extra statement because 13 is an unlucky number.

The line between normal and abnormal behaviour cannot be clearly drawn. Not too long ago women who had children outside marriage could end up in mental hospitals and there are still some elderly patients who entered hospital for this reason. In some countries, certain types of political behaviour have been treated as symptoms of mental illness. There is a tendency to see people who do things of which we disapprove as mad. Compulsive behaviour such as washing over and over again and checking that doors are locked is common, but can, in extreme cases become debilitating and prevent people from living a normal life. Behaviour which is considered eccentric in some people is labelled as mental illness in other contexts. For example, there is a tradition of tolerance of eccentricity amongst the very wealthy. Anxiety can be useful at times of examinations or interviews or can become a totally incapacitating condition.

Neuroses and psychoses

For purposes of definition, mental illnesses are usually divided into two categories. There are *neuroses* and *psychoses*. *Neuroses* are less serious and more common, although illnesses in this category still cause a great deal of suffering to victims and their families. Neuroses typically involve an exaggeration of usual emotions, for example, sadness becomes *depression*, which is the correct term for the illness many people call a 'nervous breakdown'. Other neuroses are *phobias* which are irrational fears as in the case of *agoraphobia* which is a fear of open spaces, and *obsessions* where actions are repeated over and over again.

Psychoses affect people's ability to think and to act in a rational way. Psychotics lose touch with reality as a result of their illness. *Schizophrenia* is a psychotic illness, although it is a descriptive term for a collection of symptoms rather than a clearly defined condition. It does not mean split personality, which is a very much less common mental illness. Schizophrenia typically involves a split between feelings and actions, and a schizophrenic may suffer from hallucinations and delusions. People who suffer from *paranoia* wrongly believe they are being persecuted. *Psychotic depression* is a more serious type of depression, totally incapacitating the sufferer who experiences feelings of self-hatred and worthlessness. *Manic depression* is an illness in which the person experiences swings of mood from elation to deep depression.

Personality disorders

A separate category covers people suffering from a *personality disorder*, sometimes described as *psychopaths*. Such conditions are more likely to be permanent and involve a lack of social development resulting in anti-social behaviour.

All the terms in the field of mental illness are used loosely and are open to dispute and disagreement. There is a tendency in some hospitals and amongst some psychiatrists for diagnoses not to be made, as the terms can become labels which lead to further suffering and perhaps to a loss of hope. For example, to be labelled a schizophrenic can have adverse consequences since there exists a false belief that such a person cannot be helped and can never again live a normal life.

Activity 11.3

Create a mental picture of a person suffering from a mental illness and describe your image of that person.

The portraits in fiction and myth of mental illness affect the way we think of psychiatric disorders. Such images include Mrs Rochester in *Jane Eyre* who was thought to be 'mad' and the scientist with the split personality in *Dr Jekyll and Mr Hyde*. The power of these images is unfortunate since they have little in common with reality and lead to unnecessary fears and misapprehensions. The following account of a person, whose illness posed no threat to others and could easily have gone unnoticed, is far more realistic.

> Take James Wilkins. Twenty-one-years old, in his final year at university. Intelligent, but not brilliant, he has to work hard to keep up with his Modern Languages course. He is not bad-looking, quiet, enjoys playing and watching football, and is also interested in politics and films. Three months before final exams, his girl-friend dropped him. His revision suffered immediately. A week later he heard that his father had to go into hospital for an exploratory operation to find out whether a tumour was cancerous or benign. His work stopped completely for a week, he went home but was urged by his parents to return to university and prepare for his finals. He tried, but was totally unable to concentrate. He got some pills from the university medical centre but by now, well into a state of anxiety and depression, he was beginning to contemplate suicide.[4]
>
> James was referred by a friend to the university counselling service which resulted in his receiving psychiatric treatment as an out-patient and deferring his examinations.

11.2 The causes of mental illness

The causes of mental illness are not fully understood and there is considerable disagreement among doctors and others on this issue.

Activity 11.4

What factors do you think may be causes of mental illness?

It is likely that any one person's illness results from a combination of factors, difficult to isolate and identify. Stress is one possible cause of illness, resulting from examinations, pressure of work or the need to appear successful or to be coping with problems. However, different people react differently in different situations and stress does not lead to breakdown in everyone. Social factors are relevant in understanding mental illness in a variety of ways. Statistics show that women are more vulnerable than men to psychiatric problems; it may be that women's lives are more stressful or it may be that it is more acceptable for women to define their feelings in terms of an illness such as depression and to seek medical help, where men perhaps turn to alcohol and express their emotions through violence rather than introverted depression. There is also a perspective which seeks to explain the higher incidence of mental illness among women and working-class people in terms of social control. Mental illness, according to this viewpoint, is a means of controlling less powerful groups in society and dealing with behaviour which does not conform.

Environmental factors such as poverty and inadequate housing may lead people to become unable to cope and cause them to sink into illness. Much of the psychology of mental illness is concerned with relating experiences in childhood to later symptoms and breakdowns.

11.3   The law and mental illness

Current mental health legislation is based on principles established by the 1957 Royal Commission on the Law relating to Mental Illness and Mental Deficiency. The recommendations of the Commission became law in the *1959 Mental Health Act*. Several important principles were established in the Act. Where possible, care was to be provided without compulsion, on a voluntary or informal basis. Admission for treatment would be on the same basis as admission for a physical illness, with no special forms to fill in and no loss of rights. In cases where compulsion was necessary, this would be at the discretion of the medical profession. Finally, tribunals were established to review medical decision-making.

The 1959 legislation remained essentially unchanged until 1982 when the Mental Health (Amendment) Act was passed. In 1983, the legislation in the 1959 and 1982 acts was brought together in a new Mental Health Act. The *1983 Mental Health Act* covers most aspects of mental health law, retaining much of the 1959 Act, but including changes fought for by pressure groups such as MIND. Like most aspects of the law, legislation concerning mental health is complex. A summary of basic points is provided here, but this does not constitute a guide to the law.[5]

Section 1 of the 1983 Mental Health Act defines mental disorder as 'mental illness' arrested or incomplete development of mind, psychopathic disorder and any other disorder or disability of mind'. The Act begins with the legal position of informal patients. In hospitals in Britain, 90 per cent of admissions are informal,[6] [6]although there is often pressure to enter hospital voluntarily, perhaps under threat of compulsory admission, so this figure is misleading. Informal patients are legally free to leave hospital and can refuse treatment in the same way as any other patients. However, 'holding powers' are available to medical practitioners in the event of a patient wishing to leave. A doctor can hold a patient for 72 hours and, where the doctor is not available, a nurse can detain a patient for 6 hours.

Part II of the Mental Health Act 1983 deals with compulsory admission to mental hospital in various categories, allowing detention for differing periods of time. Applications for admission are made by the nearest relative or a social worker approved by the local authority as being competent in working with the mentally disordered. Emergency 72-hour admissions can be made on the written recommendation of one doctor in cases of urgent necessity. Admissions for assessment for up to 28 days can be made on the recommendations of two doctors, one of which must be a doctor approved by the Secretary of State for Social Services as having special expertise in diagnosis and treatment of mental disorder. On the same basis, a patient can be detained for 6 months, renewable for a further 6 months and then for periods of 1 year at a time.

Mental Health Review Tribunals hear applications from patients concerning decisions made by medical practitioners. There is a tribunal for each Regional Health Authority. A tribunal usually has three members – a lawyer, a doctor, and a lay person experienced in administration or social services. The 1983 Act covers other areas of law such as patients' rights regarding treatment, the role of the Mental Health Act Commission in reviewing the working of the law and the position of the criminally insane.

11.4   Treatment of mental illness

Provision for people who suffer from a mental illness is the responsibility of the NHS and the local social services departments. In less serious cases, treatment has always been provided in the community, by GPs with support and help given from social workers. Hospital-based psychiatrists were also seen by out-patients. More serious cases involved hospitalisation. Unfortunately many of the psychiatric hospitals are large and old-fashioned, dating from the Victorian era when the solution to the problem of mental illness involved locking people up away from centres of population. Even in more recent times it was too easy for people to be admitted to hospital and to remain there longer than necessary, sometimes even a life-time.

For some time, it has been believed that these out-of-date buildings are not the best form of provision. Doctors and others began to be aware of the problem of institutionalisation (see chapter 9). This happens when people become dependent on the routines and structure of the hospital and get used to people doing things for them, to the extent that they are unable to cope for themselves. Institutionalisation can happen in any institution such as a prison, Borstal or hospital. Many hospitals try to overcome the situation by running rehabilitation programmes which attempt to get people to take responsibility for their lives and teach coping skills, such budgeting, and social skills. However, there remain a number of elderly people in

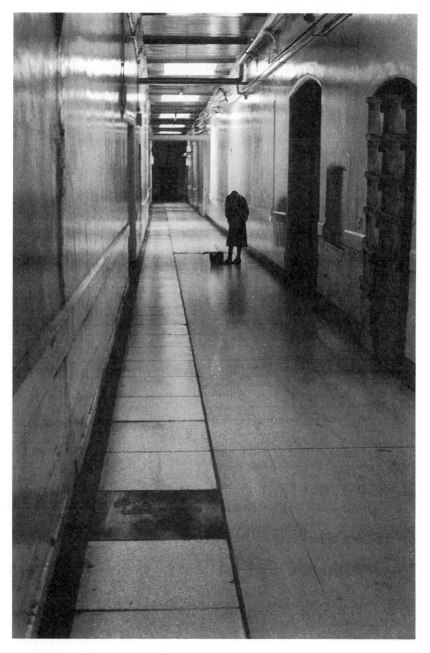

Source: Gina Glover, Photofusion
Old-fashioned psychiatric hospitals are being closed down

hospital who have been there for many years and who have no symptoms of illness but who would find it impossible to live in the community.

A government White Paper 'Better Services for the Mentally Ill', published in 1975, recommended a move towards community care and day-hospital provision. In the 1980s patients began to be moved out of the hospitals and into the community. The 1991 NHS and Community Care Act, implemented in 1993, has given further impetus to this policy (see chapter 9 for more details on this area). Where the large psychiatric hospitals have closed, new units have often opened within district general hospitals.

Services in the community

- Some areas have *mental health centres*, which act as a kind of gateway for all mental health services. These are multi-disciplinary, with a number of different workers based at the centre. These might include a psychiatrist, a psychologist, community psychiatric nurses and perhaps a social worker. In other cases, these services might be based at a hospital. The mental health centre will provide some services and treatments itself and in other cases refer people on to other services.
- *Social workers* help people with mental health problems. They can provide information and advice. They offer support for individuals and families. *Approved social workers (ASWs)* can also be involved in admitting someone to a psychiatric hospital.
- *Community psychiatric nurses (CPNs)* also provide support and counselling for people in the community. They can also administer drugs.
- There are *residential homes* and *hostels* for people with mental illnesses. These may be run by the social services department, perhaps together with the health authority, or by private or voluntary organisations. Generally the trend is towards smaller homes in which residents are involved in decision-making. Voluntary organisations such as the Richmond Fellowship run therapeutic communities providing a supportive environment, preventative care and rehabilitation for people with emotional and psychiatric problems.
- In many areas there are *day centres* and *clubs*. These provide recreational facilities and also help in training and preparation for work.
- *Counselling and psychotherapy* are available privately for those who can afford to pay and in some cases is available free through the health service or a voluntary organisation such as MIND.

Looking at the list of services described above, it appears that people with mental illnesses are well catered for in the community. Sadly, this is not the case in all areas of the country. There have been many reports on television and in the newspapers of people dumped in bed-and-breakfast or other accommodation and left pretty much to their own devices. In some cases people with mental illnesses end up in prisons. The following extracts from an article in the *Guardian* illustrate the inadequacies of care in the community for some people. The article is written by a neighbour.[7]

His name is Clifford – a huge black panther of a man – he has been my neighbour for four years now, since he was released from a mental institution under the euphemism of 'care in the community' to be housed on a large rundown South London estate.

The council gave him a flat on the top floor of my block which they probably thought would keep him out of the way.

. . .

We grew used to his ways. We had to. Several petitions were put together in the first couple of years when he continually tormented, abused and assaulted those in his immediate vicinity. But the petitions were misplaced by the housing officer. Some learnt to face up to him, others, like myself, just scattered when he came too close.

. . .

This was care in the community. Nobody came to check on him or to see he was taking his medication. No one ever contacted us, Clifford's neighbours, to explain, reassure, warn us of what to expect and how to deal with it. As far as I could see, the only care involved was that with which we, his immediate community, took to avoid him. Then the police would arrive every few months to make a forcible arrest and haul him away in a straightjacket.

Activity 11.5

What is the local availability of community provision for the mentally ill and people leaving mental hospitals?

Chapter 9 looks in more detail at the advantages and disadvantages of community care for people with mental illness.

Clinical treatment

There are several types of treatment available to the medical profession for treating mental illness. Since the illnesses are so little understood, the treatments are in a sense experimental and may or may not produce results.

Chemotherapy

Chemotherapy – or treatment with drugs – is probably the most common form of treatment. The use of psychotropic drugs, which affect emotions, began in the 1930s and expanded rapidly in the 1950s. Drugs are useful in so far as they can bring emotions to a level where problems can be tackled. The danger of drug therapy is that people can become dependent on the drugs and lose the motivation to deal with problems. The drugs may bring feelings of numbness and lack of energy, making it more difficult to take on real problems. Many drugs also have unpleasant side-effects, some of which are quite serious.

Critics of physical treatment argue that drugs are over-used in hospitals and at times are given, not to help the patient, but to enable the ward to run more smoothly. As one doctor writes:

For a time I studied the use of sedatives in a hospital practice, and discussed with the nurses the events which led up to each act of sedation. It ultimately became clear to me and to them that no matter what the rationale was, a nurse would give a sedative only at the moment when she had reached the limit of her human resources and was no longer able to stand the patient's problems without anxiety, impatience, guilt, anger or despair.[8]

It is a small step from this observation to the suggestion that it is nurses and doctors instead of patients who should take sedatives and tranquillisers!

Electro-convulsive treatment (ECT)

Shock treatment has a long history in psychiatric medicine; for example, at one time patients used to be immersed in cold water as a form of treatment for mental illness. The modern version of ECT was developed in the 1930s. ECT is used in cases of depression and schizophrenia. It involves the passing of an electric current through the brain to produce a seizure; this is done while the patient is under anaesthetic and no pain is involved. Usually the treatment will be repeated in a course of three or six 'doses'. While some people believe that ECT has no side-effects, others recognise that it can cause loss of memory and feelings of disorientation.

ECT can produce dramatic results, especially in cases of severe depression, although the explanation for such cures is unknown. It was originally thought that people who were epileptic were never also schizophrenic although this has since been disproved. ECT sometimes produces no results at all and there is a story of a hospital where the machine in use was found not to have been working for two years, and no-one had noticed. ECT is much criticised for its dubious value and punitive use but continues to be a popular form of treatment in hospitals.

Psychosurgery

This form of treatment is less popular than it used to be although it is in use. It is based on the unproven idea that certain parts of the brain are responsible for certain sorts of behaviour. These are various types of psychosurgery, also known as *lobotomy*, including removal of part of the brain, severing connections between areas of the brain, and destroying parts of the brain. Psychosurgery is not especially safe and cannot be proved to be effective.

Psychotherapy

Psychotherapy covers treatment by talking, either one-to-one with a specialist or in group discussions. The aim is to uncover reasons for illness and to get well through this new understanding. Other forms of treatment which may be available in hospitals include drama therapy and therapy through art and music. All these types of therapy aim to increase self-understanding, build up confidence and introduce the patient to new ways of releasing emotions.

Activity 11.6 _____

Imagine you have a friend who is very depressed and has been told that she must go into hospital. She is very worried about this. What could you say to her, and how could you help her?

Activity 11.7

Role-play:

The situation

A voluntary group in the town has proposed setting up a half-way house for psychiatric patients. The council is considering donating premises and social services could provide a grant for a full-time worker. There is some local opposition to the plan so a public meeting has been called to discuss the project.

The characters

1   A psychiatric hospital patient who experienced loneliness on leaving hospital and had difficulty in finding a job and a place to live.

2   A team-leader from the social services department who is prepared to give special responsibility for the residents to one of the social workers in the area team.

3   The local vicar who believes the idea should be supported in a Christian spirit of charity and community support.

4   A member of the voluntary group who believes that mental health is the responsibility of the whole community and should not be left to paid professionals only.

5   A local resident who has young children and is concerned for the safety of children in the area.

6   A Labour councillor who supports the idea and believes the council could easily allocate a house bought for a redevelopment scheme which was abandoned.

7   A local resident with experience of voluntary work in a psychiatric hospital who believes that the fears of local people are based on mis-understandings about the nature of mental illness.

8   A local resident concerned about the reputation of the area and fearful that house prices will fall if the scheme goes ahead.

9   The headmaster of a private school near to the house which is rumoured to be a possible home for the project, who believes that the safety of the children means that the half-way home should be located elsewhere.

10   A psychiatrist at the local hospital who believes that people who are mentally ill need professional help from trained people and that the volunteers, whilst well-meaning, are naive in thinking such a project is feasible.

11   A conservative councillor who sees health as the concern of the NHS and is anxious about the costs to the council.

12   An elderly local resident suspicious about the sort of people who will live in the home and fearful of an increase in violence and crime in the area.

Activity 11.8

Make sure that you understand the following expressions, used in this chapter. Check in the glossary on p. 363 if you need to.

approved social worker	community care
day hospital	depression
district general hospital	ECT
half-way hostel	informal patient
institutionalisation	learning disability
lobotomy	manic depression
multi-disciplinary	neurosis
obsession	paranoia
phobia	pressure group
psychiatric social worker	psychiatrist
psychopath	psychosis
psychosurgery	psychotherapy
psychotropic drug	senile dementia
stigma	tranquillisers
tribunal	voluntary organisation

Further reading

Sally Burningham, *Not on Your Own: The MIND Guide to Mental Health* is written by Sally Burningham (London: Penguin, 1989). It provides a clear and straightforward explanation of the various conditions. It also lists sources of help and gives practical advice on coping with mental illness. MIND also produce leaflets on most aspects of mental health. These are available from MIND (see below). The Department of Health also have a free booklet – available from BAPS.

Useful addresses

MIND: Granta House, 15–19 Broadway, Stratford,
London E15 4B4
tel. 0181 5192122

BAPS: Health Publications Unit, Storage and Distribution Centre, Heywood Stores, Manchester Road, Heywood, Lancs OL10 2PZ
tel. 01706 366287

The Richmond Fellowship: 8 Addison Road, London W14 8DL
tel. 0171 603 6373

Mental Health Foundation: 37 Mortimer Street, London W1N 6DH
tel. 0171 580 0145

⬡12 Learning disability

'Learning disability' has replaced the older term 'mental handicap'. This chapter will in most cases use the new and preferred term. (See chapter 1 for a discussion of the importance of language.) However there are points at which the old term will appear – where there is a reference to provision in the past, or where quotations date from earlier years.

12.1 Defining 'learning disability'

What does the term 'learning disability' mean? Mencap – the organisation which works for people with learning disabilities – uses the following definition.

> Someone is described as having a learning disability if they have considerably more difficulty in understanding and managing their day-to-day lives than other people of the same age, and their social skills are also deficient. In general, someone with a learning disability will not learn as quickly as other children, and will not attain the full intellectual capacities normally associated with an adult.[1]

Mencap go on to stress however that all people are individuals and the use of a category such as 'learning disability' should not lead us to lose sight of people's individuality. People with a learning disability need to be seen as people first. They should not be defined purely in terms of their disability.

More than 1 million people in the UK have some form of learning disability. The degree of disability varies widely from a person who lives a normal life but is perhaps regarded as not very bright, to someone who needs a great deal of care and cannot cope with simple tasks such as dressing. There are 190 000 people in the UK with severe learning disabilities. Learning disabilities cannot be cured but care and education can do a great deal to allow a person with a learning disability to reach his or her full potential.[2]

There is no single cause of learning disability. In many cases people are born with their disability, although it can result from a severe injury affecting the brain or from certain infections. Not all the causes of learning disability are known, although the most common condition, Down's Syndrome, is known to be genetically caused. While the risks of a child being born with a learning disability increase if the mother is over 40 at the time of the birth, anyone can have a child with a learning disability.

Many people with learning disability are quite capable of coping with life in society and their problems are sometimes solely related to the reactions of other people. Here a man tells of his longing to be treated as a normal person:

> I don't see why people don't treat me as a normal person instead of some kind of – well, you know, some kind of crazy person. I try so hard to act like a normal person.[3]

In the following quotation, the writer explains that people with a learning disability may lack skills in communication but that this is not a one-sided problem:

> You [the one non-disabled person] will be embarrassed, you won't be able to think of anything to say, you will tend to talk in an inappropriate tone of voice, you will tend to have a wide grin on your face and ask questions without being really interested in the answers. The handicap is thus a mutual one.

However there is a difference in the position of the two people, both unskilled in communicating with each other:

> The trouble is that you have lots of opportunity to go off and form relationships more easily. We don't. You can deny your handicap. We can't – we live with it all the time.[4]

There is a tendency in our society for anything which is different to be seen in a negative way, as something to be avoided and feared.

Many people with a learning disability look after themselves or are cared for by relatives. This can put strain on a family and such families need support and help in coping.

Activity 12.1

Imagine you are a child and you have a brother or sister who has a learning disability. Write about your life.

12.2   Provision for people with a learning disability

'Mental handicap hospitals'

As was stated at the beginning of the chapter, 'mental handicap' is now an old-fashioned and unacceptable term. The old institutions in which many people with a learning disability lived were however known as 'mental handicap hospitals' – so this term will be used in talking about these institutions.

In 1993 some 21 000 people lived in mental handicap hospitals – half the number of 20 years ago, but still a lot of people.[5]

Some of these hospitals provide a high level of care but problems of finance, shortage of staff, and general lack of interest in the needs of handicapped people have led to a number of scandals being reported.

In 1967, allegations of ill-treatment led to an enquiry at Ely Hospital in Cardiff. The report found some incidence of ill-treatment and much to criticise in terms of standards of facilities and care. As a result the Hospital Advisory Service was set up in 1969 to visit hospitals, assess facilities and make constructive criticisms. Pressure continued for a reappraisal of the policy for people with a learning disability in hospitals, and in 1971 a government White Paper 'Better Services for the Mentally Handicapped' expressed a commitment to community care. However, it is not possible simply to close hospitals without the establishment of alternative forms of care and support.

In 1978 the Committee of Inquiry in Normansfield Hospital found the physical environment unsatisfactory, the standard of nursing poor and a lack of clothing and facilities for patients. The Jay Committee, set up by the DHSS, reported in 1979 and recommended that nursing staff be replaced by holders of a new social work qualification, staff numbers be doubled and hospitals be replaced by homes. In the financial climate of the time with cuts in spending and learning disability not treated as a priority need, these proposals were unrealistic. In 1975, a Development Team for Mentally Handicapped had been established. The team carried out a survey of 50 hospitals and 30 homes between 1976 and 1982. The confidential findings were printed in the *Guardian* in July 1983,[6] and revealed that previous inquiries and reports had resulted in a deterioration of staff morale but little improvement in services.

Problems with institutional provision

There are many problems in hospital provision for people with a learning disability. Typically, the hospitals are large, old, and located away from towns and cities. Learning disability has low status in medicine, since the medical profession is geared towards the idea of cure and is frustrated by conditions for which there is no cure. Hospital life has a tendency to take away individuality – in the opinion of the resident quoted here this was the worst kind of deprivation:

> The real pain came from always being in a group. I was never a person. I was part of a group to eat, sleep and everything. As a kid I couldn't figure out who I was. I was part of a group. It was sad.[7]

Lack of privacy and forced group life make it very difficult for people to form relationships. There is a theory which suggests that humans need a territory of their own and without this people are too insecure to be able to relate to others.[8] It is certainly true that a large number of people in institutions are socially isolated despite the fact that they are constantly surrounded by others. Another basic need, the need for sexual relationships is denied by hospitals. This does not mean that sexual liaisons do not occur –

'us never got caught once' remembers one woman who has since married the man she met in an institution, 'we used to get out night times in the wood, and then if we heard someone coming, I'd run one way and he'd go over the hedge'.[9]

In hospitals there is a tendency for routines to dominate the lives of the staff and the patients. A nurse describes how the residents in the hospital where he worked always had to get up at 7 a.m. and follow a strict routine and order of events. The nurse says:

> Imagine a 'normal' person at home being told that for the next thirty years he must get up at seven o'clock sharp every single day . . . The prospect of a patient ever being allowed the privilege of staying in bed until eight or even nine o'clock and still getting his breakfast when he wakes up is a remote dream.[10]

The rationale for the strict following of routines is in terms of the shift system, the argument that any variation would create more work, and of course the idea that things must be the way they always have been.

The shift system, unavoidable in hospitals, can also create problems where shifts are rigidly separated and operate in quite different ways. It is astonishing at times how well patients cope with such confusing aspects of hospital life. In institutions, the standards of behaviour expected are often higher than those met by people living at home. There is further a tendency for all behaviour to be monitored and analysed in terms of symptoms. The nurse already quoted tells how he observed that ordinary people could make mistakes or be clumsy, but similar behaviour in patients would lead to criticism or punishment. Similarly, the same behaviour could be classified as normal or abnormal, depending on who was doing it:

> Some of the lads spend hours on end twirling pieces of string and gaining enormous pleasure from this. It is classified as 'self-stimulating' behaviour and considered to be a characteristic of the severely subnormal. The staff also twirl pieces of string. But this is considered normal because there's a key on the end of it.[11]

In many hospitals needs like food and clothing are met in the most basic way. Food is often served lukewarm and may have been spoiled in the course of the journey from the kitchen to the ward. Many hospitals do not use clothes which are individually owned by the patients but which form the ward stock of clothing. Such clothes are frequently washed and become shrunk and soiled. Staff who are overworked fail to ensure that clothing fits and looks presentable. In the following extract the patient is allowed no say in what he wears:

> 'This'll do. He'll never know the difference.'
> A coat covered in stains with no buttons. The coat in question would fit someone a foot taller and several stone heavier. Simon looks a terrible sight.
> 'I'd like one with buttons,' he said.
> 'We've got no time to sort out one specially for you. Take this one.'
> 'It's too big.'
> 'Never mind that. It'll keep you warm.'[12]

As in psychiatric hospitals, drugs may be given to patients not for their benefit but to keep them quiet and facilitate the smooth running of the ward.

This description of life in mental handicap hospitals has focused on the worst aspects and obviously there are some hospitals where standards are very high. However, those staff who are committed to helping people to get the most out of life are battling against problems of lack of funds, inappropriate buildings and staff shortages. In these conditions it is easy for staff to become demoralised and begin to treat residents cruelly, providing for physical existence but failing to treat people as human beings with rights. As the numbers of people in hospitals have been reduced, improvements have been made and staff are now rather more aware of the need to preserve individuality and self-determination. But there will always be a tendency within an institution for the needs of the institution to become dominant over the needs of individuals.

Community care

For some time now community care has been the accepted official policy for people with a learning disability. The 1971 White Paper 'Better Services for the Mentally Handicapped' emphasised the importance of community care and set a programme for the next 20 years. This programme turned out to be rather optimistic and initiatives in the community were slower to develop than was anticipated. (See chapter 9 for more details on the development of community care.) Other government documents followed but the real impetus for community care came with the Griffiths report in 1988 and the resulting White Paper 'Caring for People'. This became law in the 1990 NHS and Community Care Act, implemented in April 1993. (see also chapter 9).

The 1990 Act makes local authorities responsible for assessment and provision of care in the community. Where someone needs a lot of help to live in the community a care manager will be appointed to put together a mix of services providing support and care. These services will be organised into a care plan and will be monitored and reviewed by the care manager. It is government policy that increasingly the services should be provided by the independent sector – private and voluntary organisations – rather than by social services themselves.

The following extract is a case described by Mencap to illustrate how families can use the assessment provision of the 1990 Act to obtain an assessment covering all aspects of need.[13]

M is a young man who is described as severely mentally handicapped. He has a diagnosis of autism and attended special schools for many years. When he was 15 he was diagnosed as suffering from a psychiatric breakdown and was admitted to hospital. He was prescribed anti-psychotic medicine and spent several periods in hospital as an inpatient. A residential placement was secured for him which was funded by the Local Authority. He has continued to live in community care placements for the last 10 years. He is now 25 years old. M's parents are concerned that his medical needs have been poorly managed over the last 10 years and that he has now become extremely dependent on his anti-psychotic medicine which is beginning to show quite serious side-effects. They have asked the Local Authority responsible for his care to conduct a full assessment to include education, housing, medical and social needs. They are unhappy that their son's needs have not been addressed in previous assessments. They are planning to go to his next review meeting with a request that all aspects of his care be assessed. They have also asked the Local Authority to liaise with the health and housing authorities, to consider a more appropriate placement for him. In their view his current community placement is one of containment not of care. The medical aspects of his programme are minimal. They are concerned that his behaviour needs are not being treated but are simply being suppressed by medication. They are now looking to the NHS and Community Care Act to get a comprehensive assessment with targeted services for their son's needs.

Education and housing

Since 1971, education authorities have been obliged to provide education for all children. Many children with learning disabilities are educated in special schools by teachers trained in meeting special needs. The emphasis in these schools is on teaching children to communicate, to develop social skills and to learn how to survive and function in society. The merits and dangers of special education are discussed in chapter 7. Some colleges offer further education for people with a learning disability, although there is a need for expansion of such provision.

Social education centres (previously known as adult training centres and orig- inally based around work activities) are increasingly focused on helping people with a learning disability find supported employment, training and educational

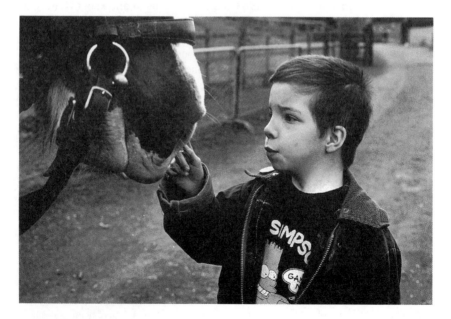

Source: Helen Stone, Photofusion
Children with learning disabilities benefit from leisure activities

opportunities. This is done by sharing courses outside the main centre with non-disabled people. Centres usually provide recreational and skill programmes and may have care facilities for people with severe learning disabilities.

Social clubs are provided sometimes by social services and sometimes by voluntary organisations. Some integrate people with a learning disability and others. An example of this approach is the Gateway clubs.

There are various types of *residential accommodation*. Many areas have hostels which provide a sheltered environment but allow a considerable measure of self-determination and do not segregate people with a learning disability from the rest of society. Many small residential care homes are privately run and cannot be distinguished from ordinary houses. Some 35 000 people live in residential homes run by the NHS, local authorities, voluntary bodies or private home owners. However the majority of adults and nearly all children with a learning disability live with their parents.[14] For people living at home respite care is available. This involves a temporary stay in a residential home either in an emergency or on a planned basis. There are also in many areas schemes for lodgings or placements with families. Landlords or landladies are especially selected and supported in providing a home for a person with a learning disability. Family placements are more commonly for children and involve a child being placed with another family for an agreed number of days each year. This scheme, as with respite care, allows carers a break.

There are employment schemes providing work in sheltered workshops and in sheltered placements in ordinary workplaces. These may be organised by a voluntary organisation such as Mencap and are supported through government schemes (some of which are described in chapter 4). The disability working allowance is a means-tested benefit to help disabled people in work.

12.3 Advocacy

A relatively new concept in this country is *advocacy*. Advocacy simply means someone speaking up for someone's needs. The term is used in a number of different ways. Citizen advocates are independent people who speak up for someone unable to do so for themselves, staff advocates defend the interests of people they are paid to look after; legal advocates are lawyers. Self-advocacy can mean people speaking up for themselves – perhaps with support and preparation in a self-advocacy group – but is also used when people with a disability speak up for another person with a disability.

In the following quotations, some people with learning disabilities write about what self-advocacy means to them.[15]

To me, self-advocacy means that I can speak out for myself and tell other people to speak out for themselves. It means to help them to speak out to better themselves in the world. Part of it is to get other people to listen to us, to see what we want.

To me, self-advocacy means learning to speak out for what you believe in and having a good life. Since I got involved an awful lot of good has happened inside of me. I've gotten better at helping other people by listening to their problems, and I'm better at listening to people to get advice from them. I'm also better at speaking up for myself.

To me, self-advocacy is getting out, getting everything going and getting things done. It's helping out other people. I like to help the handicapped who can't do as much for themselves. Now I'm better at speaking up for other people. If I see someone being mean to a handicapped person, I jump in and say: 'Hey! If you don't know how to treat him, leave him alone and find someone who does!' I believe everyone should have their rights, and they should get out and do it for themselves. If they can't do it for themselves, they can try to learn.

Activity 12.2

Make sure you understand the following expressions used in this chapter. Check the glossary on p. 363 if you need to.

advocacy	learning disability
care manager	respite care
care plan	sheltered workshop
community care	social education centre
further education	special school
independent sector	voluntary organisation

Further reading

Mencap is the best source of information on learning disabilities (see below). They have a number of useful publications of their own and can supply others from their bookshop.

Useful address

Mencap: Mencap National Centre, 123 Golden Lane, London EC1Y ORT
tel. 0171 454 0454

⬡13 Old age

The chapter on elderly people in Muriel Brown's *Introduction to Social Administration in Britain* begins with the statement, 'Simply to grow old is not in itself a problem'.[1] Ageing is a natural process which happens to everyone. It brings needs and it is the failure of society to recognise and meet these needs adequately which causes problems for older people. As a group, elderly people have limited political power, they are not organised and cannot go on strike for better pensions. Pressure groups such as Age Concern are active in campaigning on behalf of the elderly, but to a large extent, meeting needs relies on the good-will and commitment of society.

In this chapter, the terms 'older' and 'elderly' are used synonymously to refer to people over retirement age. Whilst there is a tendency for these terms to carry negative connotations, this is not the intention in this context. This section first examines population trends with regard to age and then looks at feelings and needs of elderly people in relation to poverty, housing, health and segregation from the rest of the community.

13.1 Population trends

Statistics on population show there to be an increase in the number of elderly people. In Britain, the 1901 census showed there to be 1.7 million people over the age of 65, whilst the 1991 census counted almost 10 million.[2] This increase is not simply an increase in the population as a whole, but represents an increase in the proportion of elderly people in relation to the rest of society. In 1901, 5 per cent of the population were aged 65 or over, compared with 18 per cent in 1991 and a predicted 26 per cent by 2031.[3] A distinction is often made between 'young elderly' people aged 65–74 and 'old elderly' people aged 74 plus. This is partly because the needs and situations of the two groups can be very different but also because the statistics show a significant trend towards a higher proportion of 'old elderly' in the elderly population. Figure 13.1 and Table 13.1 show the details.[4]

Whilst the figures showing the increase in the number of elderly people are in one sense a cause for celebration, the lack of provision for the elderly means that they are also a cause for concern.

Activity 13.1

Why do you think a greater number of people are living longer?

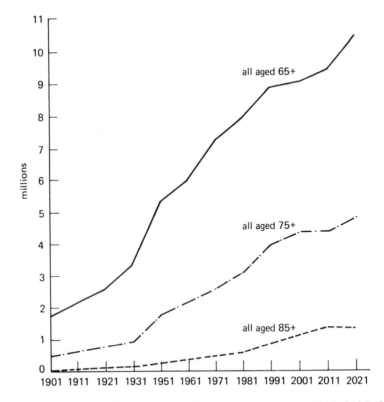

Source: Population projections by the Government Actuary, 1985–2025, OPCS
PP2, 15 (London: HMSO, 1988, © Crown copyright).

Figure 13.1   The elderly population Great Britain, 1901–2021

TABLE 13.1   The elderly population, Great Britain, 1901–2025 (000)

	65+	%	75+	%	85+	%
	Historical trends 1901–1981					
1901	1734	4.7	507	1.4	57	0.15
1931	3316	7.4	920	2.1	108	0.24
1951	5332	10.9	1731	3.5	218	0.45
1961	6046	11.8	2167	4.2	329	0.64
1971	7140	13.2	2536	4.7	462	0.86
1981	7985	15.0	3053	5.7	552	1.03
	Projections (1985 based)					
1985	8371	15.2	3544	6.4	671	1.22
1991	8847	15.8	3925	7.0	865	1.55
2001	8995	15.7	4320	7.5	1146	2.00
2011	9404	16.3	4374	7.6	1301	2.30
2021	10 562	18.2	4678	8.0	1300	2.23
2025	11 013	18.9	5177	8.9	1331	2.28

Sources: 1901–81 Census data OPCS, Population projections by the Government
Actuary 1985–2025 PP2, 15 (London: HMSO, 1988)

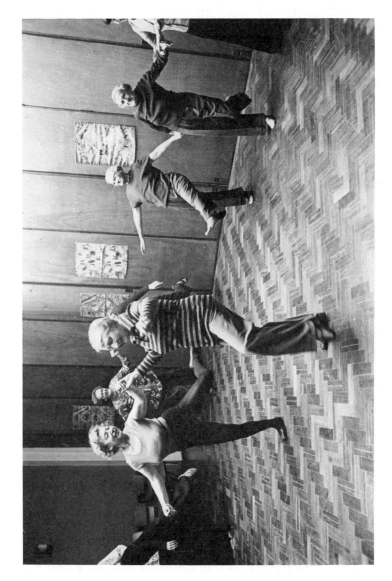

Growing old and staying fit

There have been two basic reasons for increased life expectancy since the beginning of the century. The first and most important has been improvements in general living standards: less poverty leading, in particular, to better housing and better nutrition. This has meant that very many more people live to retirement age and beyond. Secondly there have been improvements in medical science, the availability of medical provision and in welfare. This means that some health problems can be cured and that elderly people are better cared for than previously.

Activity 13.2

What problems with health, housing, etc. can occur when people get older?

13.2   Attitudes to old age

Some of the problems associated with old age are practical in nature, relating to increase frailty. There are also emotional difficulties in coming to terms with various kinds of change. Finally attitudes towards the elderly can cause problems which are not found in societies in which the elderly occupy a position of prestige and power.

This society is not one in which the experience of older people is respected and their continued contribution to society encouraged, although there are exceptions to this idea – for example, judges and politicians are predominantly older people. However, most people do not look forward to old age and the images held of the elderly are rarely attractive ones. With a few exceptions, such as the Queen Mother, images of elderly people in the media tend to focus on negative characteristics such as vulnerability, for example, in showing people as victims of crimes.

The psychological problems of growing older include adjusting to retirement which, as well as involving a reduction in income, may require getting used to loss of status, and to living an active life without the structure and routines of the working week. There are courses designed to help people to prepare for retirement, sometimes provided by companies and sometimes by colleges of further education. Many older women have given over their lives to child-rearing and it may be equally hard to adjust to the loss of this role. There are no courses laid on to help women deal with the 'empty nest' syndrome, equivalent to those provided for people leaving paid employment.

Some older people find it difficult to keep up with the rapid process of change which is a characteristic of modern society. In addition, old age may be a time of loneliness and bereavement as brothers, sisters, wives and husbands are lost. A person who lives to be 80 will probably experience the loss of a number of relatives and friends. These emotional challenges have to be met in a context of increasing practical difficulties.

13.3   Elderly people and poverty

Several studies have found a high proportion of elderly people live in poverty.[5] In May 1993 1 736 000 people aged 60 or over were receiving income support because of their low incomes. The Department of Social Security has estimated that between 22 per cent and 33 per cent of older people eligible for income support do not claim it. Older people spend a higher proportion of their income on housing, fuel and food (basic necessities) than do others in the community.[6]

Pension benefits

Women are particularly vulnerable to poverty in old age. The basic reason for poverty among elderly people is that almost universal compulsory retirement prevents people from working and an adequate replacement for earnings is not provided. The reasons for the number of people living below the poverty line include the fact that many people are unaware of benefits they could claim and others are reluctant to claim their rights since they feel benefits are a form of charity.

The provision of pensions is complex and only a brief summary of the main points can be given here. Women over 60 and men over 65 who have stopped work and paid sufficient contributions are entitled to receive a national insurance pension. (Legislation has been introduced to equalise the age limits for men and women; this will affect women retiring in 2010 who will no longer receive a pension at age 60.) In the year beginning April 1994, the rates were £57.60 for a single pensioner and £92.10 for a couple (claiming on the husband's contributions). People who live on the national insurance pension alone are likely to fall below the poverty line. In this case income support can be claimed.

Some people receive a second pension because they have paid into an occupational pension scheme whilst in work. Between 1961 and 1975 the national insurance contribution included a graduated scheme and people who paid into this receive an extra sum of money. The amount payable is small and often occupational pensions are relatively small. In 1975, the government produced a White Paper called 'Better Pensions'. This introduced a new pensions scheme which began in 1978 and will be fully in operation in 1998. The new government pensions scheme was for people who are not already adequately provided for by an occupational scheme. These people pay extra national insurance contributions and receive a second pension at a rate determined by their contributions. The amount is based on the best 20 years of the person's working life. This will involve an improvement in the position of women since the new scheme recognises that many women leave work for a period to care for young children and does not penalise them for this.

Whilst this system will be an improvement in the financial situation of the elderly, the problem of people who are now retired remains, and there will always be people who are excluded from any scheme based on employment, because for one reason or another, they have not paid sufficient contributions.

Activity 13.3 _____

Are the financial needs of older people likely to be greater or less than those of the rest of the community? Why is this?

Living costs

Comparative financial needs cannot be evaluated in any definitive sense. Whilst elderly people are less likely to have dependants and those who are home-owners may have paid off their mortgage, full employment of the leisure time provided by retirement requires adequate income. Fuel costs can be a major problem for the elderly. Costs have risen sharply in recent years and the elderly are more inclined to feel the cold than young people. Old houses are also often hard to heat. Hypothermia is a serious problem, particularly in a severe winter.[7]

13.4 Housing

The majority of old people live at home. However, many live in unsuitable housing which is too large for their needs and not adapted to take account of increasing infirmity. Gardens can become a worry instead of a pleasure if the owner is no longer able to work in a garden and has no source of help. Old people tend to live in older properties which are hard to heat and difficult to maintain. Townsend found that, particularly in the case of the older elderly, many lived in housing lacking basic amenities.[8] A government survey on housing revealed the following:

- 473 000 (43 per cent) of all unfit properties were occupied by elderly households.
- 500 500 (55 per cent) of all properties lacking amenities were occupied by elderly households.
- 223 000 (47 per cent) of unfit properties and those in serious disrepair were occupied by elderly households.
- 283 000 (27 per cent) of all properties requiring at least £7000 of repairs were occupied by elderly households.

  More recent figures do not reveal any significant improvements to the situation.[9]

Social services provision of care

About a third of people over 65 and a greater proportion of women and people over 75 live alone.[10] This can lead to problems of isolation, loneliness and practical difficulties when people are unable to manage for themselves because of ill-health or infirmity. Social isolation is greater in redeveloped areas where communities do not exist to provide support.

Most older people living at home do not require or receive any special services. Provision varies from area to area and may include some or all of the services described below. Care in the community is the responsibility of the local authority social services (as has been explained in chapter 9). Under the 1990 NHS and Community Care Act it is expected that services will be increasingly provided by the independent sector – private and voluntary organisations – rather than by social services. Social services are however responsible for monitoring service provision.

In 1985 7 per cent of those aged over 65 were receiving home help services.[11] Since that time there have been changes in the home help service. Most people are now expected to pay for the service and the emphasis has shifted from help with housework to personal care. The old home help service was a particularly popular service, providing company as well as practical help and many people have regretted the changes, which have been motivated by increasing costs and demands for savings in public expenditure. In 1985 3 per cent of people over 65 received home meals. The meals-on-wheels service may be provided by the local authority or by a voluntary group. This is a good example of a service initially provided on a voluntary basis and then taken over by social services, or run jointly by social services and volunteers. Day centres provide company and help for those who do not require residential accommodation or for whom no accommodation is available. Some local authorities offer holidays for the elderly which provide a valuable break for both the older people and the caring relatives. Social workers and health visitors are involved in the support of the elderly in the community, although both have many other demands on their time. Other forms of provision include luncheon clubs which offer company and a mid-day meal, voluntary visiting services, laundry facilities, social clubs and home nursing.

When older people do need help to remain at home, most of the help they receive is provided by their family, neighbours and friends. Many carers are husbands or wives, but there are also children who look after their parents. As was discussed in chapter 9, in this case carers are most likely to be women. Many carers are themselves elderly. In 1990, 28 per cent of carers who devoted over 20 hours a week to caring were over 65 themselves.[12]

Sheltered or residential accommodation

Some elderly people move into sheltered accommodation. This enables people to live independently, usually in a flat, with the security of a warden on hand if needed and without the whole responsibility of upkeep and maintenance of a house. There is some local authority sheltered accommodation but not enough to meet the need. Some sheltered accommodation is provided by voluntary organisations such as housing associations and there was a boom in the building of private sheltered accommodation for sale in the late 1980s.

  ___ **Activity 13.4** _____

  Is there sheltered accommodation locally? Who is it provided by? What
  services are offered? What are the costs to residents?

A minority of older people – about 250 000 in 1994 – live in residential homes.
These can be provided by local authorities, voluntary organisations or privately.
Table 13.2 shows numbers and the trend for the years 1979 and 1985.[13] The
increase was partly due to the fact that income support was available to pay for
fees of residential and nursing care but money to pay for care at home was not
easily available. This situation was however changed as a result of the NHS and
Community Care Act and it can be expected that future trends will also change.
More people should be able to receive care services in their own homes.

Standards in elderly persons' homes vary considerably, but many are old, too
large and unable to offer a sufficient degree of privacy. It is common for people
to have to share rooms. There is also a tendency for life to become routine and
lacking in stimulation and for residents to become institutionalised. Social services are responsible for inspecting all residential homes for elderly people. In
the past they also provided homes, but this is now discouraged by the government. Social services are encouraged to take the role of purchaser of services
from others, no longer as provider. The social service inspection units are
expected to work at 'arm's length' from the provider of the services, in this case
residential home owners.

**TABLE 13.2   Residential places for elderly and younger disabled persons,
England, 1979 and 1986**

	1979	*1986*	*% Change*
Local Authority	113 564	115 609	+1.8
Voluntary	33 898	36 000	+6.2
Private	31 999	92 605	+189.4

  ___ **Activity 13.5** _____

  Draw up a design for an ideal development for elderly people and decide
  how the accommodation will be managed. Include ideas about the admission policy for the housing.

The shrinking family

Some 12 per cent of old people live without a spouse in the homes of relatives.[14]
This is not always a happy situation either for the elderly person or for the rela-

tives. Changes in society have made it more difficult for relatives to provide care, although the trend towards community care, examined in chapter 9, is increasing expectations that families will care for elderly relatives.

Activity 13.6

What changes in society may mean that people are now less able to provide care for elderly relatives?

Several social and economic changes have reduced the abilities of families to provide care. Families are smaller than they used to be, so there are fewer relatives to help out in time of need. Changes in the position of women – for example, in employment – mean that many women are unable to be carers. The tendency for people to move to find work is another factor leading to difficulties in supporting elderly relatives. Finally, housing patterns reduce the possibilities for care – for example, estates of three-bedroomed houses mean that housing is too large for an elderly person alone, but too small to accommodate a family and an old person comfortably.

Activity 13.7

Role play
The situation
The Browns live in a four-bedroomed house in the suburbs of a large town. The family consists of John and Sylvia Brown, their three children and their dog. John's father lives alone (since the recent death of his wife) in the village he has lived in all his life. The village is about 30 miles from the Brown family's home. Since the death of his wife, Mr Brown Senior is finding it increasingly difficult to cope.

The decision
Should the family take John's father in to live with them or should he be moved to a home? Are there any other possibilities?

The characters
Harry Brown, aged 70, suffers from arthritis which means that he has difficulty in dressing and cooking as he cannot grip properly. Most of his friends in the village are also elderly, although he enjoys their company and visits to the local pub. He doesn't want to be a burden on his son's family, but neither does he want to go into a home.
John Brown, aged 38, sales director in a job he enjoys and which means quite a lot of travelling. He does not feel happy about his father going into a

home and would like him to move in with the family. He gets on well with his father when he sees him, which, at the moment, is most weekends.

Sylvia Brown, aged 35, has a good job in a local nursery, which she started after the children were in school. In a year or two, she expects to be promoted to deputy head. She knows of a good private home for elderly people quite near which the family could just about afford.

Jane Brown, aged 15, is afraid she will no longer have a bedroom of her own if her grandfather moves in. She is doing GCSEs at school and plans to stay on into the sixth form.

Susan Brown, aged 11, has just started at a new school which she likes. She is fond of her grandfather, but has a friend whose grandfather lives with the family and she always has to be quiet and can never have friends round to play records.

Peter Brown, aged 9, is very fond of his grandfather who always plays with him. He would love his grandfather to come and live with the family.

The dog has no opinion on the subject.

13.5   Health

Many older people are perfectly fit and some extremely so. In sports such as running, show-jumping and swimming there are many examples of older people who can put youngsters to shame. However, it is also true that, as a group, older people are in poorer health than the rest of the population. This is especially the case with the older age group – those over 75. In 1992, 66 per cent of people aged 75 and over in a government survey had a long-standing illness, compared with 32 per cent of people of all ages. 51 per cent said that they had a long-standing illness which limited their lives.[15] Older people rely more on the services of doctors and district nurses.

A growing problem which affects a minority of people in later life is Alzheimer's Disease. This is a physical disease which causes a progressive decline in the ability to remember, to learn, to think and to reason. The prevalence of dementia (Alzheimer's disease is the most common form of dementia) is as follows:

Age   40–65 Less than one in 1000
      65–70 Two in 100
      70–80 Five in 100
      Over 80 Twenty in 100[16]

The causes of the disease are not understood and it occurs equally in all social groups and areas of the country. The symptoms of the disease vary but the commonest early sign is loss of short-term memory. Disorientation and confusion are also common. The course of the disease also varies: for some people decline is quicker than others and for some people the pace of decline is uneven.

Alzheimer's disease, especially in the early stages, causes great distress to the sufferer. Enormous stress is also placed on relatives and friends. In the later stages the sufferer may be unable to recognise close relatives and may develop anti-social behaviour. Wandering is common and can be dangerous. This short account is taken from one of the leaflets of the Alzheimer's Disease Society:

> Ron is suffering from dementia caused by Alzheimer's disease. Although he can remember events which happened 20 years ago, sometimes he can't recall what he did two minutes ago. He forgets whether he had breakfast, whether he dressed, even where the kitchen is.
>
> At first Ron's wife thought he was merely getting forgetful. Then one day he forgot the way home. Yesterday he was so confused he didn't know who she was.

13.6 Segregation

In the past it was common for elderly people to end up living on hospital wards. This is less likely to happen now as a result of changes in policy within the NHS and the move to community care. In fact things have turned around so much that, instead of concern about older people staying too long in hospital, the worry is now that patients are discharged too quickly into situations where convalescent nursing care is not available. The two poems which follow are both said to have been written by elderly residents in hospital settings. Even if the messages regarding the inappropriateness of hospital as a place to live are not so relevant today, the points about dignity and humanity are still just as important.

> That I should come to this strange place
> To finish up my days
> O God I've prayed for help that I
> May fit in with their ways
>
> I've washed. I've dressed
> I've stood, I've sat
> I've learned to toe the line
> My mouth is washed, eyes swabbed, nails cut
> To suit the nurses' time
>
> I've smiled at 'Pop' and 'Dad' and 'Dear'
> They mean well, I know
> But will I ever hear my name
> Before I have to go?
>
> The Staff are few, and they are rushed
> And mostly they are kind,
> They walk me, bath me, feed my frame
> But do not feed my mind.

Deaf ears, dim eyes imprison me
Just memories remain
But they are not enough, Oh Lord
Please take me, whence I came.

I have been, I am, grateful
For food and warmth and light
But now I have no dignity
No privacy, no right.

We even have our bottoms wiped
In full view of the wards
I used to say 'please screen me off'
My words were never heard.

The patients say a nurse was blamed,
For letting someone fall
So now the screens are stored away
And they can watch us all.

Today I soiled my pants and chair
Is this the end of me?
The lost control, was it a sign of my senility?
No, it was not my fault at all
I called the nurse for sure
But she was busy, said to wait
She'd see me to the door

Was I so helpless, burdensome
The family sent me here?
I only asked to share their home
To feel my loved ones near.

The first time when Dot was gone,
They seemed to want me there,
I smoked outside, I held my tongue and never took his chair;
But soon their feelings changed for me,
Their eyes said, 'In the way,

We can't go out, the car's too small
No friend can come and stay.[17]

The writer of this poem was unable to speak, but occasionally wrote. Again the poem was allegedly found in a locker, after her death.

What do you see nurses
    What do you see?
Are you thinking
    when you are looking at me
A crabbit old woman

not very wise,
Uncertain of habit
   with far-away eyes,
Who dribbles her food
   and makes no reply?
When you say in a loud voice
'I do wish you'd try'
Who seems not to notice
   the things that you do,
And forever is losing
   a stocking or shoe,
Who unresisting or not
   lets you do as you will
with bathing and feeding
   the long day to fill,
Is that what you're thinking
   is that what you see?
Then open your eyes nurse,
   You're not looking at me,
I'll tell you who I am
   as I sit here so still,
As I use at your bidding
   as I eat at your will.
I'm a small child of ten
   with a father and a mother,
Brothers and sisters who
   love one another,
A young girl of sixteen
   with wings on her feet,
Dreaming that soon now
   a lover she'll meet:
A bride soon at twenty
   my heart gives a leap,
Remembering the vows
   that I promised to keep:
At twenty-five now
   I have young of my own
Who need me to build
   a secure happy home.
A young woman of thirty
   my young now grow fast,
Bound to each other
   with ties that should last;
At forty my young ones
   now grown will soon be gone,
But my man stays beside me
   to see I don't mourn:
At fifty once more
   babies play around my knee,
Again we know children

my loved one and me.
Dark days are upon me,
    my husband is dead,
I look at the future
    I shudder with dread,
For my young are all busy
    rearing young of their own,
And I think of the years
    and the love I have known.
I'm an old woman now
    and nature is cruel
'Tis her jest to make
    old age look like a fool.
The body it crumbles,
    grace and vigour depart,
There now is a stone
    Where once I had a heart:
But inside this old carcase
    a young girl still dwells,
And now and again
    my battered heart swells
I remember the joys,
    I remember the pain,
And I'm loving and living
    life over again,
I think of the years
    all too few – gone too fast,
And accept the stark fact
    that nothing can last.
So open your eyes nurses,
    Open and see,
Not a crabbit old woman,
    look closer – see ME.[18]

Activity 13.8

Discussion questions on the two poems.
1   What complaint is made by both writers?
2   What improvements in care could be made in the light of the feelings
    expressed in the first poem?
3   What are the needs of elderly people, whether or not they are infirm?

Ellen Newton lived for part of her life in homes for elderly people, where she kept a diary which was later published. This book captures much of the suffering felt by an older person forced to live away from the community. Ellen Newton writes:

The sense of segregation is so palpable, you feel as if at any moment you will be tightly enclosed in a cocoon of isolation. Except for the milkman, before dawn, there's no sound of traffic passing by. Everything is negative. You never hear young people singing, speeding recklessly home from late parties, or even the stereophonic calls of philandering tomcats. Never the sound of children's voices, laughing and calling to each other as they race down the street.

Later in the book she writes, 'Very soon you know that the complete human being that you still hope you are, is slowly beginning to perish.[19]

The segregation of elderly people results in a loss of all, although it is more keenly felt by elderly people. This point is illustrated in the following extract from a report by Julie Winters, after a placement undertaken as part of the Preliminary Course in Social Care. Julie states honestly, 'I did not make it a secret that I was not looking forward to my old people's placement. It was something that I had to do'. She goes on to describe how she benefited from the experience:

However, I not only feel that it helped me, I thoroughly enjoyed it. The things that I have learnt through this placement could be put into practice at any time, not only through a job but in society. There are lots of old people that we meet, on buses, in the street, etc. and a lot of them love to talk to young people. When this happened before I sometimes found myself embarrassed or I did not know how to react to them . . . The placement has given me insight into the needs and emotions of the elderly and I feel that now I know what to do and how to do it. My professional and personal development has progressed.

This extract shows how much people have to learn from each other in breaking down barriers between different groups of people.

Activity 13.9

Imagine you are 80. Describe how you are living and look back on your life.

Activity 13.9

Make sure you understand the following expressions used in this chapter. Check the glossary on p. 363 if you need to.

carer	occupational pension
domiciliary service	pressure group
housing association	segregation
hypothermia	sheltered accommodation
life expectancy	status
national insurance contributions	voluntary organisation

Further reading

Age Concern is the best source of up-to-date information on issues to do with ageing (see below). An interesting sociological approach is provided in Graham Fennell, Chris Phillippson and Helen Evers, *The Sociology of Old Age* (Milton Keynes: The Open University, 1988). Another useful text from the Open University is Christina R. Victor, *Health and Health Care in Later Life* (Milton Keynes: The Open University, 1991).

Useful addresses

Age Concern: 1268 London Road, London SW16 4ER
tel. 0181 679 8000

Centre for Policy on Ageing: 25–31 Ironmonger Row, London EC1V 3QP
tel. 0171 253 1787

⬡14 Disability

14.1　What is a 'disability'?

There is no clear dividing line between those who have a disability and the rest of society. Everybody experiences disability to some extent at some point in their lives and most people are 'able' in some situations and not in others. The line from 'normality' to 'abnormality' is a continuum with no sharp cut-off point. Labelling some people as 'the disabled' is part of the problem of disability. Whilst it is impossible to reach any clear and unambiguous definition of disability, it includes conditions like blindness, deafness, congenital abnormalities, arthritis and loss of ability resulting from accidents. Several writers make a distinction between a disability and a handicap. For example, Ann Shearer suggests that disability must be taken as given, but handicap, 'is something that is imposed on that disability to make it more limiting than it must necessarily be'.[1] The extent to which a disability is a handicap depends on a number of factors such as the type of job a person has, the services which exist to help, the attitudes of society and the personality of the person with the disability. Ann Shearer illustrates this point by arguing that not being able to run for a bus would not be a handicap if buses waited for their passengers.

The number of people in this country who have disabilities is unknown, partly because of the lack of a clear definition for the term, and partly because no comprehensive survey has been carried out. This is a major problem, since without this information it is impossible to assess the adequacy of provision. Registers of people with disabilities are maintained by local authority social services departments, but registration is voluntary and these figures do not provide a complete picture. The duty of local authorities to maintain registers was initially established in the 1948 National Assistance Act. The 1970 Chronically Sick and Disabled Persons Act gave local authorities a statutory duty to inform themselves of the needs of local people with disabilities. However, the procedure for implementation of this duty was vague and few local authorities carried out comprehensive surveys. Various surveys have produced differing figures – probably depending on how they have defined disability. A government survey in the mid-1980s put the figure at 6 million adults.[2]

Activity 14.1

Where are the common areas of need for people with disabilities? Are they being met by provision in the 1990s?

14.2   Acceptance

Needs vary but may include financial support, special educational facilities, sheltered employment, support, help in making social contacts and aids and help in the practicalities of daily life. However, the greatest need for many people is to be accepted and not rejected as somehow 'abnormal'. Often the greatest problem is not the disability itself, but other people's attitudes which may then be internalised by the sufferer. This society is one of ideals, for example the ideal of slim 'perfect' women, and to be noticeably less than ideal brings suffering when society is intolerant and rejecting of those who fail to meet the standard. Reactions which hurt and damage include fear, withdrawal, embarrassment, pity and low expectations. In the following extract, a woman with multiple sclerosis explains how she felt about categories of normality after the onset of the disease.

> I was confused, I still felt fundamentally the same. My body was different, I know that all right, but inside it was me. Normality is after all what you know. The male who is very short is normal to himself, it is other people who make him aware of an 'abnormality'. The ugly female is 'normal' to herself (try denying your own being), it's the others who make her 'abnormal'. After all if we were all very short and ugly (decide for yourself what that means) a person unlike that would be 'abnormal'. 'Normality' and 'abnormality' are socially defined. it also has to be a relative concept, we are all normal/abnormal to the social norm, in varying degrees. Disability can and sometimes does interfere with the practical running of a life, but it is the reaction of and non-action of society which causes disablement. There is no such thing as THE DISABLED, there are just people.

The woman goes on to tell how powerful an effect the reactions of other people have on the person:

> On leaving hospital and finding the mantle of 'disabled' placed firmly upon my unwilling shoulders I entered a world which was alien, absurd and ultimately defeating. My weak grasp on my identity was no real match for the massed forces of society who firmly believed themselves as 'normal' and myself just as firmly as 'abnormal'. I found myself inhabiting a stereotype. I became my illness.[3]

There are many ways in which people make others feel abnormal. The woman quoted above tells how she and her problem became public property such that strangers approached her to discuss it, whilst at the same time friends were incapable of talking about her disability without embarrassment or joking. Various expectations of their limitations and their feelings are placed on people with a disability. Many people with a physical disability complain of assumptions made about their mental abilities, and the BBC radio programme. 'Does he take sugar?' is aptly titled, referring to the tendency for people to refuse to address a person who has a disability directly.

Attitudes to disability can be clearly seen in attitudes to sexuality. The experience of the woman told in the following extract is echoed in many other accounts of similar experiences. Angie has cerebral palsy and is unable to walk.

One day while Tony was at work the gas man came to read the meter . . . As he was leaving the flat he turned and asked if I was married? I told him I was, then a funny look came into his eyes and he asked if I had sex? I was shocked at his question and at first stuck for words. Then I was angry and said the first thing that came into my head, 'Yes, do you?' He look embarrassed and turned away. During the rest of the day I kept thinking what a cheek he had asking me such a question. Since then I have been asked that question several times in different ways, most often by men, and I answer them in the same way.[4]

Attitudes to people with disability who want to have children are similarly misinformed and hurtful. There is no reason why the right to have children should be denied to people with a disability. The idea that it is wrong for such people to have children cannot be connected to fear of a disability being passed on, since cerebral palsy and many other disabilities are not hereditary. The basis for such attitudes can only be denial that people with a disability are human beings in the same way as everyone else and only different to the extent that they suffer from a particular condition.

Activity 14.2

What can be done to improve attitudes to disability? How would you set about educating people's attitudes?

Fear and prejudice are often based on ignorance and unfamiliarity. Many fears would be eliminated if people with disabilities were further integrated into the community. The media could play a role in changing attitudes by portraying people with a disability in everyday situations, leading a normal life. There is a tendency for the media to overdo the 'tragedy' aspect of disability. Schools could help young people by extending community projects and encouraging young people to get to know people with disabilities.

14.3 Finance

Some people with disabilities are unable to work, others have limited earning power and many have extra costs. These include wear and tear on clothes caused by appliances, costs of special equipment, and money to pay people to do tasks such as decorating which other people are able to do for themselves.

In the last decade, several new benefits have been introduced, reducing the number of people dependent on income support. Benefits for people with disabilities include contributory benefits such as invalidity benefit and the invalidity allowance paid to people receiving a retirement pension. Non-contributory benefits include the severe disablement allowance, the invalid care allowance (for carers), the disability living allowance and the disability working allowance.

The rates for benefits are not especially high and have been given in Chapter 3. State provision of benefits is patchy and, as the above list demonstrates, complex. It has been criticised for creating distinctions based not on the extent of the disability, but on the source of the condition. For example, people with disabilities resulting from an industrial accident or a war injury receive superior provision to those with a disability from birth or caused by a non-industrial injury. These distinctions are based on value judgements about different people's contribution to society, and on a tendency to reward the able and penalise those with a disability. The emphasis on contribution to society through employment can be criticised if a consideration is given to the amount of time spent at work and the nature of many jobs. There are many ways in which people contribute to society through activities outside employment.

Other criticisms of provision for people with disabilities include the kind of tests people have to pass or fail in order to qualify for benefits. The mobility allowance, for example, was fenced in with rules and regulations. A man with one leg was refused the benefit and decided to appeal:

> To do that, he had to go to an office set up for the purpose. And to reach the office, he had to take himself and his crutches, slowly, with difficulty, up no fewer than twenty-eight stairs. And when he at last got to the top, he eventually lost his appeal, because he had, slowly and with difficulty, made his way up twenty-eight stairs to lodge it.[5]

The old mobility allowance is now incorporated into the disability living allowance but the rules are still strict and sometimes can seem unfair.

The Family Fund is a source of finance for families with a child with a severe disability. The money is from the government but is administered by the Joseph Rowntree Memorial Trust.

The complexity of the benefits system causes suffering as the following extract, from a woman with multiple sclerosis raising a family alone on benefits, shows. She experienced many difficulties in claiming her rights and had to fight all the way:

> My main feelings about my experience are anger and frustration. Anger because not only do I have to cope with the physical and mental difficulties of being a person with a disability, but I have to use precious energy struggling to make ends meet. Frustration because there seems very little prospect of improvement in this situation. The long-term effects of this social security system are extremely detrimental to families. The children, in particular, suffer as they are unable to compete with their friends on any level. Not only do they have a disabled parent but they are also poorer than anyone else.[6]

The Disability Alliance campaigns for three long-term policy objectives. The first is to eliminate poverty, the second to bring the incomes of those with disabilities up to the level of the non-disabled and the third to have funds distributed equally, not on the basis of the cause of the disability or the place where it happened. A common feature of campaigns on disability is the demand for a single comprehensive benefit paid as of right.

14.4 Employment

Employment is very important in our society as a source of income, status and a way of meeting people and feeling part of society. A woman who had to give up work because of her disability tells how she felt:

> it was the most shattering experience I had had, because going out to work, you felt part of society, you were contributing, you were earning your own money. You also had your friends that you went to work with, and then suddenly you were cut off, you were in the house alone. Also of course financially you were worse off. You were lonely, you felt useless, on the scrap heap, finished, and it really was a very bad time.[7]

People with disabilities are more vulnerable to unemployment, especially in times of recession.

The 1944 and 1958 Disabled Persons (Employment) Acts provided a system of special help for people with disabilities. People can register for employment purposes, but as with social services registers, registration is voluntary so the registers cannot be used as a measure of the total numbers of disabled people. The 1944 Act established a quota system whereby employers with a staff of 20 or more people must employ 3 per cent of people with disabilities. Employers can apply for a permit for exemption if there are no suitably qualified people to do the job. There are penalties for breaking the law although many employers ignore the quota and few are prosecuted. It is disappointing that government departments and nationalised industries fail to set an example and are not better than employers in the private sector. The Act also provided for occupations to be designated for people with disabilities, but so far only two have been named, those of lift operator and car park attendant.

The failure of the law as an effective measure to combat discrimination, has led to proposals for changes. These have included abolishing the quota system, improving the quota by including a weighting in favour of people with severe disabilities, and proposals for stricter enforcement of the law. Other suggestions include anti-discrimination legislation and a system whereby employers opting out of the quota pay a levy into a special fund. This last proposal is implemented in West Germany where the money is used for the establishment of sheltered workshops.

Disablement Resettlement Officers (DROs) have responsibility for helping people with disabilities to find suitable employment and providing support. DROs can recommend that a person attends a course at an employment rehabilitation centre. The centres provide short courses to assess needs and to familiarise the person with the routines of work. This can be followed with vocational training at a training centre or college. If a person is unable to find work, the DRO can arrange a placement in one of the government-run sheltered workshops, known as Remploy. Some local authorities and voluntary organisations also run places of employment. There is also a Sheltered Placement Scheme to enable people with severe disabilities to work alongside able-bodied people. This scheme works through a 'sponsor' (the local authority or a

Source: Vicky White, Photofusion
This cycle mechanic has no sight or hearing

voluntary organisation) who is legally the employer and who places the worker with a 'host' employer.

Sheltered workshops have been criticised for a number of reasons. They tend to be biased towards industrial work, which may not be the most suitable type of employment. It may be more helpful for people with disabilities to be trained to work in areas where their experience is an advantage, for example in counselling or welfare rights work. Other forms of provision related to employment include places on Department of Employment programmes and in special residential colleges.

The disability living allowance is a means-tested benefit which can be claimed by people with disabilities in work.

Activity 14.3

You want to implement a new policy on employment for people with disabilities in your area. Draw up a programme for action.

14.5 Education

The provision of education for children with disabilities was reviewed by the Warnock Committee and legislation was introduced in 1981. The Warnock Report encouraged integration of children with disabilities and learning difficulties into mainstream schools, but also allowed for a variety of other methods of education (see chapter 7).

Thee are disadvantages and advantages of educating children and young people with disabilities in separate schools. A girl with restricted movement in one side tells how the cruelty of other girls in school led her to ask if she could attend a special school. She says that in the special school:

> It was much easier to make friends and I didn't feel an outsider any more. Everyone had a disability and no-one was self-conscious about it. They treated each other as human beings and you could be friends with anyone.[8]

This young woman is however aware of her loss of contact with the outside world. Another woman who suffered from a disease called brittle bones tells of her isolation until she went to a boarding school for girls with disabilities. Here she learned the joy of sharing doubts and fears:

> Our boarding school had rows of adjacent loos. One day, very soon after my arrival at the school, I was sitting in one loo whilst a new friend was sitting in the loo next door. 'Micheline' she said, 'Do you think you will ever get married?' A flood of relief came over me then. I knew the question was coming from someone who asked herself the same question many times already. There were other people who had gone through all that doubting too! Nice people! Other young women who had had their self-image as women so severely damaged that they too had wondered if they were entitled to any-thing life had to offer.[9]

These women were lucky in that they attended schools which set high acade-mic standards and provided an education equal to that of ordinary schools.

Others are not so lucky and go to schools where little is expected of children with disabilities and where the teaching is of a lower academic standard. This is part of the 'cycle of expectation' whereby little is expected of people and, as a result, they achieve little. It takes great personal strength and confidence to overcome such a handicap. Another disadvantage of special education is the way in which it segregates people with a disability from the rest of society. This is as much a loss to the able-bodied as to the people with disabilities. Finally, there is a need for greater provision in further and higher education for people with disabilities.

The 1981 Education Act set up procedures for children with disabilities to be assessed in order to decide if special provision should be made. If it is thought that special educational provision is required the local authority must make a statement of special educational needs. This process is known as 'statementing' and must involve the parents of the child (see p. 183 above).

14.6   Aids and support services

If people with a disability are to lead a full life in the community, practical help and support is needed. These services are provided either by health authorities or by local social services departments. The duty to make provision was strengthened in the 1970 Chronically Sick and Disabled Persons Act. The act gave local authorities the responsibility of informing themselves of the number of such people in their area and providing for their needs. There was a great deal of optimism about the potential of the Act but the implementation of the legislation has been disappointing and provision remains inadequate, fragmented and patchy. Local authority social services departments may provide aids to households such as telephones and can finance adaptations to homes, although there may be a requirement for the recipient to meet part of the cost. Other services include home helps, holidays and day centres. These services have been vulnerable to cuts in expenditure in recent years. A survey by the Disability Alliance found that the number of telephone installations had fallen and fewer council homes had been adapted.[10]

The duties of the local authorities have been strengthened by the 1986 Disabled Persons Act and the 1990 NHS and Community Care Act. Under these Acts the local authority must make an assessment of needs if asked to do so and decide what provision, if any, to make. In complex cases requiring the co-ordination of a number of services, a care manager will be appointed to work on a care plan and to monitor and review the provision. Services vary from area to area but are likely to include the following:

- Social workers providing advice, information and counselling
- Home care staff to help with personal care at home
- Meals-on-wheels
- Occupational therapists who provide advice on the practicalities of daily living and organise aids and adaptations for the home

- Day centres offering a variety of educational, therapeutic and recreational facilities.

All of these services may be charged for, although usually on a means-tested basis. Again this varies from area to area. As the following account shows these charges are resented by many people:[11]

> To get in and out of bed, Joanna Buckle needs the assistance of two home helps. Multiple sclerosis prevents her from standing alone and she is unable to dress herself to get to work.
>
> For this help Ms Buckle is now expecting to have to pay more than £500 a month. 'I will have to pay all this money just to get into and out of bed each day which is pretty obscene to me,' she said.
>
> 'I did not ask to have multiple sclerosis – now I am being penalised for being disabled.'
>
> . . .
>
> She has held down a professional job with neighbouring Waltham Forest council for almost 10 years. Now she faces a stark choice – either to sit in bed or in a wheelchair all day, or to carry on with her job and make severe economies in her budget.
>
> . . . Ms Buckle does not want people to think of her as a tragic victim. All she wants, she says, is some simple help at an affordable price so she can lead a normal life.

Wheelchairs are provided by the Artificial Limb and Appliance Centres. People who suffer from weakness in hands and limbs can be given electrically-propelled wheelchairs. Mobility is a key problem for many people with disabilities. In 1976,

Source: Crispin Hughes, Photofusion
New technology helps people with disabilities

the policy of providing invalid vehicles ended and the mobility allowance was introduced (later changed to be incorporated into the disability living allowance.) The introduction of an allowance initially posed some problems as it was difficult to use the allowance to buy a car. However, a scheme called *Motability* is now operated by a voluntary organisation. Under this scheme, the mobility component of the disability living allowance is paid to the organisation and a car can be hired or bought on hire purchase. There is also the well-known Orange Badge scheme which allows people with disabilities greater freedom in parking.

14.7 Access

The 1970 Chronically Sick and Disabled Persons Act included clauses concerned with making the community more accessible to people with a disability. The Act refers to buildings of public use and states that where new buildings are planned or old ones adapted, the building should be made accessible to people with disabilities. However, the Act allows that this should be done where it is reasonable or practical to do so. Words like 'practicable' and 'reasonable' weaken legislation and allow for the spirit of law to be ignored. Progress in opening up the community has been slow and there are many instances of ramps which lead into areas from which there is no exit and of special toilets which cannot be reached.

A further development came in 1981. The 1981 Disabled Persons Act gave planning authorities the duty of drawing people's attention to provisions relating to access. This must be done when planning permission is granted. These provision were later extended in 1985. Certain new buildings must now provide access and facilities for people with disabilities. These include offices, shops, single-storey factories, educational buildings and others which admit the public. Local authorities have begun to employ *Access Officers* to oversee these regulations.

14.8 Residential accommodation

Residential homes for people with disabilities are provided by social services, voluntary organisations and by profit-making organisations. This form of provision shares the problems of institutions already described in other contexts.

__ **Activity 14.4** _____

Make sure that you understand the following expressions, used in this chapter. Check the glossary on p. 363 if you need to.

care manager	mainstream education
care plan	multiple sclerosis
cerebral palsy	non-contributary benefit

contributary benefit	quota system
cycle of expectation	rehabilitation
hereditary	sheltered employment
invalidity benefit	'statementing'

Further reading

Three books on people with disabilities are; Joe Campling (ed.), *Images of Ourselves* (London: Routledge & Kegan Paul, 1981); Alan Walker and Peter Townsend (eds), *Disability in Britain* (Oxford: Martin Robertson, 1981) and Ann Shearer, *Disability: Whose Handicap?* (Oxford: Blackwell, 1981). The first is a compilation of first-hand accounts of disability, the second is a diverse collection of articles and the third combines mental handicap and physical disability in an interesting exploration of the issues.

More up-to-date information on all aspects of rights of people with disabilities can be found in the *Disability Rights Handbook*. This is updated each year and produced by the Disability Alliance ERA (see below).

Useful addresses

Disability Alliance ERA: Universal House, 88–94 Wentworth Street, London E1 7SA
tel. 0171 247 8776

Royal Association for Disability and Rehabilitation (RADAR):
25 Mortimer Street, London W1N 8AB
tel. 0171 637 5400

Motability: Castlewood House, 77 New Oxford Street, London WC1A 1PP
tel. 0171 831 1171

Disability Alliance: Universal House, 88–94 Wentworth Street, London E1 7SA
tel. 0171 247 8776

The Family Fund: PO Box 50, York YO1 1UY
tel. 01904 621115

John Grooms Association for Disabled People: 10 Gloucester Drive, Finsbury Park, London N4 2LP
tel. 0181 802 7272

⬡15 Health and the health services

15.1   Health, society and the environment

In this society, there is a tendency to see health as very much an individual issue. This leads to an emphasis on the biological causes of ill-health together with the recent stress on personal factors such as smoking and weight. Improvements in health are seen as resulting from intervention by doctors at the level of the individual, or changes in personal life-style. This chapter looks at health and health care from a different point of view, focusing on social, political, economic and environmental aspects of health. It will become apparent that health is not a purely personal matter, but an area of considerable national and social concern.

There are various ways in which the significance of this perspective on health can be illustrated. The meaning people give to the term 'good health' varies over time and from one society to another. One way of defining health was offered by the World Health Organisation in 1965. This definition sees health as a 'state of complete physical, mental and social wellbeing'. It is probably more common, however, for health to be seen as the absence of disease, although the definition of disease also varies.

Whilst the biological causes of ill-health are obviously important in combating disease, many health problems are social, economic or environmental in origin.

__ Activity 15.1 _____

What environmental factors affecting health can you think of? List them, and ways in which they can be overcome.

There are many ways in which health can be related to social factors. Working environments can cause health problems through industrial injuries and industrial diseases like asbestosis. Work can also be a cause of stress-related illnesses, as can unemployment. In addition, environmental factors such as pollution, transport, and dangerous or damp housing are also important in relation to health. The analysis, later in this chapter, of the link between social class and health illustrates the significance of social and economic factors in any discussion of health.

Whilst individuals can improve their own health to a certain extent, national policies and programmes can achieve more significant results. For example, life expectancy at birth is now 74 years for boys and 79 years for girls, compared with 48 and 52 years respectively for those born around the turn of the century.[1]

Admittedly, it is difficult to isolate particular policies or factors which increase life expectancy, but variations between countries and over time indicate the importance of factors greater than the individual.

Health also has economic implications. The economics of health and health care are immediately obvious to people who live in countries where there is no public provision of health services. In Britain, the economic aspects are perhaps less apparent, but planners and policy-makers in the health service are very conscious that health is a commodity which has to be bought, and about which choices are made as to the allocation of limited resources. There are points at which a price is put on life itself, for example in deciding whether or not to offer a heart transplant operation to a dying patient. Other economic aspects of health can be seen in lost production through ill-health, or the costs to society of supporting people who cannot work because of disablement or sickness.

Health and health care provision are both very much political issues. This can be seen in the way the two main political parties differ in their policies and priorities for health. At the simplest level, the Conservatives are more concerned to control public expenditure and to encourage private initiatives in health care. The Labour Party demonstrates a greater commitment to the original principles of the National Health Service (NHS) seeking to abolish charges and to increase funding.

15.2   The aims and organisation of the NHS

In Britain, most aspects of the health care come within the scope of the NHS, and therefore this chapter is primarily concerned with the development, future and aims of this service. The NHS has been in existence for almost fifty years, since its inception on 5 July 1948.

Activity 15.2

Consult older relatives, neighbours and friends to find out about life in the period before the NHS was established. Report your findings to the class.

Before the NHS

There were some state-provided services prior to 1948. For example, public health, in the form of water and sewage systems, was provided under the 1848

Public Health Act. Services for pregnant women and young children were introduced at the beginning of this century. From 1911, employment-linked insurance provided cover for doctors' services for people in work. Local authorities ran Poor Law infirmaries, public hospitals and mental hospitals. Hospitals were also provided by voluntary organisations.

However, there was great variation in the standards of care provided by these services, and considerable stigma attached to much of the provision. The insurance system only covered the person in employment and did not extend to the families of workers. The following quotations based on accounts of people living in Sheffield give some indication of the quality of life in the period before 1948:

> [In] Attercliffe in Sheffield's East End which housed the heavy industry of the Don Valley and the workforce which operated it – bronchitis was a way of life. People expected to live with it, suffer from it and eventually die from it, with only their weekly bottle of medicine for relief.[2]

Two women described their memories as follows:

> Bills from general practitioners were always hard to meet ... Kay remembered especially a doctor in the Crookesmoor district of Sheffield who employed a debt collector ... The effects were particularly severe for working-class women, who due to a policy of not employing married women in Sheffield always tended to fall outside the insurance scheme. 'Mother never had the doctor.' 'You just didn't go to the doctor until you were on your last legs.' Kay recalled how her own mother hadn't gone to the doctor even though she was in bed with asthma. And Jessie likewise how her mother continued to suffer with high blood pressure, even though she knew that tablets were available which could have helped to lessen her condition.[3]

Looking at health from the other side, the extracts below are from a doctor who worked as a GP before the beginning of the National Health Service.[4]
Dr Arnold Elliot remembers:

> I ran my practice from a small house in Ilford, but most surgeries were lock-up shops in industrial areas. On the whole, most of them were awful, with no running water, heat, lighting or toilets, some with no couches.
>
> I knew one East End doctor who had a cigarette machine in his waiting room. Many doctors had two doors; one for 'panel' patients (the insured workers) and one for private patients, who weren't kept waiting.
>
> Doctors didn't speak to each other, because they were deadly enemies. They went in for head-hunting the breadwinning panel patient, who would often bring in the rest of his family.
>
> Various private arrangements were set up for his dependants – so-called 'clubs' – where they paid a small amount a week for a doctor and medicine. For the destitute, there were dispensaries, which engaged the services of a doctor for a small annual payment ... Doctors used to dispense their own medicines too. The pharmaceutical firms came round and filled up the big 'Winchester' bottles every week. Many of the medicines were placebos; aspirin, for instance, which was available in a red or yellow mixture. You had to give the same colour to a patient every week, and sometimes

there'd be trouble when you had a locum in and he gave out the wrong one. It sounds immoral, but that was trade.

From another perspective, Sir George Godber was involved in setting up the National Health Service. In 1942, before the NHS, he surveyed hospitals in Britain. He tells what his survey found.[5]

You must remember hospitals in those days were very different from today. An isolation hospital might only have five beds. There was a hospital for scarlet fever in the Prime Minister's [Margaret Thatcher's] home town of Grantham that was housed in a wooden hut on the top of a hill without sewers or water – the water was delivered by cart once a week. The system in 1942 was incapable of delivering modern medicine. There were dilapidated buildings, insanitary conditions on the wards, inadequate space for radiology and laboratory services.

There were casual wards where tramps stayed overnight and even more depressing house wards where elderly residential patients waited to die in the most uncivilised conditions – the nights spent in narrow and dark dormitories of 20 to 30 beds and the daytime sitting on hard benches in a different room looking at their feet.

Organisation of the NHS

The National Health Service Act was passed in 1946, for implementation in 1948. Aneurin Bevan is seen as the individual politician responsible for designing the health service, but it is important to understand that the system was not created by Bevan alone, but formulated as a result of bargaining and compromise between the government and various interest groups. Doctors were, and are, a powerful and well-organised group and were able to get what they wanted to a considerable extent. The doctors won a number of concessions, which continue to influence the running and development of the NHS. For example, doctors are not salaried workers in the health service, but retain an independent status, contracting to provide services. Also, the option of private practice was included in the service, and access allowed to pay-beds within NHS hospitals. Further, doctors won for themselves a major role in the administration of the NHS.

The idea behind the NHS was that it should bring together all aspects of health care in one organisation in an attempt to achieve certain aims. The most important principle was that health care should be available to all, irrespective of ability to pay. National planning of resources was intended to reduce overlaps in services and ensure that there were no gaps in provision.

The NHS is organised under the Department of Health (the Department of Health and Social Security until 1988, and originally the Ministry of Health). Several changes have been made to the local structure of planning and management. Originally, the administrative structure consisted of three parts. First, GPs, dentists, pharmacists and opticians were administered by executive Councils, appointed by local professionals, local authorities and the Ministry of Health. Second, personal and environmental services, including maternity and child welfare clinics, health visitors, midwives, health education, vaccination programmes and ambulances, were controlled by the local authorities. The third part of the administrative structure was concerned with hospitals. Regional Health Boards were appointed by the Ministry of Health. The Boards in turn appointed Hospital Management Committees. The prestigious teaching hospitals had a separate status and were managed by Boards of Governors.

1974 and 1982 changes

This structure was criticised and in 1973 a new National Health Service Act was passed to come into force on 1 April 1974. The aim of reorganisation was to unify the NHS, to improve co-ordination between health services and related local authority services, and to improve the management of the service. The first aim was only successful to a limited extent, since GPs continued to remain outside the main structure. As a step towards achieving the second objective mentioned, the area boundaries for the health service were made the same as the new local authority boundaries which were also implemented on 1 April 1974. With regard to improving management, management experts were consulted, although the system was later criticised for relying on an over-theoretical approach to management.

The new structure consisted of three tiers organised in a hierarchy. First, *Regional Health Authorities* (RHAs) were appointed by the Secretary of State for Social Services. These were to be responsible for the planning of services and resources. The next tier was the *Area Health Authorities* (AHAs), appointed partly by the RHAs, partly by the local authorities and partly by non-medical and nursing staff. AHAs were responsible for planning and management, and were expected to work with local authorities to improve co-ordination of services. Alongside AHAs in the hierarchy, *Family Practitioner Committees* (FPCs), appointed by the AHAs, local professionals and local authorities, were to administer GPs, dentists, pharmacists and opticians. Most areas were then split into districts, and the third tier was the *District Management Teams* (DMTs).

At the district level, *Community Health Councils* (CHCs) were set up and given the task of representing the views of consumers. CHCs each consist of about 30 members, appointed by local government and chosen by voluntary organisations. The role of the CHCs includes obtaining information and visiting local health facilities. They are also consulted by the district authorities before major decisions are made. While performing an important role, CHCs have been criticised for their inability to represent public opinion adequately or to exercise any real power in the system.

Almost as soon as the new organisation began to work, it was subjected to criticism. It was said that the structure contained too many tiers and administrators, and led to unnecessary delays. It was also argued that the organisation was undemocratic, allowing too much power to professionals. The attempt at establishing a unified structure was said to have failed. After these attacks, a second new system came into being on 1 April 1982. The present organisation consists of Regional Health Authorities and District Health Authorities, the middle tier having been abolished. CHCs continue to operate at the district level of management. Family Practitioner Committees now known as Family Health Service Authorities have been further separated from the main administrative structure and are now employing authorities in their own right, responsible directly to the Department of Health.

Activity 15.3 _____

Contact your local Community Health Council. Find out how this organisation works and what its tasks are.

Activity 15.4 _____

Construct diagrams to show the three management structures of the NHS. You may like to consult Christopher Ham's book, listed in the 'Further reading' section at the end of this chapter.

1991 Changes

Major changes in the working and philosophy of the health service were implemented in April 1991, as a result of the 1990 NHS and Community Care Act. The key aspects of the Act are the creation of *independent trusts* – hospitals and other units which opt out of the control of the District Health Authority – and the possibility for doctors to hold their own budgets for spending on hospital and other services. The main theme of the reforms is that there should be a separation between the *purchasers* and the *providers* of health care. The health authorities and fund-holding doctors become purchasers from the hospitals and other units (the providers). Another way of talking about this is to use the term 'internal market'. This refers to the fact that the purchasers have a choice as to which provider to use and will therefore choose the hospital or other provider unit which offers the best value for money (as in a market-place). Purchasers can purchase health care from private hospitals or voluntary groups if they wish to.

The organisational structure of the NHS is basically unchanged from that operating after 1982, although the new Trusts and fund-holding GPs have to be added. The person who is ultimately responsible for the health service in Parliament is the Secretary of State for Health. She or he is the head of the *Department of Health Policy Board* which is responsible for running the NHS in England. In Scotland, Wales and Northern Ireland there are separate Secretaries of State. The Policy Board divides the money available for the NHS between the various regions of the country. There is also a Board of Directors of the NHS called the *NHS Management Committee*. This is in charge of the day-to-day running of the service.

England has 14 *Regional Health Authorities (RHAs)* which plan services for their region. They give money to *District Health Authorities (DHAs)*, *Family Health Service Authorities* and the GPs who manage their own budgets. The new trusts – hospitals or other services which have opted out of health authority control – are responsible directly to the NHS Management Committee.

Under the RHA are two organisations. The first is the Family Health Services Authority, which manages services provided by GPs, NHS dentists, chemists and opticians. The second is the District Health Authority. In England, there are 189 of these. Each is usually responsible for several hospitals – perhaps a district general hospital as well as several smaller ones – and the local clinics.

__ Activity 15.5 _____

What areas of health provision fall within the NHS? List them.

The role of the GP

The NHS brought many different areas of health care into one organisation. The first point of contact with the health service for most people is the local general practitioner or GP, who is the main person responsible for what is termed 'primary health care'. The role of the GP has changed since 1948, with group practices becoming more common and a move towards the concept of a *primary health care team*, including health visitors, nurses and sometimes social workers. There has also been a trend towards health centres, bringing together a variety of services. Dentists, pharmacists and opticians also operate within the health service. Problems with primary health care arise from the shortage of good GPs and the tendency for some areas of the country to have a better ratio of doctors to patients than others. The lack of GPs is related to the higher status and better pay prospects given to doctors working in hospitals.

Since the 1990 NHS and Community Care Act there are two types of GP within the health service. Budget or fund-holding GPs are financed directly from the Regional Health Authority. They are allocated a budget with which to buy services for their patients. These services include hospital treatments, drugs, mental health counselling and chiropody. (Not all the services were included in the original reforms: some were added in 1993.) Fund-holding GPs can send patients to any hospital which seems to offer the best value service. Non-budget-holding GPs are funded by the District Health Authority. They can send patients to hospitals with which the DHA has a contract. If the treatment which is needed is not available at this hospital, patients can be sent elsewhere, so long as the DHA is prepared to pay. On April 1 1991 the first wave of 306 GP fund-holding practices started managing their own budgets. In April 1993 there were 1200 fund-holding practices – about a quarter of all GPs.[6]

Hospitals

In terms of financial resources, hospitals are a very important part of the NHS, taking up about two thirds of all expenditure. It is possible that hospitals play too important a role in the NHS, and that the service could be improved by a shift of resources to community-based services. One of the reasons why hospitals take up so much of the money available to the NHS is that they quickly become out-of-date, as well as having high costs for maintenance and staffing. When the NHS was set up, it was intended that new hospitals should be built, to replace obsolete and run-down buildings and to ensure that provision was available in all areas of the country.

In the first decade of the NHS little hospital building was done and in 1962 the Hospital Building Plan was published. The plan recommended that for every 100 000–200 000 of the population, there should be a district general hospital with 600–800 beds. The hospitals would be located near the centre of the population to be served and would provide beds for all types of patients except those suffering from rare diseases. The idea of district general hospitals was approved, although there were problems of finance, or finding land at the centres of populated areas, and some local opposition to the closure of specialised hospitals, especially the small cottage hospitals. A considerable amount of hospital building was completed in the period following the publication of the plan.

Within the health service there are now two types of hospital. The traditional hospitals are run by the District Health Authority. Under the NHS and Community Care Act, implemented in 1991, they must now compete to win contracts to treat patients who are paid for by health authorities or fund-holding GPs. Then there are the NHS Trusts. These are hospitals which have opted out of the control of the health authorities. They get their money by competing to treat patients. The trusts are self-governing organisations run by a board of directors. They have considerable freedom in planning and using resources – they make their own decisions about buying and selling land and about employment of staff. Outside of the NHS there are also private hospitals, some of which are run by organisations for private health care such as BUPA. People can pay as individuals or through health insurance. Fund-holding GPs and District Health Authorities can also decide to buy services from private hospitals.

Other changes affecting hospitals in the 1990s have been the policy of community care (discussed in chapter 9) and a new system of management of hospital staff and services.

Community health services

Other important areas of NHS work come under the heading of the 'community health service'. These areas include health education, health visiting, screening and vaccinations, ante-natal and child health clinics, family planning and school health services. Local authorities can also provide home services such as sickroom equipment, help with laundry and home nursing. The planning of these services is the responsibility of the community physician.

Activity 15.6

In pairs, choose one aspect of community health and find out, either by writing to visiting local clinics or organisations, or by using the library, the work done by the service. Report your findings to the whole class.

Activity 15.7 _____

To what extent has the 1990 NHS and Community Care Act changed health care provision in your area? Which hospital and other services have become trusts? Have any of your local GP practices decided to hold their own budgets? Try to find out the reasons why (or why not), this has happened.

Activity 15.8 _____

Can you see any dangers or problems for health provision in the reforms brought in by the 1990 NHS and Community Care Act? Explain your misgivings.

The internal market

In the debate around the new internal market in the health service the following worries have been voiced. Some people have argued that decisions about health care should be made without thought to budgets. There has in fact always been some element of thought to cost somewhere along the line in health care decisions, but the 1990 reforms make costs more of a central issue. Standards in hospitals may fall as hospitals try to cut costs to make themselves more competitive to win contracts from the health authorities and doctors. Competition can lead to pointless duplication of services and in areas with more than one hospital, hospitals may close if contracts are lost. GPs with an eye to their budgets may be reluctant to take on elderly or chronically sick patients. It will cause anxiety if patients feel their doctor is thinking about the price of treatment in making decisions about their health. A more fundamental anxiety looks to the future of the NHS. Some people worry that there is an intention to privatise the health service at some future point. The creation of independent trusts and fund-holding GPs could be seen as a starting point for privatisations. Once the hospitals are independent units managing their own budgets, it would not be so difficult to take a further step and remove them from the NHS altogether. There is also a worry that overall planning of health care services is more difficult with hospitals and other units making independent decisions for financial reasons rather than in the interests of the health needs of the whole population.

15.3   Policy issues

Many of the issues concerning health and the NHS are related to problems of finance. There is a tendency for both the public and governments to support the

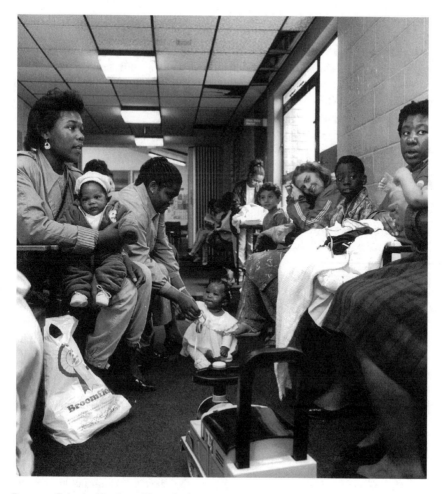

Source: Crispin Hughes, Photofusion
Long waits to see the doctor at some health centres

NHS, but to be reluctant to want to provide sufficient resources. When the NHS was established in 1948, it was believed that there would be an initial backlog of demand for services, which would then eventually stabilise and possibly even decrease. This assumption has turned out to be false and demand has continually increased. In the first year, the cost was £433 million; by 1992–3 the cost to the government was £34 912 million.[7] There are a number of different reasons for this escalation in cost. First, rather than health care demands decreasing as services are made available there is a tendency for expectations of health and health care to rise as needs are met. Also scientific and medical innovations have introduced new and often expensive possibilities for treatment. Finally, the increase in the numbers of elderly people discussed in Chapter 13 has meant increased demands on health services.

Resourcing the health service

In 1988, an all-party Commons Committee published a report on resourcing the health service.[8] The report suggested that resources had suffered a shortfall over the past few years totalling £1896 million. The report expressed concern about the ability of hospitals and other services to maintain levels of care. The MPs made the following recommendations.[9]

- An immediate £95 million to make up the shortfall in funding of pay and price inflation in the current financial year.
- An additional sum of at least £1 billion over 2 years to pay for specific developments, including information, technology, building maintenance, replacing essential equipment and community care.[10]
- A commitment to fund the coming pay awards in full, enabling health authorities to plan their budgets rather than make cuts in anticipation of underfunding.
- A guarantee to fund a 2 per cent rise in services in 1988/89.
- Urgent development of systems to measure the performance and effectiveness of the health service.

There are many examples reported of the effects of under-funding and cuts on health services. The following three examples illustrate the nature of the problems.

- In Reading, local doctors paid for a full-page advertisement in the local evening newspaper warning that 3000 operations would be cancelled as a result of a deficit in funds in their area.
- In Doncaster, 1000 non-urgent hospital admissions would be cut and 69 beds closed.
- In Mexborough two new wards and operating theatres would not be opened.

The issues discussed in the following section are the role of charges in the NHS and of private insurance, the NHS drugs bill, the allocation of resources to different client groups, and finally inequalities in health between regions and social classes. All these issues can be related to finance, although the last section examines social factors, some of which are wider than the scope of the NHS.

Charges

The original idea of the National Health Service was that services should be free to people at the time of use and financed wholly through taxation and national insurance contributions. However, it was not long before this principle was eroded and charges were introduced. Bevan resigned from the government in 1951 when the Labour Party proposed to introduce charges for glasses, drugs and dental care. Bevan believed that this threatened the most basic principle of the NHS and would be the beginning of an irreversible trend. The policy of charging for particular services was extended by later governments, although a system of exemptions was introduced in 1968.

The current situation is that charges are made for prescriptions and for services provided by dentists and opticians. In 1994, prescriptions cost £4.75 per item, with exemptions available for children under 16; older people; expectant mothers; people suffering from certain illnesses such as epilepsy where continuous treatment is required and people on a low income or in receipt of family credit or income support. There is also a system whereby people can obtain a pre-payment certificate for prescriptions. In 1994, these cost £24.60 for four months or £67.70 a year. Dental treatment is no longer free and the system introduced in 1981 means that people pay up to a maximum figure for a course of treatment. Free dental treatment is available for people under 18, or 19 if they are in full-time education, expectant mothers and mothers with children under one year of age. As with prescription charges, those receiving Family Credit, Income Support or on a low income also receive free dental treatment. The services of opticians are similarly free to those groups mentioned above, with the exception of women who are pregnant or who have small babies.

Most of the money for the NHS comes from general taxation, with a smaller amount from national insurance contributions. A very small proportion comes from charges – 4 per cent only in 1990–1.[11] The direction of change however is towards a greater emphasis on charges.

Activity 15.9

Should there be a charge for health services? List reasons for and against.

The first basis on which to argue against charges in the NHS is that charging for services goes against the basic idea that money should not be a barrier to access to health care. The NHS, despite its limitations, has achieved a great deal in improving the health of the nation and was introduced partly as a result of hard campaigning by people in the 1930s and 1940s. The introduction of charges can be seen as a betrayal of the principles of the NHS and the efforts made to achieve a free and comprehensive service.

On a more practical level, the full costs of many types of treatment and care are simply too expensive for anyone to be able to afford. Costs are also highly unpredictable and a visit to a doctor may result in treatment costing a few pounds or several thousand pounds. Charging involves administrative costs, so some of the financial saving to the country is lost.

Few patients are knowledgeable about medical matters, and this means that unscrupulous doctors are in a position to recommend expensive or unnecessary treatment in order to increase their profits. The following story from America illustrates the danger in this situation.

The *New York Times*, in an article on medical costs, recently told of an elderly woman with a temperature and bronchitis, who could have been treated in a surgery with antibiotics. Instead she was admitted to hospital for nine days and ended up with a bill for $9065.[12]

Other problems in charging for health-care concern the fact that an important part of NHS work is preventative care for which few people would be prepared to pay. A full system of charges is not feasible, since there will always be people, often those most in need of services, who are unable to pay. Examples of groups of such people are elderly people, people with chronic illnesses and people with disabilities.

Private medical insurance

There has been a recent expansion in the number of people subscribing to private insurance schemes. This expansion is supported and encouraged by the Conservative Party. There are currently three main private companies operating in the UK. These are the British United Provident Association (BUPA) the Private Patients Plan (PPP) and the Western Provident Association. The way the schemes work is that people subscribe, paying a premium and receive money for treatment when they need it. There are, however, several restrictions – for example, BUPA will not accept new subscribers over the age of 65, payments are made up to a maximum figure and are only for certain types of health care.

Activity 15.10

Contact a private medical insurance company and find out the details of their schemes. If possible, compare your findings with those of someone else in the class who has contacted a different firm.

By 1991 about 7.5 million people had private medical insurance.[13]. The rise in numbers subscribing was particularly great at the end of the 1970s and at the end of the 1980s. The early 1990s saw a fall in subscribers. Most people with private insurance join through group schemes, often provided by companies for employees as a fringe benefit.

There has also been an expansion in the numbers of beds available in private hospitals throughout the country. In 1971 there were 25 300 beds in private nursing homes, hospitals and clinics. In 1991–2 the number had grown to 147 200. The same period saw a drop in the number of private beds in NHS hospitals.[14]

Activity 15.11

What are the advantages, and the disadvantages, to individuals, and to the whole society, of private medical insurance?

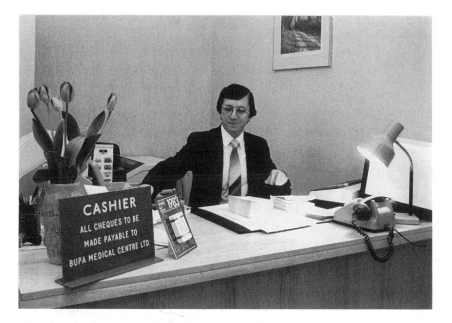

Source: Vicky White, Photofusion
Some people choose to pay privately for health care

A major problem with private insurance companies is that, as profit-making organisations, they are reluctant to accept high-risk subscribers. Also, they do not provide a comprehensive service, but concentrate on acute illnesses which can be cured by a short stay in hospital and routine surgery. They do not cover pregnancy and childbirth, and normally limit cover to a certain number of days in any one year.

In common with other forms of private health care, insurance schemes distort the priorities of NHS, shifting the emphasis from need to the ability to pay. Insurance companies exploit inadequacies in the health service, as is shown in the following passage from BUPA publicity:

> Depending where in the country you live, you can wait months for treatment under the NHS for a condition not classified as urgent. Additionally, while waiting, you may be in considerable pain or discomfort. The assurance that treatment may be received without delay is attracting more and more people to the private sector.[15]

In providing the option of private treatment for those who can pay, private insurance has the effect of reducing pressure on the government to solve problems of waiting-lists. In the past it was common for NHS hospitals to have a number of pay-beds designated for patients paying privately. Although a few still exist, recent years have seen a decrease in pay-beds as private patients are increasingly treated in private hospitals. The existence of pay-beds in the NHS hospitals encourages queue-jumping and again leads to prioritisation on the basis of ability to pay instead of need.

Private patients are subsidised by the state in a variety of ways. Doctors, nurses and other trained staff who work privately have been trained at the expense of the state. The private sector does not contribute to post-operative health and social services home care. Private hospitals tend not to have very expensive equipment and instead use NHS facilities. Finally, private medical insurance is subsidised by the state through the tax relief given to employers providing insurance for their staff.

As was mentioned earlier, high-risk groups and those suffering from chronic illnesses are excluded from private insurance cover. With or without insurance schemes it would be impossible for all health care to be provided privately. Even in the US, a country committed to private enterprise, a large public health sector exists to cater for the less fortunate and the elderly. Private health leads to a dual system of health care. People who pay expect to receive a better service, so dual standards develop. Means-testing leads to stigma in the public sector. The encouragement of the private sector in Britain could result in a system in which the principle of allowing everyone equal access to the best possible treatment and care is lost.

There is no evidence to support the idea that private hospitals can be run more effectively or cheaply than NHS hospitals. In the US, the lack of central control together with the close relationship which exists between the insurance companies and the medical profession lead to high charges for health and large profits for both parties. The administration of private treatment involves complex and costly procedures. In the US, 'admittance to hospital for a minor disorder involves an orgy of form-filling and medical insurance checking which makes filling in a car accident claim look simple.[16]

The benefits argued to result from private insurance are a reduction in NHS expenditure and therefore in taxation. Individuals who can pay are said to benefit from greater freedom of choice and the option of paying for extra services, such as individual rooms in a hospital.

In conclusion to this section, it would seem that there are advantages to some individuals in allowing a private sector to co-exist with the NHS. However, the existence of such provision constitutes a serious threat to the future of the service set up to guarantee access to high-quality medical care regardless of ability to pay.

The NHS drugs bill

Whilst the NHS is a state-run and state-financed organisation, it relies on profit-making companies for drugs, equipment and some services. The multi-national companies which manufacture drugs count amongst the most profitable enterprises in the world. Drugs prescribed by GPs cost £3.6 billion in England and Wales in 1992–3. This is 10 per cent of the NHS budget.[17].

There are several explanations for the high profits of the drug companies. Patent laws are exploited by the large companies to control markets and prices. Several different names are given to the same drug to create 'brand loyalty', resulting in confusion amongst doctors and patients and an appearance of competition where there is none.

The drug companies spend enormous sums of money on promotion of their products. New drugs are particularly widely advertised, which has the effect of increasing their cost to the NHS. This promotion is aimed at doctors and takes a variety of forms:

> The general practitioner in Great Britain receives in an average month one hundred-weight (1 cwt) of advertising literature and assorted free gifts including diaries, notepads and records, from which the drug brand-names beam out insistently. In addition, she will receive frequent visits from drug company representatives, of which there is one for every eight GPs in Britain; will be exposed to advertisements in the free medical newspapers and subscription journals; will be invited to films, drinks and conferences at home and abroad, all at drug companies' 'expense' and will receive free samples of drugs given away at an annual cost to the industry of £2 million.[18]

Drug companies also provide much of the money for post-graduate research.

A final explanation for the success of the drug companies lies with the patients and doctors themselves. Patients tend to expect a prescription from a visit to the doctor. Doctors, often under pressure of time, are too willing to prescribe drugs as an easy way of dealing with patients' problems. This is particularly the case with tranquillisers and anti-depressants. Many drugs produced by the companies are ineffective or designed to meet a 'need' created by the drug company. More worryingly, many drugs have side-effects, varying from relatively minor irritants to the devastating and tragic effects of Thalidomide. A scheme to reduce the NHS drug bill was introduced in April 1985. For certain categories of drugs there are lists from which doctors must prescribe. The categories include cough and cold medicines, minor painkillers, and tranquillisers. The drugs on the list are the cheaper, non-branded drugs. In 1993 it was announced that a further 10 categories of groups would be reviewed for potential inclusion on the list. The first new category to be accepted for inclusion was drugs for the treatment of rheumatism.

In 1994 a government report published by the Audit Commission (which monitors public spending) claimed that doctors could save the NHS £425 million by more efficient prescribing.[19] The ways of saving money suggested by the report include prescribing smaller amounts of drugs such as antibiotics, fewer prescriptions for items of limited value such as cough suppressants and the substitution of cheaper drugs with the same effect where this is possible.

'Cinderella services'

Analysis of resource allocation within the NHS shows that some client groups have been treated less favourably than others. Patients on acute and maternity wards received a greater share of NHS funds than did patients in psychiatric hospitals or those for people with a learning disability. These are the 'Cinderella services' which attract less resources and have less prestige.

Explanations for this unequal situation can be found in different attitudes towards different groups and different types of medicine. People with disabilities and mental illnesses are groups who are unable to exert pressure on the government and who fail to attract public support. Medicine tends to focus on the idea of cure and treatment. Conditions like learning disability require care, since no cures are available, and therefore have less status within the medical profession.

In 1976, a DHSS document called 'Priorities for Health and Personal Social Services in England' was published. The document set out guidelines for establishment priorities, proposing that priority be given to services for elderly people and people with disabilities and mental illnesses. A second discussion paper, called 'The Way Forward' and published in 1977, re-emphasised the points made in the 1976 document and argued that chronically sick and disabled people should be included as priority groups. These consultative documents attracted general approval, but little has been done to rectify the situation of unequal allocation of resources to different groups.

Regional inequalities in health care

One of the aims of the NHS was to make health care equally available to everyone, as the following extract from the 1946 Bill shows:

> All the service or any part of it, is to be available to everyone in England and Wales. The Bill imposes no limitation on availability – e.g. limitations based on financial means, age, sex, employment or vocation, area of residence, or insurance qualifications.[20]

In spite of this, inequalities persist within the system. We examine variation between regions of the country here, and then look at inequalities between different social classes.

One way of comparing standards of health between different areas and different social groups is by looking at death rates. The infant mortality rate refers to the number of deaths of children under 1 year of age per 1000 live births, and can be used as an indicator of general standards of health. In 1990, the infant mortality rate for the whole of England was 8.4: the highest mortality rate was in the West Midlands with a rate of 9.9 and the lowest was in East Anglia with a rate of 6.4.[21] There are also variations in adult mortality rates.

There are variations throughout the country in expenditure on health and in the numbers of health care workers. Looking at expenditure as a whole the highest rate in 1988–9 was in the North East Thames Region and the lowest rate was in the Oxford region.[22] Different regions have different health needs, according to the local population. Areas where there are larger proportions of older people, for example, will need higher *per capita* spending on health.

Often in social policy there is a tendency for areas with greatest needs to have the least resources to meet these needs. This tendency is known as the 'inverse care law'. In the 1960s and 1970s this was the case with health care expenditure; for example, there were least GPs in areas where people had the greatest health needs.

In the 1970s this problem was recognised by the government and a working party was set up to investigate and make recommendations. The Resource Allocation Working Party (RAWP) published its report in 1976. The RAWP report recommended that resources should be allocated on the basis of regional populations, taking into account factors like age, sex, mortality rates and existing provision.

The proposal for a gradual introduction of this idea was accepted, but implementation proved difficult in a time of financial cut-backs. There was also opposition from areas which would lose resources, criticism of the use of mortality rates as an indicator of need and criticism of the failure of the report to consider social deprivation factors such as housing standards and poverty. Despite these points, the RAWP report was important in reducing regional inequalities in health care provision.

In 1988 a review of the RAWP report was published.[23] This recommended different criteria for allocation of resources, resulting in a shift of resources from the North and the Midlands to the South. The report was not immediately acted upon, but its recommendations were considered within the broader review of the health service taking place that year.

The reforms in the NHS in the 1990s have led to a new way of allocating funds, but the principles developed by RAWP are still in use. Regional and district health authorities receive an amount of money based on the age, sex and mortality rates of the population in their areas.

Social class inequalities

Several surveys and reports have shown class differences in health and in access to health services.[24]. In 1980, the DHSS published a report produced by a research group chaired by Sir Douglas Black. The report takes the name of the chairperson and is thus known as the 'Black Report'. The report used the Register-General's classification of social groups by occupation and found relationships between social class and all aspects of health. In the following passage, the statistical information was translated into an account of two imaginary families.[25]

> Mr Smythe is the financial director of a large company. Mrs Smythe does not work and she is soon to give birth to her third child. They live in a pleasant suburb on the edge of the green belt with their two children, Emily aged five and Rodney aged 10. They own their own home and the area where they live is mainly populated by professional people. There are plenty of recreational and sporting facilities, good schools and a brand new health centre in the locality.
>
> Mr Jones is an unskilled labourer at a factory. His wife supplements the family income by working as an office cleaner. They live in a high-rise block of flats in the centre of the city. The flats were built in the late 1950s and are poorly serviced with play areas and parks. The Joneses also have two children, Janet, aged five, and John, aged 10. Mrs Jones is also expecting her third child. The family is registered with a local GP whose list of patients is already oversubscribed.
>
> These two imaginary families are at opposite ends of the social scale in terms of occupation, and income. In between there are different shades of grey, but how are these two families likely to fare under the existing National Health Service arrangements? Based on the Black Report these are some of the likely outcomes.

There is a 60 per cent probability that Mrs Jones will not have consulted an obstetrician by the fifth month of her pregnancy. By that time it may be too late to diagnose congenital abnormalities like spina bifida or blood disorders in her unborn baby.

Mrs Jones's poorer living standards will probably mean her standard of nutritional diet is poor. She is nearly twice as likely as Mrs Smythe to die in childbirth, or her baby to be stillborn or die within the first few months of life. If her baby is a boy and survives at birth, he is still four times more likely to die before his first birthday than is Mrs Smythe's new-born son.

Like his brother John, the new-born Jones boy is ten times more likely to die, before he is 14, through an accident involving fire, a fall or drowning, than is his counterpart Rodney Smythe. John is seven times more likely to be knocked down and killed in a road accident.

Similar disadvantages will follow him into adult life. In only one case – asthma – is Rodney more likely than John to die at an early age.

Though the statistics show that Janet Jones is not as likely to be an accident victim as her brother, her individual health and life-expectancy will tend to follow the pattern of her mother and maternal grandmother.

Mr Jones's health and life-expectancy is also considerably poorer than that of Mr Smythe – and if his son also becomes a manual worker his health is likely to follow a similar pattern too.

Although the actual health of all families has improved since the setting up of the NHS, the relative gap between professional and unskilled manual workers has actually widened.

Contrary to popular belief, Mr Jones is much more likely to die of lung cancer or duodenal ulcer than Mr Smythe. He is twice as likely to die of a disease affecting the nervous system; three times as likely to suffer and die from a parasitic disease; four times as likely to incur a mental disorder or a respiratory disease and die.

In contrast, the Smythe family are more likely to follow a nutritionally satisfactory diet, to consult preventative services such as dentists, chiropodists and opticians. Mrs Smythe is more likely to have planned her family than Mrs Jones, or to have been screened to test if she might have treatable breast or cervical cancer. The Black Report comments that health facilities tend to be geared towards the middle-class consumer rather than the working-class.

Also the high-density urban areas where working-class people live tend to have a lower *per capita* expenditure than the suburban areas which are not so densely populated. The Smythe family are likely to have frequent medical check-ups as a matter of course – the Jones are more likely to use their GP after illness has set in, and consequently visit him more often.

Activity 15.12

Discussion questions:

1   Why might a family's health suffer if the mother works as an office cleaner?

2   Why are doctors' practices in working-class areas more likely to be oversubscribed than those in middle-class areas, and what effect might this have on the service?

3   Why are middle-class women more likely than working-class women take advantage of ante-natal care facilities?

4   Why should there be a connection between level of income and standard of diet?

5   Why is it that some problems in childbirth can be traced to nutritional deficiencies in the mother?

6   Why are working-class children more likely than middle-class children to be victims of an accident?

7   There is a statistical connection between manual work and ill-health. Why should this be?

8   Why is lung-cancer more prevalent among working-class people?

9   Why are middle-class people more likely to use the preventive health service?

10 In what ways are the health services more geared to the middle-class consumer?

The Black Report made many recommendations for improvements which might help to reduce the inequalities between different social classes. These were rejected by the government, primarily on the grounds of expense. Figures released by the government in 1986 revealed that the class inequalities shown in the Black Report had widened in the years following 1980.[26]

___ Activity 15.13 _____

The government is concerned to reduce inequalities in health and has ear-marked some money for this purpose. Working in groups of three or four, make a list of policies to achieve this aim and decide the order of priority.

The main focus of this chapter has been on various aspects of the National Health Service in Britain. It is difficult to reach any final assessment of the impact of the NHS on the nation's health. Whilst there have been considerable improvements in health since the Second World War, particular factors cannot be easily isolated as causes. It may well be that improvements in the overall standard living, in housing, or in working conditions are of greater significance than developments in medicine and health care provision.

___ Activity 15.14 _____

Make sure that you understand the following expressions used in this chapter. Check the glossary on p. 363 if you need to.

acute illness   internal market
ante-natal clinic   inverse care law

anti-depressants	life-expectancy
Audit Commission	mental disorder
child health clinic	mortality rate
chronic illness	NHS Trust
'Cinderella service'	obstetrician
client group	parasitic disease
community care	patent law
congenital abnormality	*per capita*
consultative document	preventative medicine
fund-holding GP	provider
health education	purchaser
health visitor	respiratory disease
high density	social deprivation factor
infant mortality rate	stigma
insurance qualification	tranquillisers

Further reading

A useful introduction to issues relating to health is Peter Aggleton, *Health* (London: Routledge, 1990). *Inequalities in Health* (London: Penguin, 1988) is a paperback which includes the Black Report together with an updated report on inequalities called 'The Health Divide'.

A useful review of all aspects of health policy can be found in Christopher Ham, *Health Policy in Britain*, 3rd ed. (London: Macmillan, 1992). Another useful book in this area is Rob Baggott, *Health and Health Care* (London: Macmillan, 1994).

Useful addresses

Health Education Authority: Hamilton House, Mabledon Place, London WC1H 9TX
tel. 071 383 3833

National Community Health Resource: 15 Britannia Street, London WC1X 9JP
tel. 0171 837 2426

16 The voluntary sector

Voluntary provision of services for people in need has a long history. In the nineteenth and early twentieth century most health care and social provision was organised by voluntary organisations.

16.1 Statutory and voluntary organisations

The relationship between statutory and voluntary services has varied in different periods. For most of this century, the trend was for statutory organisations to take over the tasks of the voluntary sector in many areas of provision. Indeed, the expansion of state responsibility after the Second World War led to the expectation that voluntary organisations would shrink and ultimately cease to exist. However, recent years have seen a reversal in policy whereby voluntary organisations are increasingly encouraged to take responsibility for care.

The Griffiths Report and the 1990 NHS and Community Care Act had a major impact on the role of voluntary organisations (see Chapter 9 for more detail on these). A major theme in the Report and Act which followed was that there should be a separation between *purchasers* and *providers* of services in health and social care. Health authorities and social services departments would be the purchasers of services, not the providers. The providers would increasingly be the private and voluntary organisations, known collectively as the 'independent sector'. Local authorities would buy services from voluntary and other organisations on behalf of their clients.

16.2 Definitions of voluntary organisations

Activity 16.1

What do you think is meant by the term 'voluntary'? Write a definition of a voluntary organisation and list any examples you have learned about, and the work they do.

Aims, organisation and finance

It is difficult to establish a precise definition to cover all kinds of voluntary organisation. People who work in voluntary organisations may be paid, so the voluntary sector is not limited to groups staffed by volunteers. Voluntary provision is usually distinguished from statutory provision, although this distinction is not always clear-cut. For example, workers from local social services departments or health services may be involved in managing and running voluntary organisations. In many areas of work, there is close liaison between social services and non-statutory agencies. Some voluntary organisations work in areas which are also the concern of state-provided services. For example, the National Society for the Prevention of Cruelty to Children (NSPCC) will act in cases of child-abuse or neglect, overlapping with the responsibilities of social workers. Voluntary organisations cannot be distinguished in terms of being self-financing. Whilst many rely on contributions and fund-raising, a significant number of groups receive grants from central or local government to fund their work. Financial support was first given to voluntary bodies by central government in 1914. Current funding from central government totals approximately £2.4 billion.[1] In 1971–2 local authorities grant aided voluntary organisations some £1.3 million. By 1982–3 the figure was £29.5 million and by the 1990s has increased to over £250 million.[2] Despite this, voluntary organisations are different from statutory provision in the sense that they are not established through legislation and are not controlled by the government. Voluntary provision can also be defined as being non-profit-making, which distinguishes it from those aspects of provision which are independent of social services and health departments but run as business for profit. Whilst these two factors – non-profit-making motives and lack of state control – are common to all voluntary organisations, there is in other aspects considerable diversity, for example, in aims, organisations and sources of finance.

Since there is no clear definition of a voluntary organisation, estimates of the number of such groups vary. One researcher, using a broad definition, which includes voluntary schools, churches, sports clubs and trade unions, as well as charities, estimated that there were more than 350 000 groups in the voluntary sector. Of this number, some 40 per cent were registered as charities.[3]

Charities

Charities are organisations whose application for charitable status satisfies the Charity Commissioners in England, or the Inland Revenue in Scotland or Northern Ireland. Organisations wishing to become charities must show that their purposes fall within certain categories. These are the relief of poverty, the advancement of education or religion and the advancement of purposes beneficial to the community. The last category is not an all-purpose clause into which any groups excluded from the other categories can fit, but is legally defined, such that, for example, improving the welfare of the unemployed was not accepted as a charitable purpose. The law on charity has been subjected to criticism since many anomalies have been found to exist. Religion, which includes groups like the Moonies, is 'charitable', but it was only at the end of 1983 that the promotion of racial equality, which could be argued to be part of Christian teaching, was allowed as a charitable purpose. When Amnesty

International wanted to establish a fund for prisoners of conscience, this was disallowed when Mr Justice Slade ruled in the High Court that,

> The elimination of injustice has not as such ever been held to be a trust purpose which qualified for the privilege afforded to charities by British Law.[4] On the other hand, education is 'charitable', so public schools are able to establish themselves as charities.

To avoid the restrictions involved in charity law, some organisations split into two parts with separate funds and separate aims. In this way, they can engage in political activity which is not permitted to a charity. Organisations with charitable status can claim tax and rate relief, receive covenants at beneficial rates and apply for grants from charitable trusts.

16.3   The work of voluntary organisations

Whilst some charities and other voluntary groups work in areas where there is no statutory provision, others work alongside social workers and health teams. As was mentioned earlier the 1990 NHS and Community Care Act increased in the importance of voluntary organisations, so that in some areas of care they could be the major provider of a service.

Children

In the field of provision for deprived children, social service departments work with voluntary welfare groups. For example, social workers can place children in homes run by Barnardo's, the National Children's home or the Catholic Rescue Society, and social services departments will contribute to costs and inspect the homes. Similarly, in family welfare, in addition to statutory provision, many large towns have Family Welfare Associations which provide financial assistance and social work for families in need. In the same field, Family Service Units are part of a national organisation found in 1947 and based on the experience of the Pacifist Service Unit, originally concerned with problems caused by the war but continued when it was realised that problems existed not solely as a result of the war. Many Family Service Units have local authority grants and their work is mainly that of intensive casework with families referred to them by other agencies. The caseworkers each work with a small number of families, visiting regularly and offering help and support. Volunteer families work in shared care schemes in which families look after a child with a disability for a number of days each year, to give the child variety and stimulation and the family a break.

Older people and people with disabilities

Provision for elderly people is also the concern of people in both statutory and voluntary organisations. Local voluntary groups provide clubs, recreational facilities and some residential accommodation. National organisations, such as Age Concern co-ordinate the activities of local groups and also act as a pressure group trying to improve the position of elderly people in society. In the case of people with disabilities, the Royal National Institute for the Blind provides specialist facilities such as Braille literature, talking books, educational aids and homes and schools for the blind. The Royal National Institute for the Deaf has a similar role, and many other organisations exist for the needs of specific disabilities or to campaign on behalf of all disabled people.

Mental health and learning disability

The voluntary sector is also active in the fields of mental illness and learning disability. In 1946, the amalgamation of existing groups led to the creation of the National Association for Mental Health. The Association is now known as MIND and is concerned with various aspects of mental health, including spreading information, promoting research, running training courses and providing homes for mentally ill people. Mencap does similar work in its area of concern. The Richmond Fellowship runs small community hostels for mentally ill people, while Rudolf Steiner schools are well-respected for their work with people with a learning disability and the same organisation runs colonies where people can live and work, sheltered from the wider society.

Status and role of volunteers

In 1969, a report was published by the Aves Committee, which had been set up by the National Council of Social Services and the National Institute for Social Work Training. The committee was concerned with the role of the voluntary worker in personal social services. The report emphasised that voluntary workers should not be used to replace paid staff. Other areas covered by the committee were the status of volunteers in public services, motivation, and discussion of the type of people attracted to voluntary work. An important aspect of the committee's deliberation concerned the organisation of volunteers. It was recommended that voluntary bureaux be established to deal with recruitment and offer advice to potential volunteers. As a result of the report, the national volunteer foundation was set up in London in 1973, with the support of the Voluntary Services Unit, a statutory organisation, concerned primarily with co-ordinating government assistance to voluntary organisations. Volunteer bureaux now exist in most towns throughout the country and their work includes matching volunteers to needs in the community and running campaigns for voluntary workers for particular areas of work.

Voluntary groups

All the areas of provision described so far are also the responsibility of local health and social services. It would be impossible for a book, let alone a chapter, to describe all the voluntary groups which exist. In the following pages several examples of voluntary groups will be described to illustrate the diversity of organisations and demonstrate the work done by the voluntary sector. Some of the groups discussed here are mentioned in other chapters, for example, Women's Aid in chapter 2, and Shelter in chapter 5.

The National Society for the Prevention of Cruelty to Children (NSPCC)

Most people have heard of the NSPCC, although few are aware of the full range of the society's work. The NSPCC was started in London in 1884. It is a large organisation and in 1993 received 33 512 requests for help. On average, throughout the year, there were 1906 cases involving 3324 children open at any given time.[5] The NSPCC is a charity and 90 per cent of funds come from contributions from the public. The society is involved with helping families with problems in a variety of ways. The NSPCC has a Child Protection Helpline as a first point of contact for anyone who is concerned about the safety of children, including of course the children themselves. The NSPCC employs Child Protection Officers, who are qualified social workers, in 90 Child Protection Teams, Projects and Centres throughout the country. Cases may be referred by neighbours, relatives, local and other authorities, children themselves, or parents may themselves contact the society.

The work covers families in which children are deprived, neglected or at risk of abuse. The child protection officers provide advice, support, counselling and practical help such as finding places for children in playgroups or nurseries, NSPCC staff can start proceedings in the family court when children are thought to be in danger. The work of the child protection officers includes liaising with other organisations such as the police, social services and schools.

The following account from the NSPCC illustrates the type of work done by the organisation.

Two children, a boy and a girl, aged 4 and 5, were found in bedrooms which were littered with excreta and without ventilation – and from which the door-handles had been removed. The parents – who lived in perfectly normal conditions – were completely ignorant of their responsibilities as parents.

Incredible though it may seem, the NSPCC inspector's care and interest succeeded in transforming two irresponsible adults and two severely neglected children into a caring and responsible family unit.[6]

Most people are aware of the NSPCC's work in the field of child abuse. However the NSPCC is also involved in a wider range of schemes and projects, sometimes in conjunction with local authorities and other voluntary organisations. Many of these are new ideas in social care. The following are some examples of this work, from the 1993 *Annual Report*. This shows the breadth of the NSPCC's work.[7]

- In Manchester – a new black youth counselling and advocacy service to help highly vulnerable and disadvantaged people, many of whom have been in residential care and have no family support.

- In London – a joint project with Centrepoint in a new refuge for homeless children. This is the first refuge for runaways under 16 set up since the implementation of the Children Act.
- In Surrey – a witness support scheme for children facing the trauma of legal proceedings.
- In Staffordshire, Warwickshire and Gwent – independent visitor services for children who are in local authority care, using volunteers supervised by the Society's professional staff.
- In Derbyshire – the Dove project developed jointly with the probation service, to prevent the abuse of children by known perpetrators through working with known sex offenders in the community.

As well as providing immediate help for children and families, the NSPCC works as a pressure group, campaigning on behalf of children. This work involves running national campaigns to change attitudes and inform parents, giving information and evidence to the government on law and social policy matters which affect children and generally promoting children's rights. The NSPCC is also active in training workers from other organisations and in research into child abuse.

The Citizens Advice Bureau (CAB)

The CAB is another large and well-known voluntary organisation, providing a free and comprehensive information service. The CAB began in 1939 when it was recognised that people needed help in wartime conditions of ration books and bombing. During the war the CAB received funding from the government although this was withdrawn after the war ended. The organisation continued without funds for some time until the government reinstated the grant, at the time of the housing crisis in the 1950s.

Currently, the CAB consists of a national organisation known as the National Association of Citizens Advice Bureau (NACAB), area organisations and some 1300 local bureaux. Nationally the CAB deal with some 7 million enquiries each year.[8] NACAB decides the policy of the CAB, it collects and distributes information and is responsible for organising training. A government grant of £11.7 million is made to NACAB and most local bureaux have full- or part-time paid organisers as well as volunteers. Each CAB is managed by a committee and applies to the local authority for help with day-to-day running costs. The CAB deals with many different types of problems, the most common being in the areas of debt, housing, employment, planning law and social security. At the present time there has been an increase in enquiries about social security as unemployment has spread. The CAB will refer people to other agencies if necessary and some bureaux are able to represent clients at employment and social security boards.

A new development in CAB is in *outreach*. This involves taking the service into health centres, hospitals and prisons.

The Relatives' Support Group

Some voluntary groups are small and locally based, existing to meet a particular need without the back-up service of a national organisation. In Coventry, the Relatives Support Group is made up of professionals from Coventry's health and social services staff and people looking after senile relatives. The group has the support of the local authority who are aware that statutory provision for the old and senile is inadequate and that the burden of care falls on relatives. At group meetings talks are provided to give information about the condition of senile dementia and problems are shared. The Relatives' Support Group also looks at problems which require practical solution – for example, the difficulty of leaving a senile relative prevents people from being able to attend meetings. The proposed solution to this situation is to set up a 'granny-sitting' service of people trained informally and given a telephone number to ring in the event of needing assistance.

Alcoholics anonymous (AA)

Many voluntary groups operate through the principle of self-help. This involves people with the same problem helping each other. A well-known example of a self-help group is Alcoholics Anonymous, started in America in 1935. In the UK there are about 1200 local groups of people who want to solve their drink problem and who have joined the AA. Members meet once a week to discuss their problems and work on stopping drinking. The basic idea of Alcoholics Anonymous is that alcoholics and recovering alcoholics are the best people to understand the problem and to provide help. There is no fee for membership, although the organisation is funded entirely from money collected from members. The experience of Alcoholics Anonymous has led to the establishment of Al-Anon family groups which provide support for relatives of alcoholics.

Step-parent Linkline

Some of the reasons why self-help groups are popular can be seen in the way in which Step-parent Linkline was started. The founder, Mrs Mason, was living with her second husband, one child from each of their previous marriages, and a new baby. Mrs Mason suffered when she found it difficult to form a good relationship with her stepson and as a result the marriage became strained. In desperation, she wrote to *Annabel* magazine about the difficulties of being a step-parent. She received about 50 letters in reply from others in the same situation as herself. Mrs Mason explained her feelings in the first newsletter,

> those people were strangers but they saved my sanity. One thing came through loud and clear, I wasn't alone. I wasn't mad. I was and am a woman who was having a life of hell trying to rebuild two families.[9]

The organisation which resulted is a newsletter counselling service. Members pay a small fee to receive the newsletter which provides personal accounts, news of local groups and other information.

Parents' Anonymous

The self-help principle can be particularly important where the problem is one which attracts the disapproval of society. Parents' Anonymous is an organisation providing a telephone service for parents who are in danger of abusing their children. Janet's problems began when her son, later sent to a school for children with a learning disability, was born. He was put into an incubator and she was not allowed to breastfeed him. The baby was in hospital for several months by which time Janet says,

> Part of me was dying for him to come home and half was hoping for another relapse. Then within two weeks of when he did come home I'd beaten him.[10]

Janet tried to tell her husband and her doctor but both dismissed her problem. She then began to be secretive, keeping the child away from the health visitor. The situation was not recognised until the little boy went to school and a social worker put Janet in touch with Parents' Anonymous. Janet tells how her shame and fear prevented her from seeking help:

> 'I couldn't just go up to someone and say, "Hey, I keep bashing up my kid in fits of uncontrolled temper." 'They'd probably not have believed me, but if they had they'd probably have locked me up.' Janet felt that she 'was the only person, sort of isolated . . . the only person who did this, the only person in the world.'[11]

Anonymity is an important feature of Parents' Anonymous; people who phone in are not asked for their name or address or any other details usually asked for by health and social services staff. Many of the people who run the telephone service have first-hand experience of child abuse and are able to show understanding without the disapproval that most people feel for parents who hurt their children.

The Child Poverty Action Group (CPAG)

Whilst some voluntary organisations are concerned with providing immediate help to individuals in need, others are primarily involved with campaigning for change, putting pressure on the government to change laws and improve provision and trying to change attitudes towards a particular problem. One such group is the CPAG which was established in 1965 by a group of Quakers who saw a need to draw attention to the plight of the millions of people living in poverty. CPAG does not give money to the poor but is an action group in the field of welfare rights and poverty. The objectives of the CPAG are agreed as follows:

> To promote action for the relief, directly or indirectly, of poverty among children and families with children. This means: ensuring that poor people do not remain poorer than they need to be because they are not claiming (or are denied) their full entitlement to welfare benefits; educating the public and politicians about the alternative lines of government action that will increase the incomes of poor families.[12]

CPAG activity in meeting these objectives takes various forms. The group produces information to influence opinion, putting pressure on MPs and public officials and monitors changes in legislation. CPAG feeds information to the media in order to keep issues before the public. The group also provides a free information, advice and advocacy service through the Citizens Rights Office (CRO). The organisation specialises in test cases, where the law is unclear and the judgement will set a precedent for future cases. CPAG also runs courses, finances research and publishes guides to welfare rights and research findings.

The organisation is financed through membership fees, grants and donations, fees charged for courses, sales of books and raffles. There is an executive committee which sets policy and a number of local branches which take up issues, provide advice and represent claimants at tribunals.

The National Campaign for the Homeless (Shelter)

Shelter is another organisation which has an important role as a pressure group. It started in 1966 when a group of people, mainly from the clergy, were concerned about the extent of homelessness, and the aim is to fight for the right of everyone to a decent home. In the early days, Shelter was mainly involved in funding housing associations and the campaign to persuade the government to take over this role achieved success with the 1974 Housing Act (see chapter 5).

Currently, Shelter's work takes three forms. First, there are 24 housing aid centres throughout the country which provide advice and help. Second, projects are initiated and supported in response to particular needs. For example, Shelter Nightline was set up in 1991 and is an out-of-hours telephone service for people in London experiencing emergency housing problems. Calls are free. Third, Shelter campaigns for change. The group's analysis of homelessness leads to a view of the problem as one caused by the failure of the housing market, rather than personal inadequacy of people who are homeless. Shelter provides information to people in positions of power and makes suggestions for improvements in housing policy. Debates are initiated on areas of housing and Shelter produces pamphlets and books. Most of Shelter's finance comes from donations and fund-raising events.

Women's Aid

Clear-cut distinctions cannot be made among different types of voluntary groups since many combine different elements. For example, some are committed to the idea of self-help but allow people without personal experience of a problem to be involved. Also, some combine pressure-group activities with the provision of immediate help for individuals. Women's Aid is an example of an organisation which combines these different functions and philosophies. Women's Aid believes in the principle of self-help and encourages battered women to help each other. It does not however restrict involvement to those who have personal experience of marital violence. Women's Aid merges the functions of a pressure group and a provider of practical help and support. Refuges provide shelter for women and their children, while Women's Aid is also involved in fighting to improve the situation of battered women and the position of women in society generally. This more general approach to violence in marriage is explained by the early links between Women's Aid and feminism and the organisation's support of the demands of the Women's Liberation Movement.

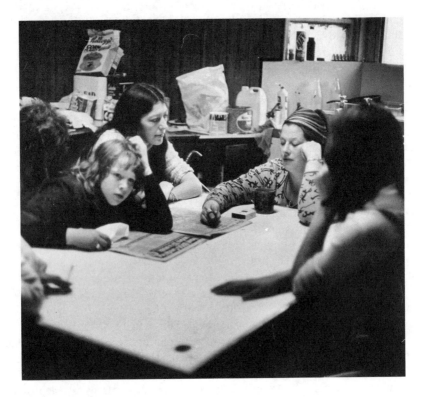

Self-help in a refuge

Women's Aid has a national organisation, Women's Aid Federation England (WAFE) which began, although with a different name, in 1975 when the 35 groups running refuges decided there was a need for a central organisation. At the present, some 100 local groups are federated in WAFE. Refuges in Scotland and Wales are separately organised. Women's Aid sets out its objectives in five aims, listed as follows:[13]

1   Promoting the development of a network of autonomous locally-based groups to provide temporary refuge on request for women and their children who have suffered mental, emotional or physical harassment in their relationships, or rape or sexual harassment or abuse.

2   Encouraging the development of facilities which offer advice, support and practical help to any woman who seeks it, whether or not she is a resident of a refuge, and which gives continuing support and after-care to women and children after they have left the refuge.

3   Researching and campaigning for the provision of facilities which meet the emotional and educational needs of children of women who seek refuge.

4   Providing information and assistance to local groups who are members of the Federation and to create a forum for the exchange of information and ideas on all aspects of the objects of the Federation.

5   Educating and informing the public, the media, the police, the courts, the social services and other authorities with respect to the violence women suffer, mindful of the fact that this is a result of the general position of women in society.

The national organisation is a federation of local groups who decide for themselves how the refuges will be run. Local Women's Aid groups are made up of women living in the refuges, paid workers and volunteers. There are also regional organisations or refuges. WAFE provides information and support and unites local groups into a political movement, campaigning on feminist issues. Women's Aid has been successful in changing the law on injunctions for battered women and in getting recognition of the problems of battered women in housing law. Both these aspects of the law are discussed in Chapter 2. WAFE receives a grant from the government to run the national office. Refuge finances vary, some groups receive Urban Aid grants, others have workers paid by the local authority, whilst some are self-supporting.

The Terence Higgins Trust

This work of the Terence Higgins Trust demonstrates how quickly voluntary organisations can spring up to meet new needs, ahead of slower-moving statutory provision. The organisation is named after Terence Higgins who died of AIDS in 1982. At that time little was known about the disease. There were few services available to meet the needs of AIDS patients. Shocked by the lack of provision, Terence Higgins' friends decided to set up an organisation to provide support and help to people with AIDS and HIV infection. The Trust grew very quickly and is now the leading AIDS charity in the country. The Terence Higgins Trust has pioneered the 'Buddy' system of support in this country. The Trust described buddying in the following way:

> Buddies are trained and skilled volunteers who are committed to providing a consistent service of emotional and practical support to a person with AIDS on a one-to-one basis. The aim is to enable a person with AIDS to live well by leading a satisfying and fulfilling life based on personal decisions and choices. The role of the buddy is always determined by the wishes of the person they work with, their individual needs and the level of support they are already receiving. Needs may range from a listening ear, companionship and help in the home to advocacy, or just having someone available and there for them.[14]

Other services provided by the Terence Higgins Trust are 'helper cells' providing more practical support on a one-off basis, counselling and various support groups for people with AIDS, their lovers and families.

Activity 16.2

Find out all you can about one of these voluntary organisations. The college or local library has various reference books describing their work and giving addresses and phone numbers. Many organisations will send information to you but you must send a stamped, addressed envelope, and in some cases you will have to pay for booklets.

16.4   The advantages and disadvantages of voluntary organisations

---
Activity 16.3 _____

Why have voluntary groups continued to exist alongside statutory provision? Make a list of reasons, using the information already provided in this chapter and any other information you may know about.

Respond to need and specialisation

Whilst many people believed that the post-war expansion of social services would mean the end of voluntary organisations, others foresaw the continuation of such work, perhaps with a change in emphasis. Beveridge, who wrote the report which formed the basis of the social security system (see chapter 3), believed that voluntary groups would continue to meet certain special needs and to act as 'society's conscience'. Both these roles are carried out by today's voluntary groups. Groups like Shelter and the CPAG keep homelessness and poverty on the agenda for debate and educate the public and those in power. Considerable success is achieved; for example, the CPAG was influential in changing family allowances to child benefit, available for all children and not just the second child and subsequent children. Voluntary groups criticise state provision and make recommendations for change.

The state is often slow in responding to new needs and inflexible in adapting to meet changing circumstances. For example, Women's Aid were able to establish refuges in most parts of the country within a few years of recognising the need which existed. In many case, the voluntary sector improves provision by experimenting with new forms of care and trying out ideas which are later adopted by statutory provision. It is probably true that, within the present structure of society, it would be impossible for the state to meet all needs and that voluntary groups fulfil an essential role in filling in gaps in state provision.

Voluntary organisations provide a specialisation in a particular area which may be lacking in state services. To take Women's Aid again as an example, its workers develop an expertise in law, housing and social security regulations relating to battered women. Similar specialisation can be seen from the experience of a woman who joined Kith and Kids, a self-help organisation for parents with children with disabilities. In the following quotation, Sheila explains how she was helped not only by being given an opportunity to share her feelings, but also by being given specialist advice from people who had developed detailed knowledge on the benefits available for parents with children with disabilities.

> Of course, you just speak and speak and if you've a few years of unspeakable things it all comes out and for the first time here was a group of people who were not only

sympathetic but seemed to think the way I did. But after you spoke your heart out in a way then comes the practicalities. I remember Mavis saying to me straight away, 'Why, haven't you got a social worker?' And at that time I hadn't. Well I should have. 'Do you know all about practical things like attendance allowance, baby buggies', things like this. I mean I'd never heard of all this and it was really like opening the floodgates.[15]

Pressure groups like the CPAG are respected as the experts on poverty issues and the quality of their information and research is recognised by MPs and government officials as well as the media.

Comprehensive and flexible response

In some areas of provision, the voluntary sector is able to offer a more comprehensive and flexible service than is provided by the state. Self-help groups provide support which is available for 24 hours a day, 7 days a week, without appointments, delay or payment. In many groups help is offered without being asked for, in contrast to health service provision, where it is extremely unlikely that a doctor would telephone a patient just to see how he or she is getting on. Self-help is also continuous, a member of CARE, an organisation for people who have or have had cancer, says:

You see the lovely part of this organisation is that they don't drop you. Lots of things, hospitals or visitors, welfare visits, they care so long and then you're left entirely. They think, 'Oh well she's going to be alright' or on the other hand 'there's nothing more that we can do'. CARE is there until a person dies. They are not given up because they are terminal.[16]

There is a tendency for statutory provision to be available only in a crisis and this is not sufficient for many problems which need continuing support. A member of Alcoholics Anonymous explains this disillusionment with help provided by friends compared with that given by AA members,

In AA I found I could talk to somebody and get a bloody answer or advice. AA and my sponsor followed it through. They saw me through the rough times. They didn't drop me in the good times. Continuity. Somebody there all the time. I found this concern. I got let down so often while I was drinking. It was all little bits here and there. I never saw anything through.[17]

For many people having a social worker involves stigma, the stigma of being a client, taking help. Most voluntary organisations are able to provide help without this feeling of stigma as the staff do not regard themselves as professionals, especially where they are working in a voluntary capacity. Self-help groups are particularly successful in this respect, in that people with similar experiences help each other, no-one is in the role of helper and no-one is being helped, much in the same way as friends provide mutual support. As a member of Relatives of the Depressed (ROD) puts it,

It's the 'them' and 'us' situation and you've got to overcome it, because you get so humiliated if you're always on the receiving end.[18]

The interaction between a professional helper and a client can lead to increased dependency and feelings of failure, in the experience of a member of Depressive Associated, the professional–client relationship is

one in which instead of being 'built-up' you are constantly being 'pulled-down'.[19]

As has already been stressed, self-help groups believe that a particular understanding and acceptance is offered by people who have first-hand experience of a problem. This is especially true in the case of problems which carry a stigma, such as incest or family violence. Whilst it is not true that it is impossible to understand a problem without personal experience, the fear of disapproval and rejection is removed in the situation where the other person has the same difficulties. Self-help groups also remove the feeling of isolation, the feeling that the sufferer is the only person in the world with a particular problem and that there must be something terribly wrong with them to feel as they do.

Here, David Townsend, the Director of Croydon social service, writes about the advantages of voluntary organisations from his viewpoint.

Voluntary activity enhances local community development and adds to social cohesion. It helps shape community care plans and children's service plans. Harnessing voluntary activity to the local authority can be very productive. Croydon social services has over 1000 registered volunteers organised in teams led by paid organisers. They are active every day in a variety of ways, from visiting recovering psychiatric patients to ferrying outpatients around. These volunteers are 'vetted'; their altruism does not suffer as a result but an unsuspecting public is offered a safeguard. Their work 'value' to the department has been estimated at up to £750 000 per year.[20]

Activity 16.4

1 Why does the state encourage voluntary organisations?
2 What criticisms can be made of the way voluntary organisations help people.

The state makes a considerable investment in voluntary organisations, for example in the generous grant made to the CAB, although it should be said that such grants are given on a temporary basis and the future for voluntary groups is always uncertain. It is to the advantage of the state to fund organisations like the CAB, since a great deal of necessary work is done, mostly by volunteers, saving the state money. Statutory provision on a scale provided by the CAB would be very costly.

Criticisms

Whilst a great deal of valuable work is done by voluntary organisations, criticism can be made of the way in which such groups allow the government to avoid responsibilities, which perhaps should be included as areas of state concern. Organisations which arise from recognised inadequacies in provision allow the gaps and areas of neglect to continue. Self-help and other groups also provide help to individuals which may have the effect of distracting attention from structural causes of problems. For example, counselling a woman who has difficulty in coping with a child with a disability shifts attention from the problems of a system which expects women in isolation, without support, to manage families.

Even if it is accepted that voluntary organisations meet some needs which could not be met by the state or which are better provided for by more informal forms of care, there is cause for concern when the state begins to turn over areas of work to voluntary organisations. Finally, it can be argued that groups providing for accepted and established needs should not have to rely wholly on contributions from members of the public, or on temporary grants in a state of uncertainty about the future.

Other criticisms of voluntary organisations include the fact that many volunteers are untrained and may be using out-of-date methods in their work. Voluntary organisations may be unreliable and inconsistent in meeting need. Linked to this, they may provide an uneven service, available in some areas and not in others. Services provided by voluntary organisations may be a duplication of services already offered by statutory organisations.

As the role of the voluntary sector has expanded and the amounts of money involved have increased more cases of mismanagement of funds and sometimes of fraudulent activities have occurred. There are few checks on staff in voluntary organisations and appointment of members of committees can be a haphazard affair. David Townsend, the director of Croydon social services writes:

> the appointment of those who become officers of voluntary organisations in a local setting is as much a matter of luck as careful choice. Once in office they may be responsible for spending grants of £25 000 per annum. The bad news is that there are often no prior checks on police records. In the case of services provided to vulnerable people that could be serious. Nor are there checks on the financial status of would be office holders. Yet they may have access to cheque books and cash. There are few questions asked about competence to manage staff or budgets, to understand employment law, or to support equal opportunities legislation. Finally the managers may have no idea how to measure the quality of what is being done by the organisation.[21]

Changing role in the 1990s

Some voluntary organisations are worried about the effects of their changing role in 1990s. As part of the changes brought about under the 1990 NHS and Community Care Act discussed earlier voluntary organisations are expected to form contracts with local authorities for the provision of services. This takes the voluntary sector into a new more formal role which particularly the small organisations have found difficult to cope with. One study found that a voluntary group had spent £30 000 in staff time negotiating a contract.[22] There is also a concern that as groups take up a bigger role in the provision of services, they will be less involved in campaigning and pressure group work. Arthritis Care, for example, have taken a political decision not to get involved with contracting. Richard Gutch, the director, said,

> We aim to make sure that the voice of people with arthritis gets heard and that is what we want to continue to focus on, rather than trying to become a provider of home help services – which is what we often get asked to do.[23]

Activity 16.5

Make sure that you understand the following expressions used in this chapter. Check the glossary on p. 363 if you need to.

advocacy service	purchaser
casework	self-help
charitable status	statutory organisation
independent sector	stigma
injunction	test case
outreach	tribunal
pressure group	voluntary organisation
provider	volunteer

Further reading

In many cases, information on voluntary organisations can be obtained from the groups themselves. Understandably, some charge for leaflets and in all cases a stamped addressed envelope should be sent.

Useful addresses

Libraries have reference books which list names and addresses of voluntary organisations.

The National Council for Voluntary Organisations (NCVO): Regent's Wharf, 8 All Saints Street, London N1 9RL
tel. 0171 713 6161

Gingerbread: 35 Wellington Street, London WC2E 7BN
tel. 0171 240 0953

National Society for the Prevention of Cruelty to Children (NSPCC): 67 Saffron Hill, London EC1N 8RS
tel. 0171 242 1626

National Association of Citizens Advice Bureaux: Myddleton House, 115–123 Pentonville Road, London N1 9LZ
tel. 0171 833 2181

The Terence Higgins Trust: 52–54 Grays Inn Road, London WC1X 8JU
tel. 0171 831 0121

⟨17⟩ Policy issues in welfare

This concluding chapter provides a more general perspective to the issues raised throughout the book. The aim is to examine the concepts and debates which influence social services provision. Whilst issues are placed under a series of headings, they are, in many cases, interrelated and the separation is an artificial one, created for the purposes of analysis.

17.1   Theoretical perspectives on welfare

Within the study of social administration and, more importantly, the political arena, there are various views of the role of the welfare state in an industrial society. The various perspectives can be summarised as follows.

Anti-collectivist

The first has been described as 'anti-collectivist'.[1] This view has its roots in the nineteenth century idea of *'laissez-faire'* but is also that of the 'new right' which includes some sections of the Conservative Party. *'Laissez-faire'* can be explained in terms of several key ideas.

Market forces
Firstly, the economy is seen as working best without any intervention from the government: it is believed that wages, for example, will find their own correct level through the workings of market forces. To understand the concept of 'market forces', imagine you are selling something – a car, perhaps. If the car you are selling is very rare – maybe is seen as a collector's item – and a lot of people want it, you can ask a high price. If however, there are many cars like yours for sale and not very many people wanting to buy, then you will have to lower your price if you want a sale. This idea is at the heart of the philosophy of capitalist economies (although not always the practice, since sellers often get together to agree prices, or sometimes there only is one seller). It can be applied to anything, including wages, as in the comment above. Under market forces, high unemployment will have the effect of pushing wages down, since a lot of people are trying to find work. On the other hand, if there is a shortage of workers, people can demand, and get, higher wages. New right economists believe that nothing should be done by governments to interfere with this process. Jobs and wage levels should not be protected by social policy.

Self-reliance, competition and efficiency

Secondly, it is believed that individuals should look after themselves and not rely on state help. Finally, the new right believe that services and goods, including welfare services are best provided by private companies. This way the firms will compete with each other and be efficient.

A speech given by John Moore as Secretary of State for Social Services, on the reform of social security, illustrates some of these points.[2] Moore explained the Conservative view of welfare as follows:

> We believe that dependence in the long run decreases human happiness and reduces human freedom. We believe the well being of individuals is best protected and promoted when they are helped to be independent, to use their talents to take care of themselves and their families, and to achieve things on their own.

For the new right, state intervention is linked with many undesirable trends. There is a tendency towards over-centralisation – power and decision-making is concentrated too much with central government. Societies with a high degree of state intervention are seen as authoritarian – government bodies bossing people about and telling them what to do unnecessarily. Competition and individual freedom are restricted – so people are not free to find the best ways of doing things, especially in terms of building successful businesses and increasing profits. Moore goes on to argue in his speech:

> For more than a quarter of a century after the last war public opinion in Britain, encouraged by politicians, travelled down an aberrant path toward ever more dependence on an ever more powerful state. Under guise of compassion people were encouraged to see themselves as 'victims of circumstance', mere putty in the grip of giant forces beyond their control. Rather than being seen as individuals, people were categorised into groups and given labels that enshrined their dependent status: 'unemployed', 'single-parent', 'handicapped'.
>
> Thus their confidence and will to help themselves was subtly undermined, and they were taught to think only Government action could affect their lives.

For the anti-collectivists, welfare is ideally seen as having a residual role. This means the welfare state will deal only with any problems that cannot possibly be solved in any other way. The welfare state will be a safety net only for a small number of people in very great need. The government is seen as having a duty to relieve poverty, but this is thought of as a necessary evil and provision should be kept to a minimum. This refers both to the level of benefits and to the categories of people receiving financial and other help. Most needs can be met on a voluntary and private basis. Moore says:

> The third important reform the (Social Security) Act makes is to focus help more sharply on people in greatest need. This is crucial as part of the long-term efforts to change the climate of opinion on welfare. The indiscriminate handing out of benefits not only spreads limited resources too thinly, it can also undermine the will to self-help, and build up pools of resentment among the tax-payers who are footing the bill, often from incomes barely larger than the money benefit recipients receive.

By targeting our welfare resources we will be able to provide more real help where need is greatest.

'Targeting' and 'dependency culture'

Two concepts which have been talked about recently and which fit within this approach are 'targeting' of benefits and a 'dependency culture'. The idea of targeting is that benefits and services should be provided only for those in greatest need. Family credit is a targeted benefit in that it goes only to families on low incomes: child benefit, by contrast, is not targeted in that it goes to everyone looking after a child, whatever their income. This issue is looked at in more detail in section 17.6 on universal or selective welfare.

The notion of a dependency culture is that welfare encourages people to become dependent on benefits and to lose motivation to do anything to improve their situation. This term is used regularly by politicians in the Conservative Party. In the following quotation, Jonathan Aitken, Chief Secretary to the Treasury, is talking about the £80 million social security budget in 1994. He described the social security budget as 'enormously high' and said

> I think most people will expect us to take a very close look at that. He went on to warn against the creation of, in effect, a benefit dependence culture and society where people became too comfortable with benefits.[3]

Collectivist

The second approach can be termed 'collectivist' but derives from two strands of thought, that of the 'reluctant collectivists' and that of the 'fabian socialists'. The first strand begins with the ideas of people such as John Maynard Keynes and William Beveridge. Keynes was concerned about the high levels of unemployment in the 1930s and believed that government economic policies could and should create work. Beveridge's report of 1942 set up the social security system after the Second World War (see chapter 8). He saw welfare as an aspect of citizenship, since all would contribute to the insurance fund and all would receive benefits as of right. These people are 'reluctant' collectivists insofar as they see the market system as the ideal and only believe in state welfare to repair minor or temporary problems.

Fabian socialists date from the beginning of the century and put a more positive stress on the role of the state to create a fairer and more equal society, gradually working towards socialism. Equality is believed to be a more important goal than individual freedom and a positive value is set on collective provision and central control. The welfare state, with comprehensive provision of national insurance, health services and education is seen as an important part of a modern industrial society. When inequality is found to exist, collectivists believe the state has a responsibility to use social policy to bring about reforms. The role of the welfare state extends beyond the relief of individual suffering and the solving of problems to redistribution of access to services such as health and education through universal provision.

Marxist

The next approach can be broadly defined as Marxist, although there are several strands within a Marxist perspective. From a radical and Marxist point of view, the economic system in Britain, capitalism, contains fundamental and inherent problems of inequality. In this context, the role of the welfare state can be seen in a variety of ways. Welfare provision can be characterised as a concession won by working-class people from those in power, a kind of ransom for the continuation of the capitalist system. Alternatively, welfare services are seen as a ploy on the part of those who rule to avert real political and economic change which would take the form of revolution. The welfare state serves to alleviate suffering and reduce inequality to the extent that tensions are removed without any real shift in power or redistribution of wealth. With a slightly different emphasis, there is a Marxist critique of the welfare state which sees welfare as helping and maintaining the capitalist system by providing healthy and educated workers at a relatively cheap price. The welfare state functions within capitalism as a form of social control and no real welfare can exist in an inherently unequal society.

Feminist and anti-racist

There are also different views of society and social policy provided by feminists, who focus on the role of women, and anti-racists, who look at the racism which is a part of this society and its welfare provision. Feminists have pointed out that more women experience more poverty than men. There are several reasons for this: women are, on average, less well-paid than men; women live longer but due to their role in the home are more likely to have gaps in pension fund contributions and therefore have poorer pensions; and more women are single parents (see chapter 2). Women's oppression is summed up in the concept of 'patriarchy' which is used to describe a society geared to the interests of men, rather than women.

Feminists have also studied the role of women in welfare. Women provide a crucial support to the welfare state. This is first in their role as informal carers. Women care for children, relatives who are sick and disabled, and for elderly people. As was shown in chapter 9, women provide the mainstay of community care. Women also provide much of the labour for the welfare state, in low-paid jobs, in hospitals and as home carers, for example.

When the welfare state was set up after the Second World War women were very clearly seen as the dependents of men and were rarely eligible for benefits in their own right. There were many examples of sexism in welfare provision, even in benefits added later. One classic example was the Invalid Care Allowance which pays a weekly income to someone caring for a person with a disability. This was payable to all except married women – presumably because this was thought to be their role in life anyway. This and many other discriminatory practices have now been removed, often as a result of cases taken to the European Court.

Anti-racist writers have studied the position of ethnic minorities in society. Black people are often in the least desirable jobs and more likely to be unemployed. They suffer more from poor housing and inner-city deprivation. They have also experienced problems in getting access to welfare services. These may be the result of language barriers or lack of knowledge or it may be that services are not geared to their needs. In the following quotations, Asian carers talk about why the services available are not helpful:[5]

> He used to have meals on wheels, but even though it was useful to have them delivered, because they were so appallingly bad. . . I don't think they had even heard of halal meat. . . it was just a waste of money.

> I see some of the old people in this area, they just sit and look out of the window all day. They have no rights. No Asian people that I know go to day centres. People have nowhere to go. In the day centres there is no food for them, culture for them, music. . . nothing. . . so they just stay as they are – housebound.

> There aren't many Asians working as home helps and my mum doesn't speak English. She doesn't want an English person who is a stranger to our ways in the house.

Activity 17.1

Apply each of these four perspectives to a specific area of social policy, for example, housing, education or personal social services.

Case study: applying the perspectives to health care policy

The *anti-collectivists* or *new right thinkers* believe that health care is best provided privately for most people. People should pay into private health insurance schemes to cover treatment from private doctors and private hospitals. Only for those who cannot afford such cover would there be a state system. This would provide a basic level of care only. This is similar to the system which has existed in America (although there are now plans for a national health service).

The *collectivist* philosophy on health is for a free national health service for all, funded completely by taxation. The NHS, as established in 1948, reflects collectivist thinking. Although there have been changes which have since moved the health service away from this philosophy, it remains an example of collectivist social policy.

The *Marxist* approach has several strands. One is to look at the causes of poor health in terms of the society in which we live and the way we work. Reluctance to take measures to prevent industrial accidents and diseases illustrates the priority placed on profit above the health of workers. The health service can also be seen as working in the interests of employers. Employers need healthy workers and under the NHS workers pay for their own health care. However another strand of Marxist thought would see the national health service as something hard won at a time when the ruling groups in society were ready to make concessions to workers. As such it should be defended.

Feminists look at the contribution made by women to health care. This is first in terms of informal care: much of the nursing of sick children, for example, is done by women outside the health service. Doctors do not actually look after sick people – women do this under their direction – and hospitals are only involved in more serious situations. Secondly, women provide most of the labour within the health service – especially in the less well-paid jobs. Another angle looks at the treatment of women by doctors. Women tend to have more needs for health care than men – partly due to their role in reproduction. Areas such as childbirth have been 'medicalised' and taken over by male professionals, often leaving women feeling a loss of control over their own bodies and a sense of frustration and bewilderment.

Anti-racists emphasise the role of black workers in the health service and the lack of provision geared to the needs of ethnic minorities.

17.2 Expenditure on social services

Expenditure on social services has increased rapidly since the Second World War. In 1991 the figure for central government spending on education, health, social security and housing and community amenities was £143.4 billion. The biggest category was social security, costing £73.9 billion.[6] Maintaining an adequate level of social welfare is expensive but need not be seen as a luxury which can be discarded in an advanced society. Education and health services can be seen as necessary to production and other areas of provision contribute to the quality of life.

Activity 17.2

Consider all the ways in which we use services and facilities which are provided by the state or state-financed organisations. Write an account to demonstrate what life would be like without state provision.

Activity 17.3

Why has the cost of welfare provision increased? Make a list of possible reasons.

It was believed that expenditure on areas like health would decrease or at least stabilise after the introduction of comprehensive services. However, there are cases where improvements in welfare lead to further demands. For example, as people live longer, more demands are made on services for elderly people. In times of economic growth, expansion in welfare costs can be met by an increase in public spending proportional to overall growth. In the present recession however, growth is rarely discussed as the emphasis is on cuts in public spending and defence of existing services.

The cuts began in 1976 under the Labour government and have continued since that time. Whilst it was initially argued that the standards could be maintained by more efficient provision, this has proved difficult to achieve in practice. Unfortunately, cuts often hit the most vulnerable sections of the community hardest. The 'Cinderella' services (see p. 309) with low status are often the first to be reduced and people who have disabilities are least able to protest in defence of services.

A radical proposal concerning public expenditure involves the move away from services provided free at the point of use and financed through taxation. In some cases – for example, prescriptions – this happened to some extent, although the exemption system shows the limitations of charging for services. The arguments about charging for health services have already been discussed in Chapter 15. At a general level, it is difficult to see why the distinction between public and private spending is a cause of such concern, since services are paid for in either case, by different means. However, there is a tendency for both governments and the public to see public spending as undesirable. People tend to be reluctant to accept taxation whilst welcoming free provision of health and other services.

Activity 17.4

Discussion question: Why do people complain about paying taxes? Are their complaints justified? How could you counter their arguments?

Activity 17.5

1 If cuts have to be made in public spending, how should choices be made.
2 Outline a policy document showing priority services that must be retained, giving reasons for your choices.

17.3   Social services: a redistributor of wealth?

The introduction, after the Second World War, of comprehensive health, education and social security services led to a belief that wealth was being redistributed from richer to poorer people. This idea continues and there is a widely-held belief that one sector of the population pays for welfare provision for the benefit of another group. This idea is based both on the belief that taxation is progressive – that is, takes a larger proportion of income from higher- than from lower-income groups – and on the belief that poorer people benefit more from social services.

Whilst there is disagreement among welfare economists on the subject, there is evidence to show that social services do not bring about a redistribution of wealth. Income tax takes the same proportion of income from most people and is only progressive in the case of very high-income groups. Since 1945, the burden of taxation has increasingly shifted to the poor. In 1949–50, a man with a wife and two children had to be earing 23 per cent more than the average wage before he started to pay tax. Today tax is payable on income well below the average and in some cases below the poverty line.[7] People with high incomes often benefit from loopholes in tax law and increase their resources by means of expense accounts and items such as health benefits schemes and company cars. Indirect taxes, such as VAT are regressive, in so far as they take a greater proportion of income from poorer people. In one study of taxation, the author concludes that

> the progressive effects of some taxes is largely offset by the regressive effects of others, and all taxes combined have little net effect on . . . inequality.[8]

In terms of benefit, there is evidence to show that people from middle- and upper-income groups receive more from certain services and those which are restricted to poorer people are low-quality services. In the health services, the quality of care is better in more middle-class areas, middle-class people are better at recognising symptoms and more effective in ensuring they get high quality services. Similarly, in education, schools in middle-class areas are often better and the middle-classes make greater use of further and higher education facilities. In housing finance, tax relief subsidises home-owners. The only clear redistribution of wealth brought about by social services is that from childless people to families with children and over the life cycle from younger to older people.

Activity 17.6

Discussion question: Should social policy be concerned with a redistribution of resources from richer to poorer people? If so, how could this be achieved?

17.4 Administration of welfare

Central and local government control

A number of different agencies are involved in the administration of state welfare services. Central government, based at Westminster, makes laws and decides on spending on welfare. Central government departments such as the Department of Health, the Department of Social Security, the Department of Employment and the Department for Education are responsible for the implementation of policies in their areas of welfare. The European Union also has a role in welfare, particularly in ensuring equality of treatment. Although the central government departments have overall responsibility for welfare, the actual provision of services is delegated to other organisations. How this is done varies in different cases.

As was discussed in Chapter 15, the health service is run by regional and district health authorities, with NHS Trusts responsible directly to central government. Personal social services are run by the county councils. Social security was run by local offices of the Department of Social Security but is increasingly being run by 'agencies' (such as the Benefits Agency) which are more independent from central government. Employment policies are carried out by local Training and Enterprise Councils (TECs), again with considerable independence. Until recently education in schools and colleges was organised by local county councils but there are now separate funding organisations and many schools have opted out of the control of the council and become grant-maintained and independent. Housing is the concern of district councils.

In some cases local authorities have a legal duty to provide a particular service – this has been the case with education for children over 5; in other cases laws give the local authority permission to provide services at their own discretion – this is the case with pre-school care facilities.

Central government control of local authorities is exercised in a variety of ways. There are circulars sent out to local authorities, inspections and of course laws setting duties for local authorities. An important source of control is through finance. Central government can send auditors into a local authority to check that money is being spent according to the intentions of central government. Central government can also control the amount of local authority borrowing. The largest part of local authority finance comes from a grant from central government – the amount of which is assessed by central government. The rest of local authority money comes from locally collected council taxes and central government can 'cap' this – set a limit to the amount which is asked for.

Changes in central–local relationship

Recent years have seen changes in the relationship between central and local government. Local authorities have less control over local services than was the case previously. This erosion of power has occurred in a number of ways. As has already been mentioned, schools and colleges have been allowed to opt out of the control of the local authorities and be financed from central sources.

Powerful new 'quangos' have been created. 'Quango' stands for 'quasi-autonomous non-governmental organisation'. It means a body set up by government but functioning with some independence from the government department to which it is responsible. Examples of new quangos are the Funding Agency for

Schools and the Further Education Funding Council – both of which are carrying out tasks previously done by local authorities. Members of quangos are appointed, not elected, and, unlike local councils, meetings are not open to the public.

The financial controls described above date mostly from the 1980s, before which time councils could set their own rates and collect more money to provide a higher level of services if they wished. Now the Secretary of State for the Department of the Environment can 'cap' councils which are thought to be spending too much money.

Activity 17.7

List arguments for and against local freedom in how council tax is collected and services are managed.

The issue of the merits and limitations of management of services by local councils is of current concern as many people perceive a move towards centralisation and control of the activities of local authorities. Where services are provided at the discretion of the authority there is a risk of too great a variation from area to area. On the other hand, this can be seen as an advantage, allowing flexibility in meeting local needs. Whilst local government may be weak, it provides a useful check on central government. However, turn-out at local elections is often low, perhaps showing a lack of interest in the activities of local authorities.

Activity 17.8

1 How can local authorities stimulate more interest and involve local communities in their work?
2 Draw up a report, with recommendations for local councillors and officers.

17.5 Privatisation

One of the key themes in social policy in the 1980s and early 1990s as we have seen in Chapter 8, was the transfer of responsibilities from state to private organisations. The means by which this policy has been pursued has included legislation, circulars to local authorities, encouragement of a belief that private provision is superior to public services, and physical conditions – for example, waiting lists for health care – which create a demand for private services by those who can afford to pay.

Privatisation is not a single policy but takes places through a variety of changes and shifts in approach. Work which is paid for by the state and was traditionally carried out by state employees is being transferred to private institutions and companies. Examples of this include private provision of school meals, the assisted places scheme for private schools and the contracting-out of hospital cleaning and laundry work. Second, state-owned property is being sold under a variety of schemes – for example, council houses to tenants, whole estates to private firms in some areas, and hospital buildings. Third the private sector received a boost with the 1990 NHS and Community Care Act. In terms of community care, local authorities are encouraged to use private and voluntary organisations as providers of care. Within the NHS, purchasers of health care (fund-holding doctors and health authorities) are free to choose private health services instead of those provided within the NHS. In both these cases, the privately provided services are paid for with public funds. Finally, there is the encouragement of the private sector in such policies as allowing tax relief on medical insurance.

The policy of privatisation is based in political ideology, although often justified in terms of efficiency and cost-cutting. Whilst complaints made of public services are in some cases valid, there is no evidence to support the view that private organisations are more efficiently run or can provide equal services more cheaply. The bureaucratic insensitivity which is often criticised in the public sector is a symptom of large-scale organisation rather than of state provision and could be reduced by policies of decentralisation.

Source: Vicky White, Photofusion
Health care in the private sector

There are many reasons for supporting state provision of welfare. State welfare is aimed at meeting social needs rather than making a profit and in the fields of health, education and other aspects of welfare this would seem to be a more appropriate approach. Services are provided for everyone and policies such as removing regional inequality can be pursued whereas a profit-making organisation would not be concerned with such aims. State services are accountable to the government and subject to inspections. High standards can be maintained without pressure to cut corners to maximise profits. Conditions of work are usually better in the public sector and high standards of training are provided for professionals such as doctors. The state can provide a continuity of provision which could be lost if a firm closed down or decided an area of work was not worthwhile.

__ Activity 17.9 __

Use library resources and your own knowledge to make a list of facilities in welfare which have been provided privately since the 1980s.

17.6 Universal or selective welfare

This area of debate concerns the basis on which services should be provided. Services can be provided universally, for all irrespective of income, or selectively on the criterion of need. The arguments in this area are complex, operating on a variety of different levels causing some confusion. Definitions of the terms 'universal' and 'selective' vary and it is sometimes argued that there are no truly universal services in the sense that all contribute and benefit equally. In terms of more commonly accepted definitions universal provision includes health and education and, within social security, benefits like child benefit which are not subject to a means-test. Examples of selective benefits are supplementary benefits and free schools meals.

The importance of the provision introduced in the years immediately after the Second World War lay not so much in the services provided but in the universality of the provision. It was this aspect which gave rise to the term 'welfare state' to describe Britain. The debate concerning universal or selective welfare continues. At an ideological level it concerns the goals of social policy. For some, social policy is concerned with the creation of a just society and state provision is the best way of providing for needs. Others see the aim of welfare provision in terms of filling gaps left by the workings of the economy, acting in a residual role as a safety-net. At a political level, universal provision is seen as an attack on freedom of choice for the individual. For those more concerned with equality, the notion of freedom is seen as illusory, since it only exists for the better-off. For example, the freedom to educate a child in a private school is only meaningful to those who can afford such a choice. There are also arguments against universal provision based on the idea that high taxation, necessary to pay for services, leads to loss of incentive. This argument is refuted by the universalists.

At a more practical level, it is argued that universal benefits are wasteful, in that they provide for people who do not need state help and mean that provision for the needy is insufficient since the available resources are spread too thinly. Against this point of view it is argued that selective provision leads to double standards of care and greater social divisions and inequality. This is based on the assumption that people who are paying demand a higher standard of services than those who receive free provision. For example, in health and education, selectivity leads to two classes of hospitals and schools, in the state and private sector. Also selectivity leads to means of distinguishing those in need, and means-testing leads to stigma and low take-up. This can be seen by comparing child benefit which is universal with a benefit like family credit which is selective.

The argument over universal or selective provision is intensified when new areas of need are discovered in a time of economic recession. These two factors lead to simultaneous demands for more spending and cuts. The trend in many areas at present is to move away from universal provision, examples of this being the assisted places scheme and the selling of council houses. However, the association of Labour politics with universalism and Conservatives with selectivity is not always maintained in practice.

17.7   Positive action

Universalism is a policy of providing welfare for all. Whilst it avoids the stigma of the means-test it does lead to resources being spread thinly over the whole population. In an unequal society, equal provision perpetuates inequality. A move towards equality and concentration of resources requires some form of positive action.

Focusing resources

Positive action is different from selectivity in that it involves the provision of extra resources or rights to areas or groups in special need. The focus on groups or areas avoids the stigma of assessment of individual need. Positive action policies which have been described in this book include Educational Priority Areas, the Urban Programme, Housing Action Areas and the Inner Cities Programmes. All these policies provide positive action on an area basis.

A further dimension to positive action is the extension of the policy to particular groups of people. This has been implemented to some extent in benefits for people with disabilities, where benefits are paid as of right, without a means-test. Arguments have been put forward for a benefit for single-parent families which is paid irrespective of income for all single parents. Whilst this was rejected, increased child benefit for the single-parent is a small example of positive action.

Access to employment

Women and black people are discriminated against in many ways. Black people are disadvantaged in terms of income, housing, employment and education, caused by institutional racism. Although there is now legislation providing for equal opportunities in areas such as employment, it is illegal to discriminate in favour of previously disadvantaged groups. This is only allowed where being black or female is seen as a 'genuine occupational qualification' – this means a situation in which the job involves providing personal services and where the services can most effectively be provided by someone from that group. An example provided by the Commission for Racial Equality is of a counselling and information service on AIDS/HIV for African women. If a large proportion of the women do not speak English and would be embarrassed to talk to a male social worker, it would be acceptable for the health authority to seek to employ an African woman.[9]

The Race Relations Act allows positive action in providing access to training for particular work for ethnic groups which have been under-represented in that work at any time during the last 12 months. For example: a health authority has a very low proportion of Afro-Caribbean health visitors. The authority can encourage Afro-Caribbean nurses to apply for training as health visitors.[10] Employers are also allowed to select people from their employees and train them to do jobs in which members of that group have been under-represented in proportion to the local population.

Employers can encourage applicants from particular social groups to 'take advantage of opportunities' for work.

Access in education

An example of positive action in education is the provision of access courses which recognise educational disadvantage and provide a route into higher education for those to whom the traditional route is closed. Whilst little has been done as yet in terms of positive action, implementation of the policy may achieve the results which were sought but not realised in policies of equality of opportunity.

Activity 17.10

Should positive action be taken on racism? List arguments for and against.

Activity 17.11

Draw up a positive action programme for a particular aspect of local authority work, for example education or personal social services.

Activity 17.11

This chapter has used a lot of complicated language which is probably unfamiliar. Make sure you understand the following expressions, used in this chapter. Check the glossary on p. 363 if you need to.

anti-collectivist	new right
'cap'	NHS trust
capitalism	patriarchy
central government	positive action
centralisation	poverty line
'Cinderella service'	progressive tax
collectivist	quango
community care	regressive tax
dependency culture	safety net
informal carer	selective
invalid care allowance	selective benefit
laissez-faire	stigma
mandatory	take-up
market forces	targeting
Marxist	Training and Enterprise Councils (TECs)
means test	universal
medicalisation	universal benefit

Further reading

A lot of the books covering the issues looked at in this chapter are quite difficult to read – they are suitable for dipping into but expect to have a bit of a struggle to understand the arguments. Such texts included Vic George and Paul Wilding, *Ideology and Social Welfare* (London: Routledge & Kegan Paul, 1976) which is quite old now but was the first to look at social policy in terms of perspectives. A much more readable introduction to some of these areas is found in Paul Trowler, *Investigating Health Welfare and Poverty* (London: Collins, 1991). There is also some useful material in Stephen Moore, *Social Welfare Alive!* (London: Stanley Thornes, 1993). As well as material on perspectives and other issues, there is quite a lot on the role of the European Union in this book. A review of feminist issues can be found in Gillian Pascal, *Social Policy: A Feminist Analysis* (London: Tavistock, 1986).

⬡ Researching and writing projects

Many courses, whether for academic or professional qualifications, require project work. Each project is a unique piece of work, chosen by the individual and worked on independently. To complete a good project is a very satisfying achievement. Starting a project can, however feel very daunting, especially to those returning to study after some years out of school. The following pages offer some guidelines to writing and researching projects in social welfare.

Choosing a project

This is the first stage in beginning work on a project. It can be very difficult and is certainly very important. It is very hard to make a good project from a bad choice of topic. There are two starting points to choosing a project. The first and probably most important is the requirements set for the work and, if available, the marking scheme. It is likely that the project will be expected to demonstrate particular skills or types of knowledge. The topic should be chosen with these criteria in mind. The second starting point concerns subject areas. It is important to choose an area which is of sufficient interest not to become boring after a few days, weeks or months. On the other hand, it is necessary to be able to be object-ive about the information and this will be difficult if the topic is one on which the author has strongly-held and passionate views.

From these starting points, there are a number of other factors to be borne in mind when choosing a topic. Firstly, the subject chosen should be large enough to provide sufficient material for the project (whatever its length) but small enough to be manageable and to study in depth. It is more common for topics to be too large and to need narrowing down than for topics to be too small. It is much better to cover a small area in depth than to deal with a large area superficially. Secondly, the topic should not be too easy, but nor should it be too difficult. This point applies particularly to the research stage. Some areas are perhaps too easy to investigate: for example a project which merely seeks to describe the work of the NSPCC can be done simply from the comprehensive and beautifully presented leaflets which are easily available to anyone who writes to the NSPCC. On the other hand, it is important not to choose a subject which is too difficult to research. Such areas would include ones about which people are too embarrassed to speak; ones about which nothing has been written or where there are only articles in obscure journals in specialist libraries; or topics which require comparisons between factors which are very sensitive and

347

difficult to identify and measure. For example, it would be very difficult to compare educational achievement with social class and intelligence in primary schools. Problems would arise in finding ways of identifying and measuring educational achievement and, even more, in measuring intelligence and social class. Such work has been done, but by professional researchers with thousand or million pound budgets and at least three years to do the research. Finally, better projects are those which seek to answer a question (even if failing to do so conclusively), rather than those which seek only to describe something. Projects based on questions are more likely to demonstrate higher skills of analysis and evaluation than those which merely describe. Another good way to demonstrate these skills is by comparison, perhaps comparing two types of provisions or by comparing what is provided with the needs of the clients.

It is important to keep a diary or log from the beginning of the project. This should start even before the topic is chosen. The diary will be vital in writing up the project.

Researching a project

Planning is an important part of project work and once the subject has been chosen plans and strategies should be made for researching and writing up. Plans should be recorded in the project diary.

A good place to start planning is by making a list of possible sources of information. These could include books, either textbooks or more specialist studies; articles, either in magazines or newspapers; interviews, with experts or others; visits and observations; minutes of meetings and other documents; leaflets and brochures; statistical sources from the government or from other agencies. Whilst not all of these sources will be relevant for every project, it is good to have a variety of different types of research methods.

There are several short-cuts to finding information on particular subjects. The first and most obvious is the catalogues in the libraries which list books under subjects. Libraries also keep annual indexes which are the quickest and easiest way to find newspaper and magazine articles on particular subjects. The *Humanities Index* is a good starting point. Once one book has been found, the bibliography can be used as a guide to further material. Libraries also keep reference books which list names, addresses and brief descriptions of voluntary and other organisations. There are sometimes local directories of organisations as well.

It is rarely necessary to read a whole book. The contents and index should be used to find the relevant parts and pages should be skimmed rather than read.

It is very easy to become overwhelmed by a huge amount of information. To minimise this problem, only information which is definitely relevant to the title of the project should be collected. This should be recorded in note-form and organised in some way. Notes kept on a computer disk or notebook PC take up a lot less space, are easy to reorganise and to copy. By keeping back-up disks or copies of your work in progress on paper you will avoid the risk of losing your work.

For each book, article or leaflet used, a note must be kept of the source. This must have all the details needed for the bibliography. Observations will also need to be recorded methodically. Interviews can be taped or notes can be taken during or immediately after the interview. Notes are easier than tapes to deal with, since tapes will have to be listened to afterwards and the information transcribed or noted. This stage is avoided if notes are taken in the first place.

Writing up a project

This is the final stage of the project and again it requires planning and organisation. Expect to write several drafts before you get it right. The process of drafting, re-writing and reorganising material is much easier on a computer where you can save one copy and edit another, delete material, add new ideas, move sections around – and always have a perfect version of your work. Another advantage of a computer is that at the end of all your hard work you can produce a very attractive and professional-looking document – something you can really feel proud of. The information needs to be selected for presentation and divided up into appropriate *chapters* and *sections*. The project is likely to include the following:

- a title page
- a contents page
- an introduction
- a description of the methods
- presentation of the findings
- a conclusion
- recommendations
- a bibliography.

The report should be written in such a way that the reader will find it easy to follow and should be presented as attractively as possible. A variety of methods of presentation should be used, including diagrams, tables, illustrations and photographs if these are appropriate to the title.

Probably the most important point about writing up the report is that it should be written in the author's *own words*. There is no value in copying out sections from other sources. Any quotations should be clearly referenced and kept short. Leaflets, etc. should not be included unless they have a definite purpose, for example demonstrating effectiveness or otherwise of communication, if this is what the project is about. Some items may be placed in the appendices, but again only for a particular purpose, not simply because they have been collected. Many projects are spoiled by the inclusion of material which seems to be no more than 'padding'.

When discussing information from different sources it is important to be aware of *biases* in the material. A pressure group, for example is likely to present information in a particular way to best represent the cause it is concerned with. The same applies to leaflets or speeches from political organisations. Some sources are more objective than others and the project should show an ability to discriminate between these. It is good to set different viewpoints against each other, for example to compare the views of social workers and clients, of the Labour Party and the Conservative Party, or of council officials and residents.

The most important part of the report will be the *conclusion*. This is where all the information is weighed up and some conclusions drawn. These are likely to be tentative but are very important nevertheless. It may also be appropriate to make some recommendations about social policy and how things might change. The project itself should be evaluated and its strengths and weaknesses identified. A statement could be made about how the project could be improved if it was to be done again.

Finally, the report will end with a list of *sources* used. For books, this should include the author, the title of the book, the publisher, the place of publication and the date. For articles, the bibliography should show the author, the title of the article, the newspaper or journal in which it appeared, the date and the page number or numbers.

Some projects will include *appendices*. Suitable contents are an interview schedule or a transcript of a tape. These are things which are necessary but which would interfere with the reading of the report if included in the main body of the project.

Notes and references

1 People in society

1. Amrit Wilson, *Finding a Voice: Asian Women in Britain* (London: Virago, 1978).
2. For example, Ivan Reid, *Social Class Differences in Britain*, 2nd edn (London: Open Books, 1981).
3. Terry Smyth, *Caring for Older People* (London Macmillan, 1992).
4. Research by Margaret Mead, reported in Ann Oakley, *Sex, Gender and Society* (London: Temple Smith, 1972), p. 54.
5. Margaret Mead, quoted in Ann Oakley, *Sex, Gender and Society*, p. 55.
6. William Davenport, quoted in Ann Oakley, *Sex, Gender and Society*, p. 58.
7. *Community Care* (18 September 1986).
8. National Opinion Polls, Bulletin, 109 (1972).
9. Ivan Reid, *Social Class Differences*.
10. Office of Population Census and Surveys, *National Monitor* (Government Statistical Office, 1992), p. 20
11. Salman Rushdie, 'The New Empire within Britain', *New Society* (9 December 1982), p. 418.
12. Amrit Wilson, *Finding a Voice*.
13. A. Bhalla and K. Blakemore, *Elders of the Ethnic Minority Groups*, (Birmingham: All Faiths for One Race, 1981). See also Yasmin Gunaratnam, 'Breaking the Silence: Asian Carers in Britain' in J. Bornat, C. Pereira, D. Pilgrim and F. Williams (eds), *Community Care* (London: Macmillan, 1993).
14. Wilson, *Finding a Voice*, p. 106
15. Berkshire County Council, *Education for Racial Equality*, Policy Paper, 1 (1983).
16. Jeremy Laurence, 'Should White Families Adopt Black Children?', *New Society* (30 June 1983), p. 499.
17. Remi Kapo, *A Savage Culture – A Black British View* (London: Quarter Books, 1981), pp. 7-8.
18. Amrit Wilson, *Finding a Voice*, p. 19.
19. Salman Rushdie, 'The New Empire', p. 418.

2 Family life

1. Central Statistical Office, *Social Trends* 1994 no. 24 (London: HMSO, 1994), p. 35.
2. Central Statistical Office, *Social Trends 1988*, 18 (London: HMSO, 1988), p. 42.
3. Michael Argyle, 'What Makes Marriage Tick?' *New Society* (12 May 1983) pp. 217–19.
4. Central Statistical Office, *Social Trends 1994*, 24, p. 38.
5. EOC, *Some Facts About Women* (London: EOC, 1993).
6. EOC, *Some Facts About Women*.

7. *Guardian* (21 December 1993), p. 6.
8. *Guardian* (6 December 1993), p. 7.
9. Central Statistical Office, *Social Trends* 1994, 24, p. 38.
10. National Council for One Parent Families, *The Child Support Agency's First Year: The Lone Parent Case* (London: NCOPF).
11. National Council for One Parent Families, *The Child Support Agency's First Year.*
12. The Guardian (29 April 1994), p. 4.
13. The Guardian (30 March 1994), p. 8.
14. The Guardian (13 September 1993), p. 4.
15. R. Emerson Dobash and Russell Dobash, *Violence Against Wives* (New York: The free press, 1979).
16. Marsden and D. Owens, 'Jekyll and Hyde Marriages', *New Society* (8 July 1975), p. 333.
17. M. Borskowski *et al., Marital Violence: the Community Response* (London: Tavistock, 1983).
18. Reported in the *Observer* (25 February 1990).
19. Dobash and Dobash, *Violence Against Wives*, pp. ii–iii.
20. Dobash and Dobash, *Violence Against Wives* (1979), p. 110.
21. Val Binney, Anna Harkell and Judy Nixon, *Leaving Violent Men* (Leeds: Women and Federation, England, 1981). , p. 3.
22. Dobash and Dobash, *Violence Against Wives.*
23. Charlotte Rampling, *Daily Mirror*, quoted in the *Guardian* (May 1983), p. 10.
24. Binney *et al., Leaving Violent Men*, p. 14.
25. Women's Aid Federation England, *Written Evidence to the House of Commons Home Affairs Committee Inquiry into Domestic Violence* (Bristol: WAFE, 1992).
26. Women's Aid Federation England, *Written Evidence*, p. 17.
27. Binney *et al., Leaving Violent Men*, p. 15.
28. Binney *et al. Leaving Violent Men*, p. 79.
29. NSPCC, *A Good Year for Children? NSPCC Annual Report* (1986) pp. 4–5.
30. The Beveridge Report (London: HMSO, 1942) quoted in Gillian Pascall, *Social Policy: A Feminist Analysis* (London: Tavistock, 1986), p. 196.
31. Department of Health and Social Security, 1975, letter to National Council for Civil Liberties, quoted in Ruth Lister, 'Income Maintenance for Families with Children', in R. N. Rapoport, M. P. Fogarty and R. Rapoport (eds), *Families in Britain* (London: Routledge & Kegan Paul, 1982), p. 23.
32. See Pascall, *Social Policy.*

3   Poverty and welfare

1. Michael Harrington, quoted in Ken Coates and Richard Silburn, *Poverty: The Forgotten Englishman* (Harmondsworth: Penguin, 1970).
2. Peter Townsend, *Poverty in the United Kingdom* (Harmondsworth: Penguin, 1979), p. 31.
3. B. S. Rowntree, *Poverty: A Study of Town Life* (London: Macmillan, 1901).
4. B. S. Rowntree, *Poverty and Progress* (London: Longman, 1941). B. S. Rowntree and G. R. Lavers, *Poverty and the Welfare State* (London: Longman, 1951).
5. Joanna Mack and Stewart Lansley, *Poor Britain* (London: Allen & Unwin, 1985), Joanna Mack and Stewart Lansley, *Breadline Britain: the findings of the television series* (London: London Weekend Television Community Education Office, 1991).

6. Mack and Lansley, *Poor Britain*, p. 9.
7. Mack and Lansley, *Breadline Britain*, p. 4.
8. Mack and Lansley, *Breadline Britain*, p. 6.
9. Mack and Lansley, *Poor Britain*, p. 98.
10. Mack and Lansley, *Breadline Britain*, p. 9.
11. Central Statistical Office, *Households Below Average Income Statistics* (London: HMSO, 1994).
12. Central Statistical Office, *Households Below Average Income*.
13. Oscar Lewis, *Five Families* (New York: Basic Books, 1959); Lewis, 'The Culture of Poverty' in D. P. Moynihan (ed.), *On Understanding Poverty* (New York: Basic Books, 1968).
14. Coates and Silburn, *Poverty*.
15. Elaine Kempson, Alex Byrson, Katherine Rowlingson, *Hard Times? How Poor Families Make Ends Meet* (London: Policy Studies Institute, 1994).
16. The *Guardian* (2 August 1994), p. 4.
17. Central Statistical Office, *Social Trends, 1994*, 24 (London: HMSO, 1994).
18. The Guardian (3 August 1994), p. 3.
19. Alissa Goodman and Steven Webb, *For Richer, For Poorer* (London: Institute of Fiscal Studies, 1994).
20. Louie Burghes, *Living from Hand to Mouth*, 1980, quoted in Child Poverty Action Group Fact Sheet *Poverty – What Poverty?* (London: Child Poverty Action Group), p. 2.
21. Ursula R. W. Henriques, *Before the Welfare State* (London: Longman, 1979), p. 12.
22. Report of the Royal Commission on the Poor Laws (1834).
23. Norman Longmate, *The Workhouse* (London: Temple Smith, 1974), p. 82.
24. Taken from Longmate, *The Workhouse*, pp. 96–7.
25. *Report on Social Insurance and Allied Service, Cmnd 6404* (London: HMSO, 1942).
26. The Child Poverty Action Group produces two books on benefits, updated each year.
27. Department of Social Security, *Income Related Benefits: Estimates of Take Up in 1991 and 1992*, Government Statistical Office (London: HMSO, 1994).
28. Lix Bisset and Jean Coussines, *Badge of Poverty, Poverty Pamphlet*, 55 (London: Child Poverty Action Group, 1982) p. 17.

4 Unemployment

1. *Employment Gazette* (March 1994).
2. *Guardian* (15 January 1988).
3. *Guardian* (15 January 1988).
4. Alan Walker, 'The Level and Distribution of Unemployment' in Louie Burghes and Ruth Lister (eds), *Unemployment: Who Pays the Price?, Poverty Pamphlet*, 53 (London: Child Poverty Action Group, 1981), p. 16.
5. All figures from Central Statistical Office, *Social Trends 1994*, 24 (London: HMSO, 1994).
6. Peter Makeham, *Youth Unemployment*, Department of Employment *Research Paper*, 10 (London: Department of Employment, 1980).
7. *Employment Gazette* (March 1994).
8. *Employment Gazette* (March 1994).
9. Central Statistical Office, *Social Trends 1994*, 24.

10. David J. Smith, *Racial Disadvantage in Britain, The PEP Report* (Harmondsworth: Penguin, 1977), p. 109.
11. Smith, *Racial Disadvantage*, p. 124.
12. Jeremy Seabrook, *Unemployment* (London: Granada, 1983), p. 113.
13. Central Statistical Office, *Social Trends 1994*, 24.
14. Seabrook, *Unemployment*, p. 144.
15. Seabrook, *Unemployment*, p. 197.
16. The Health Education Council *The Health Divide*, quoted in the *Guardian* (3 April 1987), p. 3.
17. Dr Richard Smith, *Unemployment and Health*, quoted in the *Guardian* (17 September 1987), p. 2.
18. National Association of Citizens' Advice Bureaux, *The Cost of Living* (London: NACAB, 1992).
19. Jeremy Seabrook, 'Unemployment Now and In the 1930s', in Bernard Crick (ed.), *Unemployment* (London: Methuen, 1981), p. 14.
20. Seabrook, *Unemployment*, p. 128.
21. Seabrook, *Unemployment* p. 199.
22. *Guardian* (11 September 1993).
23. *Guardian* (1 September 1993).
24. *Britain 1994: an official handbook* (London: HMSO, 1994).
25. House of Commons, *Hansard,* 24 July 1987, quoted in *Poverty* (CPAG), Winter 1987–8, p. 5.

5   Housing and homelessness

1. Central Statistical Office, *Social Trends 1988*, 18 (London: HMSO, 1988), p. 133.
2. Office of Population, Censuses and Surveys, *National Monitor 1991: Census Great Britain* (London: Government Statistical Office, 1992).
3. Stuart Lowe and Ros Day, *Housing* (York: Longman, 1985), p. 3.
4. Central Statistical Office, *Social Trends 1994*, 24 (London: HMSO, 1994), p. 110.
5. Central Statistical Office, *Social Trends 1988*, p. 132; *Britain 1994: An official guide* (London: HMSO, 1994), p. 333.
6. *Britain 1994*, p. 332.
7. Henry Aughton, *Housing Finance* (London: Shelter 1986), p. 64.
8. F. Gray, quoted in John R. Short, *Housing in Britain* (London: Methuen, 1982), p. 168.
9. *Sunday Times* (25 April 1982), p. 3.
10. *Britain 1994*, p. 332.
11. Shelter, *The Facts about Council House Sales* (London: Shelter, 1979), Appendix.
12. Central Statistical Office, *Social Trends 1988*, p. 132. *Britain 1994*, p. 330.
13. For example, *Housing Policy: A Consultative Document* (London: HMSO, 1977).
14. Central Statistical Office *Social Trends 1994*, 24, p. 117.
15. Short, *Housing in Britain*, p. 130.
16. Central Statistical Office, *Social Trends 1988*, p. 139; Joseph Rowntree Foundation, *A Competitive UK Economy: The challenges for housing policy* (June 1994).
17. Joseph Rowntree Foundation, *A Competitive UK Economy*.
18. Commission for Racial Equality, *Factsheet 2: Housing* (London: CRE, 1978), p. 1.
19. Central Statistical Office, *Social Trends, 1994* 24, p. 192.
20. Commission for Racial Equality, *Race through the 90s* (London: BBC and CRE, 1993).
21. Commission for Racial Equality, *Race.*

22. Colin Brown, *Black and White Britain* (London: Heinemann, 1984), p. 79.
23. Commission for Racial Equality, *Race*.
24. Brown, *Black and White Britain*, pp. 71–5.
25. Central Statistical Office, *Social Trends, 1994*, 24 p. 113.
26. Central Statistical Office, *Social Trends 1994*, 24, p. 114.
27. *The Sunday Times* (8 February 1981), p. 17.
28. Central Statistical Office, *Social Trends 1994*, 24, p. 114.
29. Ron Bailey, *The Homeless and Empty Houses* (Harmondsworth: Penguin, 1977), p. 21.
30. *Roof* (July/August 1987), p. 13.
31. Shelter leaflet, *Homelessness in England: the facts* (London: Shelter 1994).
32. *The Guardian* (23 January 1987), p. 3.
33. Shelter, 1982, *Ordinary People* (London: Shelter, 1982) p. 23.
34. Shelter, *Homelessness in England*.
35. Family Welfare Association, *Guide to the Social Services 1994* (London: FWA, 1994), p. 130.
36. *The Guardian* (6 June 1994), p. 3.
37. Department of the Environment, *Better Homes: The Next Priority* (London: HMSO, 1973), p. 4
38. J. Hillman 'New Houses for old-when?', *Observer*, 2 February 1969, reported in Paul N. Balchin, *Housing Policy and Housing Needs* (London: Macmillan, 1981), p. 177.
39. P. Walker, 1970, quoted in Balchin, *Housing Policy*, p. 182.
40. M. Young and P. Willmott, *Family and Kinship in East London* (London: Routledge & Kegan Paul, 1957).
41. Department of the Environment, *Old Houses into New Homes* (London: HMSO, 1968), p. 3.
42. *The Guardian* (6 June 1994), p. 3.

6 Living in cities

1. For example, L. Wirth, 'Urbanism as a Way of Life', *American Journal of Sociology* 44 (1938), pp. 1–24.
2. Central Statistical Office, *Social Trends 1988*, 18 (London: HMSO, 1988), p. 27.
3. Gill Burke, *Housing and Social Justice* (London: Longman, 1981), p. 113.
4. Lambeth Inner Area Study, quoted in Burke, *Housing and Social Justice*, p. 138.
5. Burke, *Housing and Social Justice*, p. 127.
6. Inner Cities Directorate, Department of the Environment (1981), *Census Information Note No.2, Urban Deprivation* (London: Department of the Environment, 1983).
7. Lord Scarman, *The Brixton Disorders 10–12 April 1981* (London: HMSO, 1981).
8. Paul Harrison, *Inside the Inner City* (Harmondsworth: Penguin, 1983).
9. Harrison, *Inside the Inner City*, p. 32.
10. Harrison, *Inside the Inner City*, pp. 104–5.
11. Hackney Play Association, quoted Harrison, *Inside the Inner City*, p. 310.
12. Harrison, *Inside the Inner City*, p. 345.
13. Community Development Project, *Gilding the Ghetto* (London: CDP Inter-Project Editorial Team, 1977), p. 4.
14. Benwell Community Project, *The Making of a Ruling Class* (Newcastle-upon-Tyne, 1978).

15. Reproduced by permission of the Controller of Her Majesty's Stationery Office with acknowledgement to ICD3 and the Cartographic Services of the Department of the Environment.
16. Department of the Environment, *The Urban Programme* (London: HMSO, 1981).
17. *Action for Cities* The Cabinet Office (1988), p. 15.
18. *Guardian* (9 December 1987), p. 27.
19. Quoted in the *Guardian* (10 November 1983), p. 20.
20. Information in this section taken from Central Statistical Office, *Britain 1994: an official guide* (London: HMSO, 1994).

7   Schooling in Britain

1. Central Statistical Office, *Social Trends, 1994* 24 (London: HMSO, 1994), p. 53.
2. HMSO, *Health and Personal Social Services Statistics for England* (London: HMSO, 1993), p. 72.
3. HMSO, *Health*, p. 72.
4. HMSO, *Health*, p. 72.
5. HMSO, *Health*, p. 72.
6. *Guardian* (7 December 1993), p. 4.
7. *Guardian* (7 December 1993), p. 4.
8. Quoted in the *Guardian* (18 March 1994), p. 3.
9. Central Statistical Office, *Social Trends 1988*, 18 (London: HMSO, 1988), p. 54.
10. *Guardian* (1 November 1993).
11. *Guardian* (12 May 1994), p. 3.
12. *Guardian* (18 August 1994), p. 1.
13. Central Statistical Office, *Britain 1994: an official guide* (London: HMSO, 1994) p. 416.
14. *Guardian* (3 May 1994), p. 7.
15. *Guardian* (3 May 1994), p. 7.
16. Julian Le Grand 'Is privatisation always such a bad thing?', *New Society* (7 April 1983), pp. 7–9.
17. Central Statistical Office, *Social Trends, 1994*, 24 p. 46.
18. R. Klein, 'Using the Wrong Label', *Mind Out*, 33 (March/April 1979), pp. 16–18.
19. I. Reid, *Social Class Differences in Britain* (London: Open Books, 1977), p. 172.
20. R. Davie, M. Butler and H. Goldstein, *From Birth to Seven* (The National Child Development Study) (London: Longman, 1972).
21. Central Advisory Council for Education (England), *Early Leaving* (London: HMSO, 1954); Central Advisory Council for Education (England) *15–18* (The Crowther Report) (London: HMSO, 1959); J. B. W. Douglas, *The Home and the School* (London: MacGibbon & Kee, 1964).
22. A. H. Halsey, A. F. Heath and J. M. Ridge, *Origins and Destinations: Family Class and Education in Modern Britain* (Oxford: Clarendon Press, 1980); J. Gray, A. F. McPherson and D. Raffe, *Reconstructions of Secondary Education* (London: Routledge & Kegan Paul, 1983).
23. J. B. W. Douglas, *The Home and the School*.
24. M. Young and P. Willmott, *Family and Kinship in East London* (London: Routledge & Kegan Paul, 1957).
25. B. Bernstein, 'Social Class and Linguistic Development: A Theory of Social Learning' in A. H. Halsey, B. Floud and D. Anderson, *Education, Economy and Society* (London: Macmillan, 1961), ch. 24, pp. 288–314.

26. Statistics from the Equal Opportunities Commission.
27. Central Statistical Office, *Social Trends 1994*, 24, p. 47.
28. Department of Education and Science, *Education Survey* 21 (London: HMSO, 1975).
29. N. Frazier and H. Sadker, *Sexism in School and Society* (New York: Harper & Row, 1973).
30. Pat Mahoney, *Schools for the Boys?* (London: Hutchinson, 1985).
31. Mahoney, *Schools,* pp. 37–8.
32. Mahoney, *Schools,* p. 41.
33. Mahoney, *Schools,* p. 45.
34. Mahoney, *Schools,* p. 48.
35. Commission for Racial Equality, *Race through the 90s* (London: BBC and CRE, 1993).
36. Charles Husband (ed.), *Race in Britain,* quoted in *New Society* (17 February 1983), p. ii.
37. Commission for Racial Equality, *Race,* p. 15.
38. *Guardian* (21 September 1993), p. 7.
39. *Education for All: the Report of the Committee of Enquiry into the Education of Children from Ethnic Minority Groups* (the Swann Report) (London: HMSO, 1985).
40. From *The Times Educational Supplement* (15 March, 1985), p. 12.

8   Personal social services

1. *Local Authority and Allied Personal Social Services* (The Seebohm Report) (London: HMSO, 1968).
2. Tom Crabtree: 'The Double-bind of Social Work', in New Society, *Social Work* (London: New Society, 1981), p. 5.
3. Crabtree, 'The Double-bind', p. 4.
4. Crabtree, 'The Double-bind', p. 5.
5. David Brockman, 'Trans-cultural social work: Time for attitudes to change', *Social Work Today* (24 November 1986), pp. 8–9.

9   Community care

1. Erving Goffman, *Asylums* (Harmondsworth: Penguin, 1968), p. 17.
2. Peter Townsend, *The Last Refuge* (London: Routledge & Kegan Paul, 1962).
3. Pauline Morris, *Put Away: A Sociological Study of institutions for the mentally retarded* (London: Routledge & Kegan Paul, 1969).
4. Leaflet on Elm Tree Close, Essex County Council.
5. Sir Roy Griffiths, *Community Care: An Agenda for Action* (London: HMSO, 1988).
6. Gillian Wagner, *Residential Care: A Positive Choice* (The Wagner Report) (London: HMSO, 1988), p. 60.
7. Barbara Meredith, *The Community Care Handbook* (London: Age Concern, 1993), p. 77.
8. Department of Health and Social Security, *Growing Older* (London: HMSO, 1981), p. 3.
9. N. J. Derricourt, 'Strategies of Community Care', in Martin Loney, David Boswell and John Clarke (eds), *Social Policy and Social Welfare* (Milton Keynes: Open University, 1983).

10. EOC, *Caring for the Elderly and Handicapped: Community Care Policies and Women's Lives* (Manchester: EOC, 1982), p. iii.
11. Janet Finch, *Family Obligations and Social Change* (Cambridge: Polity, 1989).
12. Finch, *Family Obligations.*
13. Carers National Association, *Community Care: Just a Fairy Tale?* (London: CNA, 1994).
14. Personal experience.

10   Children in trouble

1. Government Statistical Service, *Health and Personal Social Services Statistics for England* (London: HMSO, 1993), p. 68.
2. The *Guardian* (11 May 1994), p. 12.
3. Participation Study, Rochdale ACPC, reported on in The *Guardian* (11 May 1994), pp. 12–3.
4. Adrianne Jones and Keith Bilton, *Shape-up or Shake-up* (London: National Children's Bureau, 1994).
5. Reported in the *Guardian* (30 March 1994), p. 15.
6. Nigel Parton, *The Politics of Child Abuse* (London: Macmillan, 1985).
7. Noel Timms (ed.), *The Receiving End* (London: Routledge & Kegan Paul, 1973), p. 45.
8. Timms (ed.), *The Receiving End*, p. 47.
9. Quoted in *The Times* (28 August 1985), p. 9.
10. Commission for Racial Equality, *Fostering Black Children* (London: CRE, 1975), p. 34.
11. *Guardian* (30 July 1987), p. 20.
12. R. Page and G. Clarke, *Who Cares?* (London: National Children's Bureau, 1977), p. 16.
13. Nicola Wyld, *Living Away From Home: Your Rights* (London: The Department of Health).
14. Page and Clarke, *Who Cares?*, p. 42.
15. Page and Clarke, *Who Cares?*, p. 55.
16. Royal Philanthropic Society, *Leaving Care in the 1990s*, reported in the *Guardian* (21 April 1994), p. 8.
17. *Guardian* (27 April 1994), p. 12.
18. Page and Clarke, *Who Cares?*
19. *Black and In Care,* Conference Report (London: Children's Legal Centre, 1984, pp. 34–5).
20. *Guardian* (25 November 1994), p. 1.
21. Neale Pharoh, 'The long, blunt shock', in J. B. Mays (ed.), *The Social Treatment of Young Offenders* (Harlow: Longman, 1975), p. 57.
22. *Guardian* (19 April 1994), p. 19.
23. *Guardian* (9 March 1988), p. 38.
24. Essex County Council, *A Community Based Provision for Juvenile Offenders Subject to Supervision Orders* (1988).

11   Mental illness

1. Reported in the *Guardian* (25 August 1993), p. 14.
2. *Mental illness: what does it mean?* (London: Department of Health, 1993).

3. *Guardian* (8 March 1994), p. 21.
4. John Payne, *All in the Mind* (Oxford University Press, 1976), p. 18.
5. For a guide to the law on mental illness, see Larry Gostin, *A Practical Guide to Mental Health Law* (London: MIND, 1983).
6. Gostin, *A Practical Guide,* p. 6.
7. The *Guardian* (3 June 1994), p. 19.
8. Dr Thomas Main, 'The Ailment', quoted in Joseph H. Berke, *I Haven't Had to go Mad Here* (Harmondsworth: Penguin, 1979), p. 49.

12   Learning disability

1. *Mencap Review* (London: Mencap, 1993), p. 2.
2. *Mencap Review*, p. 2.
3. From R. Edgerton, *The Cloak of Competence,* quoted in Joanna Ryan and Frank Thomas, *The Politics of Mental Handicap* (Harmondsworth: Penguin, 1980), p. 12.
4. Paul Williams, quoted in Ann Shearer, *Disability: Whose Handicap?* Oxford: Blackwell, 1981) p. 54.
5. Mencap information, *Community Care: people and principles* (January 1993), p. 2.
6. *Guardian* (20 July 1983).
7. From R. Kugel and A. Shearer (eds), in Ryan and Thomas, *The Politics of Mental Handicap,* p. 12.
8. P. Hunt, 'Comment: Single Rooms', *Cheshire Smile* (Winter 1968–9).
9. J. Mattinson, 'Marriage and Mental Handicap' quoted in Shearer, *Disability: Whose Handicap?* p. 95.
10. Ryan and Thomas, *The Politics of Mental Handicap,* p. 58.
11. Ryan and Thomas, *The Politics of Mental Handicap,* p. 83.
12. Ryan and Thomas, *The Politics of Mental Handicap,* p. 42.
13. Mencap Resources Pack, *Community Care.*
14. Mencap information, *Community Care: people and principles, p. 2.*
15. Paul Williams and Bonnie Shoultz, *We can speak for ourselves* (London: Souvenir Press, 1982).

13   Old age

1. Muriel Brown, *Introduction to Social Administration in Britain*, 5th edn (London: Hutchinson, 1982) p. 180.
2. *Older people in the United Kingdom*, factsheet from Age Concern (1994).
3. *Older people in the United Kingdom.*
4. Family Policy Studies Centre, *An Ageing Population* (London: Family Policy Studies Centre, 1988) p. 2, 3.
5. For example, Peter Townsend, *Poverty in the United Kingdom* (London: Allen Lane, 1979).
6. *Older People in the United Kingdom.*
7. Child Poverty Action Group, *Poverty,* 52 (August 1982), p. 30.
8. Townsend, *Poverty in the United Kingdom.*
9. *Older People in the United Kingdom.*
10. *Older People in the United Kingdom.*

11. Christina R. Victor, *Health and Health Care in Late Life* (Milton Keynes: Open University, 1991).
12. Age Concern briefings, *Needs of older people* (1994).
13. Family Policy Studies Centre, *An Ageing Population,* p. 7.
14. Central Statistical Office, *Social Trends 1982,* 12 (London: HMSO, 1981) p. 238.
15. *Older People in the United Kingdom.*
16. *Alzheimer's Disease – What is it?* Information sheet from Alzheimer's Disease Society (1994).
17. Printed in *Mind Out* (March/April 1979) 33, p. 4.
18. Printed in Vida Carver and Penny Liddiard (eds), *An Ageing Population* (Kent: Hodder & Stoughton and The Open University, 1978), pp. ix–x.
19. Ellen Newton, *This Bed My Centre* (London: Virago, 1979) p. 38.

14   Disability

1. Ann Shearer, *Disability: Whose Handicap?* (Oxford Blackwell, 1981), p. 10.
2. J. Martin, H. Meltzer and D. Elliot, *The Prevalence of Disability Among Adults* (London: HMSO, 1988).
3. Sue in Jo Campling (ed.), *Images of Ourselves* (London: Routledge & Kegan Paul, 1981), pp. 47-8.
4. Angie in Campling (ed.), *Images of Ourselves,* pp. 11–12.
5. Shearer, *Disability: Whose Handicap?,* p. 178.
6. Daphne Saunders, 'Living on Benefit', in Alan Walker and Peter Townsend (eds), *Disability in Britain* (Oxford: Martin Robertson, 1981), p. 23.
7. Muriel in Campling (ed.), *Images of Ourselves,* p. 115.
8. Sarah in Campling (ed.), *Images of Ourselves,* p. 3.
9. Micheline in Campling (ed.), *Images of Ourselves,* p. 25.
10. Ros Franey, *Hard Times* (London: Disability Alliance, 1983).
11. *Guardian* (9 April 1994), p. 8.

15   Health and the health services

1. Central Statistical Office, *Social Trends 1994,* 24 (London: HMSO, 1994), p. 93.
2. Colin Thunhurst, *It Makes You Sick: The Politics of the NHS* (London: Pluto Press, 1982), p. 3.
3. Thunhurst, *It Makes you Sick,* p. 4.
4. *Guardian* (1 July 1988), p. 4.
5. *Guardian* (1 July 1988), p. 4.
6. Age Concern, *NHS Reforms – A Summary* (London: Age Concern: 1993).
7. Central Statistical Office, *Annual Abstract of Statistics* (London: HMSO, 1994).
8. *First Report of the Commons Social Services Committee on Resourcing the National Health Service* (London: HMSO: 1988).
9. Summarised in the *Guardian* (2 March 1988), p. 2.
10. *Guardian* (11 September 1987), p. 2.
11. Christopher Ham, *Health Policy in Britain,* 3rd edn (London: Macmillan, 1992) p. 61.
12. *Guardian* (4 June 1983), p. 17.

13. Central Statistical Office, *Social Trends 1994* 24 (London: HMSO, 1994), p. 105.
14. Central Statistical Office, *Social Trends 1994* 24 p. 105.
15. BUPA, *A Special BUPA Health Care Scheme* (London: BUPA, 1981).
16. *Guardian* (4 June 1983), p. 17.
17. The Audit Commission, *A Prescription for Improvement* (London: Audit Commission, 1994).
18. The Haslemere Group, 'Who Needs the Drugs Companies?', quoted in Thunhurst, *It Makes You Sick,* p. 43.
19. The Audit Commission, *A Prescription.*
20. Thunhurst, *It Makes You Sick*, p. 39.
21. OPCS figures quoted in Ham, *Health Policy in Britain*, p. 191.
22. Ham, *Health Policy in Britain*, p. 193.
23. *Review of the Resource Allocation Working Party Formula: Final Report of the NHS Management Board 1988* (London: DHSS, 1988).
24. For example, M. Stacey, 'People who are affected by the inverse law of care', *Health and Social Security Journal* (3 June 1977); A. Cartwright and M. O'Brien, 'Social Class Variations in Health Care', in M. Stacey (ed.), *The Sociology of the NHS* Keele: *Sociological Review Monograph,* 82, (1976), and M. R. Alderson, 'Social Class and the Health Service', *The Medical Officer* (17 July 1970).
25. TUC, *The Unequal Health of the Nation: A TUC Summary of the Black Report* (London: TUC, 1981).
26. Andrew Veitch and Nicky Hart 'How the government buried its dead reckoning', *Guardian* (30 July 1986), p. 21.

16 The voluntary sector

1. Family Welfare Association, *Guide to the Social Services* (London: Family Welfare Association, 1994) p.7.
2. *Guardian* (22 June 1994), p. 10.
3. David Gerard, *Charities in Britain* (London: Bedford Square Press/NCVO, 1983), p. 17.
4. Quoted in *New Society* (7 April 1983), p. 3.
5. NSPCC, *Annual Review* (London: NSPCC, 1993).
6. NSPCC, *Annual Review* (London: NSPCC, 1988).
7. NSPCC, *Annual Report* (London: NSPCC, 1993), pp. 3–4.
8. NACAB leaflet, *Seven million questions.*
9. Richard Bourne, 'Step-parent Linkline', in *Self-Help in the Social Services, New Society* (1982), p. 7.
10. David and Yvonne Robinson, *From Self-Help, to Health* (London: Concord Books, 1979), p. 21.
11. Robinson and Robinson, *From Self-Help,* p. 43.
12. Child Poverty Action Group publicity.
13. WAFE, *What is Women's Aid Federation England?* (Leeds: WAFE).
14. The Terence Higgins Trust leaflet, *Service Users Guide to the Terence Higgins Trust* (London: The Terence Higgins Trust, 1994), p. 4.
15. Robinson and Robinson, *From Self-Help,* p. 57.
16. Robinson and Robinson, *From Self-Help,* p. 78.
17. David Robinson and Stuart Henry, *Self-Help in Health* (London: Martin Robertson, 1977), p. 118.

18. Robinson and Henry *Self-Help* p. 115.
19. Robinson and Henry *Self-Help* p. 115.
20. *Guardian* (22 June 1994), p. 10.
21. *Guardian* (22 June 1994), p. 10.
22. Reported in the *Guardian* (18 May 1994), p. 12.
23. *Guardian* (18 May 1994), p. 12.

17   Policy issues in welfare

1. Vic George and Paul Wilding, *Ideology and Social Welfare* (London: Routledge & Kegan Paul, 1976).
2. Report in the *Guardian* (2 October 1987).
3. Reported in the *Guardian* (6 September 1994), p. 1.
4. George and Wilding, *Ideology and Social Welfare*.
5. Yasmin Gunaratnam, 'Breaking the Silence: Asian Carers in Britain', in J. Bornat, C. Pereira, D. Pilgrim and F. Williams (eds), *Community Care: a reader* (London: Macmillan, 1993).
6. Central Statistical Office, *Social Trends 1993*, 23 (London : HMSO, 1993).
7. David Lipsey, *The Sunday Times* (14 February 1982).
8. J. N. Nicholson, 'Distribution and Redistribution of Income in the UK', in D. Wedderburn (ed.), *Poverty, Inequality and Class Structure* (Cambridge: Cambridge University Press, 1974), p. 81.
9. Commission for Racial Equality, *Race Relations Code of Practice in Primary Health Care Services* (London: CRE, 1992).
10. Commission for Racial Equality, *Race Relations Code*.

Glossary of terms

It should be noted that the explanations given here refer only to the way in which terms have been used in the context of this book and in the study of social administration.

absolute poverty: a lack of resources for survival

acute illness: an illness which comes sharply to a crisis and is of brief duration

acronym: word made up only of initials, such as TEC

adult training centre: see *social education centre*

advocacy: speaking up for someone's needs, *self-advocacy* can mean people with disabilities speaking up for themselves – perhaps with support and preparation in a self-advocacy group – but is also used when people with a disability speak up for another person with a disability.

agency: an organisation providing a service – could be a statutory, voluntary or privately run organisation

ante-natal clinic: a service for pregnant women, providing medical checks, relaxation classes and instruction

anti-collectivist: philosophy which believes in a minimum of state provision of welfare and believes individuals and families should help themselves and buy services if needed

anti-depressants: drugs given to people suffering from depression

anti-discrimination legislation: law prohibiting unfavourable treatment of particular groups

approved social worker: social worker with special training which allows her to be involved in cases needing compulsory admission to psychiatric hospital.

arms length (inspection): local inspection teams looking at services, for example residential homes, are supposed to be independent from the managers of the service, so they will report objectively

assessment: the process of deciding what a person needs

assessment centre: social services provision for children in care, aiming to provide an analysis of needs before placement

assisted places scheme: enables pupils to attend an independent school with fees partially or fully met by the government on the basis of a means-test

at risk register: a system of local reporting of children at risk from child abuse

attendance allowance: flat-rate benefit for people with disabilities requiring supervision by day or night or both

attendance centre: provision for young offenders found guilty of an offence which, for an adult, would mean imprisonment, often run by the police on Saturdays with craft facilities, drills and sport

Audit Commission: government agency responsible for monitoring local authority and health services

binary system: a system containing two elements, as in the binary system which used to exist in higher education with polytechnics and universities. Now polytechnics have become universities.

bind over: an order of the court to a person found guilty of a crime that he or she will keep the peace and be of good behaviour or forfeit a sum of money

Borstal training: a court order now replaced by the youth custody order, it was a custodial sentence from the Crown Court for a person aged 15–21, with an emphasis on training and structured discipline

budget-holding GP: see *fund-holding GP*

bureaucratic: descriptive of administration based on rules and procedures

'cap': set a limit, for example the government can 'cap' local authority levels of council tax

capitalism: economic system which is dominant in this country and others in Europe and in America, based on private businesses employing workers to produce goods and services in order to make a profit

care manager: person responsible for someone receiving a community care package of services – involving in planning, monitoring and reviewing of services from various sources

care order: allows the local authority to take over legal custody of a minor

care package: services providing by various organisations which together allow a person needing support to remain at home

care plan: individual plan drawn up to provide care (perhaps from a variety for sources)

care proceedings: procedure in the family court for a child believed to be in need of care and control

carer: see *informal carers*

casework: a form of social work focusing on individuals and families in need of help and support

case conference: a multi-disciplinary meeting of professionals, for example from social services, education and the probation service, to discuss a case of child abuse

cash limit: the maximum supplement central government will make to local authorities through the Rate Support Grant, imposes a limit on local authority spending

census: a study of the whole population; a census is carried out by the government every 10 years

central government: as distinct from local government, includes Parliament and Whitehall

centralisation: a process of concentration of decision-making in a central authority

cerebral palsy: a condition commonly described as 'spastic' in which brain damage incurred before birth or at the time of birth results in symptoms including an inability fully to control movement

charitable status: a legal category allowing a voluntary organisation to call itself a charity and entitling it to certain benefits such as reduced rates and taxation

charter: document written by the government or other organisation setting out standards of service which users can expect and often other information such as complaints procedures

chemotherapy: treatment with drugs

child health clinic: clinic providing for routine medical care of infants, screening of pre-school children and instruction for parents

Child Support Agency: government body which assesses the financial responsibilities of 'absent' parents for their children

chronic illness: a lingering, lasting illness with slow changes in symptoms

'Cinderella service': part of provisions with less funds and less status than other services

City Technology Colleges (CTCs): secondary schools partly funded by industry and providing an emphasis on technical areas of education *class structure*: an aspect of society whereby people sharing an economic position form groups with different access to wealth, power and prestige

client groups: different groups of people provided for by a service, for example, elderly people, children or people who are mentally ill.

cohabitation: a couple living together without being married

collectivist: philosophy which believes in state provision of certain services for all

community care: exact definitions vary but basically the idea the people should be cared for at home or in small units in the community (rather than in institutions)

common-law marriage: describes a situation where a man and woman live together without being legally married, the correct term is cohabitation

community care: services provided outside institutions as an alternative to long-term residential care

community home: residential social services provision for people in the care of the local authority replacing approved schools and remand homes

community psychiatric nurse: based in the community working with people with mental illnesses living in the community

community service order: a court order requiring a person aged 16 or over to do unpaid work in the community under supervision

community work: an ill-defined term which implies social work focusing on local groups rather than on families and individuals

comprehensive: descriptive of a service or facility provided for all

comprehensive school: a school attended by all children of secondary-school age in a particular area; some people suggest a school cannot be properly termed 'comprehensive' if there is an independent school in the area

congenital abnormality: a condition present at birth

consultative document: a report prepared for discussion and comment

contact order: this replaces the old idea of 'access' to children after a divorce, this is one of the 'Section 8' orders which the court can make under the 1989 Children Act – a contact order gives a person who the child does not live with the right to contact with the child.

contempt of court: an offence, punishable by imprisonment, involving disobedience to a court, interference in court procedures or a show of disregard for the court

contract: an agreement between the provider and the purchaser of a service as to what will be provided

contributory benefit: a benefit paid only to those who have made sufficient national insurance contributions

county school: see *maintained school*

cultural differences: differences in values and acceptable behaviour between groups or societies

culture of poverty: a concept associated with Oscar Lewis' explanation of the self-perpetuating way of life developed by the poor to cope with their situation

curriculum: the content of learning

custody: (1) the guardianship of minors

custody: (2) imprisonment

cycle of deprivation: a concept associated with Sir Keith Joseph, used as a means of explaining the way in which a poor background may lead to poor prospects

cycle of expectation: a process in which little is expected of a person's achievement and consequently little is achieved

cyclical unemployment: temporary unemployment caused by periodic slumps in the economy *day hospital*: hospital care on a daily, non-residential basis – for example, for people who are mentally ill

dependency culture: a concept associated with right-wing politics, the idea of the dependency culture is that people on benefits become reliant on the state and as a result have no interest in trying to find work or living as economically as possible

depression: a mental illness, commonly described as a 'nervous breakdown' with symptoms of excessive sadness, feelings of hopelessness

deprivation: (1) individual – for example, emotional deprivation when people have been prevented from experiencing love or praise

deprivation: (2) collective – for example, urban deprivation as a result of multiple problems of poverty, poor housing, etc.

detention centre: residential provision for offenders aged 14–21 for periods of three weeks to four months

direct grant school: a form of private education which no longer exists whereby schools received finance from the Secretary of State for education and the local education authority could make use of up to 25 per cent of places

discretionary: if a service or benefit is discretionary, there is no automatic entitlement according to rules laid down by Parliament, the agency controlling the award can decide whether or not to give it.

discrimination: treatment of a person differently on the basis of particular criteria

discriminatory practice: see discrimination

district general hospital: hospital providing all aspects of health care for a particular area

disruptive unit: provision within the education system for children labelled as 'difficult'

division of labour: separation of work into different tasks to be carried out by different people

divorce rate: the number of divorces expressed either as a proportion of marriages or as a ratio to population

domiciliary service: services provided in people's homes

dyslexia: a handicap involving difficulty in recognising or reproducing shapes or sounds of words leading to impairment of reading, writing and language skills

earnings-related: benefits or contributions where the amount depends on the level of earnings

economic regeneration: financial revival

ECT: electro-convulsive therapy, a method of treatment used in cases of depression and schizophrenia which involves the passing of an electric current through electrodes fitted over the temples whilst under anaesthetic

education welfare office: a person employed by the education authority concerned with school attendance and educational welfare

eligibility: entitlement

élite: a minority group which is believed to be superior and which has power and influence

enabler: people or organisations who do not provide a service themselves but allow clients access to services provided by other organisations

equality of opportunity: a situation in which everyone has an equal chance of success

ethnic group: see *ethnic minority*

ethnic minority: a term lacking a clear definition with the implication of membership of a group possessing a culture, often carries implication of discrimination and racial difference

extended family: a family group including other relatives in addition to parents and children *fair rent*: a rent for privately rented accommodation set by a Rent Officer or Rent Assessment Committee, with regard to current prices and the condition of the property, but ignoring scarcity

family credit: a means-tested benefit for families in work

Family Health Services Authority (FHSA): looks after primary health care services – doctors, dentists, chemists, opticians

field social worker: a social worker with families and individuals in the community

foster-parent: a person providing care for children under the supervision of a social worker; technically, fostering is called 'boarding-out'

frictional unemployment: unemployment caused by time-lags in people getting jobs

fund-holding GP: doctor or practice with a budget to pay for hospital and other services for his or her patients

further education: education for people over 16, below degree-level

General Improvement Area: introduced in 1969, small areas of housing eligible for special grants and other provision for rehabilitation

General National Vocational Qualification (GNVQ): qualification gained by full-time study related to an area of work, for example Health and Social Care

generic social work: social work which is not specialised but deals with all client groups

geriatric: part of medicine dealing with illnesses associated with old age

gentrification: process whereby professional people move into inner-city areas which become fashionable and expensive, displacing poorer people

grant-maintained school: a school which has 'opted-out' of the control of the local education authority and which receives a grant directly from central government

group therapy: a form of treatment for mental illness involving group discussion of problems and possibly group living

Guardian ad litem: a person appointed at the discretion of the juvenile court in care proceedings to safeguard the welfare of children by making independent inquiries, reports and recommendations to the court

half-way hostel: residential accommodation with some supervision for people moving from an institution to the community

health education: information to persuade people to adopt a life-style believed to be more healthy

health visitor: a person trained as a nurse with experience of midwifery and knowledge of preventative health, working in the community offering advice and support

hereditary: descriptive of a characteristic biologically transmitted from one generation to another

high-density: descriptive of areas with a high population relative to size

higher education: education at a level above 'A' level

home carers: staff working with people living at home and needing personal care (other terms may also be used)

Housing Action Area: introduced in 1974, a small area of housing where the local authority can improve housing and housing associations are encouraged to buy and renovate properties

Housing Action Trust (HAT): an organisation set up by the central government to take over the running of council estates in poor condition, rehabilitate them, and sell them on to a new landlord.

housing association: a part of the voluntary housing movement with the aim of buying and improving housing for rent at a non-profit-making-price

Housing Corporation: a government organisation responsible for encouraging housing associations and distributing funds

housing tenure: the way in which properties are occupied, for example, rented or owned

housewives' non-contributory invalidity pension: a flat-rate benefit for housewives of working age suffering from a disability and not qualifying for invalidity benefit

hypothermia: accidental reduction of body temperature below normal range, particularly likely to happen to babies and old people

income support: a means-tested benefit for those not in work whose income falls below a level set by Parliament

independent school: a school not maintained by the local education authority nor in receipt of a government grant

independent sector: non-government agencies providing services, and includes voluntary organisations and private organisations

indirect discrimination: a legal concept in the Sex Discrimination and Race Relations Act referring to discrimination by rules applied to all which effectively exclude certain groups

indirect tax: tax on goods and services, for example, Value Added Tax (VAT)

industrial tribunal: an organisation, less formal than a court, which adjudicates on employment legislation, for example, unfair dismissal

infant mortality rate: number of deaths of children less than one year old as a ratio of live births

informal carers: people who care for someone who is elderly or disabled or otherwise needing care and for whom this is not a paid job, commonly just spoken of as 'carers'.

informal patient: a patient in a psychiatric hospital without legal compulsion, retaining full rights

informal social control: control of itself by a community

injunction: court order stopping someone from doing something

institutionalisation: the process of becoming dependent on the routines of a protective environment

insurance qualification: a requirement attached to a benefit that the claimant has paid sufficient national insurance payments

interest rate: the price of borrowed money

intermediate treatment: a term with no clear definition describing a sentence for young offenders or provision for young people at risk of crime involving various activities and short residential courses

internal market: idea that services within one organisation, for example the NHS, compete with each other for contracts with purchasing sections of the organisation

invalid care allowance: a flat-rate benefit payable to people staying at home to care for a relative receiving an attendance allowance

invalidity benefit: national insurance benefit payable after entitlement to sickness benefit ends

IQ: Intelligence Quotient, the score from a test measuring a type of intelligence and compared with the mean for the age group

inverse care law: idea which describes tendency for areas most in need of services to have least provision

joint-funding: arrangement whereby two organisations, for example the health service and the local authority share the cost of a project

joint roles: describes a marriage in which the husband and wife share tasks, social life and decision-making *laissez-faire*: the philosophy that the government should not intervene in the economy

learning difficulty: see learning *disability*

learning disability: someone is described as having a learning disability if they have considerably more difficulty in understanding and managing their everyday lives than others of the same age, as well as limited social skills

legal aid: means-tested financial help with the cost of legal advice and proceedings

legal system: the system of legislation and law enforcement

less eligibility: the principle, in the 1834 Poor Law, that a person receiving state help must live at a level lower than that of the poorest person living independently

life expectancy: a statistical concept giving the average number of years a person is expected to live from a given point in time

lobotomy: an operation on the brain intended to relieve a mental disorder

local authority: the local system of government run by councillors and officials

mainstream education: as distinct from special education; the education provided for most children

maintained school: a school where the running and staffing costs are met by the local education authority

maintenance payments: payments made by a divorced or separated spouse to the other for that person and/or the children of the marriage

maladjustment: a child is said to be maladjusted if he or she is unable to cope with normal situations

mandatory: compulsory

manic depression: a mental illness characterised by dramatic swings of mood from elation to depression

market forces: the idea the supply and demand for goods and services sets the price and availability of goods and services

married man's tax allowance: tax relief allowing a married man to pay less tax than a single person or a married woman

Marxist: theories based on ideas of Karl Marx, basically seeing capitalism as a system of two classes, employers and workers, in which employers exploit workers to create profit for themselves

matrifocal family: a family type consisting of a woman and her dependent children

means-tested: benefits are means-tested when they are only available to persons whose income and savings fall below a certain level

mental handicap: this term is not usually regarded as acceptable these days, see *learning disability*

modified extended family: separate nuclear families related to each other who share and provide significant services for each other

monogamy: the marriage of one man to one woman

mortality rate: the incidence of death in a population at a particular time

mortgage: a loan with property as security for the debt

mortgage default: failure to pay outstanding mortgage payments

multi-cultural education: education which relates to the cultures of ethnic minorities as well as dominant groups in a society also known as multi-racial and multi-ethnic education

multi-disciplinary: involving staff from a number of different professions, for example social workers, doctors, community psychiatric nurses

multiple deprivation: a situation where many aspects of deprivation are combined in inner-city areas, for example poverty, poor housing and unemployment *multiple sclerosis*: a chronic disease of the nervous system affecting young and middle-aged adults

national curriculum: content of education laid down by government to be taught in all state schools

national insurance contributions: payments made by employers, employees and self-employed people for national insurance benefits

National Vocational Qualification (NVQ): vocational qualifications for people in work, at various levels and covering most types of work

negative equity: the result of a fall in house prices, negative equity occurs when a house or flat has been bought with a mortgage which was higher than the current value of the property

neurosis: a less severe category of mental illness, typically involving an exaggeration of usual emotions, but retention of insight

new right: people who believe in minimal state provision, families and individuals being responsible for themselves and the private provision of services

NHS Trust: with the split of the health authorities into units which purchase services and those which provide services, most hospitals and community health services are separately managed by Trusts, the Trusts remain part of the NHS but are managed by a Board of Trustees

non-accidental injury: injury inflicted on children in their homes, also known as child abuse

non-contributory benefit: entitlement to the benefit does not depend on having paid national insurance contributions

norm: social rule for behaviour in a particular group

nuclear family: a family consisting of parents and immature children only

obsession: a mental illness where activities are taken to extremes or repeated over and over again

obstetrician: a doctor specialising in the care of woman in pregnancy, childbirth and immediately after birth

occupational pension: a pension based on payments made whilst in work to a private fund

outreach: services are taken out to where clients are, for example in prison or hospital or even on the street

paranoia: a mental illness characterised by delusions and a false belief of persecution

parasitic disease: an illness caused by an organism living the body, for example a virus

parity of esteem: descriptive of provision where different aspects are regarded as equal

Part III accommodation: accommodation provided for people needing care under Part III of the 1948 National Assistance Act

passport benefit: a social security benefit which provides automatic entitlement to other benefits

patch system: a system where small groups of social workers are based in neighbourhood offices instead of working from more centralised area offices.

paternalistic: limiting freedom by well-meant regulations and provision

patent law: gives exclusive rights over a new invention or process for a period of time

patriarchy: feminist concept seeing society as controlled by men in their own interests

per capita: per head

personal social services: provision by local authority department employing social workers and others, such as home helps *phobia*: mental illness involving an irrational fear

Placement Assessment and Counselling Teams (PACTs): provide specialist advisory services for people with disabilities

planning blight: environmental problems caused by indecision in planning

polyandry: marriage where there is one woman and several husbands

polygamy: marriage between more than one man or woman

polygyny: marriage involving one man and several wives

positive action: action to combat inequalities by giving extra resources or rights to disadvantaged groups or areas

poverty cycle: a concept describing changes in the standard of living of those near the poverty line in the course of their life, through, for example, the existence of dependent children or retirement from work

poverty line: a definition of poverty for research purposes, setting a level of income below which people are said to be in poverty

poverty trap: factors which prevent families from increasing net income through raising wages as a result of the interaction of increased income tax, national insurance payments and decreased benefits

pre-school education: education before the compulsory school age

pressure group: an organisation trying to bring about change by influencing those in power or changing public opinion

preventative medicine: medical services designed to prevent rather than cure problems

preventative services: as preventative medicine although more general in scope

primary poverty: Rowntree's term for people living below the poverty line as a result of insufficient income

private sector: services provided outside state provision

probation officer: a person employed to advise, assist and befriend offenders and those leaving prison; also involved in preparing Social Inquiry Reports for the court

progressive tax: a tax which takes proportionately more from higher income groups

prohibited steps order: This is one of the 'Section 8' orders which the court can make under the 1989 Children Act in a divorce case, a prohibited steps order stops something from being done, for example stating that the child must not be taken abroad

provider: the organisation or person providing a service (health and social services are now split into 'provider' and 'purchaser' sections following the 1990 NHS and Community Care Act)

psychiatric social worker: a social worker attached to a mental hospital or child guidance clinic, specialising in mental illness

psychiatrist: a doctor who specialises in the study and treatment of mental disorders

psycho-geriatrician: a doctor specialising in the mental illnesses associated with old age

psychological: concerned with the human mind

psychologist: a person engaged in the study of the mind or working in the field of assessment and treatment of people with mental disorders

psychopath: a person suffering from a personality disorder with symptoms of anti-social behaviour, little feeling of guilt and an inability to form relationships

psychosis: a category of severe mental illnesses in which the sufferer loses touch with reality

psychosurgery: surgery on the brain believed to cure certain types of mental illness

psychotherapy: treatment of mental illness through talking with the aim of reaching an understanding of the illness

psychotropic drug: a drug affecting moods and emotions

public school: a term with no clear definition usually used for schools whose head belongs to the Headmasters' Conference

purchaser: the organisation or individual buying a service on behalf of clients (health and social services are now split into 'provider' and 'purchaser' sections following the 1990 NHS and Community Care Act)

quango: stands for quasi-autonomous non-governmental organisation, an organisation set up by government but operating with some independence

quota system: scheme for proportional allocation to particular groups or individuals

racism: deliberate or unintentional practices, behaviour or attitudes which discriminate on the basis of race

rate support grant: grant from central government to local authorities

reconstituted family: a family including step-parents and half or step-children

redevelopment: the process of pulling down older buildings and replacing with new

red-lining: the policy of building societies of selecting areas where mortgages will not be given

redistribution of wealth: a means of achieving greater equality by transferring wealth from richer groups to poorer ones

regressive subsidy: allocation of government funds in such a way that people who are better off receive more

regressive tax: a tax which takes a decreasing proportion of income as income rises

rehabilitation: (1) programmes to help people to develop or relearn skills for independent living

rehabilitation: (2) renovation of old areas or housing, etc.

relative poverty: a lack of resources for the standard of living considered normal in a particular society

rent arrears: debts incurred as a result of not paying rent

residence order: this is one of the 'Section 8' orders which the court can make under the 1989 Children Act in a divorce case, a residence order decides where a child will live.

respiratory disease: disease affecting breathing

respite care: temporary care provided to give carers and people being cared for a break, may be in a hospital, residential home or with another family

Restart: everyone who is unemployed for 6 months is invited for an interview with a claimant advisor, this may lead to placement on a course or workshop to help with finding a job

role: set of ways of behaving in a particular social position

role-conflict: there are several definitions for this term, it is used in this book to refer to a situation in which two or more of a person's roles interact in such a way as to cause stress

role-set: a collection of roles which fit together in a particular situation, for example, student and teacher

safety net: idea of provision to support people who 'fall through' gaps in other forms of provision

schizophrenia: this is not a clearly defined term, it describes a severe mental illness characterised by loss of emotional responsiveness, loss of reality, often accompanied by delusions, hallucinations or bizarre imagery

secondary poverty: Rowntree's term for people in poverty because some of their income is spent on items not essential in terms of his definition of the poverty line

secure unit: accommodation in community homes or assessment centres for children who are violent or who continually run away *security of tenure*: where tenants of rented property cannot be evicted without cause

segregated roles: descriptive of a marriage where the husband and wife carry out separate tasks and have their own friends and social life

segregation: setting some people apart from others

selective: descriptive of provision only available to particular categories of people

selective benefit: benefit allocated on the basis of set conditions, usually involving a means-test

selective education: a system of schooling which allocates children to different types of school

self-help group: an organisation in which members have common problems and help each other

senile dementia: a mental illness of old age, characterised by vagueness and disorientation

severe disablement allowance: a non-contributory benefit for people with disabilities.

sheltered accommodation: independent housing with support from a warden or social worker if needed

sheltered employment: a protective work environment for people with disabilities

sheltered workshop: see *sheltered employment*

shorthold tenancy: tenancy of private rented property for a fixed period

shortlife property: property due for demolition or renovation let cheaply or for free for a short period

social deprivation factors: characteristics, for example, poor housing, which are used to measure need in an area

social education centre: (previously known as adult training centre) provides support in finding work, training or education for people with a learning disability, may include other facilities for people with severe disability

social indicator: see *social deprivation factors*.

social inquiry report: a report written by a social worker or probation officer (for a court) on the circumstances and home environment of a person

socialisation: the process of learning the values and accepted behaviour of a society

social policy: government action in the field of welfare

social security: the system of financial benefits for income maintenance, that is national insurance benefits and other means-tested benefits

social services: welfare provision, including education, the health services, social security, sometimes incorrectly used to refer to the personal social services alone

special education: educational provision for children with learning difficulties

special school: a school for children with learning disabilities

specific issue order: This is one of the 'Section 8' orders which the court can make under the 1989 Children Act in a divorce case, a specific issue order takes away the parents' responsibility over particular issues and means decisions must be made by the court – an example of this could be decisions on education, it is quite rare for this order to be used

speech therapy clinic: provision to help people with speech problems

squatting: unauthorized occupation of empty properties

state sector: services and enterprises provided by the government rather than private individuals or organisations

'statementing': procedure under the 1981 Education Act whereby children with more complex learning disabilities are assessed by the local education authority

status: social position relative to others

statutory: by law

statutory duty: obligation by law

statutory organisation: organisation established by legislation *stereotype*: type-cast mental impression

stigma: something which sets apart or results in unfavourable treatment

structural unemployment: unemployment caused by basic long-term changes in the economy

subnormality: see *mental handicap, learning disability*

supervision order: a court order that a child being looked after by his or her family be allocated a social worker or probation officer to provide help

take-up: the proportion of those eligible for a benefit who receive it

targeting: the policy of focusing services on those thought to be in greatest need, usually meaning the poorest only

tax relief: freedom from taxation for specific reasons

tenure: see housing tenure

tertiary college: an education institution providing further education for all over 16, replacing sixth forms and colleges of further education

test case: a legal case brought to court in order to establish a ruling on an aspect of law

therapist: a person providing treatment, sometimes used to refer to psychotherapy, but also speech therapist, etc.

total institution: Goffman's term for an institution in which people live their whole lives, e.g. prison, army barracks

Training and Enterprise Councils (TECs): local organisations led by employers and responsible for training schemes and support for new businesses in their areas (LECs in Scotland)

tranquilliser: a drug which has a calming effect; major tranquillisers are used in the treatment of schizophrenia and other psychoses, minor tranquillisers are used for neuroses such as anxiety

tribunal: a decision-making body for example in the fields of mental health, social security, rent, employment

tripartite system: organisation into three parts, for example, secondary education consisting of technical, grammar and secondary modern schools

universal: welfare provision is said to be universal when it is available for all

universal benefit: benefit available for all without a means-test

voluntary organisation: a non-profit making organisation not established by legislation

voluntary school: a school established by a voluntary organisation but maintained by the local education authority

volunteer: an unpaid worker choosing to give services

welfare provision: a vague term for services provided to help people

welfare state: a term with no clear definition, originating in the 1940s after the introduction of the health service, national insurance, etc.; refers to all welfare provision or a state which provides welfare

White Paper: a document stating the government's policy prior to legislation

workhouse:institution in which poor people were provided for under the 1834 Poor Law

work-sharing: a means of reducing unemployment by dividing work among the population, perhaps by shortening the working week

Index